TURF WARS

New Directions in Ethnography is a series of contemporary, original works. Each title has been selected and developed to meet the needs of readers seeking finely grained ethnographies that treat key areas of anthropological study. What sets these books apart from other ethnographies is their form and style. They have been written with care to allow both specialists and nonspecialists to delve into theoretically sophisticated work. This objective is achieved by structuring each book so that one portion of the text is ethnographic narrative while another portion unpacks the theoretical arguments and offers some basic intellectual genealogy for the theories underpinning the work.

Each volume in *New Directions in Ethnography* aims to immerse readers in fundamental anthropological ideas, as well as to illuminate and engage more advanced concepts. Inasmuch, these volumes are designed to serve not only as scholarly texts, but also as teaching tools and as vibrant, innovative ethnographies that showcase some of the best that contemporary anthropology has to offer.

Published volumes

1. *Turf Wars: Discourse, Diversity, and the Politics of Place*
Gabriella Gahlia Modan

Forthcoming

Homegirls: The Making of Latina Youth Styles
Norma Mendoza-Denton

Allah Made Us: Sexual Outlaws in an Islamic African City
Rudolf Gaudio

TURF WARS

Discourse, Diversity, and the Politics of Place

Gabriella Gahlia Modan

Blackwell
Publishing

BLACKWELL PUBLISHING
350 Main Street, Malden, MA 02148-5020, USA
9600 Garsington Road, Oxford OX4 2DQ, UK
550 Swanston Street, Carlton, Victoria 3053, Australia

First published 2007 by Blackwell Publishing Ltd

1   2007

Library of Congress Cataloging-in-Publication Data

Modan, Gabriella Gahlia.
   Turf wars : discourse, diversity, and the politics of place / Gabriella Gahlia Modan.
      p. cm.
   Includes bibliographical references and index.
   ISBN-13: 978-1-4051-2956-5 (hardback : alk. paper)
   ISBN-10: 1-4051-2956-5 (hardback : alk. paper)
   ISBN-13: 978-1-4051-2955-8 (pbk. : alk. paper)
   ISBN-10: 1-4051-2955-7 (pbk. : alk. paper)   1.   Community development—
Washington (D.C.)   2.   Neighborhood—Social aspects—Washington (D.C.)
3.   Mount Pleasant (Washington, D.C.)   I.   Title.

HN80.W3M63 2006
307.3'36209753—dc22

2006004755

A catalogue record for this title is available from the British Library.

Set in 11.5/13.5pt Bembo
by Graphicraft Limited, Hong Kong
Printed and bound in Singapore
by Markono Print Media Pte Ltd

The publisher's policy is to use permanent paper from mills that operate a
sustainable forestry policy, and which has been manufactured from pulp processed
using acid-free and elementary chlorine-free practices. Furthermore, the publisher
ensures that the text paper and cover board used have met acceptable
environmental accreditation standards.

For further information on
Blackwell Publishing, visit our website:
www.blackwellpublishing.com

Front and back cover photographs by Jennifer Leeman

For the members of the Kenesaw Phoenix Cooperative, for illustrating that it's possible to build community across faultlines.

For my family and the stories that got me interested in neighborhood life: Ben Gurion, noodle soup, and a hot summer day; Mrs. Freiman, the professional contest winner of Windsor Hills; and lemon memories (okay, not exactly a neighborhood story, but still worthy of being memorialized).

For my comrades-in-bookwriting – Rudi, Jenny, Norma, Paul, and Jeff – for keeping me afloat.

And in memory of my grandfather, Stanley Morton Hollins, who always found a way to point out that amidst the frustrations of everyday life exist humor, art, and dignity.

CONTENTS

FIGURES

ACKNOWLEDGMENTS

I am indebted to my neighbors in Mt. Pleasant, who welcomed me into their homes, cooked me dinner, gave me advice, argued with me, and shared their hopes and their fears about the place that is such a big part of their lives. Working on this project has given me a view into the dense texture of what neighborhood life can be, and I know that I am lucky to have had my day-to-day life enriched by it. Some will no doubt disagree with the picture of Mt. Pleasant that I paint in these pages; indeed this is a selective view, but I hope that my fellow Mt. Pleasantites will find some resonance in it. I am equally indebted to my editor, Jane Huber, whose enthusiasm and support for this project were unwavering, and whose close reading and insightful comments have made this a better book. My words cannot adequately express how incredibly lucky I've been to have her as an editor.

I've also been lucky to have friends and colleagues with whom I can talk both neighborhood and theory. This book has benefited from Jenny Leeman's keen sense for the logic of an argument and her beautiful photographs (which she generously took expressly for this project), Yael Flusberg's feel for the texture of the neighborhood and the turn of a phrase, Susanna Schaller's insight into the dialectics of theory and practice, and Reina Prado's and Natalie Avery's articulations of connections between artistic expression and politically imbued scholarship. Brett Williams inspired this work by example and encouragement and opened up the world of urban anthropology to me, and she and Olivia Cadaval gave me a model for integrating personal community engagement with scholarship. Outside of

Mt. Pleasant, Norma Mendoza-Denton helped me to tease out the complexities of social categorization, Rudi Gaudio provided creative insight into the minutiae of theory as applied to the ins and outs of social interactions, and Jeff Maskovsky pushed me to better articulate the political economic dimensions of urban linguistic interactions. All of these people shared their powers of observation, editing skills, and love of a good conversation, and this book bears the marks of their suggestions, both big and small. I'm thankful for their willingness to put so much time into reading and commenting on my work, and I'm also thankful to Jenny and Reina for their help with the Spanish transcripts.

I owe my interest in community-based research to Peter Patrick. Without his enthusiasm for this kind of work and his encouragement, I probably never would have gone the academic route. And my views of ethnography were shaped in important ways by conversations in and out of the field with Isolda Carranza, Lourdes Pietrosemoli, and Limin Zheng.

At Ohio State, I found in Amy Shuman a colleague who brought incredible insight and devotion to workshopping data and developing new ideas, many of which inspired new directions in my work – particularly in chapter 5. Terry Odlin read the manuscript with the eye of a linguist as well as a former resident of Mt. Pleasant, and this combination provided many valuable suggestions. I thank Paul Reitter for his generosity and humor.

I'm grateful to Keller Magenau, Stacey Rutledge, and Iris Bogaers for always helping me to see the big picture, and to Heidi Hamilton, Deborah Schiffrin, Teun van Dijk, Deborah Tannen, and Bill Leap for their support and feedback along the way. I also received very useful comments from two anonymous reviewers, especially in terms of structuring Section II.

I'm thankful to Eugene McCann and Annemarie Bodaar for their very helpful feedback on the Lefebvre section in chapter 9, and to Peggy Modan and Michael Modan for aid with the healthcare statistics. I am indebted to Mara Cherkasky for her comments and suggestions on chapter 2 and her invaluable help in tracking down references. My work has also benefited from background material and feedback from Robert Frazier and Quique Avilés. I'm especially grateful to Quique for involving me in various incarnations of *Chaos Standing* and allowing me to reproduce excerpts of the original show in chapter 6. Ellen Kardy at the Mt. Pleasant library also provided invaluable aid. And at Blackwell, Emily Martin, Haze Humbert, and Annette Abel made the process easy.

Over the years my thinking on language and urban life has been shaped in numerous ways by conversations with Alys Cohen, Amanda Huron, Amanda Kleinman, Amiel Summers, Athena Viscusi, Audrey Singer, Barbara Leckie, Bob Aguirre, Bob Pohlman, Celina Treviño-Rosales, Charmaine Lee, Chris Kruger, Chris Summers, Colleen Cotter, David Pass, Diane Levy, Deborah Rosenstein, Doug Wissoker, Edward Gray, Elizabeth Utschig, Emily Williams, Gerry Borstel, Gretchen Young, Guillermo Fajardo, Heather McCrae-Woolf, Hector Emanuel, Henry Heuveling van Beek, Hilary Binder-Avilés, Itoko Kawakami, Jacques Rondeau, Jeff Deby, Jennell Williams Paris, Jessica Dominguez, John Clark, Jonathan Modan, Julie Blum, Kathy Wood, Keli Yerian, Lewis Rosman, Lisa Schirch, Lora Barnette, Lucille Coutard, Marge Landis, Marita Lee, Mike Hill, Miriam Dominguez, Najiya Shana'a, Nghi Le, Nilda Villalta, Pam Saunders, Perry King, Peter Stebbins, Ray Messick, Roxana Zepeza, Rubén Martinez, Sara Paasche-Orlow, Saskia van Groningen, Scott Kiesling, Shi-xu, Sofia Varela, Spike Ingram, Tony Lee, Toshi Hamaguchi, and Webster Young.

This research was supported by funding from the US Department of Housing and Urban Development and the Ohio State University, and a visiting scholar position at the Smithsonian Center for Folklife and Cultural Heritage. As always, the content of this work does not necessarily represent the official views of these institutions, and all shortcomings remain my own.

From the *Washington Post* editorial pages, August 21, 2001, page A22

Fake People Welcome Mr. Bush

Less forgiving souls than ourselves might take some pleasure in the wretched Washington weather that greeted President Bush upon his return yesterday. After all, he has spent the past month celebrating the values of the Heartland, in not so implicit contrast with our own. . . . Those values, he repeated this week, include "family and faith," "neighborliness," "the willingness of people to help each other in need." Which means that we Washingtonians stand for – what, exactly? Just thinking about it could make us mad.

But it hasn't – not at all. We don't hold it against Mr. Bush when his fellow Republican, former Senate majority leader Trent Lott, says that Mr. Bush left Washington to connect with "real Americans." And when the president says, "Even though we've changed addresses, Texas will always be home" – when he makes that same trite point so many times it gets downright tiresome – well, we could take offense. But, as we mentioned, we won't.

So it gave us no pleasure yesterday when the president and the first lady returned from their dry rattlesnake air to muggy, smoggy Washington. We're happy that their "batteries are charged," as Mr. Bush said they were, and we'll continue trying to get our values up to Heartland standards. In the meantime, all we really want to say, Mr. President, is: Welcome home. Or whatever you want to call this place.

PART I

THE ETHNOGRAPHY

CHAPTER 1

SKETCHING THE LANDSCAPE

Prelude

Summer has come early to Mt. Pleasant. It's Saturday morning, and I go out to run some errands. Although it's only the middle of May, the heat has everyone acting like it's July. I walk into the street around the cherry picker next to my building, where two men from the Parks Department are leaning out from the basket, putting wax on the statue of the first Methodist priest on horseback, to protect him and his horse from the tarnishing rays of the sun. Below them the mulberry trees are in bloom, and the heavy berries fall to the sidewalk, blackening the red bricks with their sticky juice and squashed pulp. The teenage bucket drummers have drifted up from Dupont Circle, their go-go rhythms bouncing off the cement, forming a background beat to the merengue from the street-side table where Frank the cassette tape vendor is selling his wares. Groups of young men are hanging out with their friends in front of the groceries and apartment buildings. Everyone is out with their literature. I'm told about a protest rally against recent INS[1] raids in Maryland; about worker exploitation under Clinton's neoliberal government; about a cheap monthly dental plan; that Jesus loves me. Everyone is out, and everyone's in a good mood. Even the tiny old woman who sits on a bench in Pigeon Park, fond of yelling at passersby for jaywalking, is in a good mood. Today she merely tells me to be careful crossing the street, and calls me "dearie." The flower man is also cheerful and smiling; he gives my neighbor Grace a good price for the bunch of red and yellow gladiolas she wants to buy.

There's a big crowd in the bakery – punk rockers in their low-slung thriftstore corduroys getting up to buy donuts for their group house breakfast, security guards in slightly rumpled uniforms on their way home after the night shift, fathers talking on cell phones as their kids pull at their shirt hems, begging them for gingerbread cookies. Young couples are talking to each other in varieties of Amharic, English, Haitian Creole, Spanish. The woman in front of me orders two conchas (Salvadoran sweet rolls), a loaf of rye bread, and, giving in to her kids' whining, three cupcakes.

At the back counter, bakery clerks are bringing cakes to customers. One man picks up a two-tiered cake, frosted in a white basketweave design on the sides, with pink roses on the top. Along the cake sides and down the columns between the two tiers, minute pink roses and thin white lines form a trellis pattern, like a climbing rose bush. Written in red gel script on the top tier of the cake, is "Feliz Quinceañera Jacqui" ("Happy Sweet 15th Jacqui").

Beside the man paying for this cake is a woman inspecting a large rectangular sheet cake, also decorated in white frosting. One of the bottom corners sports a frosting-painted scene of a woman and two children playing a circle game, while the other corner is decorated with the scene of a lake and mountains. Across the top of the cake is a skyline of the DC monuments, and in the middle, in the same script as the quinceañera cake but this time in brown frosting, is written, "Welcome to the Evvans family reunion."

Outside the store, two women tie their dog's leash to the post of a no-parking sign, walk in and to the back of the shop to pick up a strawberry shortcake. This cake is also frosted in white, but the frosting is whipped cream. As they inspect the message, "Happy B-day Netta," the bakery clerk places four plastic figures around the edges of the cake. The figures have fifties hairstyles and clothing, and they are in rock 'n roll dancing poses. Between two of the figures, the clerk anchors a miniature fifties portable style record player into the frosting.

Back out on Mt. Pleasant St., Mt. Pleasant's main shopping street, the morning sun heats the late spring air. The smell of honeysuckle from the rowhouse gardens is undercut by urine fumes from the alleys, and stray tangles of hair from the Beauty and Braiding Shop waft by in the warm breeze. Dr. Roman is in front of his office pulling a gum wrapper out from the pansies in the flower box and chatting with Mrs. Lee, the owner of the dry cleaner's next door. A woman across the street parades by in her underwear, yelling at some drunk guys on the next block, and Dr. Roman leans over to Mrs. Lee and says, "I wish I had my video camera"; sighs, and whistles through his teeth, "just another day in Mt. Pleasant."

Later, as I walk in the heat of the afternoon back to Mt. Pleasant St. from the supermarket in the neighborhood next door, my naturally quick gait elicits catcalls. I walk more slowly, adapt my rhythm so that it fits with the pace on the street, and the catcalls fade out. Downtown the gears of international bureaucracy churn away, but here the pace of life slows as the heat rises.

Mt. Pleasant is a neighborhood alive with activity of all kinds, with a main street that makes some feel unsafe, while it makes others feel at home.

I'm walking down Mt. Pleasant St. one day with a friend visiting from out of town. She stops and touches my cheek to fix a makeup smudge, and says, "I feel like I can do anything on your street."

I moved to Mt. Pleasant in the summer of 1992, after having lived for a year in the adjoining neighborhood of Adams Morgan. I was drawn to Mt. Pleasant because, in the early 1990s, it was affordable, reasonably safe, shopping and public transportation were varied and convenient, I had a lot of friends who lived in the area, and I found an apartment I really liked.

My building was towards the edge of the neighborhood, sandwiched between 16th St. – a main city thoroughfare that runs between the Maryland suburbs and the White House – and Mt. Pleasant St. A small balcony off my bedroom window overlooked this street, and here I spent many hours sitting in the sun and reading, socializing with friends, watching the world go by, and, later on, tape-recording the sounds of city life and my neighbors' treatises – some spontaneous and others prodded by interview questions – about the state of US society as evidenced by the goings-on on Mt. Pleasant St.

One evening on this balcony, I sat watching some teenagers kidding around with each other outside the variety store across the street and some drunk guys arguing at the bus stop underneath my window. On this particular day it struck me that the interactions on this street and, more generally, in the neighborhood, told an important story about the way that people define, negotiate, and redefine the places they live as particular kinds of communities populated by particular kinds of people.

In the late 1990s, as gentrification[2] in Mt. Pleasant and the city at-large picked up with relentless speed, these negotiations over claims to neighborhood identity and neighborhood space began to have serious material implications for what kind of place Mt. Pleasant was to become. Would it stay a mixed-income, multi-ethnic neighborhood? Would it retain its community-minded interactive spirit? Would its cosmopolitanism up its hipness quotient and its real estate prices to the point of no return?

What I want to capture in these pages is the importance of the way that people shape the terrains they live in as they talk with their friends and neighbors in public and private settings. Through discourse, community members struggle over what kind of place Mt. Pleasant is, what constitutes a real Mt. Pleasant person, and who gets to decide these issues. What I hope to show here is why this matters.

Turf Wars

This is a book about the politics of place. It examines how community members in Mt. Pleasant create and contest visions of their neighborhood through discourses of identity, both sociogeographic and personal. By discourse I mean ways of talking, writing, and signing; patterns of recurring themes, linguistic forms, and modes of conversational interaction. As the sociolinguist Deborah Schiffrin[3] describes it, discourse is a set of utterances that are part of a linguistic and social context. This means that any given utterance both gains its meaning from other utterances and from the social context, and it also shapes the meaning of other utterances and of the social context.

The upcoming chapters will analyze email messages on the neighborhood listserv, casual conversations, a grant proposal for public toilets, a performance piece about living in the neighborhood, and ethnographic interviews to see how Latinos, African Americans, Whites, Vietnamese, and community members of various other ethnic[4] and national backgrounds use language to negotiate conflicting ethnic and gender perspectives, class alignments, and hopes and fears for their neighborhood. Discourses about what kind of place Mt. Pleasant is or should be, and about who counts or doesn't count as an authentic Mt. Pleasant person, circulate through a wide variety of social contexts and linguistic genres. Residents draw on these discourses as resources – and reinforce or contest them – in their interactions with each other, with neighborhood institutions, and with more broad-based audiences like government offices or philanthropic organizations.

In analyzing specific examples of Mt. Pleasant discourses of place, I want to illuminate the relationship between three kinds of local identities: 1) various identities for the neighborhood itself, 2) identities that speakers create for themselves as core community members, which we can call *centralized identities*, and 3) identities that speakers create for others as lesser community members, which we can refer to as *marginalized identities*. These identities are mutually constitutive, meaning that the construction of each both relies on, and works in the interests of, the others. In other words, the construction of a legitimate identity as a neighborhood person relies on an alignment with a particular kind of identity created for the neighborhood itself: talking about the neighborhood as a safe place doesn't help one to create an image of a tough, streetsmart urbanite, just as portraying the neighborhood as homogeneous would not help you to come across as a sophisticated cosmopolitan.

Constructions of neighborhood and personal identity are key components in neighbors' struggles over rights to spatial resources and authority to determine what kinds of activities are appropriate or allowable in the public spaces of parks and streets. This means that the way we talk about the places we live has material implications for how those places develop and change. When people in Mt. Pleasant create identities for their neighborhood, they do so in order to stake a claim to community membership and the rights that community membership confers to have a say in the direction of the community's future.

Mt. Pleasant

In the 1990s, Mt. Pleasant was one of Washington DC's most economically and ethnically diverse neighborhoods. (As gentrification continues in Mt. Pleasant and the real estate market in the city as a whole has become increasingly expensive, the economic and ethnic diversity of the neighborhood has lessened. A house that could have been bought for under $200,000 in the mid-1990s now is likely to sell for upwards of $700,000.) It's been home to Latinos – mostly Salvadoran – African Americans, Whites, and fairly newly-arrived Vietnamese, to name just a few of the ethnic groups represented. There are also residents who don't fit so neatly or canonically into any of these groups: Palestinians, Kurds, Trinidadians, Somalis, Bosnians, Indians. At the time I was doing fieldwork, Mt. Pleasant was also home to groups like DC's hardcore music scene and the DC Mennonite community. Economically, residents' incomes vary from the six-figure range to below the poverty line. This span in income is very clearly reflected in the variety of housing stock in the neighborhood, which includes apartment buildings ranging from fancy condos to overcrowded and unsafe tenements, stately detached houses on the National Historic Register, and rowhouses set up as single-family dwellings, split into apartments, or used as group houses.

Mt. Pleasant community members construct the neighborhood's identity in a variety of ways. While some talk about it as a cozy, civic-minded community of tree-lined streets with neat gardens in front of Victorian rowhouses, others portray it as a dangerous inner-city neighborhood, a place of drunks passed out on the street, still living in the shadow of the city's most recent riots in 1990.

In the first half of the 20th century, Mt. Pleasant was a middle-class, majority-White neighborhood. It became a middle-class, majority African American neighborhood in the early-to-mid fifties, as school and housing desegregation enabled African Americans to move to the neighborhood and many Whites consequently decided to leave.

In her 1988 book *Upscaling Downtown*, urban anthropologist Brett Williams documents how Mt. Pleasant became both more gentrified *and* more culturally diverse, beginning in the late 1970s when young, educated professionals – who were more often than not White – bought houses that had been vacated by middle-class residents who left the neighborhood after the 1968 riots. They were joined by people immigrating mainly from the Caribbean, Central America, and East Africa. As Williams explains, in the 1970s and 80s,

> rising interest rates and a faltering housing market delayed what otherwise would have been rapid and dramatic displacement. These years of stalled gentrification framed an anomalous time when the most unlikely groups of people tried to live together as neighbors.[5]

The mid-to-late 1990s was a turning point in the process of gentrification, and in particular, a kind of gentrification that *commodified* the ethnic diversity of the neighborhood, turning ethnic diversity into a feature that brought added symbolic value to living there and added economic value to real estate prices. At this critical juncture, when neighborhood change was palpable, gentrification and diversity became overriding themes in public and private discourse in various settings throughout the neighborhood and across a variety of speakers. It was through discourse that community members hammered out their visions for the kind of place that Mt. Pleasant was and should be, through talk and writing that they contested various players' claims to public space, and, ultimately, that they laid the groundwork for what kind of place Mt. Pleasant has become at the beginning of the 21st century.

Ethnographic Research in Mt. Pleasant

I began research on the present project after I had already been living in Mt. Pleasant for five years. From spring 1996 to the end of 1998, I conducted ethnographic fieldwork in Mt. Pleasant, investigating how residents talked about their community in various speech situations. A key element in ethnographic research is the participant-observer model. As participant-observers, researchers actively partake in a wide spectrum of community activities, at the same time as they make detailed observations of the patterns of interaction in various activities, and how such patterns relate to community values and norms. The logic of the participant-observation model is twofold; first, it is easier to gain acceptance in a community if one is willing to participate in community life, including in ways that benefit the community, such as helping to weed a field or clean up a park. There is also an ethical component here: since researchers derive benefit from community members' openness to them, researchers should also give something back to the community. This is what William Labov refers to as "the principle of debt incurred."[6] Second, as norms of social interaction vary in different settings, so too does linguistic behavior. Therefore, it is only through observing and interacting with community members in a wide variety of settings that a researcher can gain a full picture of members' complete discursive repertoire (the full range of linguistic styles, registers, and strategies that a person uses). Because speakers often consider certain topics or conversational styles unsuitable or irrelevant in specific speech situations such as interviews,[7] an ethnographic, participant-observer approach can get at research topics that may be missed by survey or quantitative approaches to data gathering and analysis.

Furthermore, an ethnographic approach allows us to see the ways in which similar discourses circulate through disparate settings and among speakers who may have little interaction with each other. As sociolinguist Heidi Hamilton notes, identity is intertextual, meaning that interlocutors (people talking to each other) draw on "previous interactions in which language was used to construct particular identities for these individuals (or ones like them) in some relevant ways."[8] Although sometimes speakers make the references to previous interactions explicit, at other times the relationship between two texts can be quite subtle. It's only through familiarity with a wide range of types of interactions and discourse genres, then, that it is possible to gain a holistic understanding of a community's social structure and the complex relations of discourse and ideologies to that structure.

My status as both a researcher and community resident not only influenced my own subjective view of Mt. Pleasant, but it also impacted the ways in which other community residents related to me. These identities and other social features worked to position me in ways that both constrained and helped me in conducting ethnographic research. Many aspects of my identity were relevant at different points in the data collection: to name a few, age (early 30s), place and type of residence within the neighborhood (renter on the neighborhood's main street), phenotype (light skin and light, curly hair), gender, class, ethnicity, accent, geographical ties. However, a few of these categories were consistently brought up explicitly by community members. These categories – particularly urban/suburban/rural background, local connections, and ethnicity – were therefore important indicators of prevalent ways of constructing identity in the community. My own positioning, then, was an important component in shaping my decisions about what kind of themes to focus on in my analysis of Mt. Pleasant discourse. At the same time, however, my background shaped the kinds of questions that I was interested in, and what I was interested in also influenced how people perceived and interacted with me, which in turn influenced the kind of data that I was able to collect, in terms of both style and content. My background also influenced what caught my attention in the data at the point that I started to analyze it. This is the nature of ethnographic research; as a researcher, what you discover is necessarily refracted through the lens of who you are.

Researching in your own backyard

Geographical background, ethnicity, and place of residence and housing tenure all were important features that interlocutors drew on when positioning me within the landscape of the neighborhood. Because of community members' strong neighborhood allegiances and pro-neighborhood ideology, residence in the neighborhood – and particularly a residence which began before I started this research project – was the most important of these factors. Residence in the neighborhood confers a status of legitimacy, whether for a dinner guest, a local merchant, or a drug dealer. The same holds true for researchers.

Mt. Pleasant has a number of social scientists as members of its community, many of whom at one point or another have conducted research on or in the neighborhood. (See, for example, the work of the Youth Action Research Group 2003, Olivia Cadaval 1998, and Brett Williams 1988.) Many resident researchers have had good relationships with individuals and with organizations working in the neighborhood, and have contributed their time and expertise on an ongoing and lasting basis to projects conducted by neighborhood institutions.

While non-resident researchers have sometimes been seen as outside forces coming into the neighborhood to "get" something from the neighborhood and leaving when they get whatever it is, resident researchers have tended to be looked upon more beneficently. This is especially the case when researchers are involved in the life of the neighborhood – when they have neighborhood networks which have been formed outside of, or in addition to, their research (although such networks inevitably have played a role in their research). Researchers who are positively regarded are seen to have a connection to the neighborhood which is independent of their research. While those who are not *a priori* members of the community are seen primarily as researchers, it seems that the primary identity of researchers who are Mt. Pleasantites is as community members, who secondarily do something else. Thus, although not everyone may agree with the research findings per se, these researchers tend to be described as neighborhood chroniclers, much in the same way that some people are referred to as the neighborhood philosopher, neighborhood poet, or neighborhood curmudgeon.

Mt. Pleasant's diverse demographic makeup has also made it a popular research site among area universities. In the past ten years, departments from at least five universities have conducted research projects on such topics as conflict resolution, youth leadership, institutional capacity-building, intercultural communication, and architectural planning.

Although the foci of these projects have varied with the disciplinary background of the researchers, the projects have shared a common aim to "give something back" to a community experiencing ethnic and economic tensions, where many people have limited access to jobs, education, and healthcare. Many students working on these projects have made friendships and contributed richly to the lives of individual Mt. Pleasant residents, and Mt. Pleasant has served as an effective training ground for budding conflict mediators, linguists, anthropologists, public policy analysts, and architects. However, despite the contributions that members of such projects may have made on an individual basis (not an invaluable outcome), ultimately most in the community have not noticed any broad-based impact on social or economic conditions of the neighborhood at large; today, with no concrete reminders of these projects (such as new structures for solving community conflicts, or increased economic opportunities), their contributions have by and large vanished from Mt. Pleasant's collective memory. The failure of university research to make lasting contributions to the neighborhood as a whole has made many residents of Mt. Pleasant suspicious of researchers from local universities, and of academics in general.

For me, being a community member before I started this project brought both benefits and difficulties. By presenting myself primarily as a resident of the neighborhood, who *also* happened to be conducting research, I was usually (but not always) able to allay a fair amount of my neighbors' suspicion of researchers, and to build my legitimacy as a researcher around my status as a neighborhood resident, one who had been somewhat active in community issues, whose interest in doing research developed out of personal experiences and interactions in and with Mt. Pleasant.

But doing research in the community where I had lived for a number of years also posed challenges, because it meant that people knew me as something other than a researcher. Having pre-established networks helped enormously in collecting data, because many people with whom I interacted through fieldwork already knew me from other contexts and felt at ease with me. Consequently they were more open with me than were people who didn't know me at the outset. On the other hand, being a community member also meant that my non-research relationships with people and connections in the neighborhood sometimes got in the way of finding out information. For example, I had been involved in a (now defunct) neighborhood organization that had taken somewhat polarized stances on a number of controversial issues. When I talked about some of these issues in sociolinguistic interviews or taped conversations with other former members of this group, it was extremely difficult to elicit narratives about past neighborhood events, because they assumed 1) that I knew as much as they did about the events, 2) that I knew their positions regarding these events, and 3) that I agreed with them. Whether or not these assumptions were accurate (sometimes they were and sometimes they weren't), they resulted in people not discussing information about Mt. Pleasant that they considered to be shared background knowledge.

My association with this organization also impacted research relationships that I had with people who had opposed the stances of this group. Such people sometimes aligned me with the positions of the organization, which was evidenced through evaluations in their stories that were often implicitly directed towards disagreeing with, or disdaining, policies which this organization had supported; this happened even when they were not explicitly discussing the organization. Other people were less open towards me because of my affiliation with this organization.

My identity as a neighborhood resident also created challenges because it enabled people to categorize me in specific ways which they might have been less likely to do if they had seen me solely as a researcher. When this happened, community members related to me according to the norms for interaction with someone in the particular category within which they placed me. While this categorization was beneficial in some cases (for example, being seen as a neighbor who was friendly with long-term residents and rented from a former president of the condominium was very helpful in doing fieldwork in my apartment building), in other cases it had some deleterious effects: In order to be an effective community researcher, I could not position myself as a disinterested observer. Because my legitimacy as a researcher was based on my legitimacy as a community resident, I had to construct myself as just that – a legitimate community resident. In Mt. Pleasant, community members are expected to have opinions about the goings-on in the neighborhood. So showing myself as a legitimate community member meant that I had to have opinions, and having opinions entailed positioning myself – and being positioned by others – in ways that distinctly influenced data collection and the shape of interviews that I conducted.

The idea of a sociolinguistic interview is that the researcher has a bunch of questions to start off with, but otherwise more or less tries to sit back and let the interlocutor talk and develop the conversation as they like. When I did interviews, however, I was asked as many questions as I posed – there was a much more equal distribution of the discursive labor, or the division of who asks and answers questions. There was also a fair amount of differentiation in the types of discourse data that I could collect among different community members. For example, people who saw me as having similar political leanings told many moral outrage stories about the way that others had acted in neighborhood controversies. People who saw me as having opposing political positions told me virtually no moral outrage stories. Instead, I got stories with lengthy explanations and justifications for political positions; such narratives were not told to me by people who aligned themselves politically with me.

"Where do you live?"

Not only residence in the neighborhood in general, but the particular location and circumstances of residence are important factors in shaping neighborhood identity. Mt. Pleasant St., the neighborhood's commercial corridor, serves as somewhat of a dividing line between the richer and Whiter western part of the neighborhood, and the poorer and more multi-ethnic eastern part of the neighborhood. The majority of Mt. Pleasant's apartment buildings are on Mt. Pleasant St. and to the east, while the western part of the neighborhood sports townhouses and rowhouses. Rental property is also more prevalent on Mt. Pleasant St. and to the east. In the neighborhood, the owner–renter dichotomy has strong social meaning, although it is interpreted differently by different community members. Much of the social meaning of place of residence has to do with class and politics, two important characteristics of the local landscape. My class positioning was ambiguous – as a graduate student I was poor, but I had significant cultural capital and the potential for at least a middle-class salary in the future. My place of residence also gave off ambiguous signs; I lived on Mt. Pleasant St. in the poorer part of the neighborhood, but my building was a co-op/condo building (more about that in chapter 7) that was a microcosm of the neighborhood in terms of economic and ethno-racial makeup.

My status as a renter who lived on Mt. Pleasant St., coupled with my age (early thirties when I started fieldwork), formed a text for me which people interpreted in a number of ways; some viewed these characteristics in terms of my politics, assuming that I would have an anti-gentrification stance, that my relationship to the neighborhood was based on something more community-oriented than a concern for property values, and, because I lived on Mt. Pleasant St., that I was more "authentically" Mt. Pleasant. Others interpreted renting on Mt. Pleasant St. in terms of my dedication to the neighborhood – that, because I did not have an economic investment in the neighborhood, I was not committed to Mt. Pleasant and had no plans on staying. Some people also drew this interpretation from the fact that I was a researcher, assuming that once I finished my project, I would move to a fancier neighborhood. Alternately, some thought that because I lived on Mt. Pleasant St. I had no concern for "quality of life" issues that affected people west of Mt. Pleasant St. These various attributions are testament to the way that social beings imbue the details of everyday life with immense cultural meaning, a phenomenon we'll see much more of in the chapters to come.

In addition to current place of residence, past connections with places also play a strong role in people's perceptions of each other's identity. An example of this can be seen at social gatherings, where the most frequent conversation-starter questions are "Where do you live?" and "Where are you from?" As I was asked these questions numerous times, I found that "Where are you from?" could mean many different things. When I answered that I had grown up in Massachusetts, people wanted to know what kind of town; I quickly learned that it was to my benefit that I'd come from a small city and not a suburb, giving me some insight into the ideological import-ance of the urban–suburban contrast in the neighborhood. But I also found that that answer did not always satisfy my interlocutors, as people frequently followed up my response with questions about where my *family* was from. So I similarly discovered that my mother's being from Baltimore (a Maryland city about an hour away from DC) often worked in my favor, as it established a kind of historical local connection for me, as well as an urban connection. The urban –suburban theme sometimes found its way again into this line of questioning among people who knew Baltimore well and would ask if my mother grew up in Baltimore City (which she did) or Baltimore County (the suburbs).

So while "Where do you live?" gives an interlocutor information about whether someone lives in Mt. Pleasant and where in the neigh-borhood geography they're located, "Where are you from?" can reveal whether or not the person is native to DC or the larger Washington area, as well as what their national or ethnic background is. One example of this is an interaction that occurred at a party given by a woman named Claudia in Columbia Heights, the neighborhood just to the east of Mt. Pleasant. On the southwest side of Mt. Pleasant is the neighborhood Adams Morgan. Although many people do not make a distinction between Adams Morgan and Mt. Pleasant (and, for that matter, parts of Columbia Heights), and the border between the three neighborhoods is very fuzzy, overall there is a common perception that Adams Morgan is more upscale than Mt. Pleasant. (However, the image of Adams Morgan as more upscale or gentrified than Mt. Pleasant does not bear out in the details of who lives in the two neighborhoods. According to local realtors, the housing stock in Mt. Pleasant is primarily single-family homes, many of which were built as luxury houses at the turn of the 20th century. In Adams Morgan, the housing stock is mostly apartments, and the single-family houses there were built primarily after the First and Second World Wars as housing for working and middle-class families. While prices for comparable properties are higher in Adams Morgan, however, the overall amount of money invested in property is higher in Mt. Pleasant, because of the number of large houses. Thus, some local realtors have the view that Mt. Pleasant, with its wide assortment of large renovated old homes, is actually more gentrified than Adams Morgan.)

At a conversation at Claudia's party, her friend Miriam exploited the view that Adams Morgan is more upscale than Mt. Pleasant, as she tied person and place identity together by characterizing the people under discussion as certain kinds of people based on their neighborhood residence:

La Crème de la Crème
At Claudia's party, Miriam, Yadira, and I, all from Mt. Pleasant, were talking in the back yard with Aviva, who lived in Adams Morgan. Javier, a colleague of Claudia's, came outside and started talking with Miriam:

JAVIER: ¿Dónde viven?
          Where do you$_{pl}$ live?
MIRIAM: En Mt. Pleasant. Ay, perdón, **nosotros** vivimos en Mt. Pleasant, **ella**
          *In Mt. Pleasant. Oh, excuse me, **we** live in Mt. Pleasant, **she**

          vive in Adams Morgan. **Ella** es la crème de la crème. **Nosotros** somos
          *lives in Adams Morgan. **She's** the crème de la crème. **We're**

          la crème de la merde.
          the crème de la merde.
[laughter]
JAVIER: ¿Y de dónde son?
          And where are you$_p$ from?

> MIRIAM: Yo soy de Puerto Rico, ella es de El Salvador, ella es judía de New York, ella es judía de Massachusetts.
> *I'm from Puerto Rico, she's from El Salvador, she's Jewish from New York, she's Jewish from Massachusetts.*

Miriam's answer to Javier shows that "Where are you from?" is a question not just about geography, but also about ethnicity. It is enough for Miriam to say that she is from Puerto Rico and Yadira is from El Salvador, for this implies that they are Latina. However, Miriam deems it insufficient to answer Javier's question in the same way for Aviva and me, because simply telling him where we grew up would not supply any information about our particular ethnic background. In order to be maximally relevant, then, Miriam includes our ethnic identities in her answer. So this exchange points to the salience of ethnicity in placing people in the Mt. Pleasant landscape.

While my mother's place of origin contributed to my positioning in terms of local urban connections, talk of my father's place of origin was used (sometimes by me, sometimes by others) in the construction of my ethnic identity, as can be seen in the following example. The conversation in question, which started out as a discussion of old stereo speakers, occurred one night in my apartment after dinner at some friends'. The friends wanted to go to sleep, so those guests who wanted to continue the evening came to my apartment. The conversation shows the complexity of local musings on ethnicity. And perhaps these particular speakers' own ethnic backgrounds (Afro-Dominican, Jewish Honduran, Salvadoran-Mexican American) influence their awareness of such complexity.

FREDDY:	What's wrong with them big speakers?
GALEY:	They don't work anymore. My father bought them when he was twenty-five.
ERNESTO:	Twenty-five. How old is he now?
FREDDY:	/???/old they look- They look like, back in the sixties.[9]
GALEY:	Sixty
ERNESTO:	Sixty
FREDDY:	Yeah, they look a lot like in the sixties.
GALEY:	They were good speakers, but they don't work anymore. So now they're just holding stuff.

ERNESTO: Pero [*but*], it's nice to have a:, something from the family. From far away, from, from home.

GALEY: Yeah, yeah.

ERNESTO: From long ago.

FREDDY: But I was looking at the speakers because they do look like something they would do in the sixties.

GALEY: They were like the first thing my father bought in the United States.

ERNESTO: Oh yeah? He emigrate from Israel?

GALEY: Yeah.

ERNESTO: Really?

GALEY: Yeah.

FREDDY: Where you from?

ERNESTO: Do you speak um, Hebrew?

GALEY: A little.

ERNESTO: A little bit.

GALEY: My father's from Israel.

ERNESTO: My brother was there. He was in, como se llama [*what's it called*], the big hill where the, uh, the, Masada.

GALEY: Masada.

ERNESTO: He was there.

FREDDY: I thought she was White, man. See I thought she was, I thought she was White. You know? =

ERNESTO: Yeah. Uh-huh, I saw you a few times before, and I =

FREDDY: = And, and, she said she's from-

ERNESTO: = thought then you were a Gringa, you know? Pero, ésa, ésa es la confusión, es lo que te digo, que [*But that, that's the confusion, it's what I'm saying, that*] el color- You know something, there is a lot of racism against Africans, descending Africans, and African Americans, and African Hondurans, and African Dominicans, and African Cubans. And a lot, a lot of Africans, you know? Pero este- [*but uh*], after all, a lot of Africans also have shown that =

FREDDY: Yeah, and now it's like, =

ERNESTO: = they are eh, igual to un blanco, igual to cualquier =

FREDDY: = a /picture/

ERNESTO: = raza, cualquier cabrón [*the same as / equal to Whites, the same as / equal to whatever race, to whoever*], in many, in many- many ways, man. Entonces, ya no hay [*So, there's no longer*]- I think that there is no more reason to think about, to fight against, what color or which color or what-ever, si no [*if not*], against, el que tiene el poder, y cómo

	se puede distribuir, entre [*the one who has the power, and how to distribute it, among*] the people who need it? You know? How many millions my friend over here he had to share with us, because we are from third world countries and we miss that money?
FREDDY:	But I bet you one thing is that-
ERNESTO:	And that if you don't give us that money, you gonna have five million El Salvadorians in your country, so you should share- why you don't share with us?

[. . .]

OSWALDO:	But see what I was getting at, you know, about the Black – about the Black thing, is that this-
FREDDY:	Who made that shit up?
OSWALDO:	And not only that, it's like Victoria, I keep going back to Victoria – you know when you talk to Victoria, and you ask her, where you from? Well, you know, my family's from Guatemala. We're from Guatemala. And you know, we're Indian, we're Mayan. Okay? Right. Well then, Victoria, how did you come to talk English the way you talk English? Because, because I grew up with Blacks – alright? So when she says – when I ask her where she's from and she says <in Spanish accent: Guatemala>, that doesn't tell me about her, having lived in a part of DC where she grew up with Black- kids, and how she learned to talk English like Black kids talk English.
FREDDY:	Yeah
OSWALDO:	So you see what I'm sayin?
FREDDY:	Yeah, and how she, grew up with Black kids, but she never grew up with Guatemalans.
OSWALDO:	Exactly.
GALEY:	Right, exactly.
FREDDY:	And that's the confusing ^thing. And that's what we saying. See, you not White- you- **this** [pointing to white notebook paper] is white. You know what I'm sayin? But we call it White.
GALEY:	But, do you think I'm White? Like if –
FREDDY:	I thought so, I didn't know, I didn't know. You know, it's, this, this [color thing, that we all are,
ERNESTO:	[Well if I- if

GALEY: I could, let me, let me tell you something-
So **now**, do you think I'm White? Or not.

FREDDY: No, I don't think you're White. I don't think you're completely White. But you probably have some White in you.

ERNESTO: Pero [*But*] let- Freddy, mira, /espere/ me [*look, wait*]- let me tell you something – si tu pusieras [*if you put*] two teeth of gold here, and you walk in Mt. Pleasant con otro- con trenzas y un vestido short, y unos huaraches, [*with other, with braids, and a short dress, and some sandals*], she will look Salvadorian,

FREDDY: Yeah

ERNESTO: ¿Sí? ¿O de Honduras? O de Costa Rica. O de Costa Rica. Yeah. Una chelita. Uh huh. [*Right? Or from Honduras, or Costa Rica. Yeah. a light-skinned girl.*] Éso es la onda. [*That's the thing.*] Really, que la onda- de- hay que- [*that the idea, that- we have to-*] we have to focus – quando hacemos idea, y ideología o whatever, nosotros tenemos que enfocar mas a dentro de el color. [*When we're forming ideas, and ideology or whatever, we have to focus beyond color.*]

I offer this excerpt here to give some insight into the way that the topic of race/ethnicity and color often crops up in casual conversation in Mt. Pleasant. The excerpt also shows how "Where are you from?" is often interpreted as a question about familial origins; this is clear both from my answer "My father's from Israel" to Freddy's question "Where are you from?" and Oswaldo's voicing of Victoria's answer "my family's from Guatemala" to his posing of the same question.

What was interesting to me at the time of the interaction (which can be seen by the fact that I pushed the question) was how my attributed identity as White and Gringa became reclassified with the information that "my father's from Israel." At the time of the interaction I assumed that the reclassification was based on my being Jewish,[10] but it is also possible that the reassignment here to "not (completely) White" and non-Gringa is based on what we might call inherited immigrant status. Indeed, in Mt. Pleasant it is not uncommon for people to use *White* as synonymous with White *American*; a German (white-skinned, blond-haired, blue-eyed) friend of mine with a German accent (and an American mother) related to me that often people told her that they didn't consider her White, because she was not "from here," and also because she spoke Spanish. Similarly, while some people use the term *Gringa* to mean *American*, others use it to mean *White American*, or sometimes *White Westerner not of Latin American descent*. (For example, an Anglo-Australian might count as a Gringa for some people.)

Perhaps because I don't have stereotypical Jewish coloring or what is considered in the US to be a canonical Jewish name (i.e., an Eastern European or German Jewish name), people in Mt. Pleasant did not always assume that I was Jewish; they read my ethno-racial identity generally as White. This put me in an interesting position, since not infrequently interactions took a different turn when people found out that I was Jewish.[11] This was the case particularly for members of minority groups who were around my age (again highlighting the significance of age as a factor influencing social interaction).

What I noticed particularly was that some people used less monitored speech around me, making more ethnic-related in-group jokes in my presence, and more stereotyped and/or negative statements about members of their own ethnic group. In the case of Jews, in addition to this behavior, many were also intensely interested in how members of other minority groups related to me in interviews. While it was common for community members of all backgrounds to ask what kinds of things I was finding out in my research, Jewish interlocutors frequently asked me questions like, "What about other minorities you talked to? Did they have the typical stereotypes of us?" (But this was the case only with people who identified themselves on-record as Jewish. Others – people who for various reasons I assumed were Jewish – seemed to scrupulously avoid saying anything that would identify them as Jews, for example changing the subject abruptly.)

Another extremely important factor in how people related to me was my level of linguistic competence in Spanish. The dominant languages in the neighborhood are English and Spanish, therefore it would have been quite useful for me to speak Spanish while doing fieldwork. I took an intensive Spanish class at the beginning of my fieldwork and at the time had pretty good comprehension, but my speaking was a long way away from fluent. While speaking Spanish of course would have aided my data collection, the politics of Spanish and English led me to avoid such an endeavor except, at times, with monolingual Spanish speakers. However, bilingual native Spanish speakers, especially in conversations with multiple participants, sometimes spoke Spanish to me and frequently code-switched[12] between English and Spanish in their conversations with me, even though I tended to reply only in English.

Obviously my linguistic skills were a major constraint in this research, as it made it hard to develop deeper relationships with monolingual Spanish speakers. (Of course the same holds true for speakers of other languages, particularly Vietnamese, but I focus on Spanish here because it plays such a large role in the public discourse of the neighborhood), and it made it more difficult to conduct interviews in Spanish (although I did conduct a few). On the other hand, however, my marginal competence in Spanish gave me insight into the politics of speaking non-fluent Spanish as a native English speaker, and the wide range of opinions among native Spanish speakers about this issue. Some people – particularly elderly community members – encouraged me to speak Spanish, telling me it was the only way to improve my speaking skills. These were the same people who were generally positively disposed towards native English speakers who spontaneously spoke Spanish to them, even if they had started a conversation in English. These community members evaluated such behavior as a solidarity move. As one woman said, "Oh, I like it, ah, la gringuita habla Español. There are many people here who know about our countries, so they tolerate – they know how we are."

Others had quite negative reactions towards native English speakers not fluent in Spanish who spoke Spanish to them.[13] Many with high competence in English explained that it was just annoying, since it was so much easier to hold a conversation in English. Others called it insulting, interpreting it as an implicit critique of their English. Some voiced resentment at having to play Spanish conversational partner for a free Spanish lesson. Another common explanation, particularly among US-identified native Spanish speakers (generally, people who grew up in the US or came to the US in childhood or their early teens), was that native English speakers speaking (non-fluent) Spanish were trying to be cool. This attributed "coolness move" in turn was described as exotifying a stereotypical Latino culture, simply the flip side of negative stereotyping. Given these dynamics, it seemed somehow more comfortable for me to avoid speaking Spanish, as it narrowed the ways in which community members interpreted me. This is not to say that an ethnographer should always go for comfort, since there's a lot to learn by making yourself uncomfortable. But in the context of the politics of this neighborhood, I felt that, given my limited competence in Spanish, I would be able to build better relationships if I stuck to English.[14]

Linguistic Data

The data on which this book is based are written and spoken texts taken from a wide range of discourse settings and genres, as well as detailed fieldnotes of local speech events. Spoken data include meetings of neighborhood civic organizations and the local business association; casual conversations at parties and other social gatherings such as dinner or "hanging out" on streets, stoops, or front porches; get-togethers for particular interest groups such as a Mennonite women's group or a monthly potluck among a group of friends with ties to local Latino community-based organizations; 60 ethnographic interviews; and artistic performances. The members of the civic organizations were by and large White, college-educated (with many holding graduate degrees) homeowners who tended to live west of Mt. Pleasant St., the neighborhood's main commercial corridor. The business association membership was multi-ethnic (White, Black, Latino from a number of different countries, Pakistani, Korean, Iranian). Participants in the casual conversations reflected the demographics of those in the interview data: Most belonged to the neighborhood's three major ethnic groups (Latino, White, and African American). They ranged in age from 7 to 72, although most were in their thirties and forties. Some had lived in Mt. Pleasant all their lives, while others had been there for as little as two years. Most had been in the neighborhood for at least a decade. There were an equal number of owners and renters (with some people renting apartments by themselves or with their families, and others renting rooms in group houses with unrelated housemates).

The written part of the corpus consists of a grant proposal; messages posted to the Mt. Pleasant community email list; and articles, flyers, and other literature put out by community-based organizations, individuals, and the local press about events in the neighborhood. This written data is an important companion to the spoken data of the study. Much of the written data, such as the grant proposal analyzed in chapter 4, emerged as a result of discussions carried on in the spheres where spoken data was recorded. The grant proposal and other data were written to be put to argumentative and persuasive uses, and in this capacity they offer a distillation and crystallization of particular ideologies and attitudes circulating in the community. They also serve as an enduring record of which views won out over others in the spheres from which the written data emerged and in which the texts were being read and used for rhetorical purposes.

A Note to the Reader: The Structure of the Book

In keeping with the overall structure of the *New Directions* series, this book is divided into two parts – Part I, the ethnography proper, and Part II, which provides an intellectual/scholarly context and background to the ethnography. An addendum also appears at the back. There are a number of ways to approach reading this book. If you want to jump right into the story and analysis, then you can continue reading the rest of Part I. If you want to know more about the terminology I'm using and why I've chosen the terms I have, you might want to turn to the book's addendum, *Defining Terms*. Many of the terms that I use in this ethnography have multiple and/or contested meanings. The addendum therefore lays out how I distinguish between *community* and *neighborhood*, or why I use certain ethnic or racial terms and not others (or why I use the terms *ethnoracial* or *ethnic* rather than *racial*), and what I mean by *space*, *place*, and *public discourse*.

If you'd like to get oriented to the theoretical frameworks that undergird the ethnography you can turn to Part II, which consists of chapters 8 and 9. As an ethnographer who lived in the neighborhood I studied before I started the research, and as someone who believes in the fieldwork principle that the knowledge an ethnographer gains is directly connected to their own social positioning in the neighborhood, in Part I of the book I've tried to be explicit about my own position in this neighborhood, and to narrate events in a way that shows my status as a participant in those events. In Part II I set out to do the same thing in terms of the theoretical frameworks that I'm bringing to this analysis of neighborhood life; I discuss those frameworks by explaining how I became interested in them – what aspects of my disciplinary training and, later, of what I was finding out in my fieldwork, led me to investigate the various theories that I use here.

My training is in discourse analysis, a field that has developed out of sociolinguistics and linguistic anthropology. When I started getting interested in the politics of urban identity and how urbanites use language in political struggles, I turned to research in urban anthropology. I quickly realized that many of the struggles that were going on in the neighborhood were struggles over space – over access to space and over who got to define what kind of place a given space was or should be. I wanted to analyze the processes of place-making, and theories from cultural geography helped me do this.

Because this is an interdisciplinary project, I imagine that few readers will have a background in all the disciplines that have influenced my research. Part II is meant to introduce the various theories that I'm drawing from to a range of audiences. In chapter 8 I explain how I became interested in community-based fieldwork and the notion that, somewhat simplistically stated, language shapes reality. I then discuss current sociolinguistic/linguistic anthropological theory on discourse. This part might be particularly useful for non-discourse analysts, who often have a somewhat different understanding of what constitutes discourse analysis. Chapter 9 is a discussion of theories and research on place identity from sociolinguistics/linguistic anthropology, urban anthropology, and cultural geography.

I was trained in discourse analysis in a linguistics department, whereas my interest in urban anthropology and cultural geography developed out of conducting research in Mt. Pleasant, which means that my orientation to the former fields differs from my orientation to the latter. What I have endeavored to do in discussing urban anthropology and cultural geography is to give an account of the major theoretical frameworks and scholars in these latter fields who have influenced my thinking about how we construct identities for the places we live, work, struggle, and play in.[15]

Discussion of theory is not limited to Part II, however. Much of the analysis in the ethnography chapters uses somewhat technical sociolinguistic theories. So that the analyses will make sense to readers without a background in this area, I provide explanations of the theories I am using at the point where they are relevant within each chapter. The difference between these explanations and the discussions in Part II is that Part II is concerned with a more general description of past research that bears on the current study, while the explanations within the ethnography itself (Part I) provide the details of particular theories so that readers will understand the specifics of how I'm applying these theories to what people in Mt. Pleasant have said or written about life in the neighborhood.

I also want to make a brief note about the writing style I'm using. My goal in writing this book is to make ethnography and theory engaging and accessible to a wide variety of readers. Part of that approach means writing in a less formal style than I would use for, say, an article in an academic journal. And part of that style includes choices such as using "they" and its associated forms as a third person singular pronoun (in order not to invoke gender where it is not relevant), structuring a sentence with a pronoun at the end (in order to avoid a more convoluted construction), or splitting an infinitive (for aesthetic purposes). Singular *they* has been widespread in English since at least the early 16th century, and its use mirrors the similar shift of the pronoun *you* from an exclusively plural pronoun to a pronoun that represents the second person in both singular and plural cases (making *thou*, which originally marked second person singular, obsolete). The rules against putting a preposition at the end of a sentence or splitting an infinitive are arbitrary constraints dreamed up by 18th-century pundits who wanted to make English more like Latin. This book aims to bring to a wider audience an understanding of how language works, and writing against prescriptivist conventions is a way to promote a wider acceptance of sometimes-stigmatized but perfectly grammatical and instrumentally and aesthetically useful forms of English.

Topics in the Ethnography: What's in the Rest of Part I

In order to understand the world which Mt. Pleasantites both create and live in, it is important to know the "lay of the land," both literally and metaphorically. Chapter 2 provides a comprehensive history of the neighborhood within the context of the development of the District of Columbia, as well as a discussion of the neighborhood's current physical and social landscape. It focuses on the contrast between Washington as a federal city and DC as a local city; demographic shifts and tensions that went hand-in-hand with desegregation, Northern migration, immigration reform, suburbanization, war in Central America, and gentrification. The chapter also discusses civic activism in the neighborhood and city.

Chapter 3 investigates how community members draw contrasts between the categories *City* and *Suburb*, and to a lesser extent between Mt. Pleasant and other DC neighborhoods. In their talk, locals construe the city as a place of heterogeneity in terms of ethnicity, economics, and architecture, as well as a dense, disorderly, dirty, and dangerous place. In contrast, they construct the suburbs as homogeneous ethnically, economically, and architecturally, and as orderly and safe, but bland. City and suburb are also opposed to each other in terms of gendered identity – in local discourse cities are constructed as masculine spaces, while suburbs are feminized. This chapter traces the roots of these contrasts from the rise of industrial capitalism in Europe, which led to new conceptions of the private and public sphere, the development of suburbia, and the limitations of women's presence on city streets. This delineation of gendered space leads to a local discourse of fear in which suburban people are constructed as fearful of public spaces in the city, whereas city people are talked about as streetsmart and fearless. An analysis of messages posted to the Mt. Pleasant email listserv shows how community members use this system of contrasts to construct a moral geography that disparages the suburbs and delegitimizes some neighborhood residents' claims to neighborhood membership by characterizing them as suburban people.

Chapters 4 and 5 focus on examples of public discourse about place, in order to see how community members across the local political spectrum use similar themes to construct an identity for the neighborhood, while centralizing and marginalizing different groups of people in relation to legitimate community membership. The data in these chapters shares what we can call a *discursive arena*: Chapter 4 examines a grant for public toilets, while Chapter 5 analyzes a play by a local performance artist. The grant proposal was submitted to the same funder that funded the play. Thus, through these two media, the contestation of place is brought into an arena with material implications – which vision of place wins out in convincing funders what kinds of projects should be financially supported in the neighborhood.

More specifically, chapter 4 – the analysis of a grant proposal for public toilets – examines themes of filth, geographic distancing, ethnicity, and behavior on Mt. Pleasant St. Through the use of a number of different linguistic structures, the writers of this proposal (not necessarily consciously) align Latino men with foreign and rural places, with filth, and with inappropriate behavior (urinating and making comments to women) on the street. These alignments peripheralize Latino men in the moral geography of the neighborhood. At the same time, through these same strategies the writers oppose other community members (among which they count themselves) to the above themes. Instead, they align themselves with urban environments, and with responsible and appropriate behavior vis-à-vis the built environment. These alignments and oppositions construct them as core community members.

Chapter 5, an analysis of two scenes from a play performed by a local Latino performance artist, shows how a speaker can use the same themes discussed above to marginalize a different set of people. In a section of the play on fear, the author characterizes the neighborhood as a place in which crime, men commenting to women on the street, and danger are inherent features of the neighborhood. This writer uses the same linguistic forms and themes as the grantwriters in chapter 4, but he uses them to position a White woman – and by extension Whites in general – on the margins of the neighborhood's moral geography. In contrast, the writer aligns the Latino narrator to what's cast as the inherent characteristics of the neighborhood. This constructs the Latino narrator – and by extension Latinos in general – as a core community member. Similarly, in a section about joy, the writer uses the same themes of ethnicity, behavior on the street, and geographic distancing to construct a Latina woman who takes an aggressive stance in her interactions in public space as a core community member who finds joy in public interaction and embodies the neighborhood's character.

Whereas ethnicity plays a central role in the texts analyzed in chapters 3, 4, and 5, chapter 6 examines a model of community construction which de-emphasizes ethnic boundaries and ethnic tensions.

The data in this chapter consists of stories about how a multi-ethnic group of tenants who formed a co-op[16] association and won ownership of their formerly decrepit apartment building. As a kind of "mini-Mt. Pleasant," the co-op and the co-op stories provide a smaller stage upon which to view the interaction of place and person identities in Mt. Pleasant. In these stories, co-op members use a discourse of family to construct a social structure which, rather than separating the members along ethnic lines, links people together through actual and fictive kinship ties. This family discourse, in bringing with it ideologies about the roles and responsibilities of different types of family members (e.g., mothers, adult sons), also served as an effective means of housing organizing. The narratives of the co-op members promote a view of urban fearlessness which differs greatly from that seen in the public discourse analyzed in previous chapters; co-op members connect an orientation of fearlessness to feminized roles of being a good mother and caretaker, and construe fearlessness as a position that is needed in order to confront (rather than valorize) crime and danger in order to get rid of it and make the neighborhood safer.

At the same time that co-op members de-emphasize (without ignoring) ethnic differences in their stories, centralization and marginalization of community members occur in other ways. The co-op members set up a system of community values that are linked to influences of the physical environment of the building at the time of the struggle for ownership. Through strategies of contrast and reference, co-op members align themselves to the building value system, and oppose new, wealthier residents to the values the co-op members have set up as integral to the building community. Thus, class becomes an important component in the construction of (centralized) self and (marginalized) other identities.

Chapter 7, the epilogue, brings us up to the present, exploring the changes that have occurred in the period between the speed-up of gentrification and the height of the real estate boom in 2004 and 2005. Rather than focusing on analysis, this chapter presents the stories of Mt. Pleasant residents, in order to show multiple ways that community members have dealt with the changes. It also gives insight into what community members would like a larger audience to know about their neighborhood.

As messages from neighborhood listservs find their way into metro section stories in the *Washington Post*[17] and city council members and beat police make comments like "Zero-tolerance policing is what people want in this neighborhood, don't you read the website bulletin boards?", I hope to show in the following chapters how the discourses of the mid- to late 1990s have played a role in the development of the neighborhood in light of what continues to be massive upheaval, and what contributions discourse analytic work can make to urban planning and policy issues.

Notes

1　Immigration and Naturalization Service
2　Briefly put, gentrification is the "upscaling" of a neighborhood. It is a process whereby poor neighborhoods with well-built but generally rundown housing stock gain new, comparatively more well off residents. This results in individual and commercial housing rehabilitation and investment, which drives up real estate prices and displaces the original, poorer, residents who cannot afford increased rent or property taxes. Gentrification prototypically occurs in central city neighborhoods, although this is not always the case. (For other definitions of gentrification, see David Ley (2003:2527) and Robert A. Beauregard (1989:1).)
3　Schiffrin (1994)
4　In Mt. Pleasant people tend to use *ethnicity* and *race* interchangeably and in ways that seem to have more to do with shared group identity and peoplehood. Therefore, I choose to use the term *ethnic/ethnic* or sometimes *ethnoracial*. For a fuller discussion of these terms in local discourse, see the book's addendum, *Defining Terms*.
5　Williams (1988:1)
6　In his article *Objectivity and Commitment in Linguistic Science* (1982), Labov is talking more specifically about using the particular *linguistic* knowledge gained from research to benefit a community. However, not all researchers necessarily limit the means of contributing to applying linguistic knowledge. For a discussion of ethics in linguistic anthropological work, see Wolfram (1993) and Cameron et al. (1992).
7　See Nessa Wolfson (1976) and Charles Briggs (1986).
8　Hamilton (1996:65–66). Amy Shuman (1992) makes a similar point.) For more on intertextuality, see Bauman (2004).
9　Transcription key:

.	falling intonation and brief pause
,	level or fall-rise intonation and brief pause

..	slightly longer pause
...	longer pause
–	cut-off word, false start
,	fall–rise intonation
?	utterance-final rising intonation
"quote"	"quoting" intonation
^	pitch rise on syllable
/???/	unintelligible
/word/	author's guess of difficult-to-interpret word
:	lengthened vowel
italic	English translation
bold	emphatic stress
<loud>	stretch of discourse said in a certain way: loud, with Spanish accent, etc.
<u>underline</u>	draws attention to a particular feature under analysis
[brackets]	author's comments or additions for clarity, or non-verbal sounds
[. . .]	ellipsed talk
=	turn continues on speaker's next line
indented line	Second speaker starts talking during first speaker's turn, at the point above the beginning of the indentation
[	overlapping talk that comes at a page break

10 One reason I interpreted it this way was because, when people found out my father was Israeli, they often asked me, "Is your mother Jewish, too?"

11 While some people seemed to consider Jewishness as a subcategory of Whiteness, others seemed to consider it a distinct category.

12 Codeswitching is the process whereby interlocutors interweave multiple languages within the same conversational turn and often within a sentence. Ernesto's speech in the previous excerpt is a good example.

13 While these attitudes were generally applied regardless of native English speakers' ethnic background, some native Spanish speakers made different evaluations for native English speakers who were Latino. Sometimes people were more accommodating, seeing native English speaking Latinos' use of Spanish as a legitimate claim to identity or as something that was important for them to learn. However, others were more critical of Latino native English speakers, finding the move to speak Spanish an illegitimate claim to identity if the people in question had limited competence.

14 Ideally I would have liked to have been fluent in both Spanish and Vietnamese before starting fieldwork, but budget and time constraints did not allow this.

15   Readers interested in a more comprehensive discussion of place identity in urban anthropology and cultural geography might want to read Setha Low and Denise Lawrence-Zúñiga's edited volume, *The Anthropology of Space and Place: Locating Culture* (2003) or Don Mitchell's *Cultural Geography: A Critical Introduction* (2000).

16   A co-op, short for cooperative, is an association that owns real estate, usually an apartment building. Rather than owning a specific, individual unit, as is the case in a condominium, members of co-ops own shares in their buildings.

17   See for example Schwartzman (2005).

CHAPTER 2

MT. PLEASANT HISTORY AND SOCIAL GEOGRAPHY

Washington, DC

Within the boundaries of the District of Columbia lie two distinct, and yet connected, places: Washington, and DC. If you ask for directions in Washington, people on their lunch break in sensible shoes and government IDs swinging from lanyards around their necks will tell you that your destination is three blocks from DOT (the Department of Transportation), or around the corner from the FBI building. You may have to wait in traffic as Vladimir Putin's motorcade travels from the White House to the Russian Embassy, or make a twisty detour around a World Bank/International Monetary Fund protest. And apropos of such a protest, your cab driver with a master's degree in political science, the nephew of a former Ethiopian member of parliament, is likely to debate with you about the extent to which the IMF's privatization policies (where countries that borrowed money from the IMF were pushed to privatize utilities, pensions, national industries, social services, etc.) caused Argentina's economy to collapse in 2002. In Washington people know politics, and they know lobbyists, and if you say that you are a GS 9,[1] everyone knows what you're talking about.

As people around here are wont to say, it's a company town. A third of the city's workers work directly for the federal government, and many more work as analysts, bureaucrats, and support staff in non-profits, think tanks, pressure groups, lobbying organizations, or trade associations – places like the Service Employees International

Union, Rubber Manufacturers Association, International Association of Fire Fighters, The Urban Institute, African American Women Business Owners Association, Red Cross, Institute of Shortening and Edible Oils, Irish American Information Network, Manufactured Housing Association for Regulatory Reform, and Kids Cultural Action Network.

Then there's the international side of things – embassies, interest groups like the Khalistan Affairs Center and United States New Zealand Council, as well as major international organizations like the World Bank and IMF.

In the national eye, Washington is often seen as *only* a federal city, a transient place where the population changes with every new political administration, and where life is centered around the goings-on on Capital Hill. This view can be heard in the rhetoric of politicians who – often strategically – use the terms *Washington* and *inside the beltway* (the highway that encircles the city and inner suburbs) to refer to the *federal government*, rather than to an east-coast metropolitan city and its residents.

The affairs of official Washington *do* permeate life in the city; locals often joke that the real story of any national or international current event can be found not on the front page of *The Washington Post*, but in the paper's Style section. To be sure, *The Post* has its share of gossip, but with a decidedly Washington flavor. A 2005 *Reliable Source* column,[2] for example, dished that "social Washington has been buzzing for months about the discrete romance between Deputy Defense Secretary Paul Wolfowitz and Shaha Riza, an Arab feminist and a communications advisor at the World Bank." Although the *Post* article gives scant details on the couple, it does attempt to satisfy the curious mind with these tidbits: "Wolfowitz, 61, and Riza, who's said to be in her mid-fifties, are both divorced. They have declined to publicly discuss their relationship but share a desire to democratize the Middle East."

Clearly, the "social Washington" being referred to here is Washington as federal city. *The Washington Post* follows local custom by using the term *Washington* to refer to those residents or that part of local life that are somehow connected to national or international political affairs, as well as to refer to the entire metropolitan area, which includes suburbs in Virginia and Maryland. It's a metropolitan area that has among the highest median income and level of education in the country.

So there's *Washington*, and then there's *DC*.[3] DC is an east-coast city of about 500,000 with a majority African American population, on the cultural and more or less geographic border between North and South. It's a place with neighborhoods and neighborhood identities of long standing, of residents whose families have lived in the city for generations and those who are the first in their families to live in the United States. DC is the home of go-go music legend Chuck Brown and hardcore rockers Fugazi, the birthplace of the half-smoke hotdog, the capital of arguably the richest country in the world where the infant mortality rate rivals that of Costa Rica and Bulgaria[4] (15 deaths per 1,000 live births in 1999, 11.5 in 2002[5]), where 37 percent of adults read at or below a third grade level,[6] and 20.2 percent of all individuals live below the poverty line.[7] In the city where George W. Bush holds court from his perch overlooking Pennsylvania Avenue (when he's not in Crawford, Texas), 91 percent of his neighbors voted against him in the 2004 elections. DC is not Washington.

DC is not Washington, but Washington affects the lives of DC residents in myriad ways. The daily needs of the Federal City have spawned a large service sector, including hotels, restaurants, and maintenance and cleaning companies. The fortnight-long federal government shutdown of 1996 devastated the local economy. One hundred and fifty thousand federal workers and many more thousands of contractors were furloughed.

And because the federal government shut down before Congress had approved the District's annual budget, the DC government shut down as well, furloughing 13,000 non-essential workers including librarians, trash collectors,[8] and health inspectors, and making it impossible to apply for any new Welfare, Social Security, or Medicaid benefits. An outraged spokesperson for Mayor Barry declared,

> It's another example of the differences between Washington D.C., and other municipal jurisdictions, where our own money is tied up in the federal process. This is not federal funds we're talking about. This is our own tax money. It doesn't happen anywhere else in America.[9]

Small businesses like luncheonettes and cab drivers also suffered, and welfare, veteran's and social security applications and in some cases payments were held up. As a woman working at the District's shutdown-hotline explained,

"Earlier today, a guy was angry because he didn't get his food stamps
. . . He had been trying to get in touch with his caseworker – and
now, of course, that's really impossible." After giving the man an emergency telephone number for people needing food, "I just told him
to [rely on] Jesus and something good would happen. That seemed
to calm him down."[10]

Washington wields a powerful force on the city politically. Because
of the relationship of the city and the federal government, residents
of DC live under some of the least democratic conditions in all of
the United States.[11] District residents have no voting congressional
representation, and have only been able to vote in presidential
elections since 1964. The US Congress has the authority to approve
or deny the city's annual budget, as well as the power to repeal any
law passed by the city council within one month of its enactment,
for any reason. For example, in 1997 Congress repealed the District's domestic partners law which accorded insurance and other
benefits to the partners of city employees;[12] and in 1998, Congress
prohibited the District Board of Elections from tallying the votes of
a municipal medical marijuana referendum. Although District residents were accorded (limited) home rule in 1973, in 1995 Congress
established a Federal Control Board to oversee the city government,
ultimately taking control away from the mayor of all city agencies
but three (tourism, recreation, and libraries).

Although the Control Board was dismantled in 2001, DC residents
continue to lack the representation and autonomy that residents
of the nation's 50 states have. At the same time, they pay federal
taxes that residents of US territories don't.[13] In fact, taxes in the district are among the highest in the nation: *Money Magazine* ranked
Washingtonians in the lowest tax bracket as paying the 144th highest
taxes of 1,260 cities, and those in the highest tax bracket as paying
216th highest of 1,260 cities. This does not mean that DC is rolling
in tax dollars, however: the 70 percent of the city's workforce who
live in the Maryland and Virginia suburbs do not pay a commuter
tax to DC on the income they earn in the city. This is a big loss in
tax dollars, as DC has the highest rate of workers living outside its
territory of any city in the country.[14]

The presence of so many federal buildings, national associations,
and non-profit organizations (including universities and religious

institutions) also takes a large toll on the city's tax base, since these organizations are exempt from property taxes. Non-profit organizations own 14.3 percent of the city's "real property base"; in combination with the 26.5 percent that the federal government owns, this means that no property taxes are paid on 41 percent of the city's land. The federal government does give an annual payment to DC to – in theory – cover the government's use of tax-funded city resources (police, fire fighters, public works and utilities, etc.), but the payment does not make up for the loss in tax revenue. For example, the presence of federal government targets in the city poses a high security threat to the city. To help DC protect itself, the city was given federal "homeland security" funds to implement measures to safeguard the District's residents from threat. But the Bush administration forced the city to spend 11.9 million dollars of this money on security for Bush's 2004 inauguration festivities. Perhaps it's not surprising that the car that chauffeurs Bush around the city sports an alternate license plate, not the standard issue that spells out the colonial status of DC for all to see (Figure 2.1).

The disenfranchisement of DC residents in their own backyard is the political and geographical context within which goings-on in DC neighborhoods like Mt. Pleasant are located. Because there is no possibility to affect change at a state level and no representation at a national level, what people in DC have is the local. Where we can vote and where our votes count is in elections for mayor, city council, school board, and advisory neighborhood commissioners. This means that city and neighborhood struggle take on an urgency for people that they might not otherwise. And in a neighborhood with residents who have sought refuge from wars across the world, in a city with a huge gap between rich and poor, the connection between the local and the global becomes crystal clear when you're 16 blocks away from the White House where social welfare cuts are proposed and immigration policy is hashed out. In order to understand the struggles in Mt. Pleasant, then, it's important to understand the history of local disenfranchisement. The history of disenfranchisement, along with that of migration patterns into the neighborhood, lays the groundwork for understanding something about why the struggles over rights and representation are so intense in Mt. Pleasant. And because so many local struggles are about public space, it's crucial to know something about the neighborhood's built

Figure 2.1   DC license plate © Jennifer Leeman

environment. The rest of this chapter, then, describes the history of the city and the neighborhood, as well as how spaces in the neighborhood are structured and how people use and navigate them.

Part I: The History

Founding the city and roots of alienation

Today it may seem odd to have a city that exists on its own without the structural support of a state, but there was a motivated reason behind this: the US constitution called for the capital to be placed within a district that was located outside of any state borders, so that national concerns would not be colored by the local interests of representatives who were residents of a state that housed the capital. The idea was to balance power at the national level, and perhaps this made

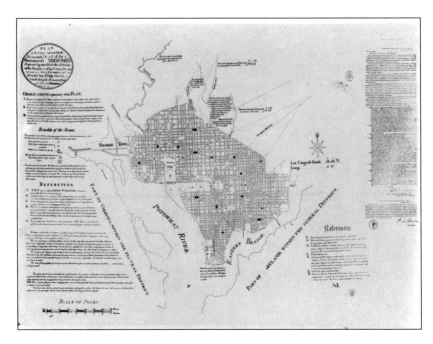

Figure 2.2   Pierre L'Enfant's original plan for Washington, DC
Library of Congress collections

sense from the perspective of congressmen who never established residency in the city, but rather stayed in boarding houses and hotels when Congress was in session.

In 1791 Maryland and Virginia offered up 10 square miles of their choicest partially submerged swampland to the federal government to form the country's new capital city. This diamond-shaped parcel of former estate land around the Potomac River became the District of Columbia. Originally the city of Washington was the area at the center of the diamond; the rest of the land was split up into the city of Georgetown (now a Northwest-quadrant neighborhood), the city of Alexandria (the part of the diamond south of the Potomac that has now returned to Virginia), and Washington County. Mt. Pleasant started off as a suburb of Washington City, located in Washington County (Figure 2.2).

The choice of Washington as the federal city was a compromise between Northern and Southern interests: Thomas Jefferson wanted a capital in the South, and Alexander Hamilton agreed to lobby

Northern lawmakers to support this plan if Jefferson agreed to Hamilton's proposal that the federal government take over state debts. George Washington chose the actual site, thinking that a location like Washington – free of big-city phenomena such as "commerce, local politics, luxury and mobs,"[15] by a major river, reasonably near the Atlantic Ocean, and located on the cultural and geographic border between North and South – would be well situated to exercise a unifying effect on the country.

Initially, local residents voted in the counties that the land they lived on had originally come from. This continued until Congress assumed its new home in 1800, and passed an act that stripped District residents of their rights to congressional representation and, what's more, to vote in national elections. Residents also had little power to vote for local officials.[16]

Things took a turn for the worse in 1871. In 1848 Congress had ruled that property ownership was no longer a criterion for voting in the District, and in 1866 Congress overrode President Johnson's veto and extended the right to vote to African American men.[17] Compared to other areas of the country at this time, African Americans in DC were well educated and prosperous. As the historical sociologist L.E. Horton argues,[18] the federal government feared that these residents' wealth and education would enable them to attain political power, and it was this fear that led Congress to pass the District Territorial Act in 1871. This act radically altered citizen rights in DC. Under this act, the president – whom DC residents had no role in electing – appointed a DC governor and an upper house of local representatives. In addition, Congress appointed various Boards to oversee city functions. Residents were allowed to elect a lower house of representatives and a Shadow District delegate to the federal House of Representatives who was not allowed to participate in any votes that the House took.[19]

The case for DC's self-determination and representation has been debated in Congress over 150 times.[20] Almost since its beginnings, then, there's been a glaring discrepancy between national ideals of freedom and the colonial reality of life in DC, and this discrepancy has not been lost on the city's residents, who have fought for the right to self-determination and representation throughout the 20th century.

DC residents have always linked their own struggles for self-determination to the national values and government endeavors at a given time. For example, right after World War I, residents of DC used national issues as a rhetorical resource to promote the case for local self-determination. Consider the remarks of a District of Columbia Supreme Court Justice at a gathering of activists lobbying for DC rights:

> We and the other free nations have just come out of a great war waged for the defense and extension of th[e] principle [of self-determination]. It would appear, therefore, that even the people of the District of Columbia might expect a fair and sympathetic hearing as they renew their modest claim. Their claim will not be weakened if we consider for a moment the part they took in that supreme struggle for democracy . . . She sent into the [military] a little short of eighteen thousand men, nearly one-half of whom saw service overseas. She outstripped seven sovereign states of the Union in the number of her forces. She outstripped eight in the number of her enlistments . . . Her dead lie tonight upon the fields of France and Flanders or sleep beneath the sea. Her maimed and shattered sons have come back to walk or hobble through her Streets, wearing the proofs of their valor which they will carry to their graves, bearing about in their bodies the marks of complete devotion to their country. And yet she cannot lift her voice in the assembly of the nation she gave her best to save. She cannot have a word to say when laws are being passed that may put a stain upon her honor or cut her to the quick.[21]

Washington society folk who led organizations like the Society of Natives and the Association of Oldest Inhabitants combined themes of freedom and patriotism with talk of the relative lack of immigrant communities in the city to publicly create a xenophobic image of the District population as "truly American" and thus deserving of American civil rights:

> The population of the National Capital, Mr. Noyes [president of the Association of Oldest Inhabitants] pointed out, is distinctly safe and sane American, lacking the unstable element which weakens so many of our great cities, he said.[22]

Despite appealing to both national and local themes and preying on the country's xenophobic fears, however, The Society of Natives and their ilk had little real impact; Congress failed to substantively address self-determination in the District for forty more years.

In 1961, with the ratification of the 23rd Amendment, DC residents gained the right to vote for president and vice-president. In 1967 the Reorganization Plan for the District of Columbia abolished the three-person council of District commissioners,[23] and in 1978 both the House and the Senate passed the Civil Rights Act of 1978. This act would create two Senators to be elected by the people of DC and either one or two representatives, depending on population numbers. When the Senate approved the amendment in August,[24] the issue then passed to state legislatures. To go into effect, the amendment needed to be ratified by 38 states in seven years. When in those seven years only 16 states out of 50 had managed to ratify it, many politicians, pundits, and residents of DC echoed Ted Kennedy's view of a national

"fear that senators elected from the District of Columbia may be too liberal, too urban, too black, or too Democratic."

The notion that the rest of the country found DC too African American and too Democrat was likely alive and well in local discourse before 1978, but discussions in Congress, state legislatures, and press conferences reinforced this characterization and made it part of national discourse.

Ted Kennedy first characterized DC as a Democrat, African American city when he bypassed the Senate Judiciary committee and brought discussion of the Civil Rights Act amendment directly to the Senate floor:[25]

After the voting representation amendment was brought onto the Senate floor yesterday, Kennedy led off the debate by asserting that opposition to the proposal "has seemed to arise from . . . [sic] the fear that senators elected from the District of Columbia may be too liberal, too urban, too black, or too Democratic." (*Washington Star* 1978b)

In many of the arguments that Kennedy and others put forth, the issue of District voting rights thus became characterized not as an issue of general civil rights for District residents, but rather as one of African American civil rights. This characterization relied on two factors: first, the name of the proposed amendment (*Civil Rights Act of 1978*) and US east-coast post-war associations of the term *civil rights* with struggles for African American civil rights in particular; and second, the presupposition that DC was an African American city. Thus, the argument both drew on a construction of DC as an African American city, and, critically, reproduced this construction at both a local and a national level.

The sociolinguist Barbara Johnstone[26] has shown that newspaper accounts of cities get picked up and recirculated in public and private conversations in those cities, thus contributing to widespread constructions of particular city identities. This is what happened with the Kennedy quote. Politicians and media throughout the country reproduced Kennedy's words, and this contributed not only to a local, but also a national construction of DC as an African American city. For example, when the New Jersey state legislature voted on the Civil Rights Act amendment, a DC journalist reported that

> Assemblyman Charles Mays, one of four blacks in the Assembly, warned that the opponents would vote no only because the District is "too urban, too Democratic, and too black."[27]

As media commentators spread Kennedy's words through national public discourse, the quote became delinked from the politician himself. For example, in an editorial written a few days after Congress approved the amendment, a prominent Washington columnist wrote,

> The Senate debate brought out some of the real reasons why some members don't want the District to have two voting senators and two representatives. "Washington is too black, too liberal, too urban, and too Democratic," is the catch-phrase.[28]

And an editorial printed in North Carolina's *Greensboro Daily News*, reprinted in the *Washington Post* for consumption by District residents, declared,

> As each [state] body takes [the amendment] up, the same ghosts that haunted the bill in Congress doubtless will haunt it in the provinces. These are the four horsemen, if you will, of a perceived apocalypse: that Washington's prospective representation will be 1) too urban, 2) too liberal, 3) too Democratic and 4) too black.[29]

Journalists characterized voting rights for the District as a specifically African American issue in other ways, for example in discourse about how the amendment vote had played out among congresspeople from the Carolinas. It was widely speculated that South Carolina Senator Strom Thurmond had voted in favor of the amendment in order to gain the African American vote in his upcoming election:

> Senator Strom Thurmond's endorsement of the amendment the other day was a potent one. The South Carolina Republican's support may, of course, have been influenced by his tight race for re-election and the one-quarter black voter registration there – and let's not be coy about it, the District's predominantly black population has been an element in this issue.[30]

Newspaper writers also reported on North Carolina Senator Jesse Helms's criticism of Thurmond and other amendment supporters, by calling their votes "a mad scramble for political advantage with a minority group."[31] Other writers detailed the state-level ratification debates, describing, for example, a memo written by a Michigan state legislature staffer to Republican representatives advising that

> any Republican who is seeking black support or who is dependent upon black support must certainly support the amendment.[32]

By investigating how discussions about congressional representation contributed to the construction of DC as an African American city, I don't mean to claim that DC is *not* a majority African American city, or that voting rights is not a critical issue for African Americans because of the US government's history of legislated and informal barriers to African American voting. And I also agree with Ted Kennedy that fear of enfranchising a majority African American city *has* been a major factor in federal and state government's denying representation to the District. So my point in analyzing the circulation of Kennedy's remarks is not to contradict what he said, but rather to show how the discussion of voting rights created a particular image of the city, an image that cast ethnoracial relations *in general* as Black–White relations *specifically*. For the purposes of the present study, this is important because characterizing ethnoracial relations as simply Black–White relations influences the way that the city addresses ethnoracial issues in Mt. Pleasant, a neighborhood with a large Latino and significant Vietnamese population in addition to Whites and Blacks.

Politics on the streets of DC: the history of Mt. Pleasant

Mt. Pleasant had its origins in the bucolic estate land aptly called Pleasant Plains, which had been passed down through generations of prominent Maryland families since its annexation by George Calvert, Lord Baltimore, in the 1600s. Set up high above the city in the north-west part of Washington County, Mt. Pleasant was considered by many of its early residents to be the area's first suburb.

In 1850 William Selden, former US Treasurer and Marshal of the District of Columbia, bought 73 acres of Pleasant Plains. Selden was a Virginian with strong Confederate sympathies and finances sunk deep into southern real estate. The Civil War cut him off from his financial resources and flung him into debt, so in 1862 he sold his property to an army supplier from Maine named Samuel P. Brown (Figure 2.3) who renamed the lot *Mt. Pleasant*.[33]

Brown had been a dealer in lumber and granite and had been engaged in the shipbuilding business in his native Maine before the vice-president offered him the position of navy agent – the main buyer for naval supplies – in 1861. In addition to his financial endeavors, Brown was also engaged in politics both in Maine and in the District; he'd served a number of times in the Maine legislature and had made a bid for Congress. Over the course of his time in DC he served as a member of the Board of School Trustees and the Board of Public Works, as well as a judge on the levy court. His prominence at the local and national level is illustrated by the range of individuals who served as pallbearers at his funeral – a senator, an ex-governor, two ex-mayors, and one commissioner from DC.

It was after the end of the war that the groundwork was laid for Mt. Pleasant to be settled as a suburban village. As the Annals of Mt. Pleasant explain,

> [I]mmediately after the close of the war, real estate began to recover from its depression and industry and enterprise to resume their accustomed channels. Hence there were frequent inquiries for suburban

Figure 2.3   Samuel P. Brown, founder of Mt. Pleasant
Library of Congress collections

property; and as these multiplied it occurred to Mr. Brown that he might do good service to the public and to himself by selling off a portion of his farm in lots suitable for suburban residences.

The Civil War led to the first wave of urbanization in Washington as a whole. As Union territory below the Mason–Dixon line, the District became a destination for a wide range of people: slaves fleeing to freedom, farmers driven from their land by war battles, equipment suppliers like Samuel Brown, journalists in hopes of a good story, and seekers of newly created government jobs that supported the war effort. Among this last group were many young single women who sought their fortunes as federal jobs became open to them.[34]

After the war, over 30,000 newly free African Americans moved to the city[35] and many of the people who'd come for military and civil service jobs decided to stay after the war's end. The city's growing population and the resulting explosion of building to house the city's new residents created a post-war economic boom.

It was during this moment of economic prosperity that Samuel Brown developed his land, selling divided plots of his estate to well-to-do New Englanders who were current and former members of government or the military, and (mostly) upper-level civil servants. In Mt. Pleasant's early years residents could access the central city by a horse-drawn streetcar that made its way back and forth twice a day, and many residents had their own horses and carriages.[36] But it was still quite a distance from the city; the village's isolation and its relatively homogeneous New Englander population created a strong communal identity from the beginning. A number of students of the neighborhood's history have observed that "the area acquired many aspects of a New England village,"[37] and the sense of community – as well as political activism – in these early years is reflected in the many neighborhood civic associations that they created, including the Mt. Pleasant Division Sons of Temperance, meetings to promote territorial government in the District, Mt. Pleasant Dramatic Club, Mt. Pleasant Citizens Association, and Christian Society of Mt. Pleasant. The village had its own school and Union Hall, where community members met for political meetings (for example to agitate for public works improvements or territorial government in the District), religious meetings, and social events. Upon the grand occasion of the nation's centennial, Mt. Pleasantites compiled and printed an extensive history of what they called their "young village."[38]

Today DC is a segregated city, but this has not always been the case. Before public transportation arrived at the beginning of the 20th century, Washingtonians of all ethnicities and classes lived within walking distance of their workplaces. This meant that commercial and residential sites existed in the same neighborhoods, and Black and White, rich, poor, and middle-class employees and employers, and property owners and tenants shared physical city spaces – although their housing conditions were vastly unequal and their social worlds remained distinct, and African Americans had many fewer avenues of opportunity than did Whites. Mt. Pleasant, however, was quite homogeneous in its early years.

There is little information about African Americans living in Mt. Pleasant in the 1800s, although the 1900 census and the 1876 Annals of Mt. Pleasant do make mention of a few African American residents. We do know, however, that Mt. Pleasant community members founded a Sunday School for African Americans in 1871,[39] and one newspaper article notes that, in the late 1800s, African American children and White children from the general area attended school together in Mt. Pleasant.[40] No records relate precisely when integrated schooling stopped in Mt. Pleasant, but it is likely that it came to an end under President Wilson.

On the national front, in 1913 Wilson halted the practice of designating African American political appointees for government policy positions. In addition, he limited African American employment opportunities in the federal government to blue-collar and very low-level white-collar jobs.[41] Locally, Wilson lent his support to residential segregation. As restrictive housing covenants and racist zoning ordinances and bank lending policies in the city flourished[42] and African American employment opportunities drastically decreased, the city began to experience "the systematic erosion of the social and economic fortunes of the African American community."[43]

The trolley brings change

Mt. Pleasant's elite status began to change at the turn of the 20th century, with the inauguration of the 42 trolley line.[44] Soon shops began opening up along the last five blocks of the trolley route, and a business corridor developed. The trolley made travel to and from Washington City easier, and therefore the neighborhood became more attractive to a wider range of people. This spurred some of the estate owners in the neighborhood to begin selling off parcels of land, and more middle-class Washingtonians started to move to Mt. Pleasant. Real estate developers chopped up large parcels into smaller lots, where they built large and luxurious Victorian-style rowhouses, many with six bedrooms, sitting rooms, and large dining rooms and kitchens. A few detached houses were also built at this time, although most of the detached houses in the neighborhood predate the trolley (Figure 2.4).

Promoting segregation

As public transportation made it easier for Washingtonians to live farther away from where they worked, many people started to move

Figure 2.4 Fancy houses on hill   © Jennifer Leeman

out of the downtown area, and longstanding residents of outlying areas reacted by pushing for *restrictive housing covenants*, agreements that barred African Americans (and in some cases, Jews and Italians) from buying or renting property. Developers who built new neighborhoods in one phase put restrictive covenants on all their properties at once. Covenants worked differently in neighborhoods like Mt. Pleasant that were built in spurts, however. In order for covenants in such neighborhoods to be valid, the law required that neighbors of individual blocks get together to put covenants on all houses of a block, thereby creating segregated areas block by block.

No histories of Mt. Pleasant deal with housing covenants explicitly, but housing deeds and minutes of the local *Citizens Association* show that Mount Pleasant had a large share of residents who were zealous about restricting African Americans from owning, renting, or inheriting property in the neighborhood.

Because of the relative lack of elected government bodies in the city, in the early part of the 20th century neighborhood Citizens Associations held an enormous amount of political influence and sway. In order to have a stronger voice at the city level, in 1910 a number of Mt. Pleasant's prominent families revived a moribund Citizens Association in Mt. Pleasant. The Association spoke out on reappointments of superior court judges and plans for city hospitals, and they also devoted their energies to neighborhood endeavors like opposing the construction of apartment buildings (which were thought to block views and attract a different (i.e., poorer) kind of neighbor), creating a park at the trolley turnaround station, and building a new library and elementary school.

The Association was deeply invested in maintaining the racial and economic status quo at a time when the city's ethnoracial landscape was in flux. In the 1920s and 1930s, African Americans from the South were moving to the District in increasing numbers in search of better job opportunities. At the same time, the new affordability of automobiles and consequent easy commuting made the idea of living in the suburbs seem manageable, and freshly built suburban houses with modern amenities like gas furnaces, gas stoves, and bathtubs with showers made suburban living attractive to many city residents.[45] The migration of White DC residents to the suburbs left many empty rowhouses, and many of these were turned into rental property and often divided up into smaller units.

Historian Dennis Gale notes that in the 1930s the population in the area southeast of Mt. Pleasant started to become more African American. During this time the Citizens Association was extremely active in campaigning against apartment buildings and for restrictive covenants. Although Mt. Pleasant and the adjoining Columbia Heights neighborhood remained predominantly White, it is clear that Citizens Association members were strongly opposed to the possibility of living next to African American neighbors. It was possibly this opposition that motivated the Association in 1923 to re-envision the territory covered by the Association as ending at 16th St. rather than 14th St., as the African American population east of 14th St. was starting to grow.[46]

The Citizens Association also worked to keep Mt. Pleasant White through a concerted campaign to induce property owners to enter into agreements with their neighbors to put restrictive covenants on their properties.[47] Starting around 1927, the Citizens Association began organizing owners by block or street to sign agreements that restricted their property from being sold, rented, or bequeathed to "any person of negro race or blood," as the covenants put it, for 50 years after the date the contract was signed[48]. In addition to their own voluntary efforts, the Association also hired a representative to engage in door-to-door canvassing to obtain signatures. According to Citizens Association minutes, any property owners who declined to sign were sent a letter encouraging them to reconsider; the Association, which was nothing if not persistent, followed up with a home visit by members of the Restrictive Covenants Committee.

The Association also had procedures in place to address neighbors' possible objections to signing an agreement. (Although, strikingly, the minutes do not address how the Association might respond to community members who refused to sign based on an opposition to segregation.) For example, the Association's representative did the work of drawing up all the documents and filing them at the Recorder of Deeds. She also collected the $1.50 filing fee that the city charged. (It was the exchange of this money that validated the agreement.) If property owners declined to sign because they didn't want to pay the fee, the Citizens Association's policy was to pony up the money themselves.

The Citizens Association cast a watchful eye over all real estate transactions in the neighborhood, because restrictive covenants became invalid on any property that underwent foreclosure. Ever vigilant, they engaged the services of a clerk at the Assessor's Office, who notified the Citizens Association every time that property in the neighborhood changed hands. And because real estate developers bought vacant property to build new dwellings on, the Association worked hard to persuade developers to put restrictive covenants on their new properties. Sometimes the Association secured agreements by offering in exchange not to oppose the developers' plans to construct new properties. Through their vigilance and heavy-handed signature-gathering tactics, by 1932 the Citizens Association had managed to put restrictive covenants onto around 90 percent of the neighborhood's properties.[49]

Through the 1920s and 1930s, DC – including Mt. Pleasant – continued to grow steadily. With the government's New Deal programs and a new administrative workforce coming to DC to find their fortune, as it were, once again infill houses[50] began to appear on the streets of Mt. Pleasant and other growing neighborhoods.

But the depression had been felt in the District as it was elsewhere, and the new houses were substantially more modest than the

Victorian rowhouses of decades past. The neighborhood increasingly became a middle-class community of primarily civil servants. With its own busy shopping street, merchants who lived near their stores,[51] and active community organizations, Mt. Pleasant retained the strong sense of community identity that it had had in the 19th century, although the characteristics that made up that identity were shifting.

During World War II, the labor needs of the war effort brought a similar influx of new residents to the neighborhood, looking to find shelter in an acute housing market. Mt. Pleasant responded to this need in various ways. Some residents took boarders into their homes.[52] Many landlords subdivided their houses into apartments or turned them into boarding houses, where newly minted government workers – many of them single women – shared hallway conversations and evening meals with elderly District residents looking for smaller accommodations.[53] The neighborhood remained almost completely White during the war period.

After integration

The decades after World War II brought to Mt. Pleasant demographic shifts larger than the neighborhood had experienced at any other time in its history. After the war, new housing for war workers who decided to stay in the city and for returning veterans and their families was built on a number of Mt. Pleasant's remaining lots. These homes, many of them designed with the heavy gables and cross-hatched timbering of the Tudor style popular at the time, were much more modest than the older and more majestic neighboring rowhouses. According to local real estate agents, in order to appeal to owners at a time when the suburbs were seen as extremely attractive, developers included some luxury and custom features in many of these houses. For example, some had finished basements with 10-foot ceilings, which were advertised as "ballrooms." In other houses, new owners were able to design individual color schemes for their bathrooms from a range of tiles, tubs, toilets, and sinks in any combination of grass green, bright purple, and shiny mary-jane black. These smaller houses and the modern apartment buildings that were built around the same time clearly proclaimed Mt. Pleasant's post-war status as a solidly middle-class neighborhood, rather than the more upper-class or mixed upper- to middle-class enclave it had been in the century's early years.

While the suburbs continued to lure White residents away from DC and Mt. Pleasant at a faster and faster pace, African Americans (who by and large were excluded from suburban mortgage financing) started moving into Mt. Pleasant. This trend began slowly with the *Bolling v. Sharpe* ruling in 1948, which made housing covenants legally unenforceable. According to residents who lived in the neighborhood at that time, however, it was not until around 1956, after school desegregation, that African Americans started moving to Mt. Pleasant in greater numbers, and Whites consequently began moving out.

These Supreme Court rulings did not mean that integration happened easily in Mt. Pleasant. While many White residents may have supported integration, the Citizens Association remained active as a promoter of de facto segregation well into the 1960s. The Association vocally opposed civic projects – such as the Barney House settlement house – that they thought might cast the neighborhood in a negative light or attract African Americans to the neighborhood.[54] They also promoted informal discriminatory housing practices.

Although the 1948 Supreme Court ruling had declared housing covenants to be unenforceable by law, it left open the possibility for property owners to refuse, on an ad-hoc basis, to sell their properties to people they didn't want to sell to. In light of this loophole, the Citizens Association printed and promoted voluntary contracts that neighbors could sign asserting that they would not sell their properties to "anyone not of the Caucasian race."[55] These contracts explained the loophole and asserted that, in contrast to previously legal housing covenants, the contracts would not be filed with the Recorder of Deeds.[56] In October of 1948 the Association presented a five-paragraph sample agreement at a special meeting of the organization. This document outlined what the Association feared and what they planned to do about it:

> Whereas it is deemed necessary to continue in the spirit of such covenants for the protection of the value of our properties and the character of the community, and to preserve what we believe to be our inherent right and prerogative,
>
> We, the undersigned, owners of the real estate in the Mt. Pleasant area of the District of Columbia identified opposite our names, in

consideration of the mutual agreement of other property owners in the Mt. Pleasant area hereby agree that we will not sell, transfer or lease such properties, or any part thereof, to any person or persons other than those of the Caucasian race.

We further agree to furnish the Mt. Pleasant Citizens Association promptly with all information we may receive of any attempt by any person not of the Caucasian race to purchase, acquire, or occupy any such property, and to cooperate with said Association in the preservation of the integrity of our community in accordance with the tenor of this agreement.

The historical record is unclear about the extent to which such agreements were implemented. No later mention of the agreements appears in the Association's minutes, but the Association worked to maintain segregation in a number of other ways. In 1950 – two years after restrictive covenants were ruled unenforceable – they established a "Real Estate Protective Committee," and this committee established a fund which would enable the organization to obtain options on properties that were potentially going to be sold to African Americans.

Despite their efforts, Mt. Pleasant did become increasingly integrated. By 1960, DC had become a majority African American city, with 60 percent of the population. At that time Mt. Pleasant was still a largely homogeneous neighborhood, with Whites constituting 73 percent of the population.[57] By the middle of the decade, however, the neighborhood's residential and commercial population would become majority African American.

In the beginning of the 1960s the feel of Mt. Pleasant's streets also began to change, as absentee landlords and property speculators avoided maintenance work and allowed their properties to fall into disrepair (cf. Figure 2.5).

In 1961 a group of residents formed a community group to protest this state of affairs and encourage property renovation. Newspaper articles of the time convey the sense that this effort was also an attempt to upscale the neighborhood:

Mt. Pleasant Citizens Plan a "Georgetown".

Mrs. Frances R. Valeo, wife of the assistant to [the] Senate Majority leader [. . .] is sparking a citizen effort to make a "Georgetown" out of Mt. Pleasant. . . . [T]he century-old neighborhood of large old homes,

Figure 2.5   Apartment building off Mt. Pleasant St.

rowhouses and apartments, now faces a slide into shabbiness, Mrs. Valeo said last week.

To halt and reverse this, Mrs. Valeo, a sociology graduate who lives at 3420 17th St NW, has formed some 60 neighbors into three committees to:

- Get homeowners to turn on porch lights on Friday nights, starting next Friday, to make things safer and cheerful and to instill an esprit de Mt. Pleasant.
- Work on code enforcement in a drive on the speculators and absentee landlords who, Mrs. Valeo said, are responsible for the blight that now exists.
- Encourage home renovation by homeowners, realtors and, possibly, foundations that might want to fix up "mansions" of the area for embassy use.

. . .

With its own shopping area (Mt. Pleasant St.), schools (Bancroft Elementary and Sacred Heart) and churches (on 16th St.), tree-laced

Mt. Pleasant offers to Mrs. Valeo the pleasing prospect of suburban living in the city. On her block it's already a reality, which she would like to share with her neighbors.[58]

The reference to Georgetown in this article shows Mrs. Valeo's group's desire to align itself with – and consequently portray itself as – a well-to-do neighborhood. The reference to Georgetown calls up connotations of both class and ethnicity: Georgetown in 1961 was a congressionally-decreed historic district with fancy shops and boutiques along its main thoroughfares. The neighborhood had undergone an intense gentrification process from the 1930s to the 1950s, which had brought with it an enormous decrease in what had been a large African American community. From 1940 to 1960, the African American proportion of the Georgetown population decreased from 22 to 3 percent.[59] (As I'll discuss in later chapters, the strategy of comparing Mt. Pleasant to Georgetown is still alive today.)

Although one of the main issues in the article is Mt. Pleasant's impending "slide into shabbiness," the neighborhood's potential to be a stately community is enhanced through exemplars of its history and built environment: a "century-old neighborhood of large old homes, rowhouses and apartments," and the "'mansions' of the area [suitable] for embassy use."

The article's author also implicitly acknowledges the role that migration to the suburbs has had in the changes in the neighborhood's physical and social landscape. By focusing on neighborhood institutions within convenient reach ("shopping, schools, churches"), and on "tree-laced streets," the author implicitly draws a parallel between the atmosphere in Mt. Pleasant and the environmental priorities of many who live in the suburbs. The parallel is made more explicit in the reference to "the pleasing prospect of suburban living in the city."

In the second half of the 1960s greater numbers of middle-class White residents as well as some middle-class African American residents traded Mt. Pleasant for suburban living. Owner-occupied properties became rental housing, and poorer residents, mostly African American, started moving in. Whereas before the 1968 Martin Luther King riots the neighborhood was 65 percent White, in 1970 this proportion dropped to 32 percent. The 80 percent proportion of renter-occupied property in 1970 hints that the neighborhood's socioeconomic makeup was also changing.[60]

The segregationist Citizens Association had started to lose clout in the 1950s, and with the demographic shift of the late 1960s, it became even more unpopular. As was common in other neighborhoods at this time, in Mt. Pleasant pro-integration neighbors created a *Neighbors* Association to demonstrate their opposition to the *Citizens* Association. While the organization's founding members were by and large Whites, by the mid-1970s the group's membership was interracial, reflecting more accurately the White/African American/Latino make-up of the neighborhood.[61] Whereas the Citizens Association believed that an exclusionist agenda would promote a stable neighborhood, the Neighbors Association argued that

> Because our neighborhood is an integrated one, our organization, to be effective, must necessarily be interracial. We believe this to be our greatest strength. We also believe that when neighbors work together on common problems, the fear and distrust that exist tend to disappear and we have a healthier and more stable community.

Washington goes international

Starting in the 1950s a small Spanish-speaking community began to form in DC as Latin American statespeople and bureaucrats, along with their families and domestic workers, came to the city.[62] They joined international university students and Puerto Rican and Mexican American white-collar government employees who had come to the city during the New Deal and World War II.[63] The 1950s and 1960s also saw the arrival of Dominicans, as well as Cubans who were fleeing Castro's Revolution.

The civil rights efforts going on in the country in the 1960s also had an effect on immigration policy, leading to the Immigration and Nationality Act amendments in 1965, which allowed increased immigration from Latin America, Asia, Africa, and the Caribbean.[64] In the Mt. Pleasant area, these new immigration policies led to a larger and ever more diverse Latino community in the 1960s and 1970s, as people from a wide variety of Latin American (mostly South American) countries moved to the District, a large number of them settling around Mt. Pleasant and the adjacent Adams Morgan neighborhood.[65] Some of these residents were families of domestic workers from the previous decades who had stayed in DC after their employers left; others came for jobs or educational opportunities. Many worked in childcare and cleaning, and the community was predominantly made up of women.[66]

The folklorist Olivia Cadaval, in her study of DC Latinos, notes that an explicit sense of a Latino community began to form in the mid-1960s, as immigrants from Spanish-speaking countries "began to forge a shared identity around a common language, shared cultural values, and similar legal, housing, and employment issues."[67]

At this time, Latino community leaders were predominantly of Puerto Rican and Cuban background. They were for the most part well educated with white-collar jobs, in comparison with the majority of the Latino community who by and large came from working-class or peasant backgrounds.[68] While the 1968 riots after Martin Luther King Jr's assassination spurred some (mostly middle-class) Latinos living in the city to move to the suburbs,[69] in general the DC Latino community began to institutionalize itself in the late 1960s and the 1970s: the Mayor's Office established an Office on Latino Affairs,[70] area school districts began offering ESL classes, and new social service agencies geared towards Latino immigrants appeared on the landscape. In 1969/1970 the first Latino festival was held.[71] Winding its way from the old trolley turnaround park on Mt. Pleasant St. to Kalorama Park on Columbia Road,[72] the festival parade and other associated events drew young and old out to socialize, celebrate, and assert their presence as part of the DC landscape.

During this time, the leadership of the Latino community began to change, as younger Latinos from Puerto Rico and South America began to take active roles in community projects. Often linking US Latino communities to Latin American political struggles, these more politicized leaders from divergent national backgrounds strived to work together to get Latino perspectives on issues such as housing, language policies, and race relations onto the city's radar.

Mt. Pleasant was not experienced as a *wholly* Latino place, however, for it remained a majority African American neighborhood up until around 1980. And Latinos were not the only immigrants to the neighborhood. The 1960s and 1970s saw the beginnings of small communities from the English- and French-speaking Caribbean, particularly Jamaica, Trinidad, and Haiti, as well as some Africans, mostly from East Africa. In the late 1970s, some Indochinese immigrants also settled in the neighborhood.[73]

Hippie kids, do-gooders, and the beginnings of gentrification

By the early 1970s, middle-class and educated post–WWII baby boomers who had cut their teeth on civil rights and anti-war activism had begun to move into Mt. Pleasant, bringing a new kind of appeal to the neighborhood and city living that their parents' generation had rejected for the suburbs. Among these new community members (mostly White, and to a lesser extent Black) were relatively poor residents who most often rented houses or rooms in group houses and cooperatives, and more well-off white-collar workers who bought formerly luxurious, large rowhouses which they then renovated, often doing the work themselves.[74]

In the late 1960s and 1970s, it was possible to buy a six-bedroom Victorian house for as little as $15,000.[75] In 2006 these same houses were selling for upwards of $800,000, an increase of roughly 4,570 percent in just three decades. It was in these decades that many of the old houses that had been converted into apartments or rooming houses during World War II were reconverted back into single-family dwellings. This move decreased the amount of available housing for low-income residents.

The baby-boomer residents were by and large well educated and civil-rights minded. Many had been involved in the social struggles of the 1960s, particularly the anti-war, feminist, and Black power movements. Their liberal to leftist politics attracted them to a multi-ethnic and integrated neighborhood, while their particular sense of aesthetics lured them to the neighborhood's pre-war housing stock, and their economic interests drew them to bargain property values.[76] The neighborhood in many ways was a center of counter-culture politics and art. As one resident from that time reminisces,

> Adams Morgan and Mount Pleasant became places that students eager to move away from dorms looked to in the Sixties and Seventies (and counterculture bookstores and other "infrastructure" came around the same time). The corner of 18th and Columbia had an old movie

theater-turned-disco, where Norman Mailer spoke (stoned) to a crowd on the eve of a famous anti-war protest in the fall of 1967.

But while many of the neighborhood's new residents were organizing themselves around local activities like Marxist reading groups, a significant number of their homeowner cohorts and reading partners were also learning about 19th-century ornamental moldings and becoming concerned with historically accurate renovation. As group house residents became more settled in the city and started earning more money, a significant portion of them joined the ranks of the homeowners. Others, especially those with school-aged children, migrated to the suburbs and their better-funded school systems.

Despite the sentiments of working-class solidarity that the middle-class-background baby-boomer residents often felt, they themselves inadvertently contributed to making Mt. Pleasant less hospitable to people in working-class circumstances. As geographer David Ley points out in his study of gentrification in Canadian cities,

> the youth culture of the 1960s included not only the *last* in a long line of poorer households occupying the inner city, but also the *first* in a new sequence of residents for whom the inner city would not be the site of last resort for households with few choices, but rather the preferred location of a middle-class cohort . . . whose residential location was part of the repertoire of their cultural identity[.][77]

By turning multi-unit dwellings into single ones, fixing up houses, and contributing to a new identity for the neighborhood as bohemian and artsy, the baby-boomer residents increased both property values and property taxes. This put a strain on moderate income renters and homeowners in the neighborhood. By 1977, some Mt. Pleasant rowhouses were selling for as much as $100,000.[78,79]

In the 1970s Mt. Pleasant renters were by-and-large a mix of African American, Latino, and White residents. Old-time homeowners, on the other hand, were predominantly African American. Some of these homeowners welcomed the increase in their property values, but higher property values also meant higher property taxes. This meant that higher property values did not benefit people who did not want to move. Former neighborhood residents – mostly African American

– tell stories of having to move to the suburbs because they could not pay the property tax increases. New homeowners were overwhelmingly White. These divisions between owners and renters and old and new homeowners cast class differences and the tensions that they caused in an ethnoracial light.

The challenges of diversity

During the late 1970s and the 1980s, neighborhood tensions and conflict tended to be indicative of increasingly disparate views about what kind of place Mt. Pleasant was and should be. The Latino community in these decades both grew in numbers and became more established. This led to an increasing sense of neighborhood ownership on the part of many Latinos. At the same time, many of the baby-boomer White homeowners began to replace their 1960s-era idealism with concerns about property values and neighborhood activities such as socializing or drinking on the street in large groups.[80] A number of these residents organized into community organizations to address the issues they felt were community problems. These organizations' undertakings often led to feelings of resentment among some of the neighborhood's longstanding African American residents (as well as the smaller groups of longtime residents of other ethnicities, including White and Latino), who felt their voice in community issues was being overshadowed or ignored by their more recent, and usually more wealthy, neighbors.

For Latinos, carving out a space in the neighborhood also involved resolving tensions that grew out of animosity towards them on the part of some of Mt. Pleasant's longer-term residents. Longtime African American community members often remark on the many ways in which the neighborhood has changed from an African American to a Latino place. Latinos who grew up in the neighborhood in the late 1970s and early 1980s have noted that some African American community members did not welcome their presence. For example, a number of Latino men have told me of schoolyard fights that African American boys instigated against Latino boys.[81]

Others have reported how a largely White group of residents in neighboring Adams Morgan petitioned the city to prohibit the Latino

Festival from using space in a neighborhood park, arguing that "the crowds would ruin newly planted bushes."[82] This park played a large role in neighborhood discourse about gentrification and the growing White population. The residents who petitioned against the festival had also raised objections to Latino boys playing soccer in the same park. In talking about gentrification, those soccer players have made comments to me such as, "I knew the neighborhood was changing when they kicked us out of Kalorama Park."

Although anti-Latino attitudes did not disappear, by the mid-1980s it was clear to all Mt. Pleasant residents that the neighborhood's Latino presence was to be an enduring one. In the 1980s many African American shopkeepers closed their doors, to be replaced by Latino and Korean merchants who opened many stores that catered to Latino consumers. With these stores came street signs and advertisements in Spanish, which gave the street a new look. Mt. Pleasant also gained Latino community institutions like churches and daily newspapers available in most businesses on the street.

The strong Latino presence in Mt. Pleasant in the 1980s was also influenced by a vast increase in Mt. Pleasant's Latino population as a result of civil wars in Central America, particularly El Salvador. Salvadorans had been in DC and its suburbs since the late 1960s, and when war broke out in the 1980s, the Washington area became one of the key destinations for people fleeing the country.

The large-scale migration of Salvadorans changed not only the face of Mt. Pleasant (and, indeed the Washington metropolitan area as a whole), but also of the Latino community. What had previously been a heterogeneous and multicultural community now became heavily Salvadoran. Many argue that the community also became more politicized, with a significant number of new community members who had been active in political struggles in El Salvador. From 1980 to 1990, the city's Latino population increased from 13 to 26 percent.[83,84] Although by population alone more Salvadorans or Salvadoran Americans live in Los Angeles, DC is the only city in the country where the dominant Latino culture is Salvadoran.[85] In fact, in the 1990s, fully half of the immigrants to the Mt. Pleasant/Adams Morgan area were from either El Salvador or Vietnam.[86]

Many of the new Latino immigrants were young men who had either been involved in political movements or were fleeing army conscription.[87] Whereas the Latino community had been predominantly female up until the mid-1980s, the predominantly young and male Salvadoran immigrants changed the shape of the community by the end of the decade, contributing to a demographic where the older members of the community were predominantly female, while younger adults were predominantly male.

Mt. Pleasant's large Salvadoran community made the area a prime location for political organizing; in the late 1980s, a number of organizers and intellectuals affiliated with the FMLN (Frente Militar de Liberación Nacional, or Military Front for National Liberation, the Salvadoran leftist political party which had fought the government during the Civil War) were sent by the political party from Los Angeles to DC to organize in the newly forming community.[88]

During the 1990s frustrations built among DC Latinos regarding their place in the city, their struggles under a growing national "war on the poor" which included budget cuts for social services that affected minority groups disproportionately (because minorities are disproportionately represented among the poor), and increasingly restrictive policies regarding immigrant opportunities. These frustrations culminated in civil disturbances in the Mt. Pleasant area in the spring of 1991. On May 5 of that year, an African American rookie police officer shot a Salvadoran man whom she was in the process of arresting for drinking on Mt. Pleasant St. While the officer said she shot the man because he was lunging at her with a knife, many witnesses reported that he was handcuffed when he was shot. A public consensus was never reached about what actually happened,[89] and the particular details of the shooting came to be a minor issue as this event became part of the neighborhood's story. Many Mt. Pleasant community members, particularly Latinos, saw the shooting to be another example of abuse, disregard, and neglect that they felt was indicative of the District police and government's attitude towards the Latino community.[90] The shooting set off a night of violent protest aimed at symbols of the city government: police cars were set on fire and a bus was overturned. Only two stores were targeted; these were franchises of national corporations. Stores owned by people well known in the neighborhood remained untouched.

In addition to aggressively asserting a Latino presence in the city, these civil disturbances also had a large effect on the identity of Mt. Pleasant at a city-wide level. While the political aspects of the disturbances highlight Mt. Pleasant as a Latino place (rather than as an ethnically diverse one), many reporters and city residents used the violent aspects of the disturbances to characterize the neighborhood as a dangerous place. This image came to carry much weight in the city-wide discourse on Mt. Pleasant, despite the fact that the details of the disturbances did not fully support this image.

Although the disturbances during the night of the shooting were directed at the city government, unrest continued for two more nights. These subsequent nights were much different in tone; the disturbances for the most part moved out of Mt. Pleasant and into adjacent Adams Morgan, and the activities focused on looting stores (also mostly, but not exclusively, chains), rather than on civic protest. The actors during the subsequent nights were also different; while witnesses described the first night protesters as predominantly from the neighborhood and predominantly Latino, community members described those on the second and third nights as coming from elsewhere in the city and suburbs, and predominantly African American and, to a lesser extent, White. Many community members complained about the cars with Maryland and Virginia license plates, their owners driving in as "riot tourists" to join in the fray and have a good time. As one girl living on Mt. Pleasant St. exclaimed, "People were coming in from other areas like this was some big party, just to come in and do anarchy. It even spread to my school – teenagers in my school [across Rock Creek Park] wanted to come down here."

Out of the disturbances grew a new young, mostly Salvadoran, leadership that formed an organization called the DC Latino Civil Rights Task Force. These leaders were somewhat successful in putting Latino issues on the city agenda. The creation of the Task Force was another factor that contributed to the identity of the Latino community as Salvadoran. This characterization was also aided by the migration of large numbers of Los Angeles Salvadorans to DC after the 1992 Rodney King riots in that city.[91] While Latinos of various other backgrounds moved to DC in the 1990s – including significant numbers of Dominicans in the 1990s and Mexicans after 2000 – many Latinos moving to the area (87 percent[92]) chose the Maryland and Virginia suburbs over the District as a place to live.

Part II: Mt. Pleasant Today

The ethnoracial landscape

In DC, the Mt. Pleasant/Adams Morgan area is the number one destination for immigrants of many backgrounds, and it is the second most popular area in the Washington metropolitan region. Immigrants in the neighborhood hail from 136 different countries.[93] The demographic breakdown of Mt. Pleasant residents as compared with the rest of the city shows that there is ample justification for Mt. Pleasant's reputation as an ethnically diverse neighborhood.[94]

Although there had been a small Southeast Asian presence in Mt. Pleasant since the 1970s,[95] the Vietnamese community grew dramatically in the late 1980s, in part due to the passage of the Homecoming bill in 1989, which granted US citizenship and resettlement to Vietnamese Amerasian children of American soldiers and Vietnamese mothers, along with the children's families. In addition to members of this group, Mt. Pleasant's Vietnamese community also includes many family members of people who had been in re-education camps. This community is starting to carve out a public presence in the neighborhood, through institutions such as a Vietnamese youth center, which took over the premises of a Latino youth center in 1998 when that institution moved to larger quarters.[96] A more pronounced presence can also be seen in the activities of local schools. For example, Bancroft Elementary, the local public elementary school, prints all letters and memorandums to parents in Spanish, English, and Vietnamese, and signs in and around the school are also in these three languages. Vietnamese Mt. Pleasant residents are by and large poor, in stark contrast to the Vietnamese communities in the DC suburbs, many of whose members were active in the South Vietnamese government, military, and diplomatic corps. Those groups are better established and better off economically.

Mt. Pleasant is also home to many African immigrants, a number of whom are political exiles. The Washington area has the largest Ethiopian community in the US.[97] Many Ethiopians and Eritreans originally settled in the Mt. Pleasant/Adams Morgan area in the 1980s, and while a large number have since moved to the suburbs, they maintain a strong presence in the area through their role as local merchants and patrons of local schools, business establishments, and other neighborhood institutions.

The small English- and French-speaking Caribbean communities that formed in the 1960s have also grown large enough in Mt. Pleasant to have made a presence in neighborhood institutions like the local Catholic parish, which has a largely Haitian choir and conducts multilingual holiday masses such as Christmas partly in Haitian Creole, along with English, Spanish, and Vietnamese. On Sunday afternoons worshippers file out of the 3:00 Vietnamese mass at Sacred Heart Church as other parishioners chat outside waiting for the 4:15 mass in Haitian Creole and French. Religious services in local languages can be found at local churches of other denominations as well.

Other cultural communities

Mt. Pleasant has a number of communities which are not primarily defined ethnically, although they may correlate with ethnicity. One such group is organized around music band membership – to a large extent hardcore bands, which are quite prominent on the local music scene. Members of the band scene are primarily in their twenties and thirties and mostly White, and they often live in group houses. Within the DC music scene Mt. Pleasant plays a central symbolic role, one which is recognized among music communities even outside of DC. As the national music magazine *Spin Underground USA* writes,

> Mt. Pleasant with its roomy houses, relatively inexpensive rents, and pleasantly run-down bars and shops, is a favorite of local indie bands, who cluster in group houses.[98]

The neighborhood's ethnoracial mix, the band scene, and the ubiquity of progressive (as well as not so progressive, or apolitical) group houses inspired the *Utne Reader*[99] in the late 1990s to declare Mt. Pleasant to be DC's "soon-to-be-hot" neighborhood:

> Up the hill from U Street, another multicultural scene is gelling in the middle of a Latin barrio. Mt. Pleasant can't support a full menu of hip commerce yet, but politically progressive kids are starting to frequent its Salvadoran restaurants and old-time dive bars.[100]

Mt. Pleasant is also home to a number of faith-based communities. In addition to major denominational churches (Catholic, various protestant, Unitarian Universalist, and the Unification Church), there is also the Community of Christ church, an ecumenical congregation, members of which by and large settled in the neighborhood in the late 1960s and early 1970s. Their inclusive politics and civic mindedness are reflected in the way they use their space; they own a small storefront on Mt. Pleasant St. that they lease out to a living skills program for a multi-ethnic developmentally disabled clientele. At night and on the weekends, Community of Christ opens their space for a very minimal fee to community groups for meetings and activities, trusting an assortment of neighborhood residents with keys to the building.

Through the 1980s and 1990s, Mt. Pleasant was also a local center of the Mennonite community, as recent Mennonite college graduates, predominantly from Mennonite schools in the US and Canada, came to the city to participate in a Mennonite volunteer corps. They by and large worked in social service or peace-and-justice jobs, and many have lived in the group house that the Mennonite volunteer corps ran in the neighborhood. After their two-to-three year tenure in the volunteer corps, many volunteers stayed in Mt. Pleasant, often living in group houses through which previous volunteers had passed. More recently, many Mennonites in the neighborhood have been moving just out of the city, to areas such as Mt. Rainier in Maryland. But one community member remarked that, "There are also some more established Mennonite families in Mt. Pleasant – who have started local social service organizations and embraced the diversity of Mt. Pleasant as a place where their children could grow up to live learning to bridge cultures."

Drawing the boundaries

Despite the fifty years which have passed since the Supreme Court's *Bolling v. Sharpe* ruling, DC has largely remained a segregated city. The area to the west of Rock Creek Park, a large federal park, is the wealthiest sector of the city and predominantly White. Mt. Pleasant lies just east of this park (Figure 2.6). At the time of this study,

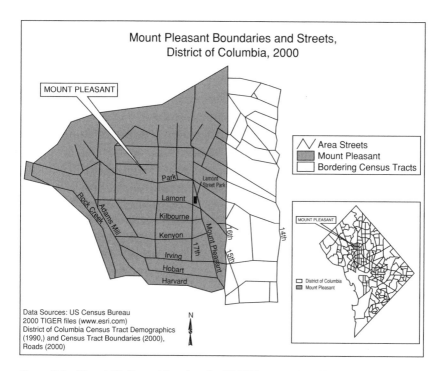

Figure 2.6   Map of Mt. Pleasant based on the US 2000 census, 2000 Tiger files

Mt. Pleasant residents often considered Rock Creek Park a kind of a semi-permeable geographical barrier to gentrification, a phenomenon seen to be encroaching on the neighborhood from the west. Even today, in DC discourse the phrases *west of the park* or, for those in Mt. Pleasant, *across the park*, often serve as shorthand for "White Washington."

Sixteenth St., a major city thoroughfare, is considered by many in Mt. Pleasant to be at or near the neighborhood's eastern border. Although the findings of the 1990 US census resulted in a reconfiguring of Mt. Pleasant's government-sanctioned borders to include three blocks on the other side of 16th St.,[101] throughout the 1990s many Mt. Pleasant community members were steadfast in their belief that 16th St. was both the official and de facto border between Mt. Pleasant and Columbia Heights to the east. Many neighbors have characterized the difference between the two sides of the street to me as "the difference between day and night." At the time that I began fieldwork for this project, community members across ethnic groups often constructed 16th St. as the border separating Mt. Pleasant from crime and poverty, as well as from a homogeneous African American community. But 16th St. is only a border for those who don't traverse it. For others who work, go to school, shop, or visit friends or family on the other side of the street, the territory at least a couple blocks east of 16th St. also counts as Mt. Pleasant. In 2005, as gentrification has increased and poor and middle-class community members of all ethnic backgrounds have been pushed east of 16th St. in search of (more) affordable housing, and as more and more Mt. Pleasantites cross 16th St. to use the new metro, more people are starting to see 16th St. as a fuzzy and permeable border, or not a border at all.[102]

While there is a range of opinion about where the eastern border lies, in the 1990s the view that the neighborhood went past 16th St. seemed to correlate roughly with age, ethnicity, and place of residence – people in their twenties and younger, Vietnamese and Latinos, and people who lived in the eastern part of the neighborhood. Today, those who still see 16th St. as an impermeable border tend to be mostly Whites,[103] homeowners, and/or people who live in the west part of the neighborhood. Furthermore, those who perceive 16th St. as the border (across ethnic and class groups) also have tended to see it as a border between African Americans and Whites/Latinos, as well as a border between more and less crime, or safer and more dangerous spaces. As one community member remarked,

> Sixteenth St. is a demarcation line. What goes on over there is usually kept over there. There are different kinds of activities. More recently the criminal element has been [decreased] because of the [Columbia Heights] metro station.

And another community member added,

> before the metro came in, I didn't have occasion to go over there very much, now I'm going over there every day. It feels safer, looks safer. It's a little peninsula, cause [the metro's] the only place to go, you or me have no other reason to go there.[104]

Mt. Pleasant's southern border is also somewhat contested. While some consider the neighborhood to end at Pigeon Park at the south end of Mt. Pleasant St., others consider the eastern part of Columbia Rd., one of the two commercial corridors of neighboring Adams Morgan, to be part of Mt. Pleasant. This is because, like Mt. Pleasant St., Columbia Rd. has many large, mixed-income apartment buildings, and a retail mix which is closer to the Mt. Pleasant commercial corridor than it is to the more upscale and entertainment-oriented 18th St., Adams Morgan's other commercial street.[105] For many in the area, the distinction between Mt. Pleasant and Adams Morgan is quite fuzzy. While some community members consider Adams Morgan and Mt. Pleasant to be basically the same neighborhood, others have a fluid determination, depending on context; as one community member remarked,

> I think there's a tendency when there's negative things to divide it, and when there's positive things, they call it Adams Morgan, [but when there's negative things] they call it Columbia Heights or Mount Pleasant. But in reality, you know, it's all one big neighborhood.

The face of the neighborhood (for better or worse)

One of the most important spaces in Mt. Pleasant's built environment is Mt. Pleasant St. As the neighborhood's main commercial corridor, Mt. Pleasant St. has an important function in symbolically representing the neighborhood as a whole; many consider it to be the "face of the neighborhood," as it were. Mt. Pleasant St.'s symbolic prominence leads to neighbors' strong focus on and concerns with the activities that take place there, as well as with its physical condition. Not surprisingly, tensions and conflicts about what kind of place Mt. Pleasant is – or should be – frequently play out in disputes about what Mt. Pleasant St. should look like and what kind of activities are appropriate there.

As Mt. Pleasant's main commercial thoroughfare, Mt. Pleasant St. is host to most of the neighborhood's public social activity. The street is a five-block-long shopping corridor of low-lying brick buildings. There are about 60 businesses on the street, including many small grocery stores, the majority of which sell beer and wine; beauty shops and barbers; restaurants/bars, most of which serve a predominantly male Latino clientele; dry cleaners; a pharmacy; a video store; a bakery; jewelry store; bank; used furniture stores; palm reader; real estate agent; dentists; laundromats; international courier services; and variety stores.[106] The merchants come from a wide range of ethnic backgrounds; the business association membership hails from over ten different countries. However, the majority of merchants are originally from Latin America or Korea. Most businesses have about four employees,[107] who in many cases are current or past neighborhood residents and/or family members of the owner. Most businesses rent their space, rather than own it.

Although not all businesses on Mt. Pleasant St. are Latino owned, they all recognize the important role that Latino consumers play in the neighborhood economy. The majority of merchants (including service providers such as dentists and doctors) either speak at least some Spanish – whether their native language is English, Korean, Farsi, Hebrew, or Chinese – or employ Spanish-speaking staff. During busy hours the bank plays Spanish-language television. In addition to Spanish-speaking tellers, this bank also has a Vietnamese-speaking teller, reflecting the increasing economic significance of the Vietnamese community in Mt. Pleasant. The video store has a room of films from Latin America (and the video store in neighboring Adams Morgan has copies of all major new Hollywood releases subtitled in Spanish), and one Chinese restaurant sells Salvadoran fast food items such as pupusas, thick tortillas stuffed with pork or cheese. Cross-ethnic marketing goes in other directions, too. For example, in an attempt to attract more of the neighborhood's White customers, one Salvadoran/Mexican restaurant for a time increased their vegetarian selections, offering such items as spinach pupusas.

Mt. Pleasant St. provides neighborhood residents with many material and social necessities, and connects them with other areas of the city through eight regular bus lines as well as an afternoon bus line for students who attend high school across the park. Three additional bus lines are available one block over on 16th St. As a group, Mt. Pleasant residents rely heavily on bus services; nearly 40 percent of the neighborhood's residents do not own cars,[108] and even those who do often report that they avoid driving in city traffic when they can. Line 42, the bus which carries Mt. Pleasantites to and from downtown jobs, is one of the most heavily traveled routes in the city – so much so that, when the local business association lobbied the transportation authority to do away with some of the bus stops on Mt. Pleasant St. in order to create more parking spaces to reduce double parking, the authority refused, explaining that each stop was being used to over its capacity at *every hour* that the bus was in service.

The 42 has one of latest schedules of any bus in the city, running until about 3 a.m. on both weekdays and weekends. During the day and evening the bus is filled with a mix of Mt. Pleasant residents going to white-collar and blue-collar jobs and running errands in the city, while late at night it is used mostly by people coming home from downtown hotel and restaurant jobs or from socializing. The 42, considered by many residents to be "the Mt. Pleasant bus," is often used as a resource in creating neighborhood identity. For example, in the performance piece discussed in chapter 5, a Latino neighborhood poet both draws on and constructs the Latino ridership of this busline in a scene where he refers to the 42 bus as "the free Spanish lesson."

In addition to transit authority customers, the bus stops on Mt. Pleasant St. are also used by homeless people and people socializing on the street and drinking. This stigmatized usage has led the transit authority to remove benches from some of the bus stops, as they have done at many bus stops throughout the city. (Although sometimes, instead of being completely removed, authorities have replaced them with shorter and narrow benches that would preclude anyone but a small child from sleeping on them, or wooden blocks are added (Figure 2.7).)

At the time of this study, one bus stop was also used late at night as an off-and-on solicitation site for female prostitutes.

The storefronts on Mt. Pleasant St. show a variety of styles and levels of upkeep. Some have crowded window displays behind clean or dusty windows, some windows are covered with blinds or tinted, some have fancy neon signs, some signs are hand-lettered with letters missing, either because they fell off or because the sign painters ran out of space. Many buildings could use a new paint job. Some residents think the main street looks rundown; others interpret these same features as contributing to a comfortable and homey feel.

Adding to the retail mix are street vendors with stands selling flowers, produce, jewelry, and a wide variety of Spanish-language music, from Dominican bachata to Los Angeles hip-hop. More vendors sell in the neighborhood on weekends than during the week. Except for the African jewelry sellers, the vendors are generally Latino. Although the vendors with the more substantially-built stands are men, there are also female street merchants; these women generally have more

Figure 2.7   A sleep-proof bus stop   © Jennifer Leeman

informal set-ups, selling items like mango with lime and chili, hor-
chata (a cold, sweet rice drink), or tamales out of coolers or wire
shopping carts. From late spring to early fall, young men, generally
African American, sell watermelons and cantaloupes out of pickup
trucks on the street.

Mt. Pleasant St. also has its share of people peddling ideology, particularly religion. Especially during weekends and in nice weather,
evangelical Christians come with megaphones and flyers to preach
in English and Spanish. Young male Mormon missionaries in starched
white shirts walk the streets in pairs, the straps of their black back-
packs sitting snugly on both shoulders. They occasionally share the space
with skittish-looking female representatives of the Unification Church.

Politics can also be found on the street. During local elections,
images of city council candidates cast their gaze out from campaign
posters plastered on lampposts and telephone poles. During elections
in El Salvador, automobile processions campaign for FMLN candidates,
supporters waving red flags out of their windows and spreading their
campaign slogans through megaphones to shoppers and residents.

Police officers from two *police service areas*[109] also cruise Mt. Pleasant's streets. Although in recent years the Metropolitan Police Department has been publicizing their *community policing* strategy, in practice I often witnessed police officers staying in their cars rather than walking a beat. In the 1990s it was not uncommon to hear officers shouting from megaphones in their cruisers for someone to stop loitering, rather than getting out of their cars and talking to the person in question. Police are sometimes seen on the street, however, and can often be found taking their breaks outside of the 7–11, which is also a daytime and nighttime gathering spot for men who are drinking coffee and socializing, and sometimes looking for work. In fact, according to the owner, the store makes most of its money on coffee. A few years ago the convenience store capitalized on the de facto police presence in front of their store, by creating a "community police desk" at the front of the store, which provided police with a warm seat and telephone, and the convenience store with good publicity.

Community policing also goes on in the neighborhood in more informal ways. For example, one store on the street gives shoplifters the choice of either being arrested by the police or having their picture taken with the items they've stolen; pictures of people staring sullenly out over a package of skirt steak or bottle of diet coke greet customers at the cash register. Another store posts the names of people who have written bad checks.

Mt. Pleasant St. is a gathering place for social life in the neighborhood, especially for people who live on it. The bus turnaround park at the north end of Mt. Pleasant St. is a site for children's events and seasonal celebrations, and every summer the business association puts on a day-long neighborhood festival on the street. At the north end of Mt. Pleasant St., the bus turnaround park is also a site of socializing and recreation. In warm weather Latino boys and young men play soccer, and Vietnamese boys and a few girls rollerblade. To a lesser extent, African American and White boys also play in the park, as do Latina, White, African American and Vietnamese girls. Adults also use the space in the park to socialize, as well as to drink.

Mt. Pleasant St. also has a number of large apartment buildings, some of which are rental buildings, and some of which are co-ops (apartments where owners own a share in the building) or condos (apartments where people own the actual space of their units). While some of these buildings are economically mixed, most house working-class or poor residents. Most are also ethnoracially mixed. Mt. Pleasant's diverse ethnic mix has made it a favorite neighborhood for a number of local refugee resettlement organizations, so that the political and ethnic conflicts on the world stage can be reconstructed through the shifting patterns of settlement in the neighborhood.

For many Mt. Pleasant St. denizens, residents of other neighborhood streets, and former Mt. Pleasantites who have moved to the suburbs, Mt. Pleasant St. is a site for running errands, socializing, and keeping up social networks. This is primarily true for men – particularly Latinos – who chat in front of apartment houses or on street corners on warm summer nights or, on weekends, sometimes watching their kids or washing or fixing cars. Except for some mildly rebellious teenage girls, women by and large do not hang out on the street. Nevertheless, women, too, renew social networks through interactions on the street, as they run into friends and acquaintances during shopping excursions, on walks, or in the beauty salons. Older women also sometimes use their time on the street as an opportunity to observe the behavior of single- or mixed-sex groups of teenagers socializing on the street, sometimes reporting their observations back to the teenagers' parents.

Up and down the ladder: class mobility

The landscape of the neighborhood is also a class-based landscape. In this regard class correlates with ethnicity, as Whites are generally better off than African Americans or Latinos.[110] As is the case elsewhere in the US, the social category of class is also complicated by other factors like age, class background and occupational culture, as well as by class alignment and upward and downward class mobility. In Mt. Pleasant there are people who grew up in poor families, went to college or graduate school, and earn sizeable incomes. There are also children of doctors who are now construction workers, for example war refugees from well-off families in Central America whose circumstances in the US – such as lack of social or family support networks, no documentation, or language barriers – prevented them from pursuing higher education and higher-status or better-paying jobs. And there are residents with the same educational background as their parents, who have fewer employment opportunities than their parents due to shifts in the region's economy, as well as residents from relatively well-off families with college-educated parents who had the opportunity to go to college, but decided to forgo it in order to pursue other endeavors such as music, and are supporting themselves by jobs such as waiting tables or working as bicycle couriers. And in addition to these residents are students, whose present low incomes are not representative of their earning potential in later years when they finish their degrees. The neighborhood also has its share of highly educated people working in low-paying jobs with relatively high cultural status, such as artists.[111] And of course education isn't the only key to a middle-class income; there are also business-people who earn substantial salaries without college degrees.

Such upward and downward class mobility means that many neighborhood residents are living in different economic conditions than those in which they were raised. In addition, even residents whose economic circumstances at present do correspond with those in which they grew up often have political, material, and aesthetic sensibilities and priorities which do not correspond neatly to the prototypical characterizations of the class culture that their economic circumstances put them in. At the same time that Ivy-League-educated 25-year-olds are making minimum wage working as bike couriers, elderly cleaning women are buying organic produce at the fancy supermarket across town and at the local farmers' market on Saturday mornings. Thus, it's important to keep in mind that class in Mt. Pleasant (as in many other places) cannot be understood simply in terms of residents' economic positions.

Spatializing class: east and west Mt. Pleasant

The housing on Mt. Pleasant St. is for the most part apartment stock, including one co-op building and one building which is mixed co-op and condominium. On the cross-streets to the east and west are rowhouses, both owner-occupied and rented. Included in the rental housing are many group houses, set up in various configurations of cooperative living. In some group houses the owner is also a resident, although these are in the minority. The properties to the east of the street are generally cheaper and to some extent smaller and in worse condition than those to the west. They also include both owner-occupied and rental properties, a few of which are detached houses, and some group houses. To the west of Mt. Pleasant St. are a few apartment buildings, some of which are condominiums, and lots of renovated houses, many of which are quite large, some detached. A few of these houses are official landmarks, listed on the National Historic Register. Rates of property ownership are geographically skewed: While 35.8 percent of property in the neighborhood as a whole is owner-occupied, in the census block-group on Mt. Pleasant St. and to the east, this number plummets to 3 percent. (However, this block group does not include a 73-unit condominium building on Mt. Pleasant St., which increases homeownership rates on the street.)

Compared with the neighborhood as a whole, per capita income is lower along Mt. Pleasant St., both overall and by ethnicity.[112] At the time of this study Mt. Pleasant St. had about the same African American population as the neighborhood as a whole, a much higher Latino population, and a much lower White population.[113] And while 32.5 percent of Mt. Pleasant's population as a whole is foreign-born, on Mt. Pleasant St. it is 60.1 percent. This statistic also points out the difference in demographics between Mt. Pleasant and the city at large, where only 9.7 percent of residents were foreign-born. The Latino population of Mt. Pleasant St. is also more Salvadoran than in the neighborhood at large – 68 percent as compared to 49 percent. Thus, while the neighborhood as a whole is about a quarter Latino, Latinos make up a little more than half the population on Mt. Pleasant St.

The differences between the east and west parts of the neighborhood are also created through discourse. In talk about the neighborhood, the west part of Mt. Pleasant is often constructed as an enclave of White homeowners (despite the many renter-occupied homes and group houses that were in this part of the neighborhood through the late 1990s), while Mt. Pleasant St. itself is often discussed as a place of Latino renters. This rendering can be seen in a quote from a White woman active for many years in Mt. Pleasant civic organizations, discussing with a newspaper reporter her view of differences in the kind of business development that owners and renters want on Mt. Pleasant St:

[An] Advisory Neighborhood Commission member . . . said Mt. Pleasant is divided between homeowners and renters on what is best for the neighborhood. The joke in the community, she said, is that

Figure 2.8　"On the street"　　　　　　　　　　　© Jennifer Leeman

"the people on the street [the renters] want food stores and the people in the neighborhood [homeowners] want flower shops." (brackets in original)[114]

In contrasting "the street" with "the neighborhood," this utterance effectively separates Mt. Pleasant St. (Figure 2.8) from the rest of Mt. Pleasant. This move, along with the geographic dichotomization of owners ("*in the neighborhood*") and renters ("*on the street*") consequently relegates renters to a status where they are not full neighborhood denizens. The reference to food stores invokes the notion popular among many active members of Mt. Pleasant civic organizations that there are too many Latino food stores on Mt. Pleasant St. Indeed, although every food store on the street sells grocery staples, every store also caters to a Latino clientele, although some market to other clienteles, in addition. For example, one store, alongside Latin American food products, sells African foods such as yam flour, palm oil, and injera (Ethiopian bread), as well as upmarket food items such as Ben and Jerry's ice cream, pesto sauce, and nutella, a European hazelnut-chocolate spread.

Mt. Pleasant History and Social Geography　79

Figure 2.9 "In the neighborhood"   © Jennifer Leeman

The split between "the street" and "the neighborhood" is a sentiment voiced by many west-siders, who dislike Mt. Pleasant St. and
consider its character at odds with the cozy tree-lined streets and
manicured gardens of the side streets (Figure 2.9).

This community split also plays out in terms of neighborhood organizations: although many of the projects that Mt. Pleasant civic organizations are engaged in focus on Mt. Pleasant St., most of these
organizations' members live in the west part of the neighborhood,
and do not use the neighborhood space as much as many of those who
live on Mt. Pleasant St. (who are largely not involved in neighborhood-
based civic organizations). In one exception to this pattern, however,
some of the most active members of a civic group focused on
fighting liquor licenses live adjacent to the street, and it is their direct
experiences of the street that motivated them to organize. Although
west-siders might pick up a quick item or two on Mt. Pleasant St.,
in general they seem to leave Mt. Pleasant in greater numbers than
those on Mt. Pleasant St. to do the bulk of their shopping (also because
more of them have cars). This contributes to resentment on the part
of many inhabitants of Mt. Pleasant St., who feel it presumptuous for

these groups to try to change things on a street where they neither live nor spend time.

These resentments are also compounded by different views about the physical space of the neighborhood. In addition to the eastern and southern borders of the neighborhood, the western border is also contested; many residents on Mt. Pleasant St. and to the east consider Mt. Pleasant St. to be the neighborhood's western border. Thus, they often consider denizens of the west part of the neighborhood not to really live in Mt. Pleasant at all.

Although many residents don't consider the area west of Mt. Pleasant St. to be Mt. Pleasant, there isn't another institutionalized name in local discourse to describe it. Latinos and Vietnamese often refer to it as "the area near Bancroft [Elementary School]," or "where the White people live." The extension of this particular view is that Whites don't live in Mt. Pleasant, and this ideology further compounds the resentment that many residents have towards the largely White civic organizations. (Neighborhood Whites who don't share the viewpoints of the civic groups also often refer to such groups as "the White forces of the neighborhood.")

What this historical and geographical overview shows is that ethnoracial and class relations in Mt. Pleasant are articulated through space. The residence patterns of different class and ethnic groups within the neighborhood's geography serve as a key component in the moral geography which neighborhood residents create, where different parts of the neighborhood, and different attitudes about using space in the neighborhood, take on moral valences. As we shall see in the following chapters, the moral quality of people's attitudes towards space and use of space both underlies and is reinforced by the way that community members engage in neighborhood conflicts.

Notes

1 A level on the government pay scale
2 March 22, 2005:C3
3 Although in local parlance *DC* tends to refer to the city itself, this is a pattern rather than a hard-and-fast rule. For example, residents also use terms like *Washingtonian* to refer to city natives.
4 March of Dimes Perinatal Center (2002)
5 District of Columbia Department of Health (2004)

6   District of Columbia Office of the Mayor (2004)

7   US census (2000)

8   Trash collection was eventually restored before the furlough ended.

9   Montgomery and Cohn (1995:A1)

10 Duggan and Parker (1995:A27)

11 Today the District's status is similar to that of other US territories such as American Samoa, Guam, Puerto Rico, and the US Virgin Islands – all of which, along with the District, have non-voting representatives in Congress. Although with President Clinton's election in 1992 Congress accorded these delegates the right to vote on floor issues that did not directly affect their constituencies, even this limited power was taken away when the Republican-majority 14th Congress came into power in 1994 and repealed this provision. Today the major differences between DC and these territories are that residents of the District may vote for president, and that residents of US territories do not pay federal income tax (following the constitutional principle of no taxation without representation). The territorial governments also have somewhat more autonomy in deciding local matters.

12 The 1992 Health Care Benefits Expansion Act provided for healthcare benefits for domestic partners of city employees. In 1997, however, Congress attached a rider to the annual DC appropriations bill that prohibited local or federal money from being spent for such benefits.

13 One symbolic exercise of power which many residents were surprised that Congress did not rescind was the creation in 2000 of a new license plate design with the motto "District of Columbia – Taxation Without Representation."

14 Ohlemacher (2005)

15 Bowling (1991:10)

16 The president of the United States appointed a DC mayor, and residents voted for a city council. (As was the case throughout the country at this time, only White male property owners were allowed to vote.) In 1804 Congress made the mayorship a directly elected office, but a new city charter eight years later took more power away from the residents by legislating that the city council choose a mayor.

17 The 14th amendment was passed, but it only went into effect elsewhere in the country when it was fully ratified in 1868.

18 Horton (1996)

19 The Act also consolidated the separate areas of Georgetown, Washington City, and Washington County into what we know today as Washington, DC.

20 cf. *Washington Star* (1978a)

21 Wendell Stafford, *Evening Star* (1919)

22 Ibid.

23 The abolition of these commissioners did not exactly create democracy, however, as it replaced the board with a presidentially appointed mayor, presidentially appointed deputy mayor, and presidentially appointed nine-member city council.

24 *Washington Star* (1978b)

25 The standard procedure for introducing an amendment was to bring it to the Senate Judiciary Committee, who would then decide whether or not the amendment merited discussion by the entire Senate. Because the Committee was headed by a strongly conservative senator (James O. Eastland of Mississippi) who had declined to bring the amendment to the Senate floor a number of times in the past, Kennedy decided to put discussion of the amendment on the Senate calendar directly.

26 Johnstone (1990)

27 Brockett (1978)

28 Rowan (1978)

29 *Washington Post* (1978)

30 *Washington Star* (1978b)

31 Rowan (1978), *Washington Star* (1978a)

32 Baker (1978)

33 Emery (1932), Harmon et al. (1876)

34 K. Smith (1988b)

35 Manning (1995)

36 Emery (1932)

37 Low and Gillette (1988:133)

38 These efforts set a precedent for early record keeping which would lead one 1950s journalist (Kennedy 1950) to remark that "Mt. Pleasant has the most completely recorded history of any area of Washington."

39 Harmon et al. (1876)

40 Kennedy (1950)

41 L.E. Horton (1996), Manning (1995)

42 L.E. Horton (1996)

43 Manning (1995:325)

44 By this time Brown was living in Dupont Circle closer in to the city; he'd moved there after an accident had left him severely disabled.

45 Gale (1987)

46 It's important to point out that this is conjecture, however, as no records exist that explicitly address why the Association decided to reconfigure the boundary. Some historians of the neighborhood disagree that the Association's motives were race-based because in 1923

14th St. was still predominantly White. However, Gale's argument about the changing local demographics, as well as the Citizens Association's hypervigilant campaign for restrictive covenants, lead me to conclude that there's a strong possibility that their motives were race-based.

47 The following account is based on the Mt. Pleasant Citizens Association meeting minutes from 1927–1957 and title records from the District of Columbia Recorder of Deeds.

48 District of Columbia Recorder of Deeds 1929, 1928

49 Mt. Pleasant Citizens' Association meeting minutes, 1923–1948

50 houses that "fill in" space between already existing buildings

51 Williams (1988)

52 Clare (1988)

53 Low and Gillette (1988), Asher (1967)

54 Low and Gillette (1988), Gale (1976b)

55 Because the neighborhood housing covenants and Citizens Association minutes of the past referred to "people of Negro blood or race," we can assume that "not of the Caucasian race" here is meant to refer specifically to only African Americans.

56 Mt. Pleasant Citizens' Association meeting minutes, 1923–1948

57 Low and Gillette (1988)

58 Washington Post (1961)

59 K. Smith (1988a)

60 Low and Gillette (1988)

61 Gale (1976b)

62 These changes in Mt. Pleasant were tied to changes on the national and international scene. The United States' victorious role in World War II had led to a new American prominence on the political and economic world stage. Washington became an international city as organizations like the World Bank and Organization of American States made their homes downtown, and delegations to the city's numerous embassies grew. Universities also expanded, and began to attract much larger numbers of international students than they had in the past (cf. Singer 2003).

63 Cadaval (1996:234) notes, however, that "for the most part, . . . the students and professional Mexican Americans separated themselves from the nascent Latino community." This was also largely true of the diplomats and international bureaucrats (World Bank employees, etc.).

64 cf. Sanjek (1998)

65 Latin American immigrants, along with immigrants from other places, also settled in the suburbs. As early as 1969, immigration figures placed the number of Latinos in the District as equal to that both in Maryland and Virginia (Shandler 1969), meaning that the Washington suburbs

were home to twice as many Latinos as the city. The number of immigrants in the suburbs continues to grow; in the 1990s, 87 percent of immigrants to the area settled in the suburbs (Singer et al. 2001).

66 Cadaval (1996)

67 Cadaval (1996:237)

68 Cadaval (1998)

69 Shandler (1969)

70 originally called the Spanish Community Advisory Committee

71 Cadaval (1996) notes that there remains a discrepancy about when the first festival was held.

72 In 1989 the festival moved downtown to Pennsylvania Avenue, site of many national marches and events.

73 Williams (1988)

74 Some of these residents also lived in rental housing, just as some owner-occupied houses were cooperatives.

75 Richardson (1990), Gilliam (1976)

76 Gale (1976a)

77 Ley (1996:175)

78 Kiernan (1977)

79 At the time of this writing, these same houses are selling for between $600,000 and $1,000,000.

80 cf. Williams (1988)

81 During this time African American–Latino tensions were addressed in a number of neighborhood endeavors, such as the LatiNegro Theater, a performing arts group founded by Latino and African American young adults.

82 Cadaval (1998:75)

83 US Census Report (1990), Farhi (1990)

84 The 1990 census was widely recognized to be skewed, especially in terms of counting members of minority groups. The US Office of the Census estimated that they undercounted the country's population by $4\frac{1}{2}$ million people (National Public Radio 1999). Nevertheless, as long as this bias is kept in mind, census figures can serve as one tool among others for examining demographics in Mt. Pleasant and comparing Mt. Pleasant to the city at-large.

85 Washington's Latino community is nevertheless one of the most heterogeneous in the country. The same holds true for the area's immigrant population at large. Numerically, there is no majority group; Salvadorans, with the highest number, make up only 10.5 percent of the area's immigrant population. In the 1990s, immigrants came to the Washington area from 193 different countries. The top ten countries of origin in the region as a whole were El Salvador, Vietnam,

India, China, the Philippines, South Korea, Ethiopia/Eritrea, Iran, Pakistan, and Peru. The top three Latin American countries of origin were El Salvador, Peru, and Bolivia. (Singer et al. 2001)

86   Singer et al. (2003)

87   Cadaval (1996)

88   Politics of El Salvador play a large role in the political landscape of Mt. Pleasant; campaign rallies are held for FMLN candidates, Salvadoran politicians come to the neighborhood to make speeches, and tensions in community organizations are often characterized as tied to national political alliances, Salvadoran and otherwise.

89   A court case in which the Salvadoran man was accused of attempted assault on the police officer ended with a hung jury and mistrial; the case was not tried again.

90   For analyses of narratives of police harassment of Latinos in the Washington area, see De Fina (1999), Carranza (1996).

91   Cadaval (1998)

92   Singer et al. (2001)

93   Singer et al. (2001)

94   (Category labels are as used by the census itself): White: 42.8 percent vs. 29.6 percent city-wide; Black: 36.6 percent vs. 65.9 percent; American Indian: 0.7 percent vs. 0.3 percent; Asian/Pacific Islander: 3.2 percent vs. 1.9 percent; Other: 16.7 percent vs. 2.4 percent; Hispanic: 26 percent vs. 5.2 percent. These data are from the 1990 census. I use the 1990 census, rather than the 2000 statistics, because the rapid gentrification that occurred in 1999 means that the 2000 numbers are less indicative of neighborhood demographics in 1996–1998. Because counts for "Hispanic" are separate from those of the other groups mentioned, there is overlap with this group and all the others. It is likely that the percentage of "other" in this count includes people who also identified as "Hispanic." Nevertheless, the discrepancy between the "other" category in Mt. Pleasant and city-wide remains striking.

95   Williams (1988)

96   The Vietnamese youth center has since moved to larger quarters, show-ing a further stage in its institutionalization in the neighborhood. Despite the increasing presence of the Vietnamese community in the public consciousness in Mt. Pleasant, during the time of this fieldwork members of this community were by and large not involved in Mt. Pleasant's public discourse. While the Vietnamese community today is currently more institutionalized than in the nineties, at present many Vietnamese who can afford it are moving to the suburbs.

97   Selassie (1996)

98 Bass (1997:387)
99 a monthly news and culture magazine which also circulates a selection of articles from the US alternative press
100 Walljasper and Kraker (1997:59)
101 After the 2000 census, the border reverted back to 16th St.
102 cf. Schaller and Modan (2005)
103 Among African Americans whom I talked to about this issue, there was no consensus about the status of 16th St. as a border.
104 Schaller and Modan (2005)
105 Because so many community members consider the eastern part of Columbia Rd. to be part of Mt. Pleasant, for the purposes of this study I also consider it part of the neighborhood. According to city districting, however, it is officially part of Adams Morgan.
106 By the year 2000, gentrification had brought such establishments as a coffee house and a bar that sells $5 glasses of Belgian artisanal beers on tap.
107 Gibson (1997)
108 According to the 1990 census, 37.3 percent of the total population, and 58.9 percent of Latinos in the neighborhood do not own cars.
109 the police department's term for police districts
110 According to the 1990 census, per capita annual income for Whites in Mt. Pleasant was $25,928, compared to $14,238 for African Americans and $9722 for Latinos. (Because the size of the Asian population counted in the 1990 census is too small and heterogeneous to be useful for describing the Vietnamese community, I have not included these statistics.)
111 cf. Ley (1996)
112 Overall population: $18,465 neighborhood-wide vs. $11,575 on Mt. Pleasant St.; African American $14,238 vs. 13,863; White $25,928 vs. 17,407; Latino $9,722 vs. $6,676. Although median income figures are not available by race, overall median income figures show a similar disparity between the west and east of Mt. Pleasant: $31,594 vs. $21,693.
113 In the 1990 census, the African American population of the neighborhood is 36.6 percent, differing only slightly from the 35.9 percent proportion along Mt. Pleasant St. Conversely, the White neighborhood-wide population of 42.8 percent is quite different from the 20.7 percent proportion on Mt. Pleasant St., as is the Latino neighborhood population of 26 percent, compared with 52.9 percent on Mt. Pleasant St.
114 Monroe (1993)

CHAPTER 3

THE MORAL GEOGRAPHY
OF MT. PLEASANT

Dear Neighbors, the problem of verbal sexual harassment of women on the streets of Mount Pleasant, a phenomenon that is all too familiar to many pedestrians in the area, was addressed at the Police Service Area (PSA) meeting on Tuesday night (7/13). Several women voiced their experiences and agreed that it has become nearly impossible to walk down Mount Pleasant Street without being subject to a barrage of insulting, offensive, and sometimes threatening comments and behavior by groups of males loitering on sidewalks, and that something has to be done.

The issue will again be raised at the ANC [Advisory Neighborhood Commission] meeting on Tuesday, July 20 at 7:00 at the Mt. Pleasant Library basement. Among topics for discussion will be possibilities for educating the public on why such behavior is unacceptable, working with cultural agencies to discourage the practice, and cooperating with local officials to stave off this trend in the most effective way possible.

It's Wednesday morning, and I'm sitting in the meeting room of the local non-profit where I'm working, discussing the meetings on "verbal sexual harassment" with my colleagues. Having attended these meetings, I mention that the woman leading this effort has been in discussions with the Metropolitan Police Department to have under-cover policewomen conduct "stings" on the street and arrest comment-making men for disturbing the public order. Gabi, a young Latina woman, remarks that this whole endeavor is ill-conceived. "In our culture, [when someone comments positively on your appear-ance], it's a compliment." Voicing her exasperation at Mount Pleasant civic activities, she continues, "White women don't understand those comments." But those of us who attended the meeting had not mentioned the ethnicity of this woman, and in point of fact she was African American.

A week later, Gabi comes into the office after having been on Mt. Pleasant St. Anna, another co-worker, comments that she looks annoyed and asks her what's the matter. "Ugh, those drunks on Mt. Pleasant St. I just want to walk down the street without being yelled at."

A similar scenario, around the same time: "Undercover cops??," Aviva says, referring to the proposed undercover cat-calling sting. "As if the cops in this city don't have anything better to do? If [that woman] can't handle walking down Mt. Pleasant St., she should move to the suburbs."

A few days later, as I'm drinking a beer with Yadira on her porch around the corner from Mt. Pleasant St., Aviva walks up the steps, plops down on a vacant chair, and complains,

> Some days, this neighborhood drives me crazy. Walking **fucking** down Mt. Pleasant St., and the amount of comments that you get even when you're **totally** covered from head to toe and you feel like **shit**. Miguel **finally** said to me, Oh, you're White, the corner of Mt. Pleasant and Irving is infamous for- and I was- no fuckin shit, as a Wh- it has nothing to do with being White – it has to do with being a **woman**. It's a **gender** issue.

What are we to make of these comments? Why did the woman who spearheaded the "verbal sexual harassment" campaign invoke *cultural agencies* as a mechanism to "educate people" about catcalling, why did Gabi and Miguel link women's dislike of being catcalled to Whiteness, why did Aviva suggest that the leader of the campaign should move to the suburbs, and why were Aviva and Gabi's reactions to this campaign so clearly at odds with their own reactions to being catcalled? In order to understand the logic of these comments, we need to examine the ways in which categories such as gender and ethnicity are imbricated or tied up in local understandings of what it means to be an urban person. This chapter will lay out the ideological framework which Mt. Pleasant community members use to create images of city and suburb, and which consequently underlie, in subtle and not-so-subtle ways, much of local debate about who has the legitimacy as a community member to weigh in on the state of the neighborhood. Because community members link their own and others' identity to the identity of the neighborhood, the work of claiming personal authority necessarily territorializes the space of the neighborhood as a place with a certain character, a place which embodies a particular set (or sets) of values.

A useful way to think about these processes is through Jane Hill's concept of *moral geography*. A moral geography is an interweaving of a moral framework with a geographical territory. Through the use of various discourse strategies and themes, community members create alignments and oppositions among people and places. These alignments and oppositions are then evaluated positively or negatively in relation to various value and belief systems circulating in the community. In other words, through linguistic moves, community members position themselves and their neighbors within a kind of abstract moral "grid" that they create for the neighborhood.

Creating a moral geography is all about showing that you fit in and how you fit in – that you and the landscape are well matched:

YADIRA: I always thought that if I'm gonna move to DC, it has to be here in Mt. Pleasant, otherwise I would be, you know, really out of- the community or whatever and um, I ended up here because I choose to be here, I guess. It wasn't by accident in any way. I wanted- I wanted to be here. [So what were the main reasons?] Main reasons? Um, the people that live in Mt. Pleasant. The Salvadorian Community. It's um, very Salvadorian and, and I like it. I like it, you know somehow it's home. [Did you feel at home in NY?] No. No, I didn't. I was. I felt out of place. There was a large Latino community there, but they're mostly, Puerto Ricans, people from the Dominican Republic, Mexicans, and other, you know- it was fun, but not as fun as here. Besides here it's like, every place that I go, I meet friends, so that's very nice. I don't feel- I don't feel, like I'm a stranger here.

GRACE: I like this neighborhood because of um, I think- It reminds me you know of Trinidad. Because Trinidad is very diverse, you know. Yeah. The culture is very diverse there. I- I fit right in. I fit right in, I mean I'm happy

here. I mean I fit right in. [. . .] I guess I feel at home-
this feels – I don't know, homey.

AVIVA: You know it wasn't like I sought out a mixed neighborhood but I don't think [as a Jew from an immigrant
family] that I would ever like, fare well? in an all White
neighborhood. [. . .] I think I'd stick out like a sore thumb.
I don't think- I just wouldn't feel comfortable.

WILLIAM: For our daughter, it's very important [as a Black–White
biracial child] to have- all ki- to have, **her** have access to
all kinds of people. Um, and that's the only way she can
really build, a sense of self. And how we can sort of build,
um, what we think is a community. U:m, there're some
people who, it's, it's just very clear. It's utterly clear, that
this is the place where they felt most comfortable
creating, a- a sense of community. Uh, and I think uh, I
think- I think that's the strength of the neighborhood. We
wanted a mixed race, mixed income kind of community.
Um, because we thought, that it would be, most interesting. And- be the best kind of neighborhood for our
children to grow up in. You know- having your kid grow
up in a place that, um, where everybody's the same, and
they aren't one of those same, creates weird identity
issues. Because- you know, you can grow up thinking that,
everybody's like one thing, but, everybody's really not, and
you're the- you're the not? And then you have to rethink
things. But if everybody is different- there is no notion
of same, so everybody's an individual. Everybody's valued
as an individual. And you develop your sense of self, within
a group of individuals.

Because fitting in is both a key and a contested component of neighborhood legitimacy, it can't always be assumed – often it must be
argued for. It's in arguing for this fit that community members make
the strongest links between the identity of the neighborhood and
their own identities. In the process of creating themselves as legitimate Mt. Pleasant people, community members devote a lot of energy
to building up an image of Mt. Pleasant as a place whose identity
is consistent with the kind of people that they are.

But this isn't always a smooth or consistent process, because
people are multifaceted; we all have multiple identities and multiple
interests, which may sometimes conflict with each other. As we saw

at the opening of this chapter, for example, Aviva's and Gabi's perspective as women may conflict with their politics on neighborhood ethnoracial relations. Since, in the context of talking about neighborhood identity, people often want to show multiple sides of themselves, and since person and place identity are linked, it's not surprising that community members talk about the neighborhood in multiple and sometimes conflicting ways.

Staking Out Territory

There are a lot of different scenes in Mt. Pleasant, and when I started my fieldwork I wanted to be able to float from one to another – from Mennonite women's group clothing-swap to Jewish Shabbat potluck dinner to White group house party to Latino jam session – without feeling out of place in any of them. One thing that this entailed was finding styles of clothing that people from various groups read as more or less neutral. My favorite outfit in this regard was a pair of button-fly jeans and a tightish gray T-shirt – paired perhaps with a cotton sweater for semi-airconditioned town-hall meetings, or dark brown lipstick[1] for weekend front-porch beer drinking. But in 1997 what I felt I was really lacking for random street-corner conversations was a good pair of clunky platform shoes. So off I traipsed to my favorite of the clothing-luggage-shoes-umbrellas-everything stores, in hopes of a little wardrobe enhancement. What I liked about this particular store was that its range of wares spanned the style spectrum of the neighborhood, and I admired the way in which the store owner, in English, Spanish, or sometimes a little French, was equally adept at finding a nice pair of dangly earrings for a White social studies teacher, fitting a Cameroonian college student with a pair of supple, three-tone leather loafers, or helping a Salvadoran line cook choose a smart new cowboy hat.

Although a little unsure about my future ability to walk in the three-inch chunky black vinyl platform sandals that I've picked out, I resolutely hand my credit card to the short, salt-and-pepper-haired store owner who is speaking Spanish on the phone.

As he hangs up, he looks down at my card. "Modan. I have a cousin who's getting married to a Modan in Tel Aviv next month."

A little taken aback, I reply, "I have a lot of cousins named Modan in Tel Aviv, but none with imminent marriage plans." I've been in this store a million times – how did it never occur to me before that this guy has a Hebrew accent?

I make an appointment to come back the next week and interview Boaz. At the appointed time, I walk in the store, glancing up at the seven-inch mezuzah[2] angled on the doorframe that I also had never noticed before, and take a seat on a vinyl-covered bench as Boaz is finishing up with his last customer of the evening. After ringing up the customer's purchase, he pulls up a chair, I turn on my tape-recorder, and he proceeds to grill me for 45 minutes on my Israeli politics.

While to someone who doesn't know Mt. Pleasant it might seem odd for Boaz to begin a discussion about his views of the neighborhood with such a topic, in fact it's quite indicative of neighborhood dynamics. One way that Mt. Pleasant gets incarnated as an immigrant place is through residents' elaborations of their immigrant ties to other locations. In a place where FMLN-placarded cars make bullhorn announcements during El Salvador's election season and exile Somali cab drivers gather in afternoons to swap the latest news about power shifts in Mogadishu, engagement with transnational politics and social life is another way that people both understand and consolidate their membership in the community. It's because of these local–global connections that it makes sense for Boaz to ask me about my Israeli politics as a way of figuring out how to locate me within the Mt. Pleasant landscape. At the same time, his own focus on this issue highlights his own status as an immigrant with translocal connections. As our discussion continues, he makes more elaborate connections between the neighborhood and his immigrant background:

Oh I love this neighborhood, it's a **great** neighborhood. You know? It's a n- as I told you, it's a neighborhood that reminds me a lot of the neighborhood I lived, as a kid in Tel Aviv. Um, you know the low-lying buildings and little shops and, and, people from all walks of life and, like when I see a woman walking down the street here, with a big watermelon on her head. Just, balancing it, you know? She's, an Indian from Peru, probably. You know. But it somehow it reminds me of my nextdoor neighbor who used to do that, with a whole bunch of things on her head and she'd walk- yeah- we knew once- you know- every day at the same time she'd be either coming or going with this thing on her head.

It's worth pointing out here that, in his move to connect his own residential history to the tenor of his current neighborhood, Boaz uses "an Indian from Peru" as the prototype of the neighborhood immigrant. In fact, in Mt. Pleasant the majority of Latinos are not from Peru (although there are many Peruvians in the suburbs). Through choosing someone from a group that does not exist in high numbers in the neighborhood, Boaz's own status as an unusual immigrant (being from Israel) gets downplayed.

Boaz continues,

> It's um, it's very unlike anywhere else in DC. Okay? And uh, it has its ups and ^downs, [. . .] but overall I mean it's- it's really a wonderful neighborhood. Um, without all the ills of a big city you know, crime and this. There's no more crime here than there is- twenty blocks away I mean, you know what I'm saying there may be a few more drunks on the street but, but that's just a that. It's no- it's, it's a lovely neighborhood it has a lot more character than any part of Connecticut Avenue [a street "west of the park" in what's commonly thought of as White DC], you know what I'm saying?

While Boaz connects his immigrant status to a description of the neighborhood as an *immigrant place*, this new image of the *Charming and Lovely Mt. Pleasant* bears on Boaz's interests as a merchant:

> Take for example this, the three people [who were shot] in Starbucks, which was a horrendous thing. If this would happen here on this street, you would have Mt. Pleasant in the news, day and night. For three weeks. Trouble in Mt. Pleasant! Things are unsafe in Mt- **fear** in Mt. Pleasant. But it happened in Georgetown [a White, wealthy neighborhood west of the park], an- you still hear about it in the news, but you don't hear **fear** in Georgetown. You don't hear- people are complaining about their safety, in Geor- they don't ^do this! But they'll do it about this place, because this place got international fame when, when it went into flames [in the 1991 riots] [. . .] That basically killed about 80% of the businesses then.
>
> Just now, this year there's a renaissance on 18th St. with the restaurants and nightclubs. [After the riots] those things were going out of business every two weeks! And uh, they had tough competition I mean a lot of these owners just went and opened in Bethesda [a wealthy Maryland suburb with a newly redeveloped downtown], which is **really** booming now. And uh, it's- it's **amaz**ing, what's

happening there. It's amazing what happens when you take this- and its an in- international flavor I mean you have as many Ethiopian restaurants in Bethesda than there are here. And Hispanic restaurants. I mean la [sic] Rincón Español, all of them- have, branches there. And more. So, if you take, this, concept, but, put it on a silver plate with public **safety**. It's a gigantic moneymaking thing. And, everybody will be happy because then the kids in the neighborhood get jobs. You know? But, when it's unsafe, and you keep, hyping the fact that it's unsafe. Then the- it does not have the chance.

While here Boaz criticizes the attitude that Mt. Pleasant is unsafe, and disdains the hype about fear, the charming, lovely, safe streetscape that he's painted seems to disappear as the topic shifts from being a merchant to Boaz's ethnic identity vis-à-vis the neighborhood:

GALEY: So how do you think that your, ethnicity, influences, how you see what goes on, around here. Or how you see what kind of neighborhood this is.

BOAZ: To put it like my wife says, you walk around like, you know, like you're in the middle of uh, attacking a, some guerrilla stronghold somewhere. I have- doesn't scare me one bit. I mean I walk through the worst, parts here. And uh, maybe because I project, you know the, sort of- you know I've learned to to project an image of, don't mess with me? I don't know. Cause I'm not very powerful physically. But um, I know how to handle myself. [. . .] The way what they project towards you if somebody project intimidation, it will be clear within the first 60 seconds that the person to be intimidated here is, you. Not me. Okay because, ^Oh, you can do this and you can do that and you can do this but you won't get away with much. Um. Cause it can get pretty scary around here. You know. [. . .] Um, . . . I think this neighborhood you you, I don't care where you're from, you have to show that- you know where you're going, and that you're not- you're not vulnerable. You know? Cause if you show a little bit of vulnerability you're done. Whether you're Black White, Hispanic. And um, my background- is such that- this world- word does not exist. I'm not vulnerable to anything. Yeah, to some-some, you know certain vices yeah, that I have! But uh, but as far as uh, be- being somebody's lamb. It's just not in the lexicon. You know. We draw blood, where we come from.

Suddenly, without warning, the scene shifts and I'm carried back through time:

I gotta tell you a funny story I was in Germany in 1976. I had a German girlfriend, and I was staying in her apartment, she was a student. And it was her birthday and we went to the cafeteria in the university one night. No it was in a bar- we went to the bar, in comes this big German guy and this big fat guy and he goes, he yells in German, Oh look what Anna got for her birthday, a Jew. This was the end of it man this guy got bottles on his head and everything we went outside and, as it was going on i- j- when I, was done with him, I told him, see we're a different breed. You made a big mistake. We're not the kind that you put on the table and you start doing experiments and then when you end up you **burn** them so there'll be nothing left. You said the wrong thing, that's why I had to beat you. I got arrested for it, and all that but. Some explaining and all that, got me off of this but. That's how I am. You know I was brought up to be this way. You know you don't turn the other cheek.

And back through time again:

And it's totally against my father's uh, you know my father lived, all his life until he was like seventeen, in an Arab country. And, they have much dislike to, the Muslim Arabs, because of all the discriminations, and the persecutions, and all that. But much of their life was- my father, being the first one, to join the Zionist movement, was the first one that said well there's no more second cheek. They can't come in here and, pogrom us. And there **was** a pogrom in Baghdad in the, in the twenties, in the late twenties. A lot of-thousands of Jews w- were, slaughtered, on the streets. And they were, mostly dirt poor, then. Uh, only a couple of, kings later, the- then at the Renaissance and, they started to make money, they were allowed to do this and that. But uh- they just went there and killed them so the thing was okay, don't upset them too much.

And now we come back to the present and the moral of the stories:

Well, you see- this, to me it doesn't exist. My being, here. What I am. Upsets you? You turn around and go. And if you want to make an issue out of it, you'll have to push me out of the way. And because of this, there is the Israeli Defense Forces, who gave me all the training, and instilled in me the confidence that, push and shove, I can push as- well as you can, without any, any any uh, qualms about it, all my- I don't think my grandfather- had that- in him. You see? That's the big difference.

Holding Your Ground

How can we understand this sudden shift, this painting of the neighborhood as a dangerous place where to fit in you must walk with a swagger, perform a violent aggressiveness, be ready to "draw blood"? Why, in explaining his ethnic take on Mt. Pleasant, does Boaz tell me about breaking bottles over some guy's head in Germany in 1976, about his father's refusal to turn the other cheek in Baghdad in the 1920s? Why does a discussion about relating to Mt. Pleasant end up as a story about pushing and shoving and holding your ground?

To fully comprehend the logic of all the stories above – of Boaz's alternating descriptions of charming and dangerous places, Aviva and Gabi's conflicting attitudes towards men's catcalls on the street, Yadira, Grace, and William's delineations of Latinoness and diversity, we need to do a little unpacking, to investigate a number of interlocking themes that lie beneath these constructions of neighborhood and personal identity. So before getting to the data, I want to lay out a framework for understanding how Mt. Pleasant community members talk about the city and the suburbs. Specifically, community members use the categories of *city* and *suburb* to organize and spatialize divergent value systems.

City vs. Suburb

People in Mt. Pleasant have many reasons for living in the city, and different ideas about what it means to be an urbanite. Community members from across a range of perspectives, however, spend a fair amount of energy on creating urban identities. One of the most common linguistic means that people use to accomplish this is the strategy of *linguistic contrast*. Through the contrast of city and suburb community members position themselves as legitimate urbanites – "city people" within an authentic urban space. They also use this strategy to delegitimize some of their fellow neighbors as "suburban people" – inauthentic urban dwellers.

Sometimes community members make this contrast between Mt. Pleasant and other areas of the city, but more frequently it is drawn between the city and the suburbs. In the process of delineating these two kinds of terrain, Mt. Pleasant people engender space – that is, they construct the city, and Mt. Pleasant in particular, as a masculine place, and the suburbs as a feminine place. These gendered constructions are frequently created through a discourse of fear.

Underlying much Mt. Pleasant discourse on place is an ideological clustering of city and suburb with what I'll call three *axes of heterogeneity*: ethnicity, economics, and architecture. The city is painted as ethnically, economically, and architecturally heterogeneous – a dense and gritty environment, a borderlands where people of all walks of life come together. The city is also considered to be a place of crime and danger – and DC's image as the murder capital of the country has certainly reinforced this image.[3]

Because the identities of places and the people who inhabit them are ideologically linked, the danger of the city fosters an image of city people as familiar with and therefore good judges of danger, and as tough, streetsmart, and fearless. This toughness often gets characterized – by both men and women – as a certain kind of masculinity. In Mt. Pleasant discourse, people often connect an orientation of fearlessness with masculinity as well as with being comfortable in a heterogeneous urban environment.

Axes of Contrast

Heterogeneity vs. homogeneity

Mt. Pleasantites contrast the urban heterotopia with images of an ethnically, economically, and architecturally homogeneous suburbia; as one more disdainful community member characterized the suburbs, a place of "cookie-cutter houses with cookie-cutter people."

The suburbs are talked about as White and wealthy, safe and clean, but bland.

Another, although less frequently invoked, category of heterogeneity is sexuality. Community members sometimes cast Mt. Pleasant as a place where a variety of sexual identities are represented. Sometimes people use symbols of gayness to help construct the diversity of the neighborhood:

GALEY: So how would you describe this neighborhood to someone who didn't know it?

RAIN: It's culturally diverse, the age, you know young people, old people, you have Black families that have been here for years and years and years, old white people, um, young progressives, young families, lesbian couples, gay men who own homes, Hispanic I- the trilingual elementary school, um, the karate school,

This quote, in casting gay men as homeowners, illustrates a common local phenomenon of talking about gay men as gentrifiers, while lesbians are more often invoked as symbols of diversity, or sometimes to reference a counter-culture/hippie identity for the neighborhood. For example, one community member told that if I was interested in diversity, "you should also talk to some lesbian group house people."[4] The difference in the ways that gay men and lesbians are talked about may have its roots in stereotypes about gay men and lesbians, the fact that, in the US as a whole, men make more money than women, or the sexual geography of the DC area, where Dupont Circle, commonly thought of as gay male space, is wealthy and trendy, while Takoma Park, sometimes considered to be lesbian space, is often described as politically progressive and hippie-ish.

Ideology vs. reality

It's important to keep in mind that the take on the suburbs as homogeneous is an ideological construct; most everyone in Mt. Pleasant has friends, family, and/or acquaintances who live in the suburbs, so community members are aware that the actual DC suburbs are quite diverse in terms of economics and sexuality, and in fact are much more ethnically diverse than the city itself. Eighty-seven percent of immigrants to the Washington metropolitan area in the 1990s moved to the suburbs, and the large suburban communities of people from China, Peru, the Philippines, Iran, India, South Korea, and Pakistan have no equivalent in the city itself.[5]

Mt. Pleasant's architectural heterogeneity is also debatable; the majority of housing stock in Mt. Pleasant was mass-produced, although at different times, so that on any given block the housing layouts are often as similar to each other as are those in the suburbs. People sometimes joke that, if you've been in enough houses in the neighborhood, you never have to ask where the bathroom is.

Order vs. disorder

The ideological divide between suburb and city is also accomplished through the contrast between order and disorder. This theme can be broken down into two sub-themes: cleanliness and filth[6] (which appears in Mt. Pleasant discourse as dirt, noise, and cursing, or "dirty language"), and safety and danger. As numerous scholars have remarked, cities have long been associated with chaos, trash, noise, and other kinds of filth. The geographer Yi-Fu Tuan[7] traces complaints about city noise from Imperial Rome to medieval London, and grievances about urban disorder from 18th-century Paris to colonial Boston. Sandra Walklate notes that "presumptions concerning the socially disorganized and disorderly nature of inner-city life have become embedded in more contemporary social and political thought,"[8] encapsulated in such expressions as "the urban jungle" or "the unwashed masses." It's quite common for both city dwellers and suburbanites to read rundown or dirty physical environments as areas of crime,[9] even though the evidence on crime locations does not support this reading. For example, in a study of a low-income housing project in Boston, Sally Engle Merry[10] found that residents viewed a rundown playground where teenagers hung out as the most dangerous part of the neighborhood. However, crime statistics showed that the majority of crimes were committed right in front of people's houses, areas that most people had rated as safest in the neighborhood.

The ideas that circulate about safe and dangerous places rub off on attitudes about people who live or spend time in such places. The person corollary of safe and dangerous places is that city people are fearless, and suburban people are fearful.

Interaction vs. individualism

A third contrast that Mt. Pleasant people make between city and suburb is that of interaction and solidarity vs. autonomy and individualism. The roots of this contrast seem to lie in the imputed density of the city vs. the spaciousness of the suburbs, as well as differing choices or options for transportation. This city/suburb dichotomy is ideological, rather than factual – many of the inner suburbs are quite dense, with thousands of people who use public transportation and live in 10-story apartment buildings. The ideology goes that city people come across and interact with each other in apartment hallways and busses or subway cars, and walking on the street, whereas suburban people solitarily drive from their detached homes into work and retreat back into their fenced suburban yards, without seeing a soul. This image is also rooted in developers' historical marketing of suburbs as a personal haven from the public work world;[11] indeed many scholars of urban studies have found that people conceptually map spheres of public and private onto urban and suburban territories.[12]

Public vs. private

The personal identity corollary of these imputed different life modes is that city people value social interaction and joint problem solving regarding neighborhood disputes, while suburban people value autonomy. In Mt. Pleasant, people link these values with imputed attitudes about public and private space; Mt. Pleasantites talk about city people as valuing public space and the lively street-life and interaction that can occur in it, while suburban people are said to value private space, the quiet of empty streets, and the sanitized commercial environments of shopping malls.

The linking of the interaction–individualism axis to the axis of public and private also plays into neighbors' evaluations about each others' behavior. The linguistic anthropologist Susan Gal[13] writes that ideological distinctions between public and private can project recursively onto larger and larger or smaller and smaller domains (a phenomenon she calls *fractal recursivity*). In the case of Mt. Pleasant, Mt. Pleasant and the city at large is constructed as public space, while the suburbs are constructed as private space (as outlined in the discussion of the urban/suburban ideological split above). *Within* Mt. Pleasant, however, Mt. Pleasant St., with its commercial strip and street activity, is often discussed as the public sphere and site of public life, in contrast to the side streets which get ideologically associated with domestic and private activities. A side street, however, can itself be divided into the public sidewalk and street and the private home. Similarly, houses themselves show this split in the public front stoop and the private back deck.

Gal notes that "a fractal private/public split can be shown to operate . . . as a discursive resource."[14] In Mt. Pleasant, community members use public/private distinctions to assign moral attributions to other people's uses of neighborhood space at different times. Interaction-oriented Mt. Pleasantites who value public space criticize their neighbors who don't go to Mt. Pleasant St., or who don't spend time on the public areas of their own side streets to interact with their neighbors, or who socialize on their back decks rather than their front stoops. Conversely, more individualism/autonomy-oriented community members may criticize their neighbors for what they consider to be "loitering" on Mt. Pleasant St., or for playing football on a side street, or for talking loudly on their front stoop, rather than inside.

A similar recursivity occurs among apartment dwellers, who divide public from private space first along the property lines of the building grounds, then between the yard or stoop and the interior of the building, and finally between the lobby, stairwells, laundry room and hallways, on the one hand, and individual apartments on the other.

As with house dwellers, in apartment buildings different attitudes about using public space also lead to tensions between neighbors at each of these recursive levels. In the Danforth building discussed in chapter 7, for example, more interaction-oriented residents objected when the condominium association put up a fence along a brick ledge at the edge of the property, so that people waiting for the bus or hanging out on Mt. Pleasant St. could no longer sit on the ledge. Individualism/autonomy-minded residents objected to others – particularly teenagers – hanging out on the building's front steps. Some in fact objected so strongly that the condominium association banned gathering there. (This ban was rarely enforced against adults, however.) This policy shows, as Gal notes, that ideological distinctions between public and private "can be turned into institutional structures and routinized organizations."[15] At the most micro level, neighbors inclined towards interaction voiced disregard for their neighbors who did not use the public spaces of hallways, elevators, or the laundry room to engage in conversation with them ("Say 'good morning'!"), while autonomy-oriented residents criticized neighbors who "use[d] the stairwell like their living room."

Social control vs. law-and-order

The linking of the interaction–individualism dichotomy also gets connected with imputed attitudes about appropriate ways to deal with neighborhood problems like noise or crime. The two main models of confronting such issues are the *social control* method versus the *institutional authority* or *law-and-order* method. The social control method gets associated with public interaction and, ideologically, with urban identity. In this method, neighbors take a personal role in dealing with problems – for example by asking a neighbor to turn down their music, or by disciplining a child causing trouble on the street. The institutional authority method is associated with valuing privacy (e.g., avoiding direct contact with neighbors) and, ideologically, with suburban identity. This approach entails appealing to an institution to mediate a problem, for example calling the police to complain about a neighbor's loud music.

These models are not mutually exclusive, and individual community members follow both of them. For example, as mentioned earlier, one merchant on Mt. Pleasant St. offers shoplifters the option of being arrested and prosecuted by the police, or having their picture taken with stolen items and mounted at the cash register for other shoppers to see.

There are certain infractions that Mt. Pleasantites across the political spectrum are likely to call the police for – namely violent crime. However, the law-and-order approach seems to be more often favored by more wealthy residents. For example, different groups of residents in the apartment building discussed in chapter 7 put forth solutions that showed these different orientations when discussing how to deal with a string of burglaries in the building. While the more wealthy condominium association lobbied to get a new state-of-the-art keycard system to replace the door locks, the working-class members of the coop association started a campaign urging people to get to know their neighbors and to ask strangers entering the building who they were coming to see.

Because the law-and-order model is seen to be indicative of wealthy neighbors, this model is often used to convey the idea of wealth, which in turn can invoke a suburban identity. Furthermore, because the law and order model entails eschewing or avoiding interaction with neighbors, this model then gets associated with an individualistic orientation. Finally, that individualistic orientation is often associated with the imputed private sphere of the suburbs.

Social ties and fear

Community members also link these models of dealing with nuisances and crime to fearful and fearless orientations to the neighborhood and to public space. Because the social control model entails interaction with other community members, those using this model are likely to know their neighbors, and to have stronger social networks than those preferring the law-and-order model. Local ideology holds that those with strong local connections tend to be less afraid in the neighborhood. While I'm not focusing here on the extent to which this ideology is rooted in fact, research on social networks and fear shows that social ties often do impact orientations towards fear. The geographers Hille Koskela and Gil Valentine, along with criminologists Ralph Taylor, Stephen Gottfredson, and Sidney Brower[16] found that people who knew an area well or who had strong social ties were less fearful than others. Similarly, Merry found that people in the Boston housing project where she conducted research who were not afraid of the area explained their lack of fear by the fact that they knew everyone in the complex, while those expressing more fear had weaker social ties. Taylor et al. also found that areas with strong social networks had less actual crime.

People's participation in social networks and in-depth knowledge of an area are also tied up with their use of space. As Koskela found in a study of women's fearlessness in Helsinki, women who felt fearless in urban spaces were those who used the space frequently, and felt "at home" in it. Furthermore, the women in her study felt that using the space conveyed on them rights of ownership to it. As she explains,

In an urban environment part of the feeling of taking possession of space is "an urban mentality." Women in my research described "the urban" as . . . being at home in the city and having roots there and being able to accept differences.[17]

Neighborhood Legitimacy

In Mt. Pleasant, using public space comes to be linked both ideologically and, I would argue, actually, with strong local social networks, a knowledge of the environment which enables one to be a good judge of safety and danger, and an appreciation of public life. For many in Mt. Pleasant, these characteristics in turn come to be associated with insider status, an orientation of fearlessness, and an urban identity. For some, then, neighborhood legitimacy is rooted in a deep knowledge of the built environment and the people who live in it, and a strong level of comfort in the neighborhood's public spaces. For community members with this attitude, the right to work for change in the neighborhood is one that has to be earned through a history of interaction with the people and the space.

Other community members, however, don't see use of space as key in defining neighborhood identity. For many property owners, especially those who follow the law-and-order model, it is the investment of money in housing and time in civic organization endeavors that show a commitment to the neighborhood. The kind of endeavors that this group of community members works on tend to focus on institutional channels, for example lobbying the Department of Public Works for more street-cleaning, or urging the police to arrest people for loitering or for making sexually explicit remarks to women on Mt. Pleasant St. However, a significant number of property owners embrace both models, placing a value on both legislating for better city services and promoting interaction among neighbors. Indeed, many residents bought property in Mt. Pleasant *because of* its strong community mindedness.

Divergent attitudes about what constitutes commitment to, and ownership of, the neighborhood cause a lot of conflict, as each group resents the other for trying to promote their vision of the neighborhood without (in the eyes of the other group) having the legitimacy as a community insider that would confer on them the right to decide what is appropriate for the neighborhood's public spaces.

To sum, up Mt. Pleasant community members delineate the city and the suburb through the following systems of ideological contrast. These systems of contrast underlie much of neighbors' discourse about their neighborhood.

City	Suburb
Heterogeneous	**Homogeneous**
Multi-ethnic ("diverse")	White
Multi-class	Wealthy
Architecturally varied	Architecturally uniform
Multiple sexual identities	Heterosexual
Disorderly	**Orderly**
Filthy	Clean
Dirty streets	Clean streets
Noisy	Quiet
Dirty language (cursing)	Clean language
Dangerous	**Safe**
Fearless people	Fearful people
Masculine	**Feminine**
Public	**Private**
Interaction	**Individualism**
Social control	Law-and-order
Strong local social networks	Weak local social networks

Indexing the Suburbs

In her analysis of the linguistic signaling of gender, Elinor Ochs[18] explains that when linguistic devices convey gender meanings, there is not always a direct relationship between a given linguistic structure and a gender category. Rather, linguistic structures can *indirectly index* gender identities. Indexicality is a process by which a linguistic structure (a word, grammatical form, pronunciation or accent, etc.) gets ideologically associated with an attitude, set of assumptions, personality type, social domain, etc. That linguistic structure then comes to signal or *index* the attitude, set of assumptions, etc. Indexicality can be either direct or indirect. Direct indexicality can be seen in the sentences, "That's a pretty mannequin," and "That's a handsome mannequin." In the first sentence, "pretty" directly indexes female gender, whereas "handsome" in the second sentence directly indexes male gender. In *indirect indexicality*, the social domain, stance, or attitude that a particular linguistic structure or strategy signals is mediated by another social domain, stance, or attitude. This is possible when a first stance or attitude is ideologically linked with another social domain (for example, gender identity). Thus, through a process of transitivity, that linguistic structure comes to signal the second social domain.[19] For example, cursing (a linguistic strategy) is ideologically associated with gruffness or toughness. Toughness, in turn, is often associated with masculinity. Because of these connections, cursing can then serve to indirectly index masculine identity.

Similarly, clustering ethnic, economic, and architectural homogeneity/heterogeneity, fearlessness and fear, order and disorder, etc., around the constructs of city and suburb enables social actors to use any of these characteristics to index any of the others, or to index urban or suburban identity. For example, Whiteness can be used to index fear, fear can be used to index gender, wealth can be used to index order, and any of these can be – and are – used by community members to index a suburban identity.

The poles of ideological contrast between city and suburb are often deeply intertwined in neighborhood talk, as can be seen from one community member's description of the neighborhood:

GALEY: So how would you describe Mt. Pleasant, to someone who didn't know DC?

SAM: I think the operative word is, diverse. It's diverse in every respect you know in terms of, eco**no**mics, in terms of **races**, u:m, you got- gay couples living next to, families, and, you know- you **name** it, th- the reason I was attracted to it when I first came to Washington, I'm from New York, and it was the only part of Washington that, at all reminded me of New York. And- the reason it did was because it's- diverse, I mean wherever you go in New York, God there's people from all over. A:nd, this is the only part of Washington- this- Mt. Pleasant and Adams Morgan, where you can get that kind of feeling. A:nd, it's not for everybody. There are people who come here and they just- freak out and run away. And then there are other people who, fall in love with the place. At first sight. U:m,. There's one lady in the building, in the Danforth, who, **left** the neighborhood to go to the suburbs, she bought a house in the suburbs, thinking, she wanted some peace and quiet, almost **immediately** regretted her decision. A:nd, started- making the effort to move back into the neighborhood and she- and she bought an apartment in our building. And moved back in, she's been there ever since. A:nd,. You know- she's the- she typifies the kind of person, that fits into the neighborhood. A number of the new people who came into the building, I could see right off the bat, they did **not** fit in the neighborhood.

GALEY: How could you tell?

SAM: They just, I don't know, I can't articulate it, it's just- intuitive. And, sure enough, it didn't take them long to leave![laughs] O:h, my.

GALEY: And what about this woman, what makes her fit in so well?

SAM: I don't know what it is that makes you fit in. But um, you just happen to like, diversity. I mean I don't know how else to describe it. That's- what you like. You know- **I** like it. I- I don't **like** the suburbs. And the reason I don't like the suburbs, is that everybody looks- like they came out of the same cookie cutter. And all the houses look like they came out of the same cookie cutter. I mean there just is no diversity. I can't stand it- it's just boring. But there are people who just crave it.

Sam's description neatly lines up the contrast between Mt. Pleasant people and people who "do not fit in the neighborhood" along the axes of city and suburb, ethnic, sexual, and architectural variety and sameness, and comfort and fear (illustrated by the people who "freaked out" and moved away"[20]).[21]

Physical and Moral Disorder

The cultural critics Peter Stallybrass and Allon White[22] have noted that physical disorder is often ideologically associated with moral disorder. In Mt. Pleasant, community members may use this arbitrary connection to create identities as bad neighbors for people whom they consider to be creating disorder. Others contest these constructions, however, through characterizing disorder as integral to city life. In the process of such characterizations, the original complainants' claims to urban identity are often delegitimized. Witness the following exchanges from the Mt. Pleasant listserv: One resident complains,

> The late-night, inordinately loud concerts have continued through the summer at the Youth Center. Beginning no earlier than 11:30 p.m. and lasting until at least 3–4:00 a.m., these concerts cannot be argued to "keep kids off the street." Moreover, they are unreasonably and unnecessarily loud. I would like the Youth Center to continue to be granted event permits but, in light of its violation of the scope of those permits, see their ability to hold any event as being in jeopardy. Those who have any information or interest in this issue, please respond.

And a neighbor responds,

> I do not want to begin by lecturing the benefits the concerts bring to both the community and the young people. I am one who is very pleased to see young people involved in these sort [sic] of activity. I am also one of those who would rather not have anyone making noise in the neighborhood before 12 noon on any day of the week; but we know we have to accept the fact that we live in a neighborhood with many diverse cultural expectations. I feel like it is unnecessary to remind neighbors that when you commit to living in the city, off of a major thoroughfare, at a major intersection, by an urban park, across from a school, and a former "youth community center" that one can expect their Saturday evenings to be [sic] bit more louder than other places one could choose to live.

As this response shows, the ostensible dirt and disorder of the city are also often valorized as an emblem of city identity. One common theme which Mt. Pleasant residents use to create an urban identity for both the neighborhood at large, and themselves in particular, is experiences with rats. For example, one summer night as I stood outside my apartment building chatting with my neighbors Kevin and Grace, we noticed a group of rats on the patch of grass next to us running back and forth, engaged in what looked like a game of leapfrog. As we watched them, Kevin remarked, "The rats are our squirrels."

While rats are associated with gritty urban areas and spreading disease, squirrels are more likely to be associated with trees and green areas, which in turn are associated with non-urban areas: squirrels like hiding nuts under the grass, not scurrying around in garbage. Thus Kevin used animals associated with urban and suburban – rats and squirrels, respectively – to contrast Mt. Pleasant with non-urban, and in particular suburban, places. And, by characterizing the rats as *our* squirrels, he linked *us* with urban Mt. Pleasant, consequently constructing us as urban people.

Fearlessness and Fear

The theme of fear is closely related to the theme of disorder and danger. The logic goes that the city is a place of ethnic and economic heterogeneity and disorder, and this creates a landscape of danger. Therefore, following this logic, city people are good judges of danger. On the other hand, since suburbanites are aligned with the alleged safety of the suburbs and ostensibly have little experience identifying danger, they are therefore bad judges of it. Sometimes this attitude results in outsiders being characterized as underestimating danger. This can be seen in a discussion with two African American community members, Kevin and Maurice. Kevin has been talking about changing racial demographics in neighboring Adams Morgan, and voicing fears Mt. Pleasant will follow the same path, and that African Americans will be pushed out of the neighborhood.

KEVIN: It's just moving up, same thing happening in Mt. Pleasant.
GALEY: How can you tell?
KEVIN: U:m, I see more White people they're, they're walking. [. . .] You see more White people walking, at night. You know what I mean? Carefree. And, just like they're not s- like me, I tell my mom and my wife, don't go out at night. Cause I know it's crime out there.

Kevin's description of Whites on the street as being carefree posits Whites as unable to read the neighborhood's geography of risk, and this peripheralizes Whites from core community membership.

Furthermore, in his utterance "Like **me**, I tell my mom and my wife, don't go out at night. Cause I know it's crime out there," Kevin emphasizes the contrast between himself and the "carefree White people." In talking about his advice to his mother and wife, rather than his own practices on the street, Kevin also indexes the notion that it's more dangerous for women on the street at night.

Kevin's description of Whites who can't read the landscape is followed by a narrative of Maurice's on the same topic:

> M: I mean it's weird because like, you know today, I saw this photographer, and, he's taking a picture of this church over here? And, one of the- the guys in the- over here in Pigeon Park, one of the, um drunks or whatever, tells the guy that, what's that it was like, y- you don't want that camera, do you? I stood there at the bus stop cause I heard him say that and I was like, he was like, you **must** not want that camera, you know around here! You know you gonna get that camera stolen. The guy was like, are you sure? He was like, don't come- come through this park! Don't come through this park. And this guy looked like, around 40, 42. Told this guy he gonna steal his camera! And it was two of 'em. You know, it was two White guys. And, some, Spanish guy in the park, was like, you gonna, you gonna lose that camera.

Here, the phrase "one of the drunks [in the park]" sets the scene for Maurice's narrative by presupposing that the park (Figure 3.1) is indeed peopled by drunks. In actuality lots of people hang out in this park who are not drunk. Maurice's characterization builds on Kevin's delineation of the dangerous city to create a picture of disorder. In Maurice's narration, the "Spanish guy" pokes fun at the photographer's inability to judge the danger of the park (thus again reinforcing the image of the neighborhood as dangerous). Maurice's narrative evaluation that "it was two White guys" connects back to Kevin's discussion of Whites as bad judges of the neighborhood's imputed danger. Through the utterance's position at the end of the narrative after the plot description, it becomes the first part of a two-part *coda*, or a concluding narrative structure that explains the point of a story. So the story comes to be about "two White guys" who don't know how to behave in this urban landscape, in comparison to a "Spanish guy," a regular in the park, whose narrative role of giving advice positions him as a neighborhood insider.

Figure 3.1   Two views of Pigeon Park

The Masculine City

Kevin's focus on the safety of his mother and wife, and his lack of discussion of his *own* safety on the streets, points to differential levels of access to city streets for women and men. This difference is embedded in a larger framework of relations between gender and space in which the public spaces of the city are seen to be masculine places, and the home – and, by extension, the suburbs (as we'll see below) – are feminized.

The image of the city as masculine space arose in 19th-century Europe with industrialization, when the city came to be associated with the male realms of workplace technology and monumental machinery, finance, and public political life that emerged alongside industrial capitalism. The rise in industrialization was the catalyst for a growing ideological distinction between public and private domains of social interaction, which were linked with public and private geographical spaces.[23] One of the reasons for this was that the site of productive labor moved from homes into factories, and homes became reconfigured as spaces of reproductive and domestic labor.[24] The streets of the city came increasingly to be seen as the public sphere and the domain of men, while the home came to represent the domestic sphere, and the domain of women. Consequently, women's access to the public sphere became more and more circumscribed. For a woman to be out alone in public was to risk harm, as well as disrepute to her and her family; it's no coincidence that a common term for a prostitute in the 19th century was a "public woman"[25] or a "streetwalker," a phrase still common today. The city was constructed as a place for men and a place that was dangerous or even unnatural for women; it was threatening to their physical, emotional, and social well-being, and a woman out alone in the city could bring about suspicion regarding what kind of a woman she was.

While in the 19th century public and private were associated with streets and homes, in the 20th century the trend of suburbanization stretched the scale of this division to the entire metropolitan area, so that the domestic sphere spread from the gates of the house to the borders of the suburb. In the United States, planners and developers pushed the suburb as a refuge from the masculine urban world of politics, culture, and work, and a haven from the social ills – the density, dirt, violence, and crime of the city.[26] The creation of the suburb was also key to enforcing the domestic role of women, at a time when many saw women's increased opportunities for paid employment as a threat. As the geographers Suzanne Mackenzie and Damaris Rose explain,

> Not only was this suburban environment predicated on the labour of a full-time suburban housewife, it also made it very difficult to organize the domestic economy and home life in any other way . . . Up to World War II, suburban environments were most effective in helping to entrench women's role as primarily a "private" domestic one. In this sense, the suburbs were a partial solution to the "woman question" of the early twentieth century, as the legitimate sphere of women's activities was confined to the home and neighbourhood.[27]

The suburbs became associated with domestic life, keeping women isolated and in their homes, and through this association the suburbs also became feminine spaces. This image also came about because of the suburbs' majority daytime population of women, as every morning men left the suburbs for their jobs in the city.

In addition to femininity, suburbs also came to be associated with Whiteness. Although working class suburbs and African American suburbs have existed in the US since the 1930s, the prototypical suburb is White and middle-class. In the second half of the 20th century, redlining (denying mortgages to people living in certain places) and unfair housing practices kept people of color – particularly African Americans – out of the suburbs, and "White flight" from US cities in the late 1960s reinforced the Whiteness of the suburbs, producing what Cornell West has termed "chocolate cities and vanilla suburbs."[28] Suburban developers also targeted White middle-class families in their advertising.[29] Although today the suburbs of Washington, DC are in fact more ethnically and economically diverse than the city itself, the region's suburban history keeps the ideology of the White suburb firmly in place.

In DC, urbanites frequently use feminized constructions of the suburbs – and of suburban people – to consolidate the masculinity of the city. One particularly prevalent way of doing this is through a discourse of fear. Suburbanites are characterized as unable to gauge danger in the city, and while sometimes DC urbanites articulate this inability through a fearlessness when people should be afraid, the more prevalent characterization is of fearful suburbanites in situations where fearfulness is not warranted. Through these articulations, fearfulness of city streets is presented as a suburban position. This works through the link of ideological connections discussed earlier: the city is male space, and dangerous for women, therefore women are fearful in the city. So fearfulness comes to be a feminine trait, and since the suburbs are associated with femininity, fearfulness then comes to be associated with the suburbs.

These ideological links are also grounded in the history of new suburban residents leaving the city because of fear, and a currently prevalent suburban discourse in which suburbanites voice fears of the city. One example of this is urban anthropologist Setha Low's[30] work on suburban gated communities, where she found fear of the city to be a common theme in residents' talk about their communities. In Low's research, it is notable that the majority of people in the neighborhood during the day (and thus available to be interviewed) were White women, and that the people these women characterize as fear-inducing were men – and very often, specifically African American and Latino men.

Gender, Ethnicity, Fear of the City

For suburban women like those in Low's study, fear of crime and victimization often works almost as a code for fear of the Other.[31] Witness the story that one of Low's informants uses to explain her choice to move to a gated community:

[Vanessa] illustrates her point by telling me what happened to a friend who lives "in a lovely community" outside of Washington, DC: "She said this fellow came to the door, and she was very intimidated because she was white, and he was black, and you didn't get many blacks in her neighborhood. She only bought [what he was selling] just to hurry and quick get him away from the door, because she was scared as hell. That's terrible to be put in that situation. I like the idea of having security."[32]

Examples like this strengthen the ideology that suburbanites, particularly White suburbanites, and particularly women, fear the multi-ethnic city. Such characterizations of suburbanites circulate widely in the popular consciousness of cities. From San Antonio to Toronto,[33] North American urbanites talk about the prototypical suburb as ethnically, economically, and architecturally homogeneous, safe, and bland, and the prototypical suburbanite as White, female, and scared of the city and its multi-ethnic denizens. This theme of heterogeneity, or *diversity*, particularly gets a lot of play in Mt. Pleasant, since the neighborhood is often thought of as the most ethnically diverse area of the city. As we saw in Sam's description earlier, in contrast to the suburbs, Mt. Pleasantites frequently construct the city as heterogeneous in terms of ethnicity, economics, sexuality, and architecture, and as dangerous and gritty. And the prototypical urbanite gets constructed as male, non-White, tough and fearless.

In order to understand the way that discourse of fear works rhetorically in Mt. Pleasant, it is useful to sketch out the historical development of such discourses, so we can understand how "landscapes of fear" (to use Yi-Fu Tuan's term[34]) have been created.

Fear, like other emotions, is a psychological framework that is culturally and socially mediated.[35] Fear is an emotional response to a perception of danger, and many of the situations which we perceive as dangerous are themselves culturally learned, based on the stories we are told and the warnings given us by our families, acquaintances, and the media about what constitute dangerous places and situations. Barry Glassner[36] documents how the rise in television news reporting about dangerous situations increased Americans' sense of fear, at the same time as actual crime rates dropped. Thus, as we also saw in the perceptions of the housing complex residents in Sally Engle Merry's study, our perceptions of danger are often not in line with the actual odds of risk in a given situation.

The prototypical case of urban fear is fear of physical harm. However, when speakers talk about danger and fear, these terms can often serve as glosses or substitutes for other phenomena. For example, Low found that her informants in gated communities used the word *security* (the flip side of danger) to signify not only shielding from physical harm, but also to mean privacy and "an emotional sense of feeling protected."[37] In Mt. Pleasant, women often express fear or discomfort in regard to walking on Mt. Pleasant St., the main commercial corridor, a place where men – particularly Latino men – often spend time socializing on street corners and leaning against fences. There are also often drunk men on the street, and men who are passed out on the sidewalk.

It is not always clear, however, who or what it is exactly that women on the street fear. In discussing shopping at Latino stores on Mt. Pleasant St, for example, one White woman told me that she felt "scared to go into those stores that you can't see in those windows." When I asked her why such stores made her fearful, she explained that it wasn't that she thought any harm might befall her in such places, but rather that, "You can't know before you go in what they're like, and I'm always scared that I wouldn't know what to do or how to act, how things work in them." This explanation shows both that, similar to Low's examples, fear of the city's built environment can often be fear of cultural difference, and that the term "fear" may be used to gloss a wide range of emotions from discomfort to terror. In fact, in Mt. Pleasant discourse of fear is very often used to refer to discomfort, rather than outright fright. For the purposes of my discussion, then, I consider talk of discomfort to be part of the larger local discourse of fear.[38]

It is instructive to note that the association of urban fear with women seems to be a phenomenon that is widespread.[39] As with many ideologies discussed here, it is an ideological link which is rooted in actual phenomena: Numerous researchers have found that women (along with seniors) consistently report more fear of crime than men, even though men are far more likely to be crime victims.[40] As Hille Koskela[41] notes, the explanation for this seemingly paradoxical finding lies in larger ideologies of gender and gendered power relations, as well as the previously discussed limited access that women have to public space. Similarly, geographers Anna Mehta and Liz Bondi point out that "gender-differentiated subject positions . . . influence[ ] the ways in which urban spaces are used and experienced by both . . . women and men."[42] In other words, the widespread attitudes that women do not belong alone in public space create a further ideology that women are at threat not just from random crime, but more specifically from sexual violence in public spaces – actions that highlight victims' gender, as it is gender norms which they may be seen to violate through being alone in public space.

The power of street remarks to women, then, does not lie in their signaling as a warning sign of actual danger to come, but rather in their force of turning women into sexual objects, which can create a feeling of sexual vulnerability. As geographer Gill Valentine explains, "women are told and soon learn through experience that it is inappropriate and potentially unsafe to be alone in male dominated space, especially at night."[43]

Gendered Access to Urban Space

One reason that women and men experience urban public space differently is the aforementioned delineation of public space as male space, and the consequent constraints put on women in terms of appropriate behavior in public space. The sociologist Carol Gardner analyzed a host of admonitions about women's presence in public space from the middle of the 19th century to the end of the 20th century. She found that etiquette books, advice columns, crime-prevention experts, and conventional wisdom all advise against women spending time alone in public places. These sources

> tell women to avoid public places at night, state that a "true lady" does not walk in certain neighborhoods, or observe that proper women avoid bars and other environments that connote moral laxity. Etiquette also suggests that women in public places practice an abridged agenda of activities.[44]

And Gardner's analysis of men's public street remarks to women — as well as men and women's interpretations of such remarks — shows that it is considered a matter of course for men to make comments to women on the street, but not vice versa. Such unequally distributed public address rights also constrain women's access to public space and acceptable means of self-protection. It follows from the notion that it is unladylike for women to engage in discussion with strangers on the street, that responding to street remarks is not an appropriate or viable course of action. As I'm sure many readers can attest, it is not uncommon for women to find that responding can escalate a situation and inspire hostility and aggressiveness. Many women simply try to ignore street remarks and remain silent, because it takes calculation and subtlety to figure out how to respond effectively to them,[45] and because responding opens up the door to increased interaction and potential harassment. This is why street remarks serve as an informal means of policing and gendering space.

Even positive comments that men make to women delimit women's role on the street. As Gardner writes, "public harassment [her term for street remarks] suggests that a women's unchallenged female self is still located in the home; it is at home, less so in the workplace, that a woman is still an authority on her own experience."[46]

One DC illustration of this in neighboring Adams Morgan is a man locally referred to as Compliment Man, who gives out compliments to women about their appearance when they walk by. Although the comments he makes are meant to be flattering, and many women who walk by him every day respond with such positive evaluation as stopping to talk or even hugging him, other women assert that his comments consistently hinder their ability to be autonomous and go about their business unimpeded and without their appearance being remarked on. Perhaps more interesting is what happens when a woman is walking with a man down the street, especially at night. In that case, Compliment Man's remarks are directed to the man, usually along the lines of "Oh, she's beautiful, you treat her right, don't let her get away." Compliment Man's explanation of this behavior[47] is that he has gotten into some nasty altercations when making comments to women when they are accompanied by men; this is also his reason for not giving compliments to men, which at some point he did do. Both the comments that he makes to men about the women they're with, and the fact that some men react negatively to Compliment Man's making direct comments to the women they're with, illustrate that street remarks construct women as less than capable of handling their own affairs. Likewise, what Compliment Man describes as some men's violent and aggressive reactions to receiving compliments themselves points to the way that street remarks can limit the addressee's autonomy, and suggests that there is in fact a sexual subtext to these remarks.

Street remarks can also work to police the space in more direct ways. One night, coming home late, I passed a man walking the other direction. He looked me in the eye and said, "I'm just curious, what are you doing walking home so late by yourself, girl?" When I posed the same question to him (but without the gendered vocative *girl*), he seemed taken aback, as if his question were quite an odd one indeed for *me* to pose to *him*.

Separating Gender and Ethnicity

The politics of street remarks becomes more complicated in a multicultural setting like Mt. Pleasant, where discussions of street remarks take on ethnoracial overtones, and the power relations between men and women become intertwined with local power relations among ethnic groups. This topic frequently comes up in public discourse settings like town hall meetings and Mt. Pleasant listserv discussions. By and large, the way that this happens is that White women or White men raise the issue of Latino men on Mt. Pleasant St. making insulting comments to women.[48]

> About the groups of men who hang all day on the fence on Frazier St. (Figure 3.2). They like to stare threateningly at white males who walk by, and of course they make disgusting comments to any woman who walks by. There is little the police can do about it unless there is an assault. But there are things that we can do. I'm considering asking the owner of the super market to remove the fence. I'll offer to do the work for free. If not this, a bright light cast on them might disperse them a bit. I've also considered getting several of my friends to occupy the fence for an afternoon . . . I imagine most women reading this would feel way safer on any Georgetown street than on Mount Pleasant Street. In Georgetown, they (meaning residents and businesses) do not tolerate drunken loiterers harassing pedestrians. This is not a racist or cultural attack but a discussion about making our street safe for us and our children.

In this message, we can see the individualism, law-and-order model of community "problem" solving, in which a White man who "walks by" a corner is troubled by the Latino men who are actually using the public space. He advocates instigating change by talking to the owner of the fence (thus implicitly orienting to property ownership status, rather than use status, in looking for some kind of "solution"), or by making the space uncomfortable for them to hang out in.

Figure 3.2   The current fence on Frazier St. The sign reads, "Private property: Do not lean against the fence."   © Jennifer Leeman

(Although he suggests the social control approach in his consideration of him and his friends "occupy[ing] the fence," this is not a
suggestion which he actually carries through.) I don't know if this
particular individual ever talked to the owner of the supermarket,
but since this data was collected, the owner has indeed changed the
fence to one that people cannot sit on (but people do lean on it,
despite the signs discouraging this practice).

Interestingly, although the writer talks about White men who are
ostensibly being stared at threateningly, his post focuses on safety as
an issue for women, rather than for men. Additionally, the writer
connects threats to safety with ethnicity; although the writer doesn't
explicitly reveal his ethnicity, as is typical of much White public discourse, he attributes ethnic identity to the men on the street indirectly. In this case, the attribution is based on the knowledge that the
men who hang out on the corner in question are Latino, coupled
with the implicit contrast with "white males" in the first utterance,
and the disclaimer, "this is not a racist or cultural attack" – which,
contrary to the writer's claim, brings race and culture explicitly into

the discussion, thereby *highlighting* them as potentially relevant lenses through which to read his remarks.[49]

In addition to invoking ethnicity, the writer links ethnicity to themes of gender and safety in his strategy of speaking for women ("I imagine most women reading this would feel safer on any Georgetown street") and speaking for safety for "us and our children." This move recalls colonialist and US racist discourses which cast men of color as threats to the safety and purity of White women and children.[50] Furthermore, the writer invokes Georgetown, a predominantly White and very wealthy city neighborhood, as a model neighborhood. These strategies serve to promote White interests in Mt. Pleasant, while marginalizing Latino men by constructing them as deviant.[51] Given these moves, it is difficult not to read the "us and our children" in this message as Whites in the neighborhood.

Ethnicity was similarly invoked off-record in the meeting about getting the police to use sexual harassment laws to arrest men for making comments to women on the street. At this meeting, the woman who was spearheading the effort suggested that flyers about new arrest policies be printed and put up in "both languages."[52] We can assume that "both languages" here means the most widely spoken languages in the neighborhood, which are English and Spanish. English, as the language of wider communication in DC, does not index any particular ethnic group. Conversely, Spanish specifically indexes Latinos.

The move to publish these flyers "in both languages" is notable given what kinds of civic organization announcements tend to be written only in English vs. what gets written in both English and Spanish. During the time that I was conducting fieldwork, flyers advertising civic group and town hall meetings were written only in English except when a meeting was to discuss policies for selling alcohol and drinking on the street. Similarly, in a neighborhood newsletter around the time of this alcohol policy meeting, all the stories were in English and all of the announcements except the announcement for the alcohol policy meeting were in English. Given this local pattern, publishing flyers about sexual harassment in Spanish constructs Latino identity as particularly relevant to public sexual harassment.

Another strategy for discussing street remarks is to draw upon cultural norms as a theme through which to explain the behavior of men on the street (as in Gabi's remarks at the beginning of this chapter). For instance, the woman who asked to have this item on the meeting agenda suggested that the effort to stem "verbal sexual harassment of women on the streets of Mt. Pleasant" should include "educating the public on why such behavior is unacceptable, [and] working with cultural agencies to discourage the practice."

Clearly, Mt. Pleasant discourse about street remarks is highly racialized – associated with Latino men – as well as culturalized – associated with particular aspects of Latino culture; many neighbors assert that hanging out on the street and making remarks to women walking by is acceptable in Latin American cultures. I don't deny this. However, as Carol Gardner's work shows, the practice has an equally strong tradition in the US. It would be disingenuous, then, to characterize the practice as more indicative of cultural groups with roots in Latin America than of other US groups.

Given the way that such discourse constructs Latino men and Latino culture as predatory and highly sexualized, it is little wonder that Latina women rarely criticize such behavior in public discourse settings, because to do so would reinforce cultural stereotypes. Latina women are put in a particularly difficult position in public discourse in relation to this issue, because their gender and ethnic affiliations are often put at odds with each other in such situations; if they don't want to reinforce stereotypes about their own community, they are forced to publicly show an acceptance of behaviors they often do not condone or appreciate. Latina women in Mt. Pleasant deal with this conflict in a number of ways.

Sometimes, women use this same theme of culture to delegitimize the protests that non-Latinos make about male comments on the street, as we saw with Gabi's comments in the beginning of the chapter about the town hall meeting on "sexual verbal harassment." Rather than taking those remarks at face value, however, it's useful to consider their rhetorical function within the context of racialized struggles over public space. It's important to note here that Mt. Pleasant civic groups are overwhelmingly White, and that most people in public meetings who raise the issue of comfort and safety on Mt. Pleasant St. are women. And when men do talk on this issue, as we saw in the email example above, more often than not they don't speak from their own perspectives, but instead voice the imputed complaints of actual or theoretical women. An excerpt from another message posted to the listserv illustrates this trend:

> Please come [to the meeting] and hear about the women who live in the neighborhood who can't get into their apartment buildings because drunks are blocking the doorways. Please hear from the retired ladies who cannot find a place to park their cars because people with out-of-state tags are taking all of the parking spaces and are failing to get DC tags (as required by law.")[53]

Through such phenomena, White women come to have a privileged place in the public discourse when it comes to safety talk. Considered in this light, Gabi's remark that "White women don't understand those comments" serves to delegitimize the local authority of White women, first, by constructing the woman at the meeting as White, based on no prior knowledge about this woman's (in fact African American) ethnic identity, and second, by portraying White women in general as unable to correctly interpret street activity in the neighborhood. It is not necessarily the case that Gabi's main *goal* is to delegitimize White women, however; her remark that "White women don't understand those comments" is equally, if not more so, a means of combating anti-Latino discourse. Because talk of women's attitudes towards street comments is so often anti-Latino – because such talk about gender relations is so tied up with ethnic bias – it is difficult to contest the ethnic bias without invoking gender.

It is important to keep in mind that Gabi's comments are a contestation of a particular ideology, rather than a simple description of her "true" feelings about remarks made to women on the street; remember her expression of annoyance when talking about being catcalled after a walk on Mt. Pleasant St. When the overarching topic of talk was not neighborhood politics or ethnic relations, Gabi expressed her dislike of receiving such remarks, negatively identified men making such comments as *drunks*, and expressed the desire that men on the street would "just leave me alone." In *this* context, Gabi did not refer to catcalling as part of any type of Latino culture, but rather as the behavior of drunks. Gabi's two disparate characterizations of the same behavior point to the function of behavior characterization as a strategy in arguing a point; in this case, it is a strategy to stake out a position in the battle over ethnicity and claims to public space.[54]

Gender and Ethnicity on the Street

I'm walking home with three female friends. Two of us look White, one looks Latina, and one is variously perceived as either White or Latina. We pass two African American guys, and exchange greetings. Next, two White guys in an SUV coming from the other direction stop alongside us and offer us a ride. When we say no, they try to convince us that we need a ride from them. In this process, they tell us, "You shouldn't be walking around here – it's not safe around here for girls like you." Next, one of the African American men who we just passed turns around and says to the guys in the car, "*You* shouldn't be around here – It's not safe for *you* – this is not the suburbs."

While the SUV guy's utterance constructs the street as masculine space where my female friends and I don't belong (potentially because of race? because of how we were dressed? It was not clear), the second guy's utterance contests this notion and discursively dis–places the White SUV guy from the neighborhood, highlighting the local ideological link between Whiteness and wealth (potentially represented by the SUV), and the common local attitude that links suburbanites with fear. As in Maurice and Kevin's stories earlier, the White SUV guy is interpellated as a bad judge of danger; the speaker uses the local discourse of safety and danger to make the point that the SUV guys' comments, and the guys themselves, are out of place. Another possible reading is that the African American guy is displacing the drivers because of their Whiteness – this is a dangerous place, and it's not safe for people of your ethnicity. We can also read the interaction as a threatening show of aggression which challenges the drivers' rights to be (behaving like they are) in this public space.

In addition to such informal policing,[55] policing of gendered and racialized space also goes on through the activities of actual police officers. In two and a half years of fieldwork, I heard many stories about police harassment, and most of them were about harassment of Latino men. While there were very few stories of White women getting harassed, the stories that I did hear were remarkably similar. They were about young White women getting frisked for drugs, and police officers[56] telling them that "White girls don't live around here" (despite the fact that the neighborhood has been at least one-third

White since the 1980s) – so that, if they were there, they must have been doing something illegal. This is a sort of modern-day DC version of London's public women.

Fear Discourse as Marginalization Strategy

The above examples show that discourses of fear and fearlessness can be used to marginalize various groups. When the fear is characterized as justified in neighborhood public discourse, it is usually Latinos (and occasionally African Americans) – and usually Latino men – who are being constructed as the (ostensibly justified) cause of such fear. It is this process that marginalizes Latino men.

Conversely, when fear or fearlessness is constructed as uncalled for, more often than not it's usually Whites, and usually White women in particular, who are being marginalized. I would argue that both of these processes are rooted in an ideology that holds that Whites are fearful of men of color, a phenomenon that Susan Ruddick describes as the "gendered and racialized trope of the dangerous black male who threatens the integrity of the white community through sexual or physical violence to its women."[57] As Low's White woman–Black salesman story shows, there is ample evidence in fact to support the ideology that White women are fearful of men of color.[58] For example, in a study of the effects of neighborhood racial makeup in Chicago on residents' fearfulness, Gertrude Moeller found that in Chicago "white respondents living in racially mixed neighborhoods [are] those most likely to report fear of crime."[59] Similarly, D.J. Smith and J. Gray found that Whites in "high ethnic concentration" neighborhoods in London were twice as likely to be fearful as those living in "low ethnic concentration" neighborhoods.[60] And Low comments that it was fear of what one of her informants referred to as "ethnic changes" that impelled ex-urbanites in the New York area to move to the suburbs.[61] Thus the view of White suburbanites as fearful of a multi-ethnic urban populace arises out of the historical conditions of urban and suburban migration patterns. It is this history that underlies the ideology of White fear, and which enables Mt. Pleasant community members to exploit this ideology and invoke the themes of fear and Whiteness – along with femininity – to align their neighbors with the suburbs, and therefore contest their neighbors' positions as legitimate Mt. Pleasant people.

"Girlfriend Needs to Move to the Suburbs"

If the city is set up as masculine and the suburbs as feminine, then it's not surprising that people perform masculinity as a way of constructing an urban identity, and that they index femininity in their discourse as a way to link people to the suburbs, thereby delegitimizing those people's claims to an urban identity and authority. One way in which this is done is through a performance of violence or verbal aggression. As many researchers have noted,[62] in the US, dominant images of masculinity – particularly working class masculinity – entail physical, emotional, and verbal aggressiveness – this last articulated, among other things, through "rough" language such as cursing or direct confrontation. Dominant masculinity also involves an orientation of fearlessness. In a study of socialization of fearlessness among adolescent boys, for example, Jo Goodey found that, while 11-year-old boys expressed more fear of their environment than did 11-year-old girls, this differential reversed with age. Older boys were much less likely than girls their age or than younger boys to express fear or vulnerability in the company of male peers, and when they did, it was through joking or banter.[63] Similarly, in a study of Edinburgh college students, Anna Mehta and Liz Bondi[64] found that men portrayed themselves as fearless and able to handle violent situations. Conversely, the males in Goodey's study who showed fear risked being called "a sissy" or "a girl" by their peers.

Postings on the Mt. Pleasant email discussion list illustrate how neighborhood residents perform masculinity and attribute femininity to others as they consolidate their own neighborhood identity and delegitimize others' rights to community membership. Often these gender and neighborhood identity/community membership performances are linked, implicitly or explicitly, to the suburbs. Below is an example of explicit suburb talk and contestation over community membership.

I'm replying to Joe, who railed against the precious amongst us, and I'd just like to second it. We are being colonized by suburbanites, who seem to want to legislate a Chantilly-by-the-Ghetto[65] here, and the character of the neighborhood will be the first to go. Please add your voice.

And the response:

Oh my goodness, I'd better move out of the city. I might actually be one of these horrible "suburbanites"! I grew up in Arlington, VA. I forgot that there was a law, (or is it just an attitude), that said that I wasn't allowed to live in the city! Please forgive me for also disliking crime and graffiti, and trash. I'll be sure to leave the lid off my garbage so you can have a more city-like atmosphere. Oh, also, I planted a garden – I'll uproot it and replace the weeds that were there.

Frequently, however, the attribution of the suburbs and their associated themes is more subtle. This can be seen in another email exchange, this one about activity on Mt. Pleasant St. The message under analysis here is the second one below, which is a response to the following email:

Often I have read about different struggles involving the darker element that resides within Mt. Pleasant. The problem with drunks on the 1700 block of Avery, the disgust at public defecation, the aggressive panhandling, etc. . . . What I have to offer is some small advice on how to deal with these issues that will continue to plague our neighborhood until we do something about them.

Police response: To increase police activity in the neighborhood we need to do two items.

1) Call them more often. Call the police any time you see anything suspicious. Call the non-emergency number . . . and feel guilt free. The fact is that the police gather information on which areas call the most, and then give those areas the most attention. "The squeaky wheel gets the grease" is the logic. So let's start squeakin'!! I personally take pleasure calling in minor offences such as sleeping drunks, minor vandalism and the like.

. . .

Another way to reduce the acceptability of negative street behavior is to be there. By this I mean people actively deciding to walk the routes they normally avoid due to this behavior. The more street alcoholics witness positive people walking by their "usual hangout" the less comfortable they will feel hanging out there. Possibly some of our positive energy will rub off and influence these people to get the help this neighborhood provides plenty of, via [a homeless shelter] and other such wonderful organizations.

Ideas. Ideas people. I've got plenty more about many issues. Let me say that the problems we have in this area are so minor in comparison with others. Hey, we do live in the city. It is real nice, however, to live in a place where so many people care. I love this 'hood.

F. Knox.

Many list participants wrote in to criticize this message, including the writer below. Since her response highlights many of the noteworthy elements of Knox's message, I will refrain from commenting on Knox's message itself. What I want to focus on, rather, are the discourse strategies that Sands uses to critique F. Knox, as well as to delegitimize Knox's community member standing.

F. Knox loves his 'hood?!!? Gimme a break! I found Mr. Knox's mssg. [sic] in the Mt. Pleasant Forum [the listserv] thoroughly revolting. He objects to "the darker element" that resides within Mt. Pleasant – of course you're referring to the non-lily white cast outs? . . . It's puritanical, self-righteous people like Mr. Knox who claim to love this neighborhood, but who are struggling to convert it into a replica of Takoma Park, Chevy Chase, Cleveland Park and other cutesy, pseudo-liberal areas, that "plague our neighborhood" – not the people who've been living here far longer than him, even though they may be "darker" and unsightly to Mr. Knox's delicate sensibilities. There's a lot of lip-service going on to "diversity," but too often it feels like Mt. Pleasant could do with another riot to remind all these eager new homeowners who fear for their real estate value that this IS a diverse neighborhood: economically, racially & culturally – it does NOT solely belong to upper middle class homeowners. I've never been incensed enough to respond to a Mount Pleasant List posting, but this one was definitely way over the top. Mr. Knox wants to change the neighborhood so much, it would be simpler for him to move somewhere where he and his neighbors can congratulate themselves on their lovely similarities. Oh, and calling the police and harassing harmless bums is NOT a sign of caring – it's being stuck up, scared and self-righteous.

samanthasands@yahoo.com

In this email, Sands takes up an aggressive tone and invokes violence and threat as she attacks Knox's claim to being a Mt. Pleasant person – a claim that was put forth in the original message with the remark "I love this neighborhood." The themes that she uses to delegitimize Knox's position are all in some way linked with the larger local ideology of suburbia – homogeneity, whiteness, wealth, femininity, and fear. Where Knox had professed love for the neighborhood, Sands challenges the veracity of this assertion by labeling it as a "claim," and she calls into question his alignment with Mt. Pleasant, and Mt. Pleasant identity, by aligning him with wealthy, predominantly White Maryland inner suburbs – Takoma Park and Chevy Chase – and a wealthy predominantly White DC neighborhood – Cleveland Park. Sands presupposes that Knox and those like him are "new homeowners," who haven't been living in the neighborhood for nearly as long as the people he criticizes, and who want to change the neighborhood. These presuppositions serve to dis-align Knox from the neighborhood, for if he were truly *of* the neighborhood, why would he want to change it? In addition, by posing Knox's homeownership status and tenure in the neighborhood as background information, the structure of presupposition naturalizes these imputed identities.

The alignment with the suburbs of Takoma Park and Chevy Chase, and the DC neighborhood of Cleveland Park, which further serves to characterize Knox as White and wealthy, in turn aligns him with suburbanness. Given that Knox opposed himself to what he called "the darker element," Sands' implicit definition of "the darker element" as an ethnoracial category further creates a White identity for Knox. And her suggestion that Knox move to someplace where he's similar to his neighbors highlights Mt. Pleasant as a *diverse* place, and indexes the ideological homogeneity of the suburbs, so this another way of aligning Knox with the suburbs.

Although there's no clue to Knox's gender in the original message, Sands assumes that Knox is a man. This is interesting in light of the gender work that Sands is doing in this message, particularly the subtle ways that she feminizes Knox. By attributing maleness to Knox, she's able to very subtly engage in a masculine insult ritual whereby, through attributing femininity to Knox, she calls his masculinity into question. This text would play very differently if it were addressed to a female addressee. We see the theme of femininity first in Sands' assertion that Knox is trying to turn Mt. Pleasant into a "cutesy" neighborhood, next in her attribution of Knox's "delicate" sensibilities that are threatened by "the darker element" (this harkens back to Setha Low's informant and the salesman), and finally in her suggestion that Knox move in with people with whom he shares "lovely similarities."

As Kira Hall and Rusty Barrett[66] have noted, speakers use such words to create images of femininity – and in Barrett's work, a femininity that is explicitly middle-class and White. Because of a link in the popular consciousness between femininity and male homosexuality, some could interpret Sands' words as negatively implying that Knox is gay. Indeed, in one screed against Sands' message, another listserv member writes,

[. . .] One such sign of community decay, in Mr. Knox and my opinion, at the very least, is the presence of fat, shirtless, drunken men passed out on the sidewalks . . . [sic] bottle in hand, vomit running off their chins. We should be able to express our disdain for such things without having to worry about some knee-jerk's accusations of being "puritanical" or "stuck-up." One doesn't necessarily have "delicate, (–intimating a lack of machismo, perhaps? homophobe! fascist!–), sensibilities" if one objects to being subjected to the nuisance of panhandling.

"Delicate," "cutesy," and "lovely" are prototypical of the set of *empty words* that Robin Lakoff found to be commonly considered part of women's language in her groundbreaking study *Language and Women's Place*.[67] Sands wields the words "cutesy," "lovely," and "delicate" to create for Knox a kind of "Language and Women's Place in the Suburbs." Finally, Sands' invocation of fear to describe Knox and those like him – ". . . harassing harmless bums is . . . being stuck up, scared, and self-righteous" and "eager new homeowners who fear for their real estate value" – aligns these residents with the suburbs through the indexical link of fear and suburbanness.

Since masculinity is aligned with urbanness, challenging Knox's masculinity works to challenge his claim to urban identity. Conversely, by engaging in this insult ritual, as well as by taking on an aggressive and even violent stance – proposing that the neighborhood should have another riot, Sands carves out what could be read as a masculine positionality for herself. This, in turn, works to bolster her position as a true, urban, Mt. Pleasant person whose demeanor corresponds with the identity of the neighborhood, and whose views on the neighborhood, therefore, should carry weight.

If we want to understand urban conflict, we also need to understand how and why ideologies about social identity get embedded in notions of urban life and urban problems. The following chapters analyze a wide variety of neighborhood texts in order to illuminate how community members utilize themes of gender and fear, along with disorder, orientation to public space, and attitudes about social interaction, to construct various and often conflicting characterizations of Mt. Pleasant and Mt. Pleasant people. An understanding of these processes can help us to decouple fights for personal authority from the actual issues of safety, crime, and the rampant social inequalities that are indicative of North American cities undergoing gentrification. As Vince, another writer to the Mt. Pleasant listserv, explains,

> Reading about F. Knox's comments in Samantha Sands' subsequent posting got me to thinking. We seem to have very little common ground in our neighborhood, especially on that elusive bugaboo "diversity." Everyone talks about it, but we all seem to define it solely in terms of our comfort level. I probably have been guilty of this too.
>
> If F. Knox feels like harassing homeless people is good sport, or that it is OK to talk about the "darker element" in our neighborhood, or use some other veiled, pejorative term, he's wrong. I also take exception to the idea that "another riot" is the most effective way to remind people that we live in a diverse neighborhood. That kind of statement presupposes that people of color always need to resort to violence to express their displeasure, and that all white folks are always so stupid that they don't "get it" unless their car is set afire.
>
> I feel it's counter productive to talk about neighborhoods like Chevy Chase and Bethesda as "fake." These so-called fake neighborhoods have lots of components I would like to see in our neighborhood, like regular trash pickup, recycling, trees in all the tree boxes, etc. It's

fine to prefer not to live in these places, but let's not get into the mind-set where we're looking at real problems in our neighborhood – and rampant homelessness, prostitution, and drug abuse are problems, not just "bad luck" – and convincing ourselves that we are "tougher" or "better" because we put up with more crap everyday.

Notes

1 I realize that this is not particularly neutral in terms of gender. However, as sociolinguist Deborah Tannen (Tannen 2004) notes, there often exists no neutral, unmarked category for women's fashion. For a woman, not wearing makeup makes as much of a statement as wearing a particular color or style of makeup.

2 A rolled parchment with texts from the Old Testament and the name of God, enclosed in a bar-shaped box. Mezuzahs are traditionally affixed to doorframes in Jewish homes and establishments.

3 Although DC's murder rate decreased in the early 1990s, it has remained among the top five US cities.

4 For a discussion of the myth of gay-led gentrification, see Ley (1996).

5 Singer et al. (2001)

6 For more on the ideological power of filth, see the discussion on Mary Douglas's work in chapter 4.

7 Tuan (1979)

8 Walklate (2000:50)

9 Susan Smith (1987), Skogan (1986)

10 Merry (1981)

11 cf. Monk (1992)

12 Ackelsberg (1988)

13 Gal (2002)

14 Gal (2002:90)

15 Gal (2002:90)

16 Koskela (1997), Valentine (1989), Taylor, Gottfredson, and Brower (1984)

17 Koskela (1997:308)

18 Ochs (1992)

19 See also Hill (1998), Silverstein (1976).

20 This comment refers back to an earlier discussion about newcomers to the neighborhood who were scared by crime and prostitution and left the neighborhood after only a couple of months.

21 This description also points to a limit on what kinds of diversity are appreciated even by people who promote diversity. In this case, there is less tolerance towards residents who are not open to all aspects of

city life. In an ideal sense but perhaps somewhat contradictorily, a place that was truly open to a diversity of residents would also be open to and accepting of residents who did not share attitudes towards diversity.

22 Stallybrass and White (1986)
23 Mackenzie and Rose (1983), McIlhenny (1997), Walkowitz (1992), Wilson (1992)
24 Monk (1992)
25 cf. Walkowitz (1992), Wilson (1992)
26 cf. Monk (1992), Schwartz (1976)
27 Mackenzie and Rose (1983:170)
28 West (1993)
29 Monk (1992)
30 Low (2003, 2001)
31 See chapter 8 for a discussion of this term.
32 Low (2003:145)
33 cf. Low (2003), Ley (1996), Mills (1993)
34 Tuan (1979)
35 Mehta and Bondi (1999), Susan Smith (1987), Middleton (1986)
36 Glassner (1999)
37 Low (2003:90)
38 I use *fear* as the overarching term because this is the term that appears most often in local discourse.
39 It's worth pointing out that the majority of research on urban fear has been conducted in the Americas and Europe.
40 Koskela (1997), Moeller (1989), Sacco and Glackman (1987), Susan Smith (1987), Skogan and Maxfield (1981)
41 Koskela (1997)
42 Mehta and Bondi (1999:80)
43 Valentine (1989:389)
44 Gardner (1995:19)
45 I am talking here specifically about street remarks that at least allude to women's sexuality, not remarks like "good morning," although in certain circumstances even those kinds of comments may be read – or intended – as catcalls.
46 Gardner (1995:14). A classic example that I use with my students to discuss street remarks is the case of men saying to women, "Smile!" as they walk down the street. In every class that I have discussed this, every single one of the women has had that experience, and none of the men has. Consistent with my own experience, my female students report either feeling constrained to smile in order to "be polite," or deciding not to smile or respond, which more often than not provokes hostility. The outcome of either response points fairly clearly

to the ways that even seemingly innocuous comments can limit women's autonomy.

47   to me when I asked him why he made a similar comment to a man I was walking with one day, as well as to a *Washington Post* reporter. See Reel (2003).

48   While this is the general pattern, it is not always the case. As we saw, for example, the campaign that Gabi and Aviva commented on in the beginning of this chapter was started by an African American woman.

49   cf. van Dijk (1993)

50   cf. Jacobson (1998), Stoler (1990)

51   In point of fact, the men who hang out on this particular corner are rarely drunk; at the time this message was written, the men at this fence were a group of friends who met each afternoon to socialize and talk to each other and passing acquaintances; I have never heard them make disgusting comments to women. Although I don't know the linguistic skills of this particular writer, it is also worth pointing out that many street comments are made in Spanish, and many criticisms are made by people who don't actually speak Spanish. Thus whether or not this particular writer is capable of assessing whether or not comments are "disgusting" is questionable.

52   It's worth noting that this woman also distanced herself from the neighborhood by pointing out her unfamiliarity with local behavior, saying that she had moved to the neighborhood three months earlier, and that she wasn't "used to communities where people hang out on the street." This led many to consider her an outsider.

53   It's important to point out that if people with out-of-state tags (license plates) got DC tags, the number of cars on neighborhood streets would be exactly the same, although there might be slightly less jockeying for spaces on the very few non-zoned blocks in the neighborhood. The power of this statement, then, rather than being a logical argument about how to improve parking, lies in its creation of an *us* and a *them*; retired ladies, a group ostensibly in need of protection because of its implied age and gender status (and also a group that has a certain level of income implied, as they have the financial means to stop working), are having problems because of outsiders coming from "out-of-state" who are not willing to fully align themselves with DC by getting a DC license and registering their cars in the city. Additionally, it could be argued that – because a driver's license is the primary form of identification in the US – people without DC licenses habitually mark themselves as outsiders whenever they show identification – whether walking into a municipal government building, writing a check, wiring money, or going to a bar.

54 Also important to note is that some Latina women, as well as some women of other backgrounds, articulate a clear distinction between derogatory remarks (defined for example as sexually explicit comments) which they interpret negatively, and complimentary remarks (for example comments that they look beautiful) which some women interpret positively as compliments. If some women react to some types of street remarks positively, this complicates any evaluation of men's behavior on the street as simply or unequivocally problematic.

55 Although it's possible that the African American guy here does not intend to be policing the space of the neighborhood, this is the outcome of his remarks; what speech act theorists would call the *perlocutionary effect*.

56 Police officers in these stories were either African American or White.

57 Ruddick (1996:142); see also Davis (1983).

58 See Barrett (1999) for an analysis of this stereotype in performances of African American drag queens.

59 Moeller (1989:219)

60 Smith and Gray (1985)

61 Low (2003)

62 cf. McElhinny (1995), Connell (1995)

63 Goodey (1997:411)

64 Mehta and Bondi (1999)

65 Chantilly is a suburb in Northern Virginia. It is notable that the suburb the writer chooses has a potentially feminine ring to it, based on the association of the label with chantilly lace. For some DC residents, the reference to Chantilly may also bring to mind connotations of political conservatism, as the Virginia suburbs are popularly considered to be much more conservative than the Maryland suburbs. (And the voting records of congressional representatives from these areas support these views.) Also notable in email messages to the discussion list is the tendency of anti-suburb writers to invoke suburbs in unfavorable comparisons to Mt. Pleasant, while more law-and-order writers tend to invoke Georgetown, a neighborhood which is wealthy and white but generally thought of as urban, in unfavorable comparisons.

66 Hall (1995), Barrett (1999)

67 Lakoff (1975)

CHAPTER 4

THE POLITICS OF FILTH

This dirty old street
This borderline I've
Scraped to cross and
Longed to find
They found a way to
Sterilize it

Gina, the lead singer in a Mt. Pleasant all-woman punk band, wrote this song in response to a rash of local civic group projects and campaigns to "clean up" Mt. Pleasant St. While some neighbors were cheered at the weeding and flower planting in tree-boxes along the street, others were less sanguine about the campaign to end what detractors called "noise pollution" in the form of live music in establishments on Mt. Pleasant St. These so-called "street improvement" efforts took place amidst a growing anti-immigrant sentiment nationwide. Ripples from California's proposition 187[1] had sparked similar initiatives in other states, and the immigration and welfare reform acts that Bill Clinton had signed into law were starting to see their effects in the country at-large as well as locally. In 1997, with the passing of the Nicaraguan Adjustment and Central American Relief Act,[2] Salvadoran refugees were losing the Temporary Protective Status the US government had granted them due to the Salvadoran civil war, immigrants were reporting increased police harassment, and friends who were social workers told me they were finding their immigrant clients coming to see them with ever-increasing levels of stress and anxiety. In Mt. Pleasant, many

Latinos perceived local civic group initiatives as a reflection of anti-immigrant feelings.

One night after a particularly vituperous community meeting about locked fences that a community member had erected at either end of the public alley behind his house, I walked home with my friends Esmeralda and Miguel. As we nodded to the Mariachis in their starched outfits bringing their instruments into Victor's restaurant, passed two Ethiopian men drinking coffee and arguing about politics with Miguel's cousin in front of the 7–11, waited for the stoplight with some teenagers sharing a bag of potato chips, Miguel turned to us and said, "They want to get rid of all this. They want to get rid of us."

Esmeralda agreed, citing as an example the initiative from a majority-White civic group to pressure local bars and restaurants, most of which were immigrant-owned, to sign "voluntary agreements". The civic group planned to lodge protests with the Alcohol Beverage Control Board against the liquor license renewal of every establishment that did not sign an agreement. By signing a so-called "voluntary" agreement, owners of alcohol-selling establishments had to agree not only to refuse service to inebriated customers, but, in addition, to 1) ban live music performance (the overwhelming majority of which at that time was Mariachi music in Latino restaurants and bars), 2) take out pay phones in front of their premises, 3) keep the sidewalk in front of their stores trash-free, 4) make sure that people didn't "loiter" in front of their businesses, and 5) "support community organizations which seek to alleviate alcohol abuse problems, by participation in meetings and programs, by contributions of food and financial assistance, and other assistance as the circumstances may warrant." These and other efforts to "clean up" the street were not only about filth, but were closely tied up with ethnoracial tensions, and discourse about such efforts was often used as a tool of ethnoracial discrimination.

During this time I'd been going to a lot of town hall meetings, and issues of street cleanliness were engendering a lot of discussion. At one particularly tense meeting, a White woman, a member of the liquor-license-protesting civic group, complained that the problems of the neighborhood were caused by "the Hispanic riff-raff" on the street. I had to leave this particular meeting early, but later I ran into Gina, the songwriter, who told me what happened after the meeting ended:

That woman, Linda, when we were standing in front of [Victor's restaurant], did I tell you what she said to Victor? She said- **You**, Hispanics. teach your children how to piss in the street. I have seen it. It's part of your culture. And your culture has no place here. The problem with this restaurant is not the restaurant, is not the restaurant, it's your culture. And your culture has no place here. You should have left it back in El Salvador.[3]

I was reminded of this story a few days later at another town hall meeting, this one on public toilets, in which a grant proposal was passed around applying for funding for public toilets on Mt. Pleasant St. This chapter analyzes that proposal, a crystallization of some of the dominant attitudes in circulation at the time, and a document that was presented to outside audiences who had the ability to allocate material resources to the neighborhood.

The writers of the grant proposal, a coalition of community groups, came to this project as a means of addressing complaints about public urination while at the same time attending to the interests of people hanging out on the street. A number of people in the neighborhood voiced vehement opposition to public toilets, because they thought it would bring more drunk people and homeless people to the neighborhood. As one woman[4] wrote on the Mt. Pleasant listserv,

I have a strong concern regarding the possibility of CRIME [sic] if the neighborhood were to acquire the public toilets I've been reading about here. The types of people who need the toilets most are the type who continue to keep the crime rate up in the neighborhood. How would the police deal with a possible increased threat of crime? Has the police department responded to this concern?

Those in favor of public toilets felt that such an addition to the neighborhood would help public sanitation at the same time as it would attend to the interests and welfare of the people who hung out on the street. As one supporter admonished his neighbors,

I urge all concerned to try to look at the problem from the other person's point of view: by-stander, pisser, or pissee. We've got plenty of creative, compassionate people in this neighborhood, and we ought to be able to come up with a workable solution rather than NIMBY or NOPE (Not In My Back Yard or Not On Planet Earth).

In community discussions that I attended with the individuals who wrote the grant, they often emphasized the welfare of people hanging out on the street. In the grant proposal itself, however, their concern and compassion for their neighbors was undermined by the discourse structures and topics that they used to argue their case. The grantwriters' combination of a range of linguistic structures with themes of geography and filth served to divide the Mt. Pleasant community into native-born and immigrant residents. The writers constructed a core of the community, placing themselves and people who share their values at that core, and immigrants (who were characterized as not sharing the writers' values) at the margins.

Following the geographer David Sibley,[5] we could call the grantwriters' language a discursive type of *spatial purification practice* – an activity to literally or metaphorically "purify" a space. In the proposal, the writers set up a moral and spatial order where they and other core community members were deemed to use space "appropriately" and thereby inhabit positive moral positions. On the other hand, immigrant community members' imputed "inappropriate" use of space was used to construct negative moral positions for them within what I've been referring to as the neighborhood's moral geography. While the writers decried Latino men's behavior on the street as a problem and described them as "marginal people," at the same time the writers constructed the street as male space which is intimidating to women.

Themes of Filth

Before turning to the grant proposal itself, it's useful to discuss the ideological connections between filth and morality. As many scholars have noted, filth is often portrayed as a threat to moral and spatial order. One way that people lessen what they see as threats is to marginalize – to push to the edges, or render "out of place" – the people who they think pose threats. A common way of rendering "threatening" people as out of place is to characterize them in terms of filth. Such characterizations frequently occur alongside vivid descriptions of places – for example, talking about homeless people (the people that others feel threatened by) as sleeping on garbage-strewn streets (the filth). This type of marginalization is what Sibley refers to as a *spatial purification practice*.

Spatial purification practices rely on the notion that filth is something that doesn't belong. The theoretical groundwork for this perspective was laid by the anthropologist Mary Douglas in 1966. Douglas describes filth (or dirt, in her terms) as "matter out of place":

> Shoes are not dirty in themselves, but it is dirty to place them on the dining table; food is not dirty in itself, but it is dirty to leave cooking utensils in the bedroom, or food bespattered on clothing; similarly, bathroom equipment in the drawing room; clothing lying on chairs; out-door things in-doors; upstairs things downstairs; under clothing appearing where over-clothing should be, and so on. (Douglas 1966:36)[6]

In invoking filth, speakers presuppose a system of classification that delineates between purity and order, on the one hand, and impurity and disorder on the other. In this way, themes of filth signify a breach of (a preferred) order.

Much discrimination and persecution is partially accomplished by language of cleanliness and filth. The cultural geographer Kay Anderson has illuminated how such language was used to argue for banning Chinese immigration to Canada. In the late 19th century, for example, provincial government committees protested Chinese immigration to the federal government with arguments that "the hordes of Chinese . . . carry with them the elements of disease, pestilience, and degredation over the face of the fair land."[7]

Taken to its extreme, the language of filth and pollution can be used to undergird genocide. As social scientists like Zygmunt Bauman and Alexander Hinton have observed, one of the keys ways that governments have dehumanized groups of people targeted for genocide is through a discourse of filth, pollution, and disease. For example, in Hitler's Third Reich, the metaphor of "racial hygiene" found its instantiation in the eugenics policies of the Ministry of the Interior's National Hygiene Department. As Bauman explains, the head of this department

> described as the major task of the Nazi rule "an active policy con-sistently aiming at the preservation of racial health [that must include] facilitat[ing] the propagation of healthy stock by systematic selection and by elimination of the unhealthy elements."[8]

Bauman further notes that, in Nazi discourse, the Jewish genocide was variously referred to as the "*Gesundung* (healing) of Europe, *Selbstreinigung* (self-cleansing), *Judensäubering* (cleansing-of-Jews)."[9] And Hitler himself explained,

> The discovery of the Jewish virus is one of the greatest revolutions that have [sic] taken place in the world. The battle in which we are engaged today is of the same sort as the battle waged, during the last century, by Pasteur and Koch.[10] How many diseases have their origin in the Jewish virus . . . We shall regain our health only by eliminating the Jew."[11]

Alexander Hinton has noted similar discourses among the Khmer Rouge. In an infamous speech against "traitors" to the Party, for example, Pol Pot spoke of the need for the party "to be scrubbed clean" from the "sickness inside the Party," the "ugly microbes" that would "rot us from within."[12] The more contemporary version of this discourse is the term *ethnic cleansing*, which came into the English language during the Balkan wars of the 1990s. While this term originally referred to the forced expulsion of a people from a particular territory, it has taken on the additional meaning of genocide, as genocide is often the means of such expulsion.

Cultural critics Peter Stallybrass and Allon White[13] provide a historical foundation for understanding how people in powerful positions use themes of filth *and* themes of space to marginalize others and construct groups such as prostitutes and poor people as social deviants. One of the most important aspects of their work is their tracing of the link between physical disorder and moral disorder to early 19th-century social reformer discourse about London slums. It was in these texts that reformers of the day attributed "moral depravity, disorder, and crime"[14] to the crowded conditions, sewage, disease, rodents and pigs, and crowded "mingle, mangle . . . hodge-podge streets"[15] that they saw to be characteristic of working class neighborhoods.

This sort of linking of animals like rodents and pigs both to filth and to place – as well as the further linking of this trio to people deemed to be "out of place" – is a common theme in marginalizing discourses. To justify Jewish expulsion, for example, Hitler's Propaganda Minister Joseph Goebbels stated that "the fact that the

Jew still lives among us is no proof that he also belongs with us, just as a flea[16] does not become a domestic animal because it lives in the house."[17] Similarly, the Victorian London reformer Mayhew described people living on the street – people who did not conform to the norms of living in a house and were therefore "out of place" – as having

> greater development of the animal than of the intellectual or moral nature of man . . . [lying like] a bundle of rags and filth stretched on some dirty straw [in a place] redolent of filth and pregnant with pestilential diseases, and whither all the outcasts of the metropolitan population seem to be drawn.[18]

Of course the social construction of urban density, open sewers, and rodents as something to be deplored is not completely arbitrary. Debilitating infectious diseases can flourish in areas with poor sanitation that are densely populated enough for pathogens with short life-spans to find new hosts before they die. As Lawrence Schell explains,

> Except for the rich, common people [in medieval Europe] shared their living quarters with domesticated animals, slept on straw as a family, stored grain in the home, and generally provided few barriers to rats. Once the [plague] was started in humans, it could spread from person to person by an aerosol route . . . In a crowded city, the disease would be able to spread quickly. Since the disease is often fatal and survival does not provide immunity for very long, if at all, the disease could (and did) kill millions.[19]

So clearly the associations between marginalized places like slums and filth have some relation to actual public health concerns. However, in places with modern public sanitation technologies, the *symbolic moral concerns* that themes of filth and marginalized places index are as important as, if not more important than, *actual* threats to public health. Stallybrass and White argue that reformers' focus on the filth of poor neighborhoods went hand-in-hand with a growing preoccupation with physical and moral cleanliness among the bourgeoisie. Symbolically, it was this *moral* purity that the physical filth of the slums threatened. So as notions of physical and moral hygiene became more and more closely linked, and the bourgeoisie felt threatened by the disorder which the "unwashed masses" represented, people or things which symbolized uncleanliness became more explicitly reviled.

Within cultural geography, researchers have examined spatial purification practices that deal with spatial relations among groups. David Sibley,[20] for example, analyzes themes of filth from Classical Greek treatises, through medieval, early modern, and Victorian European literature, to 20th-century US popular culture and media, to show how themes of filth have played a key historical role in creating boundaries between those who fit in and those who don't. Such boundaries serve an important function in preserving the position of those in power, and they often take spatial forms. When members of dominant groups consider others to be violating their own social, cultural, or spatial norms, they perceive such people to be a threat to (their) moral and *spatial* order, as well as to their power. This is another way in which places and the actions of people get tied together.

Tim Cresswell's work[21] on graffiti in New York and anti-nuclear activism in England reveals such links. He found that New York media texts that connected graffiti to foreign places also characterized it in terms of garbage, pollution, or disease. The connection between filth, graffiti, and foreignness served to marginalize the graffiti artists as people who did not belong. In news stories on the Greenham Women's Peace Camp – an anti-nuclear protest site – filth took the form of odor. British press reports discursively linked the Camp with the Soviet Union, and discussed in extreme detail garbage and mud in the camp. Cresswell shows the connection between filth (in this case in the form of odor) and moral transgression in a newspaper comment that "the 'final solution' to the Greenham 'problem' was Chanel No. 5."[22] The choice of Chanel No. 5 here also invokes wealth. A veneer of wealth, then, can confer respectability: the filth of mud can be mitigated by the smell of money.

Like these scholars, cultural geographer Peter Jackson[23] also found that themes of filth went hand-in-hand with themes of foreignness – often cast in racial terms – in marginalization practices. In his work on shopping malls, for example, Jackson detailed the ways in which Anglo-British women used themes of purity and cleanliness to characterize some shops and shopping experiences positively, whereas they used themes of filth and foreignness to characterize other shops negatively:

Concerns for the purity of "real linen" and "nice quality shops" are contrasted with a vocabulary of dirt and pollution, where prices are "dirt cheap", based on imported "rubbish" and other "foreign muck". Racialised fears of dirt and pollution are contrasted with an exaggerated respect for the cleanliness of established stores . . .

Having now laid out some of the functions of discourse of filth, we can better understand how such discourse works as a spatial purification practice locally, for the same processes that we've seen at work in other sites and times also occur in Mt. Pleasant. Mt. Pleasant residents in powerful positions use themes of filth to exclude some of their neighbors from membership in what they construct as the core community of Mt. Pleasant, and to consolidate their own positioning *in* that core.

The Public Toilets Project and Attitudes towards Public Urination

The text which I analyze here is a grant proposal for public toilets that a group of neighborhood organizations submitted to a philanthropic organization funding community-based collaborative projects in Mt. Pleasant and adjoining neighborhoods. At the time of the grants competition, the topic of public toilets was much discussed in Mt. Pleasant neighborhood meetings. Members of several neighborhood organizations decided that a project for public toilets might fit within the grant's parameters, and wrote a proposal together.[24]

The grant proposal for public toilets is an important neighborhood text to analyze for a number of reasons. First, although public toilets were discussed in other various public and private forums, the proposal is unique in that it is the only instance of public toilet discourse which was formally presented to an out-of-neighborhood audience.

Second, the text of the proposal was constrained by the funders' guidelines, and consequently shaped in ways that make it a particularly relevant object of study for questions of neighborhood identity. The guidelines call for a neighborhood description which begins the grant and is meant to contextualize the project. While public toilet discussions elsewhere among Mt. Pleasantites implicitly indexed[25] neighborhood identities, the grant proposal differs from those conversations in that there is considerable focus in the proposal on neighborhood description per se. This means that connections between public toilets and neighborhood identities are more fleshed out and explicit than was the case in other neighborhood discourse. Furthermore, the guidelines require grantwriters to formulate their community description in terms of diversity. Applicants for these grants are instructed to "describe present relationships among community members of diverse backgrounds" and are asked, "What impact does the diversity of the community have on the life of the community?"

Finally, as a written document produced by writers who had official positions in established neighborhood institutions, the grant proposal can be seen as an authoritative and enduring representation of Mt. Pleasant to the outside world. In this case, it is an outside audience who has the power to allocate resources to Mt. Pleasant.

Based on my discussions with a wide range of community members over the years, it is safe to say that there is nearly universal agreement that public urination is unpleasant and poses public health risks. However, in the context of the public toilets discussions ensuing around the time of the grant proposal, community members disagreed strongly about how important an issue public urination was, who was urinating in public and why, and what appropriate community responses should be. The proposed public toilets project grew out of a subset of this community talk, namely discussions in town hall and civic organization meetings about public urination. Among community members at meetings there was more consensus about these issues than there was among the community at-large. Meeting participants generally agreed about who was urinating on the street, and that public urination was a major problem in the neighborhood that they should try to do something about. Interestingly, there was never any debate about exactly who was urinating on the street. Although it's questionable whether they in general had enough eyewitness accounts to accurately ascertain who was urinating on the street, their theories were quite convergent, based as they were on who they saw spending a lot of time on the street. The three categories of people that meeting participants often focused on as public urinators[26] were homeless men, drunk men, and Latino men. Many people conflated these groups.

There was also a considerable amount of conflict as to what should be done about the issue. While some participants thought community responses should be linked to alcohol treatment and affordable/

accessible housing (a framing that focuses – at least superficially – on the interests of people urinating in public space), others were more concerned simply with how to expel purported urinators from the neighborhood (a framing focusing on the civic group members' interests).[27] This second group considered the urinators to be members of a class of "street deviants," which also included drunk and homeless people. Those whose framing of the issue included the needs of the people ostensibly urinating in public spaces were in favor of public toilets, for they considered it a means of both providing sanitary facilities to people who did not have ready access to them, as well as a way of improving the sanitation of the neighborhood. Community members who were concerned more narrowly with getting what they considered "problem people" out of the neighborhood were generally opposed to the idea of public toilets, for they thought public toilets would simply (and by that I mean in a simple, direct way) attract "deviants" from other neighborhoods to use the facilities and hang out in Mt. Pleasant.

Despite some residents' vehement opposition to public toilets, a number of people who were active in neighborhood organizations decided to work together to find a site and raise funds for toilets. These community members were deeply concerned about the social, health, and economic resources unavailable to many men who drank on the street, and they saw procuring public toilets as a small step in addressing both the needs of people who spent time on the street, and the concerns of people who were upset about public urination.[28]

The Grant Proposal

The grant proposal presented the public toilets project as one that would improve the "quality of life" of everyone in the neighborhood, and it ostensibly focused on an issue which a wide variety of people can rally around: few people enjoy living on streets which smell of urine, and urination and defecation in open streets is potentially a public health hazard. In this analysis, I don't want to focus on the merits of providing restrooms; in fact, as a neighborhood resident I supported the effort to get public toilets. Instead, I want to draw attention to the marginalizing and centralizing ideologies that the grantwriters both incorporate and obscure in the grant proposal discourse.

On the surface the grant proposal extols diversity, portraying the diverse ethnic makeup of the neighborhood as an asset. However, a closer reading reveals a less rosy picture. The writers were genuinely concerned about the well-being of their neighbors on Mt. Pleasant St., and they stated their concern in the proposal. At the same time, however, the linguistic forms – what we can call *discourse strategies* – in the proposal marginalize a significant proportion of Mt. Pleasant residents, namely immigrants.

The focus on discourse strategies in this chapter is somewhat more micro-level than the analyses in other chapters. The value of this kind of detailed analysis is that it allows us to see the very subtle ways that identities get constructed. If we were to pay attention only to the content of the proposal, it might be easier to overlook the subtleties in favor of writers' expressions of solidarity with people on the street.

A close look at the discourse strategies reveals that the text's structure works in tandem with themes of filth and geographic peripherality to set up what's known as a *deictic center* of the community. A deictic center can be considered the base point where a speaker locates themselves spatially, temporally, and socially. Deictics are a subset of indexicals (discussed in chapter 3); they are words whose reference can only be determined through context. For example, it is only possible to know which people the pronouns *I* and *you* refer to in a sentence if one knows who the speaker and addressee are.[29] Deictics like *I* and *we*; *this* and *these*; and *here* and *now* include their referents (the things in the world that the words refer to) in the deictic center. On the flip side, *that* and *those*, *there* and *then*, as well as second and third person deictics (you, she, he, it), set up a reference point outside of that deictic center; in other words, those deictics exclude their referents from the deictic center. In the grant proposal, deixis combines with other discourse strategies to set up a rigid distinction between core and marginal members of the community, and to posit diversity as something that is inherently a burden to the core community members.

The proposal itself is divided into five main sections and an appendix. Section A gives an overview of "The Mt. Pleasant Community." Section B, "The Project," describes what the toilets will look like and how public toilets will benefit the community. Section C,

"Intergroup Strengths and Assets," outlines the collaboration processes of the neighborhood organizations working on the public toilets project. The organizations in question, and their individual missions, are listed in Section D, "Intergroup Partners." Section E, "Goals," develops some of the ideas about the benefits of the project expressed in Section B, focusing on long-term outcomes. This section reiterates many of the points made in Sections A and B – that the public toilets project would result in cleaner streets and less inappropriate behavior on the street, a heightened affirmation of diversity and awareness of common interests, and improved welfare of the people who hang out on the street. The appendix of the grant consists of a project budget, timeline, and contact information for each participating organization. Sections A and B, "The Mt. Pleasant Community" and "The Project," discuss the relationship between the characteristics of Mt. Pleasant and the need for public toilets; therefore, my analysis focuses on these two sections.

Public Toilets and Diversity

The grant itself begins with a cover sheet including the title, "Public Toilets for a Diverse Neighborhood." If we follow philosopher J.P. Grice's observation[30] that the utterances speakers use are relevant to each other and that to interpret language we must assume relevance, then this title tells us that the neighborhood's diverse nature is related to its need for public toilets. Another tenet of Grice's theory, the maxim of quantity, states that we interpret language as if the amount of information given is just the right amount – not too much, and not too little. The maxim of quantity leads to interpretation of the neighborhood's diversity as needed, non-extraneous information. So even as early as the title, the proposal implies that there is an inherent link between diversity in Mt. Pleasant and the filth that public toilets would take care of, and that there needs to be a remedy (in this case, the toilets) to clean up that filth.

The theme of diversity is continued in the proposal's first section. In the first two of five paragraphs in Section A, the writers frame the discussion of public toilets within a discourse of "celebration of diversity":

We define the Mt. Pleasant community as everyone who lives, works, or visits Mt. Pleasant, including service and delivery people, shoppers, guests of residents, people attending cultural events or going to school, and service providers like police and social workers.

One of our most important strengths is our celebration of diversity, not just tolerance. Not only do we have community members from a wide range of countries (xx [sic] languages in the local elementary school[31]), but we also have great variation in socio-economic status among both native-born and immigrant members of the community. One telling difference is that many people come from rural, third-world societies and face severe culture shock living in a crowded, modern, urban environment.

The inclusive vision of community with which the first paragraph begins becomes stratified in the second utterance, which gives some specifics about the people included in this community. These specifics serve to differentiate between various types of community members: The types of people who are listed – "service and delivery people, shoppers, guests of residents," etc. – are all people who are defined in ways other than residence in Mt. Pleasant.

The construction of Mt. Pleasant as an inclusive community is reinforced in the first utterance of paragraph two: "One of our most important strengths is our celebration of diversity, not just tolerance." Here, "our celebration of diversity, not just tolerance" expresses the ideas that "we celebrate diversity" and "we don't just tolerate it" as presuppositions. Presuppositions are propositions (proposed ideas) that are expressed as background or assumed information.[32] Further, presuppositions must be true in order for the larger utterances they appear in to make sense. For example, the idea that "we celebrate diversity" must be assumed to be true for the utterance "one of our most important strengths is our celebration of diversity" to make any sense. So this utterance constructs it as a given that community members in Mt. Pleasant do indeed value (i.e., "celebrate") diversity, and that they are tolerant. The valuing of diversity is also emphasized structurally through the "X not Y" (celebration not tolerance) contrast structure in the clause in question. It's also emphasized through the semantic contrast (contrast in meaning) of *celebrate*, which involves an embracing of diversity, and *tolerate*, which means being willing to live with diversity without fully accepting it.

The presuppositions of tolerance and of valuing diversity introduce the argument for having public toilets, and they serve an important function. Presuppositions work as background information that constitutes the context within which the propositions of an utterance are interpreted. In their capacity as background information, presuppositions become naturalized, seen as taken-for-granted information. Because the pro-diversity and tolerance attitudes are presupposed, it is more difficult to explicitly contest them than it would be to contest analogous assertions.[33]

Positing that Mt. Pleasant people are tolerant and value diversity also lays a groundwork for community members' positive moral positioning. This positioning plays an important role in the grant as a whole. Since it comes at the beginning of the document, it sets up a frame of a pro-diversity community within which subsequent text is to be interpreted, despite the much less inclusive view of community that is actually propounded in the subsequent text.

After laying out this valuing of diversity, the grantwriters elaborate on what diversity entails. Diversity is defined as variety in national origin, class, and native language. The writers represent ethnic diversity by creating a dichotomy between "native born" Mt. Pleasantites and "immigrant members of the community." This portrayal compresses the multiple ethnicities of the neighborhood's population into two groups, and this move erases ethnic differences among those born in the US, as well as among those hailing from multiple other countries. Because of both the strong role of Latinos in neighborhood life and the textual indexes to Latinos that appear later in the grant proposal, we can take "immigrant members of the community" to be predominantly Latino. But the dichotomization between "native born" and "immigrant" poses a problem for the status of Latinos as a group, since many Latinos living in Mt. Pleasant are in fact US born. This dichotomization sets the stage for a discussion in which ethnicity inaccurately becomes a question of "being from here" or "being from there."[34]

In this introduction to the community, the proposal writers point out that class diversity exists within both immigrant and non-immigrant groups. However, this important point is not elaborated on at any later point in the text. In fact, as we'll see in the description of people hanging out on Mt. Pleasant Street, the writers later implicitly elide class and ethnicity when talking about immigrants.

Through what we can call geographic dichotomization, ethnic variety becomes binary rather than multiple, as well as hierarchical: The core people who belong in Mt. Pleasant are those who are native born or understand and adhere to "urban American" customs and values. The less central members of the community are those who are less familiar with what are purported to be urban American values. This dichotomization can be seen in the utterance, "One telling difference is that many people come from rural, third-world societies and face severe culture shock living in a crowded, modern, urban environment."

Opposition of the world of Mt. Pleasant to communities of origin outside the US obscures the non-local origins of the many US-born community members who have migrated from other parts of the country. The opposition also elides migrants from other parts of the US with people born and raised in Mt. Pleasant, even if the migrants have lived in the neighborhood for only a year or two (as is in fact the case for a number of active participants in local civic organizations). Conversely, this opposition marginalizes anyone born in a rural, third-world country, even when such people's length of residence in Mt. Pleasant may surpass that of some US-born local residents by decades. This characterization also obscures the fact that many Mt. Pleasant residents immigrated from urban areas. The opposition between native- and non-native-born leads to the grantwriters' portrayal of the people from "rural, third-world societies" as "a telling difference"– in other words, as a group set apart from the norm in a way worthy of remark. The people characterized in this way become marked as Other,[35] while the core, i.e., the people who they ostensibly differ *from*, is unnamed, and consequently unmarked. The immigrants' marginal status in Mt. Pleasant is reinforced through the proposition that they "face severe culture shock," which attributes to them strong unfamiliarity and difficulty with the cultural life of their "new" place, Mt. Pleasant.

It is through such strategies that the unnamed, US-born residents of Mt. Pleasant are set up as the deictic center of talk; they are the people who are already present; they must be the people who make Mt. Pleasant the "crowded, modern, urban environment" that the immigrants come to. In the proposition "Many people *come from* rural, third-world societies," the immigrants move *to* the deictic center of Mt. Pleasant. In contrast, the grantwriters – members of the "core community" – are already there. They are the ones in the deictic center position to observe that others are *coming to* (as opposed to *going to*) Mt. Pleasant.

A more accurate characterization of Mt. Pleasant's ethnic diversity might be something along the lines of, "Mt. Pleasant residents have a wide range of national and ethnic backgrounds. Ethnic diversity characterizes both residents born and raised in Mt. Pleasant, as well as those who have migrated to Mt. Pleasant from urban and rural places throughout the US and the world." In such a description, neighborhood diversity is presented as developing out of the mix of *all* community members. The description given in the grant proposal, however, places a special focus on immigrants from "third world" rural areas, and this focus serves to frame *immigrants from third-world rural areas* as particularly relevant for the discussion of public toilets to follow.

Civic Activism and Diversity

The proposal's next paragraph illustrates another common way of talking about Mt. Pleasant people, namely as independently-minded activists who are responsible for their community:

> Another strength is our civic activism. While some of the community do wish that problems would just go away, or that the government would solve them (preferably somewhere else), most people neither accept social problems as facts of life nor expect outside organizations like the government to solve them for us. For example, Mt. Pleasant runs its own recycling program and established its own community office for the Metropolitan Police. The Advisory Neighborhood Commission recently adopted a substance abuse policy that endorses community-based treatment programs.

This paragraph sets up a self-reliant identity for Mt. Pleasant people, where they are able to identify local problems and solve them with no help from outsiders. The possessive *our* in the first utterance ("Another strength is our civic activism") sets up civic activism as a characteristic shared by the community at large, and thus *representative* of the community. Neighbors who don't take an activist stance are still shown as part of the community ("some *of our community* do wish that problems would just go away, or that the government would solve them"). However, through the contrast ("while") of these members with "most people" who "neither accept social problems [. . .] nor expect outside organizations like the government to solve them," non-activists are posited as the minority, and "most people" as representative of the community.

In the utterance "Mt. Pleasant runs its own recycling program and established its own community office for the Metropolitan police," the premise of activism as a community trait is strengthened through a *metonymy* in which the place – Mt. Pleasant – stands in for Mt. Pleasant community members as the people responsible for community endeavors to promote cleanliness (through recycling, a form of trash removal) and safety (through establishing a neighborhood police office). The proposition that "the Advisory Neighborhood Commission [a body of elected community representatives] recently adopted a substance abuse policy that endorses community-based treatment programs" reinforces the notion that the community prefers local, insider approaches to local problem-solving.[36]

Through this process of metonymy, where one thing is used to stand for another, Mt. Pleasant activists are equated with the place Mt. Pleasant; thereby, members of this group become the prototypical Mt. Pleasantites, while those who don't engage in activism become marginal to the community's identity. That the activist endeavors cited relate to cleanliness and safety further implies that core community members are opposed to filth and disorder. It follows from this that those who not only are not active on cleanliness and safety issues, but who also participate in making the neighborhood feel filthy and unsafe to others, are peripheral community members. As we will see in following paragraphs of the grant proposal, this is exactly what the identity constructed for the class of people who engage in public urination is attributed to.

The next paragraph of the proposal describes benefits of activism and diversity:

> This diversity and activism gives us a much richer economic and cultural life, with a wide variety of products and services available for sale and cultural events to experience. It gives us a wider perspective from which to understand problems and recognize opportunities.

In addition to lauding a broad perspective, this section also characterizes the benefits of diversity through a consumer model of experience. In such a model, diversity becomes commodified as "a variety of products" to buy and "cultural events to experience." Researchers on diversity and neighborhood identity in gentrifying US and Canadian neighborhoods like Mt. Pleasant have found that the commodification of ethnicity into objects to be bought or experienced plays an important role in such residents' self-identities as worldly and tolerant people.[37]

"Proper" Behavior

In the next paragraph, the writers presuppose Mt. Pleasant as a diverse and inclusive community, with the noun phrase "our diversity" in the first utterance:

> At the same time, our diversity sometimes makes it harder to reach consensus on community standards and the actions that express those standards. While we believe that there is an underlying consensus on what is, and is not, proper behavior, it is not always expressed. In addition, there may not be mechanisms to either express or practice that proper behavior.

Positing the difficulty of reaching consensus on community standards implicitly includes people with differing values within the community. However, these different values are characterized as problematic: It's important to keep in mind that the assertion that "[Mt. Pleasant's] diversity . . . makes it harder to reach consensus" follows the paragraph that enumerates positive aspects of diversity. In prefacing the assertion at the beginning of the paragraph with the contrastive phrase "at the same time," the writers contrast the benefits of diversity discussed earlier with the drawbacks of diversity – difficulty in reaching consensus. Through characterizing lack of consensus as a problem, consensus itself gets constructed as desirable. Consensus implies similarity of opinion. Similarly, we see that the superficial valuing of diversity in the guise of "products for sale . . . and cultural events to experience" masks an underlying valuing of homogeneity.[38]

Furthermore, any positive value of residents' diversity in opinion is mitigated by the writers' belief that an underlying consensus indeed exists "on what is, and is not, proper behavior." Exactly what that proper behavior is, however, is left implicit. This becomes clearer if we look at the grammatical slots for the performers (agents) or experiencers of certain actions. In the utterance "In addition, there may not be mechanisms to either express or practice that proper behavior," quite a number of these slots are unfilled. The grammatical structure "there may not be" (called an *existential construction*) leaves the agent who might supply such mechanisms unnamed, while the lack of a receiver for *mechanisms* leaves implicit the question of who those mechanisms should be for. Also left unclear is just what kind of mechanisms *could* express or practice proper behavior. These grammatical structures, then, leave closed for discussion and debate the following: what the grantwriters mean by "proper behavior," which community members are aligned with that view of proper behavior, and what is needed in order for which players to express proper behavior.

As sociolinguists Jan Blommaert and Jef Verschueren[39] note, the lack of explicit definitions for terms relating to values and norms produces words with fluid meanings: terms like "proper behavior" function as in-group boundaries that can be arbitrarily shifted by those using them. By using an ill-defined term like "proper behavior," an in-group can keep excluding an out-group even in cases where out-group behavior and in-group norms may start to coincide. In other words, if people in an out-group start behaving in a way that qualifies as "proper behavior," new criteria for "proper behavior" can be developed, without changing any of the discourse.

Marginal People

The last paragraph in Section A further develops the distinction between the core community members who hold Mt. Pleasant values and are already *in* the neighborhood, on the one hand, and marginal members who have more tenuous ties with the neighborhood, on the other:

In addition, Mt. Pleasant's acceptance of a wide variety of behavior attracts marginal people who may have slipped over the line into alcohol and drug addiction or untreated mental illness. Many of these people are homeless or have nowhere to spend their days but on the streets. Others are living in overcrowded apartments and doing most of their socializing on the street, because they have no extra money to go to movies, sporting events, restaurants, and so on. One of the biggest problems these folks present is public (or semi-public) urination and defecation. Aside from the obvious aesthetic and public health problems this presents, it is demeaning for the people who have to eliminate like animals (and even the animals probably have someone to clean up after them). This perpetuates the feelings of hopelessness and low self-esteem that make another drink or drug, or failing to take medication for mental illness, seem like the only way to deaden the pain.

With the phrase, "Mt. Pleasant's acceptance of a wide variety of behavior," the writers again presuppose Mt. Pleasant residents' open-mindedness. This utterance thus reinforces the positive moral positioning of the Mt. Pleasant core community. At the same time, however, the rest of the utterance ("attracts marginal people who may have slipped over the line into alcohol and drug addiction or untreated mental illness") positions other people as peripheral in the moral geography of the community.

This utterance marginalizes community members in a number of ways. First, the verb "attracts" construes the people in question as new to Mt. Pleasant. As was the case earlier with "people coming from rural, third-world countries," the verb "attracts" locates these people as coming *to* the deictic center of Mt. Pleasant from somewhere else, outside the bounds of the neighborhood. This creates them as geographically peripheral or marginal. Grammatically, this verb places the "marginal people" in what we can call an *experiencer role*: a position where the attraction is something that *happens* to them, rather than something that they actively do. Another way to say this is that this grammatical structure denies the people in question any agency.

The people being discussed in this paragraph are not only painted as *geographically* peripheral; the noun phrase "marginal people" creates a moral peripherality, too. However, exactly who or what these people are marginal to is left implicit. Finally, geographical and moral peripherality become linked through the spatial metaphor "slipped over the line." The line that is posed here is a border between positive moral positioning – adherence to "appropriate" social norms – and negative moral positioning – deviance in the guise of mental illness and drug and alcohol addiction. (Mental illness or addiction is not a prerequisite for being marginal, however, as the marginal people only "*may* have slipped over the line.")

The grant proposal defines the marginal people as members of three groups: 1) homeless people; 2) people who "have nowhere to spend their days but on the streets"; 3) people "living in overcrowded apartments." Although the writers do not explicitly invoke ethnicity or gender in their descriptions of "marginal people," these social categories are still indexed through the propositions that the marginal people are people spending time on the street and living in overcrowded apartments. As discussed earlier, the majority of people who socialize on the street are Latino men. In addition, Mt. Pleasant Street – the main street where socializing goes on, the general site of most public urination, and the street where the grantwriters proposed putting the public toilets – is commonly constructed as a Latino place.[40] Furthermore, as mentioned above, local civic group ideology holds that overcrowded apartments are inhabited by Latinos. So for those familiar with civic group discourse, the invocation of living in overcrowded apartments and spending time on the street implicitly constructs these community members as Latino men.

The implication of "marginal people" as Latino is further reinforced through the text's earlier focus on diversity and the dichotomization of diversity into native and foreign-born. As we have seen, the proposal posits that diversity causes problems – namely that "diversity sometimes makes it harder to reach consensus on community standards," and that "there may not be mechanisms to either express or practice that proper behavior." The paragraph currently under analysis starts, "In addition, Mt. Pleasant's acceptance of a wide variety of behavior attracts marginal people . . ." By beginning this utterance with the connector or *cohesive tie* "in addition," the writers draw a connection between the diversity-caused problems mentioned earlier and the marginal people discussed here. The cohesive tie works in tandem with the implicit indexing of Latino men (through the phrases "[people who] have nowhere to spend their days but on the streets" and "people living in overcrowded apartments") and with the previous marginalization of "people com[ing] from third-world societies," to promote a reading of the marginal people as Latino men, and it posits that they are the ones responsible for public urination.

This is made clear in the next utterance, "One of the biggest problems these folks present is public (or semi-public) urination and defecation."

To sum up, the phrase "these folks" in the utterance, "one of the biggest problems these folks present is public (or semi-public) urination and defecation," comes to serve as a gloss for Latino men, and this comes about through links to both prior text (i.e., "people from rural, third-world societies") and to local beliefs and customs (i.e., that people hanging out on the street are Latino men). Crucially, this gets implied off-record, meaning that the grantwriters could declare that Latinos are never mentioned in the text.[41]

The term "folks" in the utterance "One of the biggest problems these folks present" indexes a register of solidarity towards the people in question. It's worth noting that the paragraph in which the term occurs, which has the strongest focus in the text on the welfare of people on the street, is also the only place where the term "folks" is used. A concern for the welfare of the referents is clearly evident in the second half of the last paragraph of this section, which presupposes that the people on the street are hopeless and have pain in their lives.

> This [. . .] perpetuates the feelings of hopelessness and low self-esteem that make another drink or drug, or failing to take medication for mental illness, seem like the only way to deaden the pain.

However, the grantwriters' focus on these neighbors' welfare is mitigated by the text's overall marginalization of the people on the street. Also, while "folks" may index solidarity and a consequent show of concern, the term can also index people who have a simple and down-to-earth way of life, and/or a rural lifestyle. In a reading where "folks" indexes rurality, the term can thus also marginalize the people it refers to by implicitly contrasting them with the earlier-stated urbanness of Mt. Pleasant.

The grant proposal's explanation of why people are socializing on the street is also related to the commodification and consumerism model discussed earlier. In this last paragraph of Section A, we are told that some of the "marginal people" are on the street "because they have nowhere to spend their days but on the streets," and that those who "are living in overcrowded apartments [are] doing most of their socializing on the street, because they have no money to go to movies, sporting events, restaurants, and so on." Where the earlier example of consumerism portrayed core community members as successful consumers (able to buy products and experience cultural events), the explanation here shows the people socializing on the street as unsuccessful consumers, and relies on a deficit theory which disallows the possibility that they are socializing on the street because they *enjoy* it. Socializing on the street is constructed as a social necessity which presumably would not occur if the people in question had bigger houses or more money. In other words, forms of socializing that are not rooted in the capitalist enterprise are delegitimized; legitimate social activities become only those that involve spending money – "go[ing] to movies, sporting events, [and] restaurants."[42]

The deficit explanation here contributes to the construction of socializing on the street as a *problem*. This construction in turn creates a foundation upon which to logically build the presupposition that the people socializing on the street are the *same* people who are pissing on the street. Specifically, the word "these"[43] ties together that sentence with the next sentence: "one of the biggest problems *these* folks present is public (or semi-public) urination and defecation."

Through the conjunction "and" in the phrase "urination and defecation," public urination is equated with public defecation, implying that these activities carry the same social meaning. In fact, public defecation is a much rarer phenomenon in the neighborhood than is urination. Many men[44] who urinate in an alley or a park, on occasion or frequently, and whether they admit to the practice or not, do not defecate in the street, and most people in Mt. Pleasant find public defecation more repugnant than public urination, as well as more of a health hazard. By obscuring this differentiation and giving equal weight to urination and defecation, the grant proposal has the potential to trigger readers' reactions based on their reactions to defecation, which I would argue are likely to be stronger than reactions to public urination.

In the utterance *"one of the biggest problems* these folks present is public (or semi-public) urination and defecation," the notion that "these folks" present numerous problems is presupposed – posited as a given, rather than as the opinion of the grantwriters. Calling urination problematic is a subjective interpretation. It's presented as a statement of fact, however, because the people who are interpreting it this way are not represented in the grammatical structure of the sentence. The verb *present* implies an actor – the one doing the presenting ("these folks"), a patient – the thing being presented ("the problem"), and a recipient – the person to whom the problem is being presented. But the grammar of this particular utterance leaves this last role unstated; there is no *present to X* structure to introduce the people being confronted with something that they are interpreting as a problem.

In addition, the person who is presented with a problem that someone creates is generally not the same person who presents the problem. So in characterizing the marginal people as "present[ing] a problem," the grantwriters again separate the community into those who are *presented with* a problem, and those who are *responsible for* it. "Present" also de-emphasizes the welfare of those who might actually *have* a problem.[45]

The last part of Section A's final paragraph again reinforces the marginalization of the "marginal people":

> Aside from the obvious aesthetic and public health problems this presents, it is demeaning for the people who have to eliminate like animals (and even the animals probably have someone to clean up after them). This perpetuates the feelings of hopelessness and low self-esteem that make another drink or drug, or failing to take medication for mental illness, seem like the only way to deaden the pain.

These utterances implicitly categorize those on the street as *out of place* through linking them with urination and defecation, which symbolizes both filth and out-of-place behavior. Next, the behavior of marginal people is compared with animals ("it is demeaning for the people who have to eliminate like animals"), thus dehumanizing them (albeit with some concern for the proposed "demeaning" effect of their actions). This part of the grant also relates back to the deficit model of spending time on the street, grouping together on the other side of the boundary of appropriate behavior all those who spend time on the street. The chain of logic goes as follows: People spend time on the street because of a lack of other options. If they have no other place to be but on the street, then when they need to urinate they will do it on the street. This in turn leads them to a state of hopelessness and low self-esteem, which then creates a painful state that contributes to substance abuse and untreated mental illness. This argument (for which the writers give no supporting evidence) reinforces the previous marginalization by anchoring the marginal people on the other side of the line set up between appropriate and inappropriate behavior – between cleanliness and belonging on one side, and filth and out-of-placeness on the other.

Constructing Core and Margin: Community Values

The grantwriters present public toilets as a project that has an important goal, that of supporting the diversity of the Mt. Pleasant community. But this goal is subverted by the very discourse that is used to promote it, because the linguistic structures of the text divide the community and create a hierarchical relationship between different groups of people. The dichotomization that began in Section A is reinforced in the last paragraph of Section B.

> Another critical component is development and expression of a community consensus against public urination and defecation. On the one hand we have the urban custom of not interfering in your neighbor's business, and on the other we have former rural residents who are not accustomed to having toilets readily available. One thing we hope to promote is the articulation and expression of community values, where people can say, "we don't piss (drink in public, harass women, litter) in this community. Please use the toilet (drink in the bar, respect your neighbor, use the trash can)." It will be a lot easier to ask someone to change behavior if the new behavior can be specified and is facilitated by appropriate facilities.

The first utterance of this paragraph calls into question the community consensus which the proposal has already stipulated, which harkens back to the conflict discussed earlier in this chapter over whether or not public toilets were a good thing for the neighborhood.

The second utterance in the paragraph recalls the "modern urban environment" discussed in Section A. Read within the context of the geographical discourse in Section A, the "urban custom" presupposed here in Section B must be taken to be consistent with the norms not just of any urban community in general, but of Mt. Pleasant in particular. The urban custom, and the Mt. Pleasant community members associated with it, are opposed to "former rural residents" through the contrastive construction "on the one hand, on the other hand." This contrast is enhanced through the opposition of "urban" and "rural" in the two opposing clauses. These textual contrasts strengthen the contrast between the core, urban community members, and the marginalized former rural residents (who have already been characterized as immigrants in the first section), who are identified by *previous*, rather than *present* residence. Marginalization is enhanced through the characterization of rural residents as "not accustomed to having toilets readily available." Being unaccustomed to "readily available" toilets (an exotifying claim which is never explained and for which I have uncovered no evidence in all my years in Mt. Pleasant) harkens back to the culture shock proposed for those residents in Section A. Both these characterizations portray immigrants as unfamiliar with the customs and way of life in Mt. Pleasant. This, in conjunction with identifying these people in terms of their former place of residence, constructs them as out of place in Mt. Pleasant.

The split between the core and the margins of the community can also be seen in the description of "community values" in the second half of the paragraph, starting with the utterance,

> One thing we hope to promote is the articulation and expression of community values, where people can say, "We don't piss (drink in public, harass women, litter) in this community."

While promoting restroom facilities may be an admirable public health initiative, what I want to focus on here is the hierarchical arrangement of one group of people over another that this initiative promotes. The values that the grantwriters espouse are posited as shared "community values," and those who are positioned as holding the "community values" are sanctioned to judge their neighbors' actions as appropriate or inappropriate – as "over the line" or not – and to legislate appropriate behavior. Furthermore, the parenthetical inventory of activities: "(drink[ing] in public, harass[ing] women, litter[ing])," links these activities together. This linkage reflects and reinforces the wholly unanalyzed assumption that the people who are urinating in public are the same people who are drinking and littering on the street and harassing women. Furthermore, the utterance presupposes and constructs the street as a filthy place peopled by men, where women get harassed.

What's being promoted in this segment is not simply the abolition of "piss[ing] in this community," but rather a much broader goal – the socialization of the people hanging out on the street. And the people who have the right to shape this socialization are community members who have ostensibly established the core community values and who adhere to community norms. The deictic referent of "we" in "we don't piss in this community" is strategically fluid: If the addressee of this utterance indeed uses the trash can and doesn't piss in the street, then the statement holds true for them, and they are included in the "we" of "this community." If they disobey the community norms, the statement does not hold true, the "we" in the utterance addressed to them becomes exclusive, and they are defined out of the community.

The next utterance, "It will be a lot easier to ask someone to change behavior," construes the community members who are doing the socializing as the agents of the utterance's main action. The grammatical construction "it will be a lot easier" obscures the agent doing the asking, in contrast to the patients of the action, who are named ("someone"). This unequal division of agentive labor prohibits the people being socialized (and as we've seen, these are constructed as people from rural, third-world societies, living in overcrowded apartments – indexically, Latino men) from being full, equal, core community members. If the diverse strands of the community really were unified under a *celebration of diversity and common interests* theme, the ensuing toilets discourse would be something more along the lines of, "We as a community need to stop pissing on the street", where the performers of the pissing are referentially included in the deictic "we" of "the community."

The Perils of "Diversity"

Through projects like public toilets, civic activists like the grant-writers are ostensibly trying to improve "quality of life" in Mt. Pleasant and to value the diverse makeup of the community. But the grant proposal for public toilets implies that the way to improve neighborhood life is for core community members to socialize the neighbors they've marginalized into their own vision of how Mt. Pleasant people should behave. At the same time, the proposal positions the core community members as responsible, proactive participants in civic life, worthy stewards of funds for neighborhood improvements.

The grantwriters give attention to tolerance and diversity, and are genuinely concerned about the material and psychological well-being of those they are writing about. However, the linguistic structures and themes that the writers use in their discourse threaten to undermine these values. We've seen that the grantwriters set up a deictic center for Mt. Pleasant, a core of the neighborhood in terms of person, place, and time. The linguistic strategies that set up this deictic center work together with themes of geographic peripherality and filth to locate various members of Mt. Pleasant inside or outside the deictic center. The strategies separate and contrast core and marginal community members, constructing immigrant members as a threat to civic groups' perceptions of appropriate spatial and moral order in the neighborhood.

Linking the linguistically marginalized community members with themes of filth such as public urination creates a *moral* marginality for this group, whereas the characterization of the core members as intent on "cleaning up" the neighborhood serves as a morally centralizing force. Thus community problems are linked to marginalized members (i.e., "one of the biggest problems these folks present"), and the responsibility to fix the problems is posited as resting with members aligned with the grantwriters. It is through these linkages that the diversity which was celebrated at the outset of the proposal comes to be a burden for the in-group, in this case civic group members.

The grant proposal thus serves as a spatio-discursive practice – as Henri Lefebvre explains, a social act projected onto a spatial field."[46] The grantwriters' spatio-discursive acts rely on and reconstruct locally dominant attitudes about the kind of place that Mt. Pleasant is and should be. The moral and spatial order is constructed as a given, rather than specified as a point of view propounded by particular community members, namely civic group members.

The access that these community members have to outside institutions provides for the possibility that their views become incorporated into the discourses of major governmental and non-profit organizations.[47] In this way, civic group ideologies can be incorporated into city planning policies, into the rationales for major non-profit projects, and into other spatial practices which can potentially impact life in Mt. Pleasant in numerous ways.

The ability of civic group members to put forth their views as the *communally shared* ideologies of Mt. Pleasant residents relies on both their connections outside the neighborhood and their institutional positions as neighborhood organization leaders. This is a two-way relationship: the act of writing and submitting a grant proposal like the one in question also functions to reinforce the writers' authority and institutional position as neighborhood spokespeople and experts.

While Latino men are marginalized in the proposal, however, at the same time they are constructed as inherent to the current landscape of Mt. Pleasant St. Despite the fact that the grantwriters deplore this environment, they nevertheless construct Mt. Pleasant St. as a dirty, gritty, urban space peopled by (Latino) drunk men, where women get harassed. In the next chapter, I'll illustrate how a male Latino performance artist creates this same landscape, but does so in order to contest the positioning of Latinos that is so common in public discourse. Rather than deploring the gritty landscape of Mt. Pleasant St., he speaks back to the marginalizing moves of the civic group discourse by valorizing such a landscape, and by positioning Latino masculinity as central to Mt. Pleasant identity and White femininity as marginal.

Notes

1   Proposition 187, passed in 1994, aimed to cut public services for undocumented immigrants.

2   This act granted amnesty to undocumented Nicaraguans and Cubans and enabled them to apply for permanent residency, whereas Salvadorans and Guatemalans had to prove "extreme hardship" if they were to be deported. In 1999, after the damage caused by Hurricane Mitch in El Salvador, the "extreme hardship" criterion was dropped, but Salvadorans and Guatemalans still had to argue their cases to the INS, in contrast to Nicaraguans and Cubans. In 2001, after earthquakes devastated all of El Salvador, Salvadorans were again granted Temporary Protective Status, which is set to expire in September 2006.

3   It's interesting to note that culture here is constructed as a detachable entity that can be cast off like a coat in warm weather – rather than a way of life, value system, perspective on interacting in the world.

4   Throughout this study, when I ascribe gender to email writers, it is based on the names they sign their messages with or other references to their gender.

5   Sibley (1988)

6   Sibley was also influenced by philosopher Julia Kristeva's work. In her book *The Powers of Horror* (1982), Kristeva adds to Douglas's notion of filth by directing her attention towards the *boundary* between pure and impure categories that groups create. Kristeva brings to the discussion a focus on the power relations between those who have the power to enact such marginalization, and those who are marginalized.

7   Anderson (1988:133)

8   Bauman (1989:66). Along with race, this policy was also concerned with (dis)ability and sexuality.

9   Bauman (1989:71)

10 Koch and Pasteur discovered the workings of bacteria, founding the field of bacteriology. (Koch discovered how the anthrax bacillus worked, while Pasteur developed the germ theory of disease and made important innovations in the science of inoculation.)

11 Bauman (1989:71)

12 Hinton (2005:147)

13 Stallybrass and White (1986)

14 Chadwick (1874:274), in Stallybrass and White (1986:131)

15 Ibid. (:128)

16 A creature, like the rat, that is generally associated with uncleanliness.

17 Bauman (1989:71)

18 Stallybrass and White (1986:131–132)

19 Schell (1980)

20 Sibley (1995)

21 Cresswell (1996)

22 Cresswell (1996:106)

23 Jackson (1988)

24 The proposal was ultimately rejected. Explaining that obtaining and maintaining public toilets did not fall within the goal of strengthening intergroup collaboration, the funders said that they would consider funding a process whereby community groups got together to *talk* about public toilets. The proposal writers declined to propose such a project, averring that the neighborhood did not need money to *discuss* public toilets, since community members had been doing so unpaid for months.

25 See chapter 3 for a definition and discussion of indexicality.

26 Although this may seem like an awkward term, I use it as a more neutral alternative to the grant proposal's more highly charged discourse of "pissing."

27 This is not meant to imply that civic group members and public urinators are necessarily mutually exclusive groups.

28 Seeking exclusively private investment for what in past years could have been considered a public good is typical of municipal approaches to public space under neoliberal policies. I thank Brett Williams for pointing this out. See also Maskovsky (2001).

29 But see Silverstein (1976) for an argument that all words are inherently deictic, as they carry connotations that are not part of their literal or referential meaning.

30 Grice (1975)

31 By further describing the diversity of community members' national origins with the parenthetical elaboration "xx languages in the local elementary school," the grantwriters also posit that linguistic diversity is an indicator of diversity of national origin. In fact, this is not an effective means of discerning students' national origin in the school in question. For example, according to this school's description of their students at the time the grant proposal was written, the 387 students who spoke Spanish as a first language (almost two-thirds of the student body) were born in eleven different countries in North, Central, and South America.

32 cf. Levinson (1983)

33 cf. Fairclough (1995), van Dijk (1987)

34 In the terms of sociolinguist William Labov (1972), this information serves as an *orientation*, a story structure which orients listeners to the general scene and sets up the context of a story.

35 For a discussion of this term, see note 58 in chapter 9.

36 However, the Advisory Neighborhood Commission is a government institution with a budget provided by the city, the community police station is staffed by police from the city-wide police force, and community-based treatment programs are largely supported through outside funders. These facts contradict the assertion that Mt. Pleasantites don't expect "outside organizations like the government" to solve local problems.

37 See Lees (1998), Ley (1996).

38 See Blommaert and Verschueren (1991).

39 Blommaert and Verschueren (1991)

40 See Cadaval (1998).

41 There are certainly other readings of this discourse in which Latino men are not indexed. However, a number of contextual features make

this a more common reading for those who are familiar with the neighborhood, including the funders for whom the grant proposal is written. First, Mt. Pleasant is the center of the Latino community in DC, and the area where the grant is available in Virginia also has a large Latino population, suggesting that the funders are interested in funding projects in Latino areas. Second, the proposal focuses on immigrants on Mt. Pleasant St., and the majority of immigrants who socialize on Mt. Pleasant Street are Latino men. Finally, public discourse of alcohol and drinking on the street frequently focuses, implicitly or explicitly, on Latinos. One example mentioned earlier is a neighborhood newsletter written exclusively in English, with the exception of an announcement of an upcoming alcohol policy town hall meeting written in both English and Spanish.

42   For Mt. Pleasant civic group discourse which explicitly criticizes socializing on the street without engaging in consumerism as "being up to no good," see Schaller and Modan (2005).

43   *These* here refers most directly back to "Others [who] are living in overcrowded apartments and doing most of their socializing on the street," and more distantly to "marginal people who may have slipped over the line," including "many of [whom] are homeless . . ."

44   It is rare, although not unheard of, for women to urinate or defecate in public spaces.

45   Blommaert and Verschueren (1991:528) remark that constructions that obscure agents or recipients promote a pro-homogeneism ideology, where discourse about values or norms is presented as "depersonalized and desocialized," and "objectively identifiable." They further note the unmarked nature of the group not explicitly named: "the 'we' in the debate is self-evident, stable, and atemporal."

46   Lefebvre (1991:31). See chapter 9 for a discussion of Lefebvre.

47   See Schaller and Modan (2005).

CHAPTER 5

LA LOCA VS. THE CULTURAL VAMPIRES

John is thinking of moving. He's sick of the bullshit in the neighborhood, he says. This is not how he thought it would be.

> I lived [on the other side of the park], in, an apartment building that was all White, small, uh, four stories, uh, place. And, there might have been a couple other people in there that were different- or of, different nationalities. But it was- I just thought it was the most bland living situation. [. . .] And there was, there were, **no**, minorities there, or hardly any, and people there were very intolerant, or suspicious. So, I wanted diversity and I decided, you know, this would be a perfectly wonderful diverse neighborhood.
>
> I would particularly want my family to be, to grow up in a multicultural setting where if people did speak different languages and, if it came time to- the holidays that were, generic to everyone- uh, then they could go to different houses and see how people celebrated differently. Or at least- you know, hear different languages and maybe pick up some of it. And a little bit more tolerance and patience. because I grew up in a- one I grew up in a very intolerant, Black, neighborhood. And then, I worked in a ve- I work in a very intolerant community, which is partially White, partially Black, very intolerant of each other. [. . .] I still want to live with different, groups of people. I mean I would love- still want my family to grow up with culturally diverse people. You know or- **ethnically** diverse people. And uh, I I **really** think that's one of the most important things I could ever do. And uh, one of the best gifts I could ever give to a family.

John is a border straddler – in this racially divided city he refuses to identify as either Black or White. Born white-skinned and straight-haired to parents in the Black Power movement, he's a member of the city's EMT[1] squad who wears an earring and keeps his hair long. Mt. Pleasant seemed like a place that fit him, he says, but lately things have been getting him down.

> I think the neighborhood's getting worse. You know, as far as crime, as far as uh, drug activity, uh, interpersonal skills, you know, of people being friendly to each other, or at least tolerant of each other. And, the activity that surrounds those, plus the, I guess like the panhandlers out front, and just watching people walk past each other. If someone, you know, I don't know what- what etiquette is, but you never see two people stop at once and- you know, when they're gonna run into each other walking. You know you- you never see someone stop and, waive the other person along. It's always people running into each other and looking at each other. And it just- simple, simple courtesy, like that, which, should be something you take for granted. Are, you know, there's no civility in this neighborhood. And that, I find infuriating.

But what really gets John is the attitude that Vince in chapter 3 critiqued, the idea that putting up with a bunch of crap makes you a better person, a more real urbanite. John voices nothing but the utmost disdain for those who display such an attitude:

> I think they lived around here to say how groovy they are. U:h, you know I'm **so** coo:l, and, u:h, I I think it gave them an edge, on other people, like they would go back to other communities and, you know s- talk to- this- woman that I just da- I dated, [she's moving] out to Seattle, she said [. . .] everybody out there told me I [was] moving into a really bad neighborhood, but I told them, I'm from DC, and I'm a tough bitch. Cause you know how it is in DC.

But even John is not impervious to the attitude that living in certain places makes one tougher, as he caps off his commentary with the remark, "And she lives on Connecticut Avenue!"[2]

The object of John's disdain is the flip side of racism, the hipster attitude that, particularly if you're White, then living in a neighborhood with people of color – many of whom are poor – can up your social capital. As geographer David Sibley has noted, features associated with marginalized groups, "the very features which are reviled[,] are also desired because they represent those features of the 'civilized' [quotes added] self which are repressed. Defiled peoples and places offer excitement."[3] This is a phenomenon for which John has no patience:

> There was a- there was a **big**- a big exodus of people that I knew, and I always said, they were the ones who offered, the very least for the city. and for the community. They never did anything, on the community level, except for get high and get drunk. And say how groovy they were because they were, you know dating somebody of, another race or something. You know they were, cultural vampires. And they'd come up, and, come here and, they'd hang out, say, you know, God I'm so open-minded. And eventually they'd float back to some, predominantly White, comfortable community somewhere. And say, wasn't I groovy. You know, I hung out with those people.

Continuing on about the woman he dated, John explains that

> I think she was typical of the other people I met that, would never, say, there's- you know there's problems, in this neighborhood, there's problems with the people. There's problems with what goes on there, maybe there's something, you could do to make it better. Instead it was always like, Hey I'm a real cowboy because I live up there. And uh, that makes me a real adventur- adventurous soul, and tough. So- I, pretty much- I would much rather, somebody, look at me and say You know that's a shit neighborhood you live in. From my perspective. Which I- accept as reality. You know, when, Bo-Bo and Scat, are raisin hell at the pay phone with four or five other, hoodlums, that, everybody's drinkin, and screamin at the top of their lungs, that's just not what, I think anybody should accept as indigenous of a community. I mean a, community is when you **have** a group of people that, are will to s- you know, alcohol's not a bad thing. You know, willing to share drinks, or, whatever, or food. in a, civil way. Not as, people tryin to terrorize and, enforce their opinion. And uh, that's what I see.

For John, the people he calls cultural vampires are bad for the neighborhood because they are psychologically invested in the crime, litter, drug dealing that contribute to the neighborhood's reputation as a tough and gritty place. As we've seen in chapter 3, however, others see such issues as part and parcel of city life – not something to brag about, but problems that are indicative of the poverty and unequal distribution of resources that are becoming more extreme in the District every year – and as such, they don't frighten city people away. What John shares with his neighbors who hold this alternate view, however, is the perception that many who are attracted by the neighborhood's diversity are attracted to it in a superficial way, in a way that is about creating a certain kind of identity for themselves, rather than about participating in an ongoing way in community life, and that they will eventually leave because in the end they don't feel comfortable. Both perspectives cast "cultural vampires" as feeding on the community, commodifying diversity and sucking up its exotified manifestations.

Chaos Standing

Bachata music is softly playing as the lights in the small theater on 18th St. begin to dim, and slides of the hustle and bustle around the vendors' stalls on Columbia Rd. are projected onto a white screen on the theater's brick back wall. Suddenly the measured rhythms and standardized enunciations of a female broadcast voice, somewhat giggly but with an authoritative air, flow out of the PA system:

> Peace and tranquility. A great view. Sidewalk shootings. Fresh flowers, poverty, and contradictions. Drugs, and prostitution. Incense, or sunglasses. maybe, a fake greencard. palm readers. candles for your saints. a piece of /????/, for good luck maybe fresh bagels. Or a California-style meal. Chaos, and harmony, hatred, and respect. If you wanted all of this, where would you go to find it? What if you only had, 20 to 30 minutes to get it all? After six months of interviews, research, visits, and walks through three communities locked in constant change and transition, this reporter may have found the answer. Mt. Pleasant. Columbia Heights. and Adams Morgan. This seven part series will examine different aspects of the realities in these three, culturally saturated neighborhoods. Joy, pain, fear, love, hate, happiness, anger. The ingredients. of multicultural living. My name is Pam Anderson. and I'm a reporter, for the *Washington Post*. I'm writing an article about Washington DC's, multicultural neighborhoods. and the people who live there. I must confess, Yo [pronounced "joe"] no habla [sic] Español!

So begins Quique Avilés' one-man performance piece *Chaos Standing/Caos a Pie*. *Chaos Standing*, as it is usually referred to, is a play about seven emotions and how they relate to life in the Mt. Pleasant –Adams Morgan–Columbia Heights area. Avilés performed *Chaos Standing* during a five-week run in local venues to a wide cross-section of Mt. Pleasantites and people from elsewhere in the city.

In addition to neighborhood-wide public discourse, the play also entered larger city-wide discourses about Mt. Pleasant through the media publicity it received (reviews in the *Washington Post* and local arts and entertainment publications), as well as through its connection to the granting organization which funded the play's development and performance. *Chaos Standing* was in fact funded through the same grant program that the writers of the public toilets grant had applied to. As I discussed in the previous chapter, when it comes to promoting particular views of Mt. Pleasant to a city-wide audience, civic group members have a powerful position through such channels as grant proposals and connections with non-profits. Avilés' show plays an important role in the public discourse because, as a show institutionally backed by a local performing arts organization, it was one of the few competing views of the neighborhood which had similar access to policy makers and others with resources outside the neighborhood. It's also interesting in terms of gender constructions: like some of the emails in chapter 4, three scenes in the performance piece represent the views of a male author filtered through the voice of female characters.

Through the performance of *Chaos Standing*, as well as through the original grant proposal for funding for the piece, Avilés was able to contest dominant characterizations of Mt. Pleasant in settings which provided an opportunity to undermine civic groups' facility to speak for the neighborhood; the performance also provided a forum to make an implicit criticism of dominant groups' views getting translated into funded projects or city policies.

As part of the public discourse, *Chaos Standing* was able to bring Avilés' characterizations of a cross-section of Mt. Pleasantites to a wide and diverse audience. Avilés started working on *Chaos Standing* around the same time that the issues of public toilets and voluntary agreements for liquor-selling establishments were being discussed on the Mt. Pleasant Forum listserv and in meetings of the mostly White civic groups. One of Avilés' main goals in writing *Chaos Standing* was to speak back to these public discourses that marginalized Latinos, particularly Latino men. Through the performance piece, he both implicitly contested the peripheralization of Latinos that was dominant in the public discourse, and he called into question the authority of (mostly White) civic group members to speak for and about Mt. Pleasant and Mt. Pleasant people. In other words, through the public performance of this play, Avilés' constructions of Mt. Pleasant and its community members came to stand in opposition to those of the dominant public discourse, as well as to publicly delegitimize the community members who promoted that discourse.

At the same time, however, contestations like Avilés' play that themselves occur in public discourse rarely call into question the underlying ideological linkages of urban authenticity to ethnicity, gender, filth, and fear. In fact, as we'll see in this chapter, such contestations often *rely* on these ideologically laden representations of the landscape in order to speak back to the marginalization of Latino men and call into question the legitimacy of White community members. So although *Chaos Standing* serves as an important tool in fighting against the negative positioning of Latinos in discourse like the public toilets grant proposal, Avilés' approach also reaffirms the representation of the neighborhood as dangerous and gritty because of the public interactions that take place with people hanging out on Mt. Pleasant St, and solidifies some stereotypes of them.

As in other forms of local public discourse, in *Chaos Standing* person and place identities are mutually constitutive: the construction of what we could call local stock characters or archetypes relies on character alignments with Mt. Pleasant as a certain kind of place, just as the construction of Mt. Pleasant is built upon descriptions of the characters who ostensibly people it. An integral part of the play's representation of the urban landscape is a representation of the prototypical urbanite as non-white, working-class, tough, and fearless. Avilés also uses femaleness as a site in which to develop characterizations of class and ethnic identities. In the play, the representations of two very different female characters serve to delegitimize local White positionalities, particularly feminized ones.

Chaos Standing is structured as an interview about Mt. Pleasant with a character named Pelón. A *Washington Post* journalist asks Pelón to discuss neighborhood events or people that exemplify seven emotions: love, hate, joy, anger, happiness, sadness, and fear. Each emotion is linked with a particular character. In addition to speaking in his "own" voice, the character Pelón discusses the emotions by telling the stories of these other characters. As he relates these stories, Pelón takes on the personas of each character.

The perspective of the character Pelón is loosely based on Avilés' own experiences moving to Mt. Pleasant from El Salvador as a young teenager and growing up in the neighborhood. The play's other characters are likewise loosely shaped by Avilés' experiences with community members whom he had observed or interacted with over the years, as well as on research interviews as preparation for the play. Although some of the occurrences described in these characters' narratives reflect real-world events, Avilés has stated that the characters themselves are not meant to represent actual individuals. Rather, we can consider their function to be to represent the various ideologies circulating in the neighborhood about *types* of people and the types of conflicts present in Mt. Pleasant. In my view, Avilés is playing with stereotypes; his use of stock characters points to the stereotyping power of local ideologies about different kinds of people in the neighborhood. By creating characters that represent types, rather than individuals, Avilés creates a platform for community members to address the stereotyping that goes on. Avilés has stated that an integral part of his approach to theater is engaging the audience in issues his works bring up. One of the most direct ways that this happens is through post-performance discussions among the performer and the audience members. *Chaos Standing* and the ensuing discussions provide a forum to address community tensions and conflict, as well as a potential opening for transformation.

Framing Local Perspectives

In *Chaos Standing*, the relationship of community attitudes and the moral positioning of different characters and perspectives is set up through a layering process that we can call *framing*. Framing is a concept originally developed by the anthropologist Gregory Bateson[4] to explain how people 1) signal the boundaries of activities – setting them apart from other activities so that they are identifiable as certain kinds of events – and 2) communicate exactly what kind of activity is going on. Bateson gives the example of monkeys at play. Although playing has many of the same elements as fighting, the monkeys give each other what Bateson calls *metamessages* to set up the activity's frame as one of play, signaling that the biting and swatting they're performing is not meant to be taken seriously as actual fighting. Similarly, a scene from a theatrical performance is framed as part of a play, so that audience members know that what they are seeing is actors taking on roles, not people actually engaged in spontaneous social interaction. Framing also occurs in storytelling: If someone tells a story at the dinner table about work, then that story frame exists within the larger frame of dinner-table conversation. In telling the story, that person may quote themselves as saying to a colleague at work that "I've had enough coffee today," and it will most likely be clear to listeners that that quote exists within the frame of the storyworld. However, if, while they're telling the story, the dinner host asks them if they want some coffee, they may respond in their own voice – not as a storyteller but as a dinner participant – that "I've had enough coffee today." They will use other metamessages – turning their body to the host, changing their intonation and rhythm – to signal to their listeners that this utterance is meant to be interpreted as something they are saying within the frame of the dinner conversation, and not something they as a character said within the frame of the story.

Chaos Standing is a set of stories within stories, and as such it is useful to approach the play from a framing perspective. Avilés, writing within the context of the debates circulating in the neighborhood at the time, establishes various sets of nesting frames within each scene of the play. One of the most common ways that he does this is through the strategy of reported speech, whereby various characters take on the voice of other characters, either directly – by "turning into" other characters ("I've had enough coffee today") – or indirectly, by articulating the voices of others through the lens of their own perspective ("She said she'd had enough coffee today"). These two approaches are often referred to as *direct* and *indirect discourse*. When the voice of one character is embedded within the voice of another character quoting the first, two frames are invoked: the frame of the original, or reported context (the storyworld) and the frame of the new, or reporting context (the storytelling event).

Jane Hill (1995) has observed that discourse that represents the voices of multiple participants – what we can call a *multiple voice system* –

can serve to carry different ideological positions which exist within a community's moral geography. Along with Hill, Deborah Tannen (1989) and Amy Shuman (1992) point out that reported speech is situated within both the frame of its original context, and the frame of the context of its uttering. In the storytelling example above, for instance, the first "I've had enough coffee" gains its meaning from the original interaction in which the speaker uttered it in the storyworld, as well as from the situation of the storytelling event. In other words, the reasons why the story is being told, the particular aspects of the story that the teller highlights, etc., will influence the meaning of "I've had enough coffee." As Tannen (1989:101) notes, reported speech and the context in which it is revoiced "are dynamically interrelated, [and] the meaning of [reported speech] is transformed by the reporting context." This means that reported speech often tells us less about the original speaker (who may be a fictional character, as is the case in *Chaos Standing*) than about the character who is revoicing the speech in a new context. Through this relationship between the reported and the reporting frames, speakers can take certain stances vis-à-vis the content or the utterer of the reported speech.[5]

In *Chaos Standing*, the multiple frames are used to index clashing points of view in and about neighborhood conflict. By bringing these voices together into his construction of a moral geography, Avilés positions these voices – and by extension the people they represent – in certain relationships with each other; as we'll see, the frames themselves, as well as the interaction *between* the frames, create positive and negative moral positionings for Avilés, the stock characters, and the types of community members these characters represent, within the neighborhood's moral geography.

To see how this all works, I want to focus on the two scenes in *Chaos Standing* in which women are the main characters.[6] *Joy* is represented by Camila, a Latina high-school girl, while Tiffany, a young White social worker, represents *fear*. These scenes make an important contribution to neighborhood discourse: Taken together, they invoke the gendered and ethnicized ideologies of toughness and fear that are prevalent in the neighborhood. But Avilés wields these discourses in a way that creates an alternate view of who counts as a legitimate community member.

The Camila piece has five frames: 1) Camila, as a character in two events that 2) Camila narrates herself, whose larger story is narrated

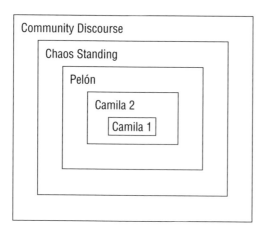

Figure 5.1   Frames in the Camila scene

and embodied by 3) Pelón, who is performed and written by 4) Avilés, who is writing within the larger context of 5) the community's public discourse (Figure 5.1).

There is also a sort of linear framing in *Chaos Standing*: The first emotion scene in the play, which portrays *joy* in the form of Camila, serves as a kind of metamessage in Bateson's sense to set up an identity for the neighborhood against which the ensuing scenes can be interpreted. Camila, as the symbol of joy and the first character in the piece, sets up a positive moral positioning for the neighborhood at large, and creates a model of insider identity against which later characters can be compared.

After Camila comes the character Tiffany. Created to symbolize the archetype of the person who fears the neighborhood, the representation of Tiffany serves to speak back to the institutional discourse we saw in chapter 4, by showing that someone with Tiffany's attitudes is not *of the neighborhood*, and therefore cannot speak from any authoritative position about what kinds of changes should happen *in* the neighborhood. The Tiffany scene has six frames: 1) Catcalling men and 2) a beer-drinking client who 3) Tiffany talks about, 4) channeled by Pelón, who again is performed and written by 5) Avilés, writing within the context of the 6) community's public discourse (Figure 5.2).

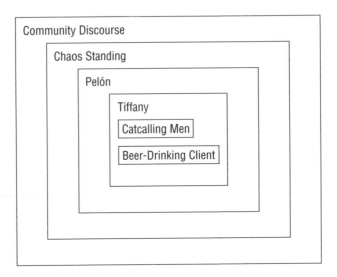

Figure 5.2 Frames in the Tiffany scene

The Pelón Frame: Danger and Diversity

The depiction of the neighborhood as a certain kind of place starts with Pelón's answers to the journalist's questions. While neighborhood identity construction goes on throughout the piece, here I want to concentrate on the way that the Pelón character talks about the neighborhood in the introduction to the Tiffany scene:

JOURNALIST: What about, fear?

PELÓN: In this place, you can either rule fear, or be ruled by it. I, have been lucky in a way. The only time I was afraid, was when I was- when I couldn't speak the language. I was in Junior High. I couldn't speak for myself, defend myself. I remember going to the post office, to get stamps, with notes written by my brother. [laughs]. <Spanish pronunciation: "Please give me two twenty-five cent stamps."> I couldn't order anything at McDonalds! I couldn't ask the bus driver for directions! Couldn't get in a cab, couldn't go to the store for a refund or exchange you know like if I had gotten the wrong size underwear. Which happened! But other than

that, I'm not afraid of anything. The ki:ds. The stree:ts.
Whi:tes,. Bla:cks,. My own Raza!

Avilés constructs Pelón as the consummate insider: he is the neighborhood expert that a journalist from a prestigious newspaper has chosen as a verbal tour-guide through the neighborhood; he has a deep knowledge of neighborhood events and of a wide range of community members, he's comfortable with everyone and performs the same kind of fearless bravado that we saw with Boaz in chapter 3.

The segment above contributes to this characterization in a number of ways. Pelón's first utterance, "In this place, you can either rule fear, or be ruled by it," presupposes and therefore sets up as a given, the notion that fear is an integral element of life in Mt. Pleasant. This is reinforced by the allusion to "the kids" and "the streets," which invokes the stereotype of dangerous inner-city youth and inner-city streets. The implication here is that there is something in the neighborhood that causes fear − in other words, that the neighborhood is a place of danger and risk. Like Boaz, the Pelón character's articulation of his own fearlessness amidst this supposed danger helps to set him up as an authentic urbanite.

Pelón's insider identity is also created through the language that Avilés puts in Pelón's mouth.[7] Pelón is bilingual in English and Spanish, and this aligns him with the multilingual and multi-ethnic neighborhood that Avilés recreates in the performance piece. Another important aspect of Pelón's language is his use of cursing. In *Chaos Standing*, cursing serves a similar function as the invocation of urination in the grant proposal; as "dirty language," it is another kind of filth in the urban landscape. While filth was deplored in the grant proposal, however, dirty language in *Chaos Standing* serves as an emblem of urbanness, which contributes to the linguistic process of constructing characters as either legitimate or non-legitimate urbanites.

After describing his own early experiences in the neighborhood, in the following stanza of the scene Pelón next recirculates the view of Mt. Pleasant as an ethnically diverse place, punctuating each aspect of attraction with a snap of his fingers:

I've known people that moved here
because they just **loved** the **place**.
the **accents**. [snap]

the **food**. [snap]
the **different** people. [snap]
the different natio**nal**ities. [snap]
the different **accents**.

Using the deictic *here*, Avilés sets up a deictic center in which Pelón
is located, and constructs other people as coming to that center, and
being attracted to it because of the diversity. These are both strategies
that we saw in the public toilets grant proposal. But, as was the case
in that proposal's description of the neighborhood, the particular type
of diversity that these people are attracted to is a commodified one
– one which can be counted and consumed, either literally or figura-
tively, as Pelón does by enumerating each of these emblems of difference with a snap of his finger. Whereas in the grant proposal such a
commodified diversity was simply presented as a given, in *Chaos Standing* Avilés gives the commodification of diversity a negative valence,
developed through three strategies. First, as the character Pelón elab-
orates the list of diverse features, he uses an exaggerated intonational
contour that implies sarcasm and hyperstresses the last word of each
item in the list. Second, he aligns this type of diversity with people
who are moving *to* the neighborhood, consequently portraying a desire
for commodified diversity as representative of outsider identity.

Third, Pelón dichotomizes the people who are attracted to
Mt. Pleasant and to a commodified diversity ("people that moved here
because they just loved the place," the different accents, food, etc.)
into two groups: people who eventually flee, and people who stay
despite their growing uncomfortableness. He explicitly characterizes
both groups as at odds with the tenor of the neighborhood. By implication, then, an attraction to commodified diversity is also at odds with
an implied *local* take on diversity:

> There are things that can happen, that can change that love affair. I've
> seen some people run like hell, just after a few months! you know,
> **then** there's the people who stay no matter **what**. But I don't think,
> that these people live at peace with themselves in the place. The fear
> stays with them.

The people described as "running like hell" receive peripheral positioning because they actually leave the neighborhood, as well as because
"running like hell" indexes the notion that people who are afraid

in the neighborhood are not true Mt. Pleasant people. But in Pelón's construction even those who *stay* are also made marginal, because they are portrayed as not "liv[ing] at peace with themselves in the place." This positing of inner turmoil constructs the identity of "these people" as inconsistent with the identity of the place. This not fitting in is reinforced in the next utterance, "the fear stays with them." Positing fear as an *enduring* characteristic of these people again constructs them not only as inauthentic urban dwellers, but also as people who will *remain* inauthentic urban dwellers.

The Camila Frame: Authentic Urban Behavior

In addition to the character of Pelón and Pelón's descriptions of the neighborhood, the image of urban authenticity is also shaped through the character of Camila. The Camila scene begins when the reporter asks Pelón, "Tell me about joy. Is there any joy in this place?" From the outset, then, as the character who represents such an unmitigatedly positive emotion, Camila is set up as a representative of what is good in the neighborhood. Pelón responds,

> Fuck yeah! Check this out. There was this girl. Camila, that was her name. This is when I was in high school. We had a lot of classes together.

With this answer, the character Pelón locates Camila along with himself in the deictic center; not only is Camila represented as simply and already being in the space of the neighborhood, but her high school connection with Pelón aligns her with the play's protagonist, and this enhances her positive moral positioning.

Camila is represented as a wild teenager who hates school, acts dumb and never does her homework, but whose personality blossoms outside institutional walls as she inhabits the urban environment. (It's important to keep in mind, however, that the piece is not so much a character study as an interrogation of archetypes and ideologies in the neighborhood.)

> [At hooky parties[8]] She. was. the sta:r. Everyone called her, la loca [*crazy girl*]. This girl, she would smoke weed, like I had never seen

before. She'd drink beer, liquor, anything, but she lo:ved, getting high. She'd get all giggly- ^Lu:::::::::. She'd start laughing and doing all kinds of things. From that time on, I always wanted to come back just to see her. She'd go ^wi:ld, man. Shit, you know, she'd start acting out, and we would encourage her, come on Camila, do la mara, do la mara! And she said, okay.

[all of the following in high pitch] Vamos, en la, Columbia R:oad. Bien pedos [*Pretty drunk*]. We're walking down Columbia Rd. [Figure 5.3]. Eh, ¿qué pasó, loca? Vamos para la dieciocho y Columbia, Joder con los bla:ncos. [*We're going to 18th and Columbia,*[9] *Fuck with the Whites*]. <creaky voice:[10] Ye:ah>, it's Friday night, la Mara wants to go to party and dance and fuck with the White girls and the White ^boy:s! Huh huh! She was a trip man, for real!

Before you knew it, she would flip the script. Vamos, en el cuarenta y dos. We're on the 42 bus, now! La clase gratuita de español. El bus del part time. [*The free Spanish class. The part-timers' bus.*] We'd get on, at the bus stop, at the 7–11, we'd sit, all the way, in the back. We're drinking sodas, and eating chips. AHH. Two girls, with jherri curls, get on, at the next stop. We start talking, shit about them. In Spanish, of course. Ah, look, mira la chava mantecosa [*look at the greasy girl*]. Ha ha ha ha! They notice what's ^up. They came to bitch at

Figure 5.3   Walking down Columbia Rd.   © Jennifer Leeman

us. We all, get up at once. Hold my shit! And walk to their seat. Yo what's up? What's the problem? Whatchyou mean we're talking shit? You talk Spanish? Well you don't know what we're saying then! Yeah- Oh, you want to talk about respect! You're the one that's disrespecting us, looking at us all funny and shit, rolling your bo- bug eyes at us and shit, Oh, you want to ^^fight? Gi:rl, we kick your jherri curl ass in a minute and use the extra grease to make some refried beans! Seven of us! Of course they shut up!

The first thing to notice about Camila's performance in this section is that it is explicitly portrayed *as a performance*: her posturing starts in response to her friends egging her on to "Do la mara, do la mara."[11] It's ambiguous to what extent Camila is just performing la mara, or performing herself as part of this group, but in any case, her ability to get the performance right, to the wide acclaim of her fellow school-skipping friends, is testament to her competence in promoting a brash urban self. We see the same ambiguity in the second section, when Pelón says, "Before you knew it, she would flip the script." Although this makes it seem like Camila is just acting a role, the narrative's closing, "Seven of us! Of course they shut up!" reframes this play-acting as a self-narrative about an activity that Camila took part in.[12]

Another aspect of the Camila character that points to the importance of performance is Pelón's characterization of Camila's homelife. While in *Chaos Standing* the characters representing urban authenticity are generally described as poor or working-class, this is not the case with Camila:

It was- weird, cause she was one of us, and she wasn't. It seemed like, the only thing bad in her life, was school! [. . .] She was the only one in our group, that lived in a house. Not in an apartment. They had a nice house, too. They had all these naked sculptures, and things, plants and things, <high pitch: my parents like to, collect old things,> she would say, <high pitch: I hate antiques.> But, they seemed to get along. They liked her, and she liked them, too. They'd give her a lot of freedom. Shit. She was hanging out with us!

Although Camila is 'one of the gang' in terms of her demeanor, her class background sets her apart. Pelón presents Camila's living in a house as noteworthy and different from the rest of Pelón's group of friends – and it's not just any house, but a house filled with antiques and art. Later in the scene, Pelón also discusses Camila as a serious, disciplined, and talented singer who spends long hours writing and revising songs. This reveals another side of the character not evident from the first anecdotes.

That Camila's hanging out with this group is portrayed as an example of the freedom that her parents give her is also noteworthy, as it invokes an image of Pelón and his group as tough, inner-city kids, who some parents might not want their children hanging around with. This consequently points up Pelón's comment that in some ways Camila "was not one of us." The discussion of Camila's class background as different from the rest of the group implicitly characterizes Pelón et al.'s class background as working class. Because Pelón, as the protagonist expert narrator, is in the center of the deictic center, working-class identity thus also becomes a marker of central and legitimate neighborhood positioning. That Camila's class background does nothing to erode her positive moral positioning is evidence that urban authenticity is not only about the social categories of class or ethnicity that someone falls into, but has a lot to do with how comfortable or competent someone is at performing a self-identity that reads as authentically urban to in-group members of the community (keeping in mind that who the in-group is varies within the community at-large). Given that Camila's story is framed by Pelón as an emblem of joy, the character's brash behavior and her Spanish nickname "la Loca" along with her own use of Spanish (which indexes her ethnic identity), as well as the contrast of her actual class background to the class identity that she performs, all work together in the scene to construct legitimate femaleness as brash, working-class, and Latina.

The linguistic themes that Avilés uses to create Camila as an authentic urbanite are ones that we've seen before: aggressiveness, use of intoxicating substances, alignment with filth (in this case, dirty language). Avilés uses these themes in ways similar to Boaz in chapter 3, and in ways diametrically opposed to the grantwriters in chapter 4.

These stories bring out the local theme of urban heterogeneity discussed in chapter 3. Through Camila's use of Spanish and comment about refried beans, her reference to jherri curls, and her desire to "fuck with the White girls and the White boys," Camila paints a picture of the neighborhood as a Latino, African American, and White place. And whereas in local public discourse talk around ethnic tension is fraught and often avoided explicitly – note the grantwriters' lack of ever discussing Latinos on-record – Camila does not pussyfoot around; instead, in these stories about confrontation, she brazenly invokes stereotypes of her own and other characters' race/ethnicity in talk about messing with them. Such confrontation serves to paint Camila as a character who is comfortable with the heterogeneity of the neighborhood; instead of it making her nervous or her shying away from it, she embraces it as a source of joyful play. This interpretation of ethnic-based, in-your-face confrontation as a positive, fun activity is of course shaped by Avilés' framing of the scene as representative of joy. It is a rebellious joy that resists the quiet, restrained street demeanor promoted by much public discourse, and therefore it functions to critique that model of public decorum.

Another way that Avilés constructs Camila's alignment with the heterogeneity of the neighborhood is through his use of Spanish –English code-switching dialogue. The character's facility with both of these languages constructs her as bilingual and therefore, again, in line with the tenor of the neighborhood. And since Camila's bilingualism recalls Pelón's bilingualism, her linguistic repertoire aligns her across frames with Pelón. This also enhances her urban legitimacy.

As mentioned above, the framing of the Columbia Rd. and 42 bus stories is ambiguous – is Camila telling stories about herself, or about others? In answer to her friends' request "Do la mara," she does not simply report on the actions she discusses in third person. Rather, she embodies la mara, putting herself in the ranks of this group through her use of the first person plural verb and pronoun in "*Vamos* en la Columbia Rd./ *We're* walking down Columbia Rd." and "Vamos en el cuarenta y dos/ We're on the 42 bus now." This alignment with la Mara is heightened by her use of the present tense in the story. As many scholars have noted,[13] narrating a story in the present tense makes a story feel more immediate. This immediacy brings the story closer to the narrator, and this closeness can serve as a type of alignment of the narrator to the characters that she narrates. The alignment is also heightened by Avilés' use of direct discourse to represent Camila's telling of both events from her own perspective. (This will become clearer in comparison to the Tiffany character's narration style.)

Avilés uses the strategy of direct discourse to align Camila with themes we've already seen that locally signify urban identity. She drinks and smokes weed and swears; she fiercely inhabits the public spaces of the streets and the city busses like she owns them; she postures aggressively and she does not shy away from physical confrontation. As the scene closes, Camila is still located firmly in the deictic center as a core community member, and she serves as counter-evidence to outsider stereotypes that urban life is miserable. Pelón ends the scene by saying,

> So you ask me,. if there's joy. You know, a lot of people think that, our lives should be, supposed to be, pathetic, **bitter** and **sad**. We:ll, not everyone. Look at Camila. She's still around. She's still the same. Crazy, and happy, still singing. And that for me, is joy. Just to watch her. Being happy. **That**, is joy.

To sum up, Avilés creates an authentic urban identity for the Latina high school girl Camila through language (Spanish, dirty language, on-record references to interlocutors' ethnicity), behavior (drinking, smoking weed), performances of class (working class) and ethnicity (Latina), deictic positioning (in the deictic center) and through a framing alignment where Camila as narrator voices herself as a character by using direct discourse and Pelón aligns Camila with himself, thus creating a closeness between the two Camila frames as well as between the Camila and Pelón frames.

The Tiffany Frame

Whereas Camila is firmly located within the deictic center at both the beginning and end of the piece, Tiffany's scene has her entering the neighborhood at the beginning, and leaving in the end. This creates a tenuous positioning for her, casting her as an outsider. Tiffany is the character who represents fear, a theme that we've already seen is commonly used in neighborhood discourse to delegitimize people's claim to community membership. Pelón introduces Tiffany as an example of people who are discomforted and discomfited by the neighborhood:

> I've seen some people run like hell, just after a few months! you know, **then** there's the people who stay no matter **what**. But I don't think, that these people live at peace with themselves in the place. The fear

stays with them. Take, Tiffany for example. She was this bright, spunky, energetic, well-meaning young woman, from the Midwest. Illinois.

Tiffany is the only character that Pelón discusses whose introduction links her with other places. This is the flip side of the strategy that we saw in the grant proposal, which cast Latinos as immigrants coming from elsewhere. In *Chaos Standing*, it is the Latina Camila who is portrayed as simply already *in* the space, and the White Tiffany who is characterized as migrating *to* the neighborhood. It's not a coincidence that Tiffany is painted as coming from the Midwest: the common American image of the Midwest as the country's "heartland" has helped in DC to construct an image of the Midwest as the center of White America. So this migration from the White homeland, as it were, is another strategy that creates an outsider status for Tiffany. Her class position also distances her from the model of neighborhood authenticity that Avilés has set up; she is characterized as someone who came to DC originally for an internship, and a college graduate with a white-collar job.

Tiffany's origin from elsewhere sets up what we can call a tenuous *anchoring* for her within the neighborhood, which becomes enhanced as Avilés the performer moves from the Pelón frame into the Tiffany frame proper, taking on the voice and mannerisms of the Tiffany character:

I've had it. Moving here was a mistake. I'm going back home. At first, I thought, my situation and this place, were idyllic. I thought I- I'd found a place where I could grow, and develop a sense of belonging. You know be good for myself and for others. But now I know I was wrong. This place is **mea:n**. **Crazy**.

Here, the utterance "I'm going back home" sets up Mt. Pleasant as a place which is not Tiffany's true home, and constructs her sojourn in the neighborhood as temporary. Similarly, the evaluation that her move to Mt. Pleasant was a mistake sets up an oppositional relationship between her and the neighborhood. This is a radically different set-up from the one we saw in the Camila scene.

Another strong difference between the Camila and Tiffany characters is their relationship to public space. While Camila revels in the public nature of the neighborhood streets, Tiffany is scared of those streets and of the public interactions that can occur in them:

This place is **mea:n. Crazy.** When I moved here, I used to drive a lot. But then I got used to walking. Short walks, long walks, you name it. Every now and then I would walk all the way to the White House, and back. Straight down 16th St., going back up through Dupont Circle, Connecticut, Columbia Rd. I would walk to the grocery, to the metro station. I'd get ice cream at Ben and Jerry's. But then,. **they** started. <high-pitched, exaggerated intonation: **Mamita**, mama**cita**, grin**guita**, amor**cita**, cap**ulla**, [kissing noises:] mw mw mw mw mw mw mw mw mw mw!> Then, they got **nasty.** Men screaming shit out. Talking about my ass, my pussy. How they wanted to fuck me, lick me, when and where and what position it was dis**gus**ting!

Tiffany's explicit reporting of sexual talk of men on the street serves a number of functions.[14] The description of such behavior constructs Mt. Pleasant as a place where sexually explicit street remarks made by men to women are part of everyday life. Furthermore, Tiffany's stance towards such behavior argues that such behavior is inappropriate, and justifies women's uncomfortableness or fear of walking on Mt. Pleasant streets. But the messages conveyed do not stop here, for we must remember that Tiffany's voicing of the men's comments is itself embedded in the Pelón frame, as part of a story which serves as an argumentation for the premise that some people do not "live at peace with themselves in the place." As part of this argumentation, Tiffany's stance towards the men on the street indexes the notion that urban people can handle "urban problems" and, conversely, that people who cannot handle the urban environment are not urban people. So even while it critiques the sexist behavior of men on the street, Tiffany's lack of tolerance for street comments (as well as, perhaps, her deeming it important or noteworthy enough to comment on) creates a non-urban identity for her. At the same time, Pelón's oppositional stance towards Tiffany distances him from her, the opposite of the way that Camila is aligned with Pelón. It is worth noting that both the alignment and the opposition, combined with the expression of his own fearlessness of these same streets, also create urban legitimacy for the Pelón character.

But Tiffany's fear is not completely irrational: Through her accounting of dangerous events in the neighborhood – which start with the street comments above – we see some legitimate reasons for her to be fearful:

After I was followed home one day, at two **in** the **morn**ing, coming back from Habana Village. I never felt safe anymore. That night, I had to run to 7–11, wait for a cop to come in and **beg** them to walk me home. After that, I didn't feel safe anymore. Day or night, it just didn't matter. **Then**, they break into my car. [. . .] Then, they had the nerve to break into the group house. [. . .] **Then**, m- my roommate, one of the housemates, the one that lives on the third floor, **she** gets robbed at knifepoint around the corner from the house.

Being followed home, robbed, and mugged at knifepoint all connect Tiffany's fear to actual dangerous events, and thus construct her fear as rational and reasonable. However, these events do not constitute Tiffany's real reasons for leaving the neighborhood, as is made clear with the utterance that begins the next segment of the scene:

But what really did it was an encounter I had with one of the kids I was working with.

With the contrastive marker "but," the dangerous incidents in Tiffany's list are distinguished from the "real" reasons for her leaving:

But what really did it- was an encounter I had with one of the kids I was working with. 16 year old kid, had been assigned to me after he punched my co-worker Li- Lino on the nose. This was an angry kid. He had already been in and out of prison for the **third** time. He was mea:n, unconsiderate, and **nasty**. I'd been trying to work with him for about a month. **Then**- I see him, smoking marijuana with his buddies, on the sidewalk. And what was I to do? I confronted him in one of our counseling sessions. And why did I do that? He- went off: Oh what right do you have to come in here, and get some sorry-ass salary at the expense of my fuckups. You know that you're doing this, not because you care, but because you want to feel **good** about yourself, don't you! He called me, a lily-White bitch. A rich do-gooder. A goody-goody White girl. He said, I like Latin dick and that's why I was here. Then- he talks loud in that deranged, way of his. And to top it off, he reaches into the inside pocket of his jacket and takes out, a beer. And starts taking swigs out of it, right there in front of me.

Despite the physical threats to person and property which Tiffany has experienced or witnessed, in the end it's not these things, but rather her client's threat to Tiffany's authority (through his smoking and drinking in front of her) and his challenge to her legitimacy as an authentic Mt. Pleasantite (through the question, "What right do you have to come in here" and his evaluation of her motives for being "here"), which she cannot abide.

Framing Relationships: Tiffany and Men on the Street

In addition to the above strategies, Avilés also accomplishes the peripheralization of the Tiffany character through his use of framing. This is clear particularly if we compare the Tiffany framing to the framing of the Camila scene.

Recall that in the Camila scene, it's Camila who engages in behavior that we've seen is characterized in public discourse (for better or for worse) as *urban* – drinking, smoking, swearing, addressing strangers confrontationally in public space. In the Tiffany scene, it is the male characters who engage in this behavior, separated from Tiffany by a more defined frame shift than is the case in the Camila piece; the frame shifts in Tiffany's narration are introduced explicitly as reported speech with the utterances, "Then, they started," and "He went off." It is also worth noting that it is these male characters who, like Camila and unlike Tiffany, are represented as being already in the space, rather than coming to it.

Tiffany's disalignment from the neighborhood is also accomplished through Avilés' choice to narrate her stories in the past tense (as opposed to the present tense in Camila's case), as well as the use of indirect discourse to represent reported speech. The Tiffany character uses both direct and indirect discourse to voice men on the street. In the case of the catcalling men, she uses direct discourse for the less sexually explicit utterances:

> But then, **they** started. **Mamita**, mama**cita**, grin**guita**, amor**cita**, cap**ulla**, [kissing noises:] mw mw mw mw mw mw mw mw mw mw!

However, the utterances that directly follow this – utterances that deal with sexuality and race – are written in indirect discourse. In the first case, the switch from direct to indirect discourse at "Men screaming shit out" serves to differentiate between vocatives which do not have a semantically negative denotation (diminutives of "mama," "gringa,"[15] and "love," and "[flower] bud" – words that can be used as terms of endearment among intimates), on the one hand, and lewd sexual comments that Tiffany explicitly defines as "nasty" and "disgusting," on the other. (Vocatives are terms used to directly address someone, often in order to get their attention. Proper names and terms of endearments are vocatives, as in "Wanna go to the movies, Honey?," or "Gretchen, what do you think?")

> Then, they got **nasty**. Men screaming shit out. Talking about my ass, my pussy. How they wanted to fuck me, lick me, when and where and what position it was dis**gus**ting!

A similar phenomenon occurs in the social work client section, which starts out in direct discourse:

> Oh what right do you have to come in here, and get some sorry-ass salary at the expense of my fuckups. You know that you're doing this, not because you care, but because you want to feel **good** about yourself, don't you!

This also is followed by a switch from direct to indirect discourse:

> He called me, a lily-White bitch. A rich do-gooder. A goody-goody White girl. He said, I like Latin dick and that's why I was here.

Here, the switch separates the client's calling into question of Tiffany's motives for coming to the neighborhood and to her job, from the more explicit insults. The switch again serves a distancing function; through it Tiffany opposes herself to the ideas and attitudes expressed by the insults, and she shows great offense at the remarks.

Additional linguistic strategies enhance Tiffany's tenuous positioning: In the first utterance of this section, "Oh, what right do you have to come here," the verb *come* and the deictic *here* set up the character of the client as located in (and part of) the deictic center of the community, while these words position Tiffany outside of that center.

Tiffany's tenuous anchoring in the neighborhood is also reinforced through the client's attention to and negative evaluation of her Whiteness, ("a lily-White bitch" and "a goody-goody White girl") and wealth ("a rich do-gooder") which contrast her to local ideologies of urbanness, and her "goody-goodyness" which contrasts with the brazenness of the beer-drinking kid whom Avilés uses in this scene to represent urban life.

The utterance "he said I like Latin dick and that's why I was here" also reinforces Tiffany's migrant status. In positing that Tiffany came to the neighborhood to satiate her desire for exotified and sexualized ethnic diversity, Avilés aligns her with the commodified diversity that Pelón disdained in the intro to the scene.[16] The "Latin dick" utterance also implies that the place she came from did not have such ethnic difference. This aligns her with an ethnically homogeneous place, and such an alignment serves to further dislocate her from the ethnically diverse Mt. Pleasant.

Also important in the analysis of this utterance is that it is placed in a compendium of the beer drinker's utterances which include comments about Tiffany's Whiteness. These comments connect Whiteness to the negative qualities of being "a bitch" and "goody-goody." By virtue of its placement, the utterance "He said I like Latin dick" also gets aligned with Whiteness, and particularly with a negative Whiteness; in this way, desire of exotified/sexualized difference is constructed as a White characteristic.

In the Tiffany scene, indirect discourse firmly locates the profane and sexual language – what we can call *dirty language* – firmly outside Tiffany's frame. Thus, the use of indirect discourse further distances the Tiffany character from such language use and the urban identity it's representing here. Even when Tiffany is shown as *wanting to* engage in this kind of talk, she can't. The scene ends with her reaction to her client's behavior, and her consequent decision to leave the neighborhood:

> Then- he talks loud in that deranged, way of his. And to top it off, he reaches into the inside pocket of his jacket and takes out, a beer. And starts taking swigs out of it, right there in front of me. At that moment. At that moment. I started trembling. My blood started **boiling**. I was furious No I was fucking pissed! I wanted to tell him to go to hell! to go fuck himself and his mother.

Here Tiffany fantasizes about hurling curse-filled and unmitigated insults at her client, insults which would match the intensity of her emotion at the moment described. The register which she imagines employing is that which Avilés has constructed (through the client as well as through other characters in the play) as the language of the street – in other words, urban language. Actually using such language, then, would be a way for Tiffany to set up an urban identity for herself. However, she is not up to this task:

> But not one word would come out. [. . .] I got up from that chair and ran out of that room because I could **fee:l** the tears coming. I passed one of the receptionists. She asked me- if everything was okay I didn't answer. By the time I got to the bathroom, I had a thunderstorm coming out of my eyes. And that- . that did it. That's it. I'm outa here.

Instead of matching the "urban" actions and discourse of her client with her own example of "urban" discourse, Tiffany flees the room and starts crying. These actions document her inability to handle urban life, and, as they are stereotypically feminine behavior, they also serve to feminize her. The fact that the incident with this client ultimately impels her to leave the neighborhood for good, only confirms her positioning as a peripheral Mt. Pleasantite and inauthentic urban dweller.

It is clear from the above excerpts that the character Tiffany is painted as having a very different relationship to "urban" activities and public spaces than Camila does. Whereas Camila revels in the public space, Tiffany narrates begging a cop to walk her home and not feeling safe day or night after being followed once. Where the Camila character uses profane language, Tiffany's profanity is used only in narration, never in direct discourse. Finally, instead of engaging in aggressive confrontation, she is represented as fleeing confrontation with the ideologically feminized behavior of crying.

Avilés' emblem of the neighborhood's White women is thus scared of the public space, she shies away from talking about race explicitly (even though she indexes it implicitly in a number of ways), she is accused of being "a goody-goody White girl" – epithets which clearly contrast her with the working-class bad-girl behaviors and markers of Latina-ness used to construct Camila.

The Tiffany character serves as a forum to air the issue of gendered inequalities in regard to rights to public space, and Tiffany's voicing of the catcalling men makes clear the sexist nature of the kinds of comments addressed to women of all ethnicities on the street. However, because of the complex voicing system that Avilés has created, because Tiffany's critique of such street behavior is embedded within the frame of Pelón's discussion of fear and people who do not live at peace with themselves, Tiffany's views are delegitimized.

This framing also serves to position Pelón in opposition to Tiffany, which consequently reinforces Pelón's own anchoring and positive positioning as a core community member who, as we remember from the beginning of the piece, is not afraid of anything.

Larger Frames of Reference: The Playwright and the Community

The last layer of *Chaos Standing* is the frame of public discourse in Mt. Pleasant within which *Chaos Standing* is situated. As discussed earlier, in publicly performed safety talk, White women civic group members often talk of being made to feel unsafe by Latino men whom these women portray as dangerous forces lurking on the street. Through this talk Latino men get marginalized as deviant and peripheral community members, and these marginalizations play out in public policy like no-loitering ordinances.

Given this context, Avilés' piece on fear becomes a contestation of the kind of marginalization which occurs in talk at public forums. Avilés turns this talk on its head in his own public venue, using the same themes – ethnicity, fear, sexualization – to switch the positioning of White women and Latino men in the moral geography of the neighborhood. In the grant proposal the men on the street's purported Latin American roots, "harrassing of women," and making women feel uncomfortable on Mt. Pleasant St. were all used to marginalize Latino men. In *Chaos Standing*, however, Tiffany's Whiteness, her fear of the men on the street, and her not being able to handle sexually explicit comments, marginalizes her. At the same time, the Camila character's performance of a tough, working-class, and Latina femininity constructs her legitimacy. Avilés thus tweaks the conflation of gender, ethnicity, class, and community belonging prevalent in public discourse, but he does not call this conflation into question, and this precludes a way of addressing actual neighborhood problems.

Audience reactions

On a number of occasions after *Chaos Standing* was performed, Avilés participated in discussions with the audience. These discussions were generally facilitated by the show's director, or by other people prominent in the DC arts scene. The discussions provided a forum for audience members to voice their reactions to *Chaos Standing*. Invariably, a few White women critiqued the Tiffany piece. (In the particular discussion I observed, the Tiffany character was actually the only character in the show that the audience commented about specifically, although a number of African American women commented about the lack of African American women characters in the play.) What was striking to me about these Tiffany critiques was that they did nothing to fundamentally challenge the conflations discussed above. For example, Robin, a White woman in the audience the night I attended the play, remarked,

> One of the things I found interesting was that – all of the, the White people **in** the piece, um, you know the yuppies moving in, the money moving in, Tiffany and um, other people, were all kind of negative and unsympathetic, and kind of- cause everybody else, I thought-even if there was not bad or good- they were very complex and rich. And, you know, um you asked at first, do you see yourself in this piece, and I see a lot of my friends and my neighbors and everybody else – but I'm not really sure that, I see myself there cause I didn't come in as an intern, I don't have a lot of money, I consider myself a community member, I work in the neighborhood, I sit there and dis all the suburbanites that come in on the weekends cause I work at a bar, you know, and we see them come in, we talk about the busses bringing them in.

Although Robin did try to delink Whiteness and class ("I didn't come as an intern [and] I don't have a lot of money"), her remark nevertheless reinforces the idea that community insiderness is connected with working-class status and an opposition to suburbia.

Because the main gist of this comment was about ethnicity and community identity, it was on that front that Avilés responded, taking the opportunity to go on record about the importance of voicing a Latino perspective in the public discourse:

> The answer to that question is like, where are you – what's your political stance, where if you're Latino, and what you see these people doing [. . .] that's part of the world.

On the heels of Avilés' remarks, the discussion facilitator, a local African American poet, commented on his own experience of portraying White characters:

> I've had the experience sometimes that, someone says, well you know you're not fleshing out your, your White characters. So sometimes what you'll find – you'll find the White [characters] are all fleshed out – they're actually **more** fleshed out than their own – characters of their own culture.

Clearly, the post-performance discussion provided an important forum for community members across ethnoracial and political divides to listen to each others' perspectives; particularly, it provided a rare community forum in which Latino and African American community members were able to publicly express their views to White community members and contest White views about ethnicity, power, and community belonging. But the discussion left submerged the problematic ways that ethnicity gets entangled in public discourse with gender, class, safety and danger, toughness, and urban legitimacy.

Taken in tandem, the *Chaos Standing* scenes on joy and fear create an alternate view of neighborhood legitimacy, a perspective that contests dominant public neighborhood discourses that marginalize Latinos, and particularly Latino men. But this alternate model, with its valorizing of danger and fearlessness, reinforces the prevalent construction of a public space to which men and women have unequal rights of access, where women can gain access rights only by enacting an aggressive, confrontational stance. The prevailing ideologies of danger and fear make it extremely difficult to have meaningful public discussions about risk and safety. In community meetings on safety, for example, it is difficult to get and keep the floor without engaging these discourses. Speakers who take a feminist stance on women's rights to public space without explicitly confronting and disclaiming stereotypes of Latino men end up reinforcing the peripheral positioning of Latinos common in local public discourse. However, those who do try to confront the ways in which these discourses marginalize Latinos are often deemed by meeting convenors as interactionally off-topic, and by meeting attendees as ideologically anti-feminist.

Alternate Views: Neighborly Loitering

Despite the limits of public discourse, however, alternate local characterizations of gender, fear, and community identity do exist. Like Gabi in chapter 3, Gabi's neighbor Grace is also not fond of being catcalled. As she explains, "Now I don't walk through Pigeon Park because I don't like – the people that sit out there I mean they always have something to say to you." But in the end, she values public interaction despite its sometime annoyances:

> I have more likes than dislikes. [. . .] People are very friendly in this neighborhood. [. . .] You can talk to anyone on the street here, I guess that's the reason why I like it. Whenever I went to the grocery store and I had like four heavy bags in my hands you know bringing home, Um like one of those fellows that will drink a lot on the corner there? Although they're drinking a lot, on about three occasions they offered to carry my bags home and I accepted it. And you know I gave them like a dollar. I think it was very nice. When they ask to carry my bags I feel really grateful about that, I appreciate it. It makes you appreciate everyone.

And Jennifer, a teenager much like the Camila character who spends a fair amount of time hanging out on Mt. Pleasant St., points to the way that public interaction can strengthen community ties, build social networks, and spread knowledge, when she complains that Mt. Pleasant is like a village, that everyone knows everyone and when you're hanging on the corner with your friends, someone's aunt is bound to walk by and report to your mother what you're doing. Similarly,

Jennifer's neighbor Veronica remarks that Mt. Pleasant St. is a good place for her son to play because the people on the street watch out for him and will tell her if anything happens.

These views show a Mt. Pleasant which is vibrant and safe because of the people who use public space for *many* purposes – not just for consumption. These views – which are virtually never represented in public discourse venues – argue for community development projects that preserve public space and consider interaction in it a resource for community building.

Notes

1 Emergency Medical Technician
2 This is a reference to the wealthy and predominantly White area on the other side of Rock Creek Park which is often considered a safe part of town. This is the same street Boaz in chapter 3 refers to.
3 Sibley (1995:51)
4 Bateson (1972)
5 These scholars all draw on the influential work of Mikhail Bakhtin (1981) on voicing and the dialogic nature of reported speech.
6 There is a third scene that has a female character, an eight-year-old girl. This character presents what the perspective of a child might be like, and gender does not play a significant role in this scene the way it does in the two scenes under analysis here.
7 It is true that, in the above excerpt, the character of Pelón describes himself as coming from El Salvador, and lists a number of things that did make him fearful upon his first coming to the neighborhood. However, as we'll see a little further on, Pelón constructs Mt. Pleasant as a Latino place. Thus, his own characterization as a Salvadoran aligns him with the identity he has constructed of the place, positioning him as a core member of the Mt. Pleasant community. Furthermore, the items which he lists as making him fearful – going to the post office, asking the bus driver for directions, taking a cab, and going to a store or restaurant where the salespeople do not speak Spanish – all relate to institutions or places *outside of* or not associated with Mt. Pleasant. Therefore, they do nothing to mitigate Pelón's identity as a Mt. Pleasantite. Also, this is an identity that grows as the character's longevity in the neighborhood grows.
8 *Hooky parties* are parties held during the day while teenagers are skipping school or *playing hooky*.

9   This can also be translated as "Let's go to 18th and Columbia."

10 Creaky-voice is a type of articulation at the lowest pitch of a speaker's pitch range, where the vocal chords vibrate irregularly and at a very low frequency, producing a "creaky" sound. Norma Mendoza-Denton found that the group of girls she studied used creaky-voice in stories about gang fights (but never, for example, in talk to teachers or parents) to create an aura of toughness.

11 Although *la mara* means *gang* in both the 'group of friends' and 'organized gang' senses, Avilés states that his intention here is to use it to refer to Camila and her friends, without any gang connotations.

12 According to Avilés, both of these narratives are meant to be interpreted as reportings of interactions the Camila character took part in.

13 See, for example, Deborah Schiffrin (1981) and Barbara Johnstone (1990).

14 It's true that Tiffany does use profane language, and Avilés's depiction of Tiffany using such language shows the character as someone who has some connection with this urban environment. She has, after all, chosen to come to the neighborhood. She made friends in the neighborhood and is described as having been friends with the protagonist character Pelón, she's voiced things about the neighborhood that she liked, and she is familiar with the way people talk and able to use profanity when talking *about* people. But she only uses profanity when talking about others who are not present. This is quite different from the Camila character, who is portrayed as cursing in direct confrontations.

15 While some Mt. Pleasantites consider this term to be offensive, others often do not. The pragmatic valence of the term is contested among both Spanish speakers and non-Spanish speakers.

16 This echoes the Pelón character's comments about Tiffany's exotification of Latino culture in his introduction to Tiffany: She "fell in **love** with the crowd at **Habana Village**. She thought that Latinos had a cool culture about them, an air about them, something. She made friends. She would visit them, on, the weekends at their group houses and their apartments. She just **loved** the feel of **things** around here."

CHAPTER 6

KEEPING IT IN THE FAMILY

Security

Again, the storage room in the basement of my apartment building, the Danforth, has been broken into. They didn't take too much from my unit — just my ex's old bike and a big backpack, I guess to help cart out the more valuable stuff they stole from the other units. What's worse, the same guys held up Lorena's son Mark and stole his keys. He's okay, but now we have to change all the locks — the storage room, the front door, the back door — some of my neighbors even want to change the laundry room lock. As usual, the opinions about how to deal with security range from the lackadaisical — we've reached the limit of how many times this can happen; to the rational — let's get new locks; to the impractical — let's have a raffle to raise money for around-the-clock security guards; to the wildly flamboyant — let's get a voice-activated key-card system. I know all this because, in my capacity as assistant floor captain of the 3rd floor, I've been subjected to a lot of pontificating as a result of my pleas and encouragements to get my neighbors to attend a security meeting that some of the building's old-timers are organizing.

My building is a microcosm of the neighborhood — half limited-equity low-income co-op, half market-rate condo,[1] with lots of renters, we span the age, class, and ethnicity spectrum of Mt. Pleasant. At the moment the spectrum has made it downstairs to the circle of folding chairs in the small basement meeting room sandwiched between the laundry facilities and the storage units. Irene, one of the longtime co-op members who's organized the meeting, suggests that we get started with a round of names. The curly blond-headed guy sitting upright next to Irene introduces himself as a new condo owner on the 6th floor, and asks who are condo owners and who are co-op owners. Sabine, the mod girl from the 5th floor with Doc Martens and henna'ed hair who I always think of as Danish despite the lack of any evidence to support that particular theory, eyes him warily, drops her chin just a bit, narrows her eyes, and says, "We're not condo owners or co-op owners or owners or renters. We're neighbors, and we're getting together to discuss our building."

Although I was primarily at this meeting to participate in the discussion of security issues in the building, the researcher in me had of course brought along a notebook for just such interactions. I opened it up and quickly jotted down, "I wonder if Sabine's been spending time with co-op members lately."

The Danforth Co-op and Condo

The history of the Danforth is not unlike that of other apartment buildings in Mt. Pleasant and elsewhere in the city that have undergone major demographic shifts in the course of the past century. The Danforth was built in 1905, at a time when Mt. Pleasant was an elite and somewhat bucolic neighborhood on the outer edges of the city. The building was commissioned by a high-ranking European diplomat and the son of a US senator. Displaying the grandeur of its times, the building boasted two parlors, a ballroom with 17-foot-high ceilings and intricately detailed moldings, two equally well-appointed public dining rooms, and a pharmacy with lunch counter which remained in business until the mid-sixties.

As the neighborhood changed through the years, so did the Danforth. With the end of legally enforceable segregation in 1948,[2] in the 1950s more African Americans, of varying class backgrounds, moved into the building, and middle- or upper-middle-class Whites moved out. In the 1960s, as was the case in the neighborhood as a whole,[3] middle-class residents left the Danforth in increasing numbers. The poor, mostly African American, residents who stayed were joined in this and the following decade by new residents originally from Latin America and the Caribbean, as well as from elsewhere in the neighborhood or the city. By the beginning of the 1970s, most of the tenants were Latino and African American, and some were White.

As the Danforth aged and the neighborhood lost its elite cachet, owning the building became increasingly less profitable. Rather than making the costly repairs that would be needed to bring the building up to code,[4] in 1964 the owners, descendants of the original building financiers, sold the building. The Danforth residents had few resources to pressure the new owner to attend to building maintenance and repair. Consequently, this new owner let the building run down to the point that the elevators ceased to work and there was frequently no heat or hot water. Finally, in the mid-1970s, this owner gave away the building and its 681 housing code violations[5] to a local law school as a tax write-off.

The school decided to turn the Danforth into dormitories or a classroom building, but abandoned those plans when faced with opposition from the both the tenants and their own law students, who sided with the tenants. They hired a management company to run the building. The company, whose leaders were eventually indicted, stole $153,821 of the tenants' rent money and neglected to pay up to $225,000 in bills.[6] In 1977, with the building in disastrous condition, the school decided to try to sell it and offered tenants $10,000 each to leave. While many tenants took the money, the residents of 28 of the 65 apartments elected to stay and fight for ownership. With the help of a local community organization and a number of law school students, these tenants formed the Danforth Cooperative Association, established an escrow fund into which they paid monthly rent, and led a difficult fight to gain ownership of their building.

The struggle for ownership was led by two women, whom I will refer to as Mrs. Wallace and Louisa.[7] Other co-op members often talked about these women as the matriarchs of the building. Although both women and men participated in activities and events to gain ownership, it tended to be predominantly women who orchestrated and took part in activities such as meetings, building cleaning, and security patrols. In many ways, organization of and participation in these activities was similar to the activities that they performed in the domestic sphere of their own apartments.

Although the co-op was ultimately successful in their fight, the road to ownership was not without its tribulations. At the end of 1978, after several nasty battles between the co-op association, the law school, and a number of developers who wanted to buy the building, the District government bought it. They agreed to renovate the Danforth and then sell it back to the tenants after the renovations were complete. The District's massive mismanagement of the project – including the hiring of contractors who stole all the original and costly brass fixtures in the hallways and apartments and all the turn-of-the-century cast-iron bathtubs – resulted in a string of different management companies and contractors, who ripped out the first renovations and started all over.

Finally, in 1984, under the direction of a private property management company, the renovations were completed, and the co-op association gained partial ownership of the building. The management company, who themselves gained ownership of three commercial units in the building's lower level, advised the co-op association that it would be very difficult to sell the remaining apartments as co-op units,[8] and encouraged them to offer them on the market as condominiums. Starting in 1984, then, new condo owners joined the original co-op members as residents in the Danforth. The building set up an organizational structure with a condo board as well as a co-op board, with two seats on the condo board occupied by members of the co-op, and the co-op voting as a block on all items to be decided by the condo association constituency.

The renovation split up some of the larger apartments, so that the original 65-unit number increased to 85. Since the renovation, the Danforth's population has included condo owners and co-op members[9] as well as tenants who rent apartments from both condo and co-op landlords. Whereas the co-op members are by and large working class,[10] the condo owners, part of the wave of gentrifiers moving into the neighborhood in increasing numbers in the mid-1980s, are generally middle- to upper-middle class. The renters are a mix. The diversity of class backgrounds causes not a small bit of tension among Danforth residents, because class backgrounds often correlate with divergent ideas about appropriate interaction with neighbors and uses of public spaces such as hallways and the front entrance. These conflicts echo larger conflicts in the neighborhood about use of public space. In terms of ethnicity, more of the condo owners are White, while the majority of the co-op members are African American, Latino, and Caribbean/Caribbean American. The renters, again, are a mix.

The story of the Danforth plays an important role in the history of housing policy in DC. It is because of this housing struggle that there now exists in DC a *right of first refusal*, which mandates that any tenant has the first right to buy their residence if the owner wants to sell it.[11]

A Different Kind of Authority

In this chapter I want to focus on the experiences of the co-op members in organizing for housing rights. These stories serve as an instructive case study of how people use discourse to include and exclude others and to construct centralized and marginalized identities, and how they put these discourses towards political purposes. Whereas in the previous chapters I've examined how neighbors in Mt. Pleasant marginalize each other through constructing and highlighting ethnic difference, in this chapter I analyze stories about my apartment building in which one group of neighborhood residents worked *across* ethnic boundaries to create a tight-knit community and organize politically. At the same time as these storytellers created positive identities for themselves as community members, however, they – like the performance artist in chapter 5 and the grantwriters in chapter 4 – also create negative and marginalized identities for some of their neighbors, namely some of the building's condo owners.

Danforth co-op members use discourse strategies that are not very common in other neighborhood talk – namely, themes of family – to accomplish the same kinds of alignments and oppositions to place that we have seen elsewhere. Through such alignments and oppositions, co-op members show themselves as adhering to a set of values that they link to the core community inhabiting the Danforth. At the same time, in these stories new residents of the building disregard the values of the Danforth community. This opposition distances them from the building community, and thus from the values of place.

The co-op members' stories fit into the larger discourse of the neighborhood in two ways. First, they accomplish the same kind of inclusion and exclusion based on value systems that they link to place. Second, in their stories of the struggle for building ownership and of the subsequent architectural alterations and population shifts that occurred after they gained ownership, co-op members describe the changes of their building as emblematic of changes occurring in the neighborhood in the same time period. Co-op members use their stories, then, to represent the meanings and implications of neighborhood change at a smaller level.

What was striking to me in analyzing the Danforth stories was the way that *family* and *kinship* terms structure both the storytellers' descriptions of the co-op association and its members, as well as their characterizations of the relationships and interactions among the members. These terms work at what I'll call both a macro and micro level. At the micro level, kinship terms construct individual co-op members as *family people*, while at the macro level, such terms serve metaphorically to construct the co-op community itself as an extended family.

In addition to discourse of family, Danforth co-op members use many of the same themes that other neighbors invoke – city vs. suburb, diversity, safety and danger, fearlessness and fear. However, one striking difference between the Danforth stories and public neighborhood discourse is the way that the co-op residents talk about danger and fearlessness. Where public discourse often constructs fearlessness as a masculine quality, the Danforth residents give it a decidedly feminine edge, linking it with female community role models and an attitude of protectiveness towards the community. As is common in other speech communities, the Danforth stories connect female power with ideas associated with the role of mothering, such as protecting and nurturing. Where public discourse of danger and fear often conflate women's interests with gentrifier interests, Danforth stories very clearly distinguish these two groups, portraying the interests and values of female co-op members as often at odds with their newer and wealthier neighbors.

Another phenomenon that I want to investigate in this chapter is the co-op members' invocations of public and private spheres. In the Danforth co-op stories, residents put the family metaphor to use in their political organizing strategies, arguing for better housing from the position of mothers with small children, for example. In so doing, they blur the boundary between the private sphere of the home and the public sphere of politics.

Many feminist scholars have noted that the ideological split between public and private does not bear out in practice. For example, it is women's traditional responsibility over children and households that often puts them in the position of interacting with public or state institutions such as schools, landlords, welfare offices, etc.[12] As the linguistic anthropologist Bonnie McIlhenny[13] notes, particularly for poor women, the scrutiny of the state into the goings-on in their private lives – for example by welfare officers evaluating qualification for aid – belies the separation of public and private spheres. As the stories below will show, Danforth residents capitalize on an inter-penetration of spheres to work in their interests in their dealings with the city government.

At the same time as they blur the distinction between public and private for organizing purposes, however, within the community the co-op members actively create a boundary between private and pub-lic, linking these constructs to insider and outsider identity. The co-op members employ a distinction between public and private space in order to demarcate the space of the building as their own, and to separate themselves from newer post-renovation residents, whom they strategically refer to as "the public." This is somewhat akin to the linguistic anthropologist Susan Gal's analysis of the ways that people distinguish between public and private in the US and East Central Europe.[14] Gal notes that the categories of public and private are ideo-logically potent across many contexts – the concepts of public and private are major categories that people use to organize space – but that there's an incredible amount of variation across time, space, and situation in what counts as private and what counts as public, and how the public and the private are seen to relate to each other. In the case of the Danforth, the malleable relationship between public and pri-vate allows the co-op members to place these constructs in different configurations in relation to each other, in order to accomplish mul-tiple political and spatial goals.

Some Background on Community Development, Gender, and Metaphor

Before jumping right into the analysis, I want to explain some of the reasons why I think these stories are important, and what an under-standing of them can contribute to affordable housing endeavors specifically and community development more generally. In order to contextualize the Danforth struggle within the larger frame of community development work in North America, it is helpful to have some background on housing organizing in general, as well as specifically on women's organizing roles. Additionally, because much of what I'll be analyzing here is metaphor, before getting into the metaphor analysis itself I want to provide a brief explanation of the mechanics of metaphors – how metaphors work, how they highlight some phenomena while obscuring others.

What co-op stories can tell us about tenant organizing

As environmental psychologist Heléne Clark found in her work on co-op movements in New York City,

> An important way that co-op members created and continue to create social integration and communication, building and reinforcing shared value systems and norms, is through talking about their experiences in what one resident referred to as "the war years."[15]

Analyzing co-op members' stories[16] can help us to better understand how residents integrated the structures of their daily social life into their political struggle and dealings with city government. In addition, such analysis can provide insight into how the co-op community is reconstructed and kept alive among Danforth residents today, at a time when the co-op association has a much weaker presence in residents' day-to-day lives, and their interactions with each other are likewise less intensive.

Because co-op members' energies were focused on fighting for ownership of their building for such a long time, and felt such a personal stake in the achievement of ownership, co-op members' identities as Danforth people have been deeply rooted in the ups and downs of the building over the years. This connection of people to place also makes co-op stories useful tools for examining how cooperatives are established. Analyzing the language that the co-op members use to talk about themselves and their struggle can help to provide detailed insight into some of the ways that empowerment works in housing organizing, and what makes a successful co-op.

Stories told about the co-op struggle relate to both present and past contexts. As stories told to people like me – newer residents of the Danforth who moved in after the building renovation – the stories socialize us into the values and social norms of the co-op community. And through members' re-tellings of these stories to *each other*, community values and norms are remembered and reinforced.

Finally, the stories can impart important information about how to wage a successful housing struggle. But a caveat is in order here: As much discourse analytic work has shown,[17] stories are anything but simple, straightforward, accurate accounts of past experiences. Discourse analysts are careful to point out that narratives should be understood not for what they tell us about the past per se, but rather for what they tell us about the relation of the *reconstruction* of a past event to a present context and narrator. For example, if I tell you a story about something stupid that I did, that story functions not to paint a picture of me as an idiot, but rather to create an image of me as someone who has the insight to reflect upon and evaluate their actions, someone who can laugh at themselves or take things in their stride, etc.

At the same time, it is significant that tellers of the Danforth stories – speakers of different generations, many of whom rarely socialize with each other anymore, and some of whom have long since moved out of the building – use the same linguistic strategies when talking about the co-op struggle almost twenty years after the fact. Their stories are filled with kinship terms that create metaphors of family, and the storytellers use these terms in remarkably similar ways to construct and deconstruct public and private spheres, and to present a co-op value system which is portrayed as integral to the co-op struggle.

Gender and organizing

The Danforth co-op stories also have much to tell us about the role of gender in community organizing. Community organizing researchers have found that much successful organizing at the neighborhood level brings "'private sphere' problems of household and family into the 'public sphere' of the broader community, demonstrating the essential integration of these spheres in daily life"[18] and that such actions often go hand-in-hand with a strategy that exploits traditional gendered roles for political purposes.[19] One particularly powerful trope in this regard is that of motherhood; women from such divergent groups as peace activists,[20] Ku Klux Klan women[21] and striking garment workers[22] have rhetorically used their identity as mothers to build legitimacy for their perspectives and positions in political struggles. As we will see in the Danforth case, this strategy can be particularly useful for women who have been disempowered because of their class or ethnic positions.

Metaphor

One last area of scholarship that it's important to know something about before getting to the stories is the study of metaphor. Metaphor is a system in which a source domain – the domain to which the metaphorical language refers – is used to explain a target domain – the domain under discussion. In the case of the co-op members' metaphors, family is the source domain, while the group of co-op members is the target domain. Linguist George Lakoff and philosopher Mark Johnson[23] use the source and target domain terminology to explain how speakers understand particular concepts by applying characteristics of a source domain to a new domain. They argue that the power of metaphor lies in its ability to invoke certain ideas about a source domain without being explicit; because interpreters understand the new target domain through the lens of the source domain, many assumptions get "snuck in" to interpreters' perceptions of the target domain. This process highlights some features of the source domain, while obscuring others. For example, the geographer Neil Smith[24] found that popular and developers' discourse of gentrification had a preponderance of "frontier" and "wild west" metaphors. These metaphors served to portray gentrifiers as "urban pioneers": The frontier metaphor constructs gentrifying areas as unknown, empty spaces to be populated by adventurers. At the same time, the metaphor obscures the fact that people already live in gentrifying neighborhoods. Also, because Cowboy–Indian discourses of the "untamed frontier" are part and parcel of the "wild west" metaphorical system, the system may work to portray people already in gentrifying neighborhoods as dangerous and unknown Others. In the case of the Danforth, the co-op members' presentation of themselves as caring people goes a long way towards working against the dehumanization of people living in gentrifying or to-be-gentrified neighborhoods that the wild west metaphor promotes.

To Lakoff and Johnson's claim that our world view is shaped by metaphor, the anthropologist Naomi Quinn[25] has responded that metaphors do not simply create speaker orientations to the world, but that they also reflect speakers' cultural models. As she explains,

> [P]articular metaphors are selected by speakers, and are favored by these speakers, just because they provide satisfying mappings onto already existing cultural understandings – that is, because elements and relations between elements in the source domain make a good match with elements and relations among them in the cultural model.

In analyzing the Danforth co-op stories, I want to argue that kinship terms – in both their metaphorical and non-metaphorical uses – reflect and promote the co-op members' communal vision of the co-op and themselves both at the time of the co-op struggle and at present. The similar use of kinship terms, metaphors, events, and themes across co-op members' stories creates a shared coherence in terms of describing the co-op's social organization and political mobilization. It is in this sense that the stories can provide insight into the Danforth residents' actual process of achieving building ownership.

The discourse strategies that co-op members use in their stories are not *only* reflective of a cultural model (cultural here referring to the culture of the co-op community); these strategies also (re)construct it. Through using such kinship and other strategies in their stories, the co-op members both present and promote the cultural model of the co-op members as a family with a particular value system.

The Co-op Stories: Home and Family

In the co-op members' stories, the most prevalent construction of the Danforth is as a home inhabited and tended to by a caring family. This characterization contrasts with media portrayals at the time of the Danforth as "a run-down . . . apartment building"[26] of "mostly low-income blacks and Hispanics"[27] or "mostly domestics, janitors, nurses and dishwashers earning no more than $150 a week."[28] Constructing the building as a home – as a private, domestic space, inhabited by kin – is empowering on a number of levels. First, in a neighborhood (and no less in a city and a country) where homeowner–renter status was and continues to be a major means of social categorization, the co-op members' talk of themselves as homeowners rather than squatters is a way for them to show themselves as conforming to a middle-class US ideology which has it that homeowners are the backbone of strong and caring communities; this consequently creates a positive moral positioning for them among other neighborhood residents and city agencies.

The application of the home and family metaphor to tenant organizing served as a general empowerment strategy, but it was especially empowering to women. Constructing the building as private or domestic space creates a structure where women often have positions of authority.[29] Within the walls of the Danforth, women were the main force behind organizing and performing building maintenance, as well as leaders in the political organizing that the co-op members were engaged in. In the public venues in which the struggle was enacted (such as city council meetings and meetings with the mayor), women were the spokespeople for the building. The family and home discourse themes thus created leadership positions which utilized the power resources that the Danforth residents already had available to them, namely the social structures in which they participated in their daily lives.

The gender dynamics in the Danforth are characteristic of successful building upkeep and tenant organizing in other low-income apartment buildings in Mt. Pleasant and elsewhere. For example, in research on an apartment building down the street from the Danforth, Brett Williams[30] found that the social networks among women residents of the building "were at the heart of efforts to resist the deterioration of the building." This is in line with urban geographer Deborah Martin's[31] research in St. Louis where successful community action was rooted in social networks maintained and promoted by women, and in a discourse which "defined community organizing in terms of responsibility, family, and the material landscape."[32] Similarly, urban planner Jacqueline Leavitt and environmental psychologist Susan Saegert found in their study of co-op organizing in Harlem that

> [t]he predominance of female leaders in the coops studied and the similarity between their approaches to leadership and women's traditional roles provided the strongest link between domestic life and the organization of the co-op buildings.[33]

The use of domestic roles and relationships in organizing is not simply a utilitarian application of a structure from one sphere to another. Rather, it involves a significant amount of identity work – much of which is accomplished through discourse. As Heléne Clark remarks,

> Struggles for identity may, as in cooperatives, be struggles simultaneously over rights to space . . . [T]he home, as a site for both material and symbolic reproduction, is an important place in which women achieve identity and empowerment.[34]

Through blurring the boundaries between the domestic (private) and political (public) spheres – organizing around their identities as responsible family members fighting to provide their children with a proper home – the Danforth women utilized the power relations of the domestic sphere to achieve political power and influence in the public sphere.

Social Structure of the Danforth Community

Through the co-op members' stories, a model of a (partly metaphorical) kinship structure of loose extended families emerges. In this structure, there is an overall hierarchy of matriarchs, parents, and older and younger children. While some of these kinship roles are actual, others are metaphorical. For example, individual parents had actual kinship relationships with individual children. However, all adults had some degree of parental-like authority over all children. But despite this universal authority, adults' individual parental and/or marital statuses influenced their overall position in the hierarchy. (In these stories, being a parent conferred a higher or more "in-group" status than being married; thus the marital status of parents was not particularly relevant. However, being partnered was more statusful than being single.)

Some positions were not related to actual kinship ties. For example, Luisa, one of the leaders of the co-op struggle, achieved the role of *building matriarch* without having any children of her own.

In order to see how these kinship structures emerge in discourse, I focus on the stories of four Danforth residents, who can be grouped into two different roles within the Danforth community. The first group is parents. Mrs. Rosales was a young mother with two young children at the time of the co-op struggle, originally from urban Central America. Mrs. Patterson, originally from a small city in the Caribbean, had two teenage children and one adult child at the time of the co-op struggle. Kevin (whom we saw in chapter 3 talking about White people walking carefree on Mt. Pleasant St.) is her youngest child, and Grace (whom we saw at the end of the last chapter) is her middle child. Both Mrs. Rosales and Mrs. Patterson have served on the co-op board, and both have been co-op members on the condo board.

The next group consists of Sam (who discussed the diversity of Mt. Pleasant in chapter 3) and Joel, who were young, single men when they moved into the building in the late 1970s. In the metaphorical kinship system, Sam and Joel functioned like older sons. They both grew up in suburbs in the Northeast US – one the son of immigrant parents, the other with a family not too far removed from immigration. Both have served on the co-op and condo boards, and at the time these narratives were collected Joel was the co-op president.

In these four speakers' stories, the two people who figure most prominently are Luisa and Mrs. Wallace.[35] These women were the leaders in organizing the co-op struggle, and they are portrayed by the co-op members as both powerful leaders and conscientious mothers. They are the matriarchs of the building.

Macro- and Micro-Kinship Relations

From this kinship structure emerge two substructures: macro-kinship relations and micro-kinship relations. Macro relations relate to co-op members' roles within the larger co-op "family," while micro relations concern the kinship ties of individual co-op members. These two structures are instantiated in talk through what I will call *macro-kinship linguistic strategies* and *micro-kinship strategies*. Macro strategies use the metaphor of family and kinship to describe relations among co-op members as a corporate group. On the other hand, micro-kinship strategies highlight co-op members as family people by pointing to individual members' kinship ties.

The kinship strategies that the co-op members use to construct their community are also an important way of building cross–ethnic ties. In positing a social structure where all community members are connected to each other through numerous social links, the kinship model overrides ethnic distinctions. This means that, while ethnic distinctions among members of course exist, and while in practice social ties were and continue to be organized also by ethnicity, the kinship model crosscuts ethnic boundaries, providing for a social organization where ethnicity is not the most important category. At the same time, we shall see that the kinship model keeps intact and in fact utilizes other social categories, particularly gender.

Grandmothers and Granddaughters: Micro-Kinship Strategies

One common micro-kinship strategy is the identification of co-op members through kinship terms. For example, when Joel talks about who he used to socialize with, he doesn't only link his best friends in the building together as brothers, but he places them in a family network by highlighting their affinal (marital) and lineal (descendant) connections:

> It was really just myself and uh the, Flying Zavala Brothers, we called ourselves the Three Banditos. It was myself and Pedro Zavala, who was Angela's husband. And Eugene, whose daughter was just-

In a discussion between Mrs. Rosales and Mrs. Patterson, the two women use a similar strategy when answering a question posed by another conversation participant about the familial status of the original co-op members. **(Bolding indicates kinship terms; underlining marks repetition.)**

MEG:[36]	Were they all families, or were some of them single people, or?
MRS. R:	Single people, no- Mrs. Wal- She was, single maybe?
MRS. P:	Wallace, I don't know.
MRS. R:	She lived with, one **daughter**, right?
MRS. P:	And then her **husband**, her **husband** passed away. And she had her, um, **children**, and **grandchildren**.
MRS. R:	**Grandchildren**, uh huh.

MRS. P:	/???/. <u>Anna</u>₄ is her **granddaughter**, is that right?
MRS. R:	I don't remember if is.
MRS. P:	Yes, <u>Anna</u>₄ is her **granddaughter** that's right because she says her **grandmother**.
MRS. R:	Oh.
MRS. P:	Mrs. Wallace was-
MRS. R:	Two **granddaughters** and one **grandson**.
MRS. P:	**Grandson**.
MRS. R:	Right.
MRS. P:	And she had a **great grandson**, Anna's **children**.

In this example, Meg, the other conversation participant, makes kinship status salient through her question. What is striking about Mrs. Rosales' and Mrs. Patterson's response, then, is not that they frame it in terms of kinship, but rather that they go into so much detail to answer the question. Instead of simply answering with something like, "They were mostly families," the women instead elaborate Mrs. Wallace's kinship ties through four generations, identifying all her descendants primarily by kinship labels, as opposed to names. Furthermore, for the one family member for whom a name *is* used ("Anna is her granddaughter, is that correct?"), Mrs. Patterson makes an effort to establish whether or not she has the kinship relationship right, and then confirms that she does, through using the kinship term that Anna purportedly uses to identify Mrs. Wallace ("She says her grandmother").

In addition to the detailed description of kinship relations, both Mrs. Patterson and Mrs. Rosales engage in extensive repetition of kinship terms, thereby emphasizing the kinship relations. By detailing the kinship relations among Mrs. Wallace and the rest of her family, the two women construct her as a family person. This identity is reinforced elsewhere in the conversation, where they refer to Mrs. Wallace as "Anna's grandmother." Through her micro-kinship position as a mother, grandmother, and great-grandmother, Mrs. Wallace gains status within the macro-kinship hierarchy of the co-op community. In this way, macro- and micro-kinship structures are linked.

The sociolinguist Deborah Tannen[37] explains that repetition serves as an involvement strategy in talk, that builds solidarity between speakers. Through the combination of 1) the repetition strategy itself, and 2) the indexical relationship of the repeated terms to social structures valued within the community, Mrs. Rosales and Mrs. Patterson reinforce their own ties to the community as well as their ties to each other as neighbors, members of the community, and interlocutors who share memories and conversational strategies.

Another way that Danforth residents emphasize the micro family structure is by referring to the co-op group as "the families" – as opposed to "the tenants" or "the residents," for example. Often co-op members use this reference method when they're describing work that was done *in* the co-op building, and *for* the co-op ownership struggle. This is another way, then, that the residents' social, every-day life is integrated with the more political cooping process. For example, in discussing building maintenance, Mrs. Rosales remarks,

> The families, they had to clean their own floors, clean the steps and everything and report to the captain instead of paying someone to come in and do that you know.

Similarly, when Mrs. Patterson explains why the residents formed the co-op association, she says that "the families wanted to purchase the building."

Melding Public and Private

A macro strategy

The integration of family discourse with talk of the domestic life of the co-op on the one hand, and the struggle for ownership on the other, is also put to work to provide a justification for better hous-ing conditions and ownership. In telling about some of their strug-gle activities, Mrs. Patterson links family life in the co-op to dealing with city political institutions. In the following example, she uses a macro-family strategy, where she focuses on people's roles within the larger co-op family:

> Because I was here when we all went down to Abilard Center, the school down there, and we invited Mayor Barry to come. Luisa- Luisa had um babies' bottles and different things and- you know, she's a spokesperson. And she told him that how the babies had- I mean

ha- no heat! No hot water! And we had a lot of babies and those things you know.

Here, Mrs. Patterson focuses on the hardships that the Danforth residents had to endure, and through this focus she presents the co-opers *as a group* as family people who care about raising their children in a good environment.[38] Note that it is the co-op as a whole that is indexed by the pronoun "we" in "We had a lot of babies"; Mrs. Patterson at that time did not have any babies, nor did Luisa, who nevertheless is constructed as the person in charge of carrying the babies' bottles. In this way, responsibility for families translates into responsibility for the building, and strategies of coping in a particular set of domestic conditions get applied to the co-oping process. By portraying Luisa, the building spokesperson, as simultaneously talking to the mayor and carrying the babies' bottles, and *talking* to the mayor *about* babies, discourse like this also emphasizes the dual role of women in general in co-op domestic life and in the co-op struggle.

A micro strategy

The intermingling of domestic and political spheres can also be seen in Joel's discussion of difficulties for families, mothers, and children in the building. He uses the hardships imposed on families to explain and justify the need for and merits of the co-op's fight to gain building ownership:

> So here we were living in the nation's capital, in supposedly the civilized center of the world, and we were living like third-world people. Without any heat or hot water and there were families there with children, and, the mothers had to, you know boil hot water to draw baths for their kids.

In this remark, Joel also locates the Danforth's movement for improved housing within the larger political framework of Federal Washington. This contextualization points out the contrast between the condition of the Danforth building and the circumstances of its residents, and the location of the Danforth less than 40 blocks from the White House, the president's mansion that represents the United States' economic and political power.

Melding Macro and Micro

Sam

Another example of the kinship model working in service of the co-op struggle is the incorporation of Sam into the co-op, an incorporation at both the macro and micro levels of the kinship structure. Sam became involved in the co-op as a law student who was helping with the legal side of the co-op struggle. He became so involved that he ended up moving into the building. Through his residence, legal know-how became incorporated into the domestic model of co-op organizing as Sam became incorporated into the co-op as a member of the family.[39]

One important way in which Sam was incorporated into the co-op community was through his becoming a godfather to two boys in the building. This position gave him a new kinship status, which he had not had when he first moved in. Equally important is the fact that it was Luisa, one of the matriarchs, who suggested and encouraged him to take on this role; in other words, his status increased because he became incorporated into the family through the actions of one of the very important people in the family hierarchy.

Sam's status in the macro-level community also changed with his individual family status. When describing some of the events that the co-op organized, he explains that he became more integrated in the community when he got married and had children:

SAM: They would have functions together I mean you know, you know- everybody would come over to one person's apartment for New Year's, and then, they'd all go over there for Christmas, and that kind of thing.

GALEY: Mm hmm

SAM: U:m, . . I didn't get too much involved in that until I got married.

GALEY: Mm hmm

SAM: A:nd, and then I just started- my wife and I started getting invited to things.

GALEY: Really.

Sam: Mm hmm. And um, . But when I was single, no.

GALEY: So why do you think that changed, when you got married?

▲

SAM: Well I was, one of them! [extended laughter]. A:nd, plus-
         uh, we got pregnant right away so- in less than a year after
         moving in, we had a baby, besides. Then we were really
         one of them! [extended laughter]

In this discussion, Sam differentiates himself from the co-op body
through his use of the exclusive pronoun *they* to refer to the people
organizing Christmas parties and such – events to which he was not
invited in the beginning – and his use of the pronoun *we* to refer
to his own nuclear family. This distinction fades, however, when his
status as an in-group member of the co-op increases upon getting
married ("I was one of them!") and having children ("Then I was
really one of them!").

Joel

As another of the young, single adults in the building, Joel also had
experiences of being incorporated into the macro-level co-op kinship structure. In his talk of life in the co-op, he also describes some
disputes over the management of co-op resources. In one example,
he constructs himself as a kind of prodigal son, who had to leave the
co-op and then come back a few years later to fully return into the
good graces of the family:

> But we felt like we were acting in the best interests of the co-op and
> eventually- you know well we were, restored to- uh, a state of accept-
> ance, <u>by the elders</u>. [. . .] Um I mean we've all sort of bonded
> with one another even though we come from different backgrounds.
> [. . .] so- and, to that extent, I'm sort of a <u>member of the family</u>.
> And, you know, it doesn't really matter if I've left. You know, they,
> they identify- and now I see the children, who are all grown up.

As outlined in the above sections, the construction of the co-op members as a family serves important rhetorical and political functions. But
for at least some members, there was also some psychological reality
to the metaphor. For example, when I told Joel of my analysis of the
family metaphor, and of his and Sam's roles as older brothers, he
responded in the following way:

You know, I thought I had thought about the Danforth from every possible angle, but you're right, they were our surrogate family, . . .[40]

And Joel went on to add, "Sometimes it could be a pretty dysfunctional family, though." The characterization of the co-op membership as at times dysfunctional points to the strength of the family model; conflicts or individual actions which have negatively impacted relationships among co-op members do not threaten the integrity of the kinship model, but rather become incorporated into it.

Children grow up

Joel's description above of seeing the co-op children all grown up is a way of showing himself to be part of the family. The *children growing up* genre of talk – describing kids getting taller, remembering how cute they used to be or beaming about how well they turned out, is a linguistic ritual that often occurs among members of extended families who aren't in contact on a day-to-day basis. Such talk, both for Joel here and in general, illustrates and at the same time reinforces family ties. These *children growing up* rituals take a number of forms.

Kin pride

One prevalent *children grow up* ritual among co-op members is descriptions of the educational and professional accomplishments of co-op children:

JOEL:	Well we've had some wonderful uh, stories, too I mean like, for example Frankie, Contreras, Isabeh- and uh, Mr. Contreras's son, I mean he went to Yale University on a full scholarship,
GALEY:	Uh huh,
JOEL:	Mr. uh, is it Mr. Peterson's son? And he's a teacher,
GALEY:	Mm hmm
JOEL:	U:m, is it Mr. Waters's son, Albert? I think it *is* Albert, Mr. Waters's son, you know who went to Berkeley Law School. And he's an artist. I mean so you know a- you know I mean it's really been, interesting to watch <u>the families</u> grow up.

In his description of the co-op "success stories," Joel embellishes on the macro-kinship structure of the *children growing up* ritual through two micro-kinship strategies. First, he labels the co-op children by their relationship to their parents ("Mr. Waters' son"). In addition, he reinforces the status of co-op members as family people by grouping the co-op members as *families* in the utterance, "It's really been interesting to watch the families grow up." Joel's comment in this example that Mr. Waters's son is an artist also strengthens the kinship construction: Mr. Waters is a well-known artist; thus, mentioning his son's talents in this field draws on and emphasizes the connection between father and son.

Kin woes

In addition to characterizations of co-op children's achievements, stories of problems that co-op children have had also use macro- and micro-kinship strategies. In other words, negative stories serve as well as positive stories to emphasize the co-op's kinship structure. We can see a macro strategy in Sam's description of the different paths of co-op kids:

> Uh, lot of them played together, lot of them went to school together, a lot of them went to jail together! [laughs] I think- we had it all! You know, guy who graduated from Yale, another guy who graduated from Berkeley Law School, all on scholarships,. Um, we had- we had a couple of- one kid is, went to jail several times for stealing cars, another couple of kids, got involved with drugs, and none of them are- I guess they're in jail now too and, so we've had it all.

In this description Sam outlines the ties among co-op children (playing together, going to school together, and going to jail together). Through the "we had it all" syntactic construction, he positions the chronicles of individual children's exploits as grammatical objects (it) that are possessed by the co-op community (we). In this way, Sam constructs the experiences of individual co-op children as experiences jointly "owned" by the co-op community, thus highlighting the coop's macro-kinship structure.

Kinship relations may also be used as a primary theme in constructing positive or negative positions for Danforth tenants. For example, when another member of the co-op told my neighbor Clara and me that a new building tenant was the sibling of our neighbor

Patricia, Clara laughed. When I asked her why, she explained that this person's sister had been a very unreliable member of the co-op. Clara told me stories about Patricia, as well as her mother and her son, thereby creating a vision of Patricia's sister based on the characteristics of her kin:

> Patricia's been, very unreliable, member of the co-op. And her son's, been in trouble. Uh, and she and her mother are always late, they've been so- we've had to have special meetings you know to get her to pay. U:m, things are better now. But Patricia kind of- does what she wants to do. So- when I learned that she was Patricia's sister, it made me just sort of chuckle.

Kinship and Change

When talking to co-op members about the co-op struggle and life in the Danforth, I was particularly interested in change in the building since the renovation. In answering my questions about this topic, co-op members frequently used changes in the structure of individual families to explain why life in the building had changed. For example, in explaining why people in the building aren't as close as they used to be, Sam says,

> [Some people have moved out], you know other people have gotten divorced, and so, and the family isn't what it used to be.

As the ties within individual families have come undone, then, so have the ties of the larger co-op family. Note that the reference to family in "the family isn't what it used to be" is ambiguous; we can take it as either a micro or a macro kinship strategy.

Mrs. Rosales and Mrs. Patterson also point to processes in individual families:

GALEY: Why do you think it's changed?
MRS. R: Before, the children was, small, now they are bigger. And, maybe that's why.
GALEY: So you think because, the children played together?

MRS. R:	Yeah, before. We used to go outside, you know, you remember?
MRS. P:	Yes.
MRS. R:	<u>With the children.</u>
MRS. P:	<u>With the children</u>, yes.
MRS. R:	They played together, and we talked, you know with the other people, instead, it was, nice! But now they are grown up, you know. Maybe that's the reason.

Here also, changes in the micro-structure of individual families – in this case, children growing up – are linked to changes in the macro co-op family as well as in the life of the building. Mrs. Patterson's repetition of Mrs. Rosales's utterance "with the children" also serves as an involvement strategy to highlight the family theme.

Wearing Slippers in the Hall: Separating Public and Private

Whereas the co-op members blur the public and private in their strategies for interaction with government institutions, they distinctly separate these spheres when it comes to delineating the building as their rightful property. The linguistic anthropologist Susan Gal remarks that definitions of public and private often seem contradictory. For example, what may seem like a public space may be privately owned. Gal explains this contradiction by pointing out that

> "public" and "private" are not particular places, domains, spheres of activity, or even types of interaction. . . . Public and private are co-constitutive cultural categories . . . [and] indexical signs that are always relative: dependent for part of their referential meaning on the interactional context in which they are used. . . . [t]he public/private dichotomy is best understood as a discursive phenomenon that, once established, can be used to characterize, categorize, organize, and contrast virtually any kind of social fact: spaces, institutions, bodies, groups, activities, interactions, relations.[41]

Here, Gal locates the source of the seemingly contradictory ways that "public" and "private" are used in the indexical nature of these terms:

their meaning comes (partly) from the particular situational context, rather than from any stable and abstract meanings inherent in the terms themselves. I would like to argue, however, that there *is* a stable meaning of public and private across different uses of these terms in the US context. Whether we speak of a private space, a privately owned space, a private sphere, a private conversation, or a private school, what these all share is the notion of rights to authority over the domain and rights to determine the exclusion of others. Thus, private spaces – whether they are private in the sense of a home where specific people are recognized as the residents, or private in the sense that someone other than the state owns it – are spaces where certain people have unlimited access to the space, as well as rights to determine who may enter it and under what circumstances. Similarly, interlocutors in a private conversation are commonly considered to have the right to determine if someone else can join their talk, in a way that is not possible in a public discussion such as a town hall meeting. This is not to say that there are no constraints on participation in the public sphere.[42] Rather, in the public sphere, at least in the US context, representatives of the state decide on access and exclusion, at least ostensibly based on the interests of "the public" and the common good.

Viewed from the point of access, it benefited the Danforth residents to utilize an interpenetration of public and private spheres in their efforts to involve the state in their housing struggle and construct their housing issues as public community issues. On the other hand, when it came to materially claiming their building, it was in the co-op members' interests to delineate it as private space over which they had authority to determine access.

The construction of the building as a private domestic space is closely linked with the characterization of the co-op members as a family. Co-op members also create the building as private space in a number of other ways. For example, when members describe events that occurred in the building's common areas, they often include activities which are commonly thought to occur within private residential spaces. We can see this in Sam's description of life in the pre-renovation days:

SAM: At any time, you could put on your slippers, just walk down the hall or take the elevator, and, you can borrow a cup of sugar, borrow some eggs.

By talking about borrowing a cup of sugar or some eggs, Sam creates a vision of group solidarity within the building by drawing on stereotypes of the way that close neighbors interact. The utterance "At any time, you could put on your slippers, just walk down the hall . . ." reframes this solidarity as not solely one of neighborhood closeness, but rather one of a sort of familial closeness: slippers are worn inside in the home, in private space, rather than outside in public. And Sam's demarcation of private space by means of discussing clothing use is in fact reflected in the current dressing behavior of a number of co-op residents, as well as some condo residents, who often wear slippers or housecoats to do the laundry, check their mail, or even (although less often) to step outside for some fresh air or to survey the flowers newly planted next to the front door. These residents do not wear slippers or housecoats to go anywhere off of the building's grounds, even to the street corner to drop a letter in the mailbox.

Patrolling the Private

The characterization of the building as private space is intensified through descriptions of activities that co-op members took part in to police and maintain the building's status as private space. One of the most important of these events was the nightly security patrols. At the time that the co-op association formed, the building was extremely run down and far from fully occupied, and the residents, because they were not paying rent to the landlord (although they were paying rent into an escrow account) were technically squatting. Thus, legally, they had the same claim to the space as anyone else who came off the street. And in fact many people did come into the building – for sheltered sleep, to do drugs, or to conduct other activities that they did not want to conduct out in plain sight. In order to keep the Danforth the purview of the co-op community, the members engaged in nightly security patrols to kick out people whom they considered not to belong there.

In addition to these trespassers, Mrs. Wallace and Luisa also kicked out people who failed to or stopped paying rent into the escrow account. Payment into this fund established, in the eyes of the co-op members, an economic basis for the co-op community's inscription of the building as private space; they were paying money for their inhabitation of the space (even if the money wasn't going to the owner of the building). Likewise, the security patrols maintained the private nature of the building through the invocation of a *trespasser* category and the consequent expulsion of the trespassers.

In the same way that these security patrols and expulsions territorialized the building as private space through actions, *stories* about the security patrols construct the building as private space discursively:

> SAM: I was walking around with Luisa, and Mrs. Wallace, the three of us were doing patrol, and, we ran into, I don't know if he was a cousin or a nephew or- some kind of- some kind of relative of one of the people in the building. Who didn't live in the building. U:m, a young guy, I don't know if he was in his- late teens early twenties, but there he was with his girlfriend, and they were making love on the floor of some empty apartment. And so we happened to walk in on them, and Luisa says, Well. well. well! [laughs] Look. at. this! And the two of them are, hobbling into their clothes and, [laughs]! And, she's carrying on like this and they're all embarrassed and, and she just didn't let up on em until they were out of the building. But um, that's what we just did that, over and over and over. For eight years.

In this narrative, Sam constructs Luisa and Mrs. Wallace as powerful forces walking through the halls and, with their footsteps, inscribing the building as private space – as their home. The story, along with Mrs. Rosales's and Mrs. Patterson's below, reinforces the image of these two women as the building matriarchs, the family leaders at the top of the hierarchy who are in charge both of the space and of the conduct of people in and around the space.

A Different Kind of Fearlessness

> MRS. R: You know Mrs. Wallace, she is not afraid to go to Mt. Pleasant St. She say everybody call her Mama!
>
> GALEY: [laughs]
>
> MRS. R: Yeah! And I told her, okay, when you go out one night, just give me a call, I go with you. Because she says, she's not afraid.

Mrs. P:	Not afraid.
Mrs. R:	With Luisa both.
Mrs. P:	Up till now she would pol um, police the building two o'clock in the morning. Ye:s:! She knows, herself and Luisa.
Mrs. R:	Yes.
Mrs. P:	They know when people put their trash outside illegally, =
Mrs. R:	yes
Mrs. P:	= you know, wee hours of the morning. I mean, they know everything. **Nothing** passes them.
Mrs. R:	Yes, that's right. They know who's coming, who's going. I don't know how they know! [laughs] I come to my apartment, I don't see nobody. Nobody! [laughs] I just watch TV, you know stay with my children talk with my children, but well maybe when you get older you don't have nothing to do!
[laughter]	
Mrs. P:	Yeah, right!
Galey:	It seems like, yeah.
Mrs. R:	I don't know.
[laughter]	
Mrs. R:	Maybe, I, No, but it's nice. because if there's somebody's do something wrong, they know, right? It's good. If =
Mrs. P:	Um hmm
Mrs. R:	= somebody has her eyes open, yeah.

In this discussion, Mrs. Patterson and Mrs. Rosales highlight Mrs. Wallace's matriarchal position by portraying her as embodying qualities associated with good mothers; she and Luisa are like the proverbial mother with eyes in the back of her head. They look out for their family by protecting the family home from intruders and disciplining the people who transgress the rules and norms of the co-op. Mrs. Wallace's status as building matriarch is further reinforced through Mrs. Rosales's remark that "she say everybody call her Mama." This utterance both sets up a community-wide acknowledgment of Mrs. Wallace's matriarch status, and, by conveying the proposition through reported speech, portrays Mrs. Wallace as fully cognizant of that position.

Mrs. Rosales's first turn further builds Mrs. Wallace's authority through the proposition that Mrs. Wallace "is not afraid to go to Mt. Pleasant St." Through the use of the negative (as in the grant proposal in chapter 4), this utterance implies the negative's opposite, i.e., that some people *are* afraid to go to Mt. Pleasant St. This in turn constructs Mt. Pleasant St. as a potentially dangerous place, and Mrs. Williams, through her fearlessness, as an authentic urbanite who fits with the neighborhood. This authority based on fearlessness is reinforced with the repetition in Mrs. Rosales's second turn, "Because she says, she's not afraid." Again, the strategy of reported speech portrays Mrs. Wallace's authority as a trait that she explicitly constructs, through both actions and words. As Penelope Eckert points out, because women often have limited access to material capital which is readily available to men,

> [W]omen's influence depends primarily on the painstaking creation and elaboration of an image of the whole self as worthy of authority . . . [W]omen must justify and define theirs on the basis of their overall character.[43]

Finally, Mrs. Rosales builds Mrs. Wallace's moral authority by contrasting Mrs. Wallace's knowing everything that goes on and patrolling the building, with Mrs. Rosales's staying in her apartment and not seeing what goes on ("I come to my apartment, I don't see nobody"). Although Mrs. Rosales's portrayal of herself here has the potential negative effect of constructing her as someone whose behavior does not exemplify co-op community values, she precludes this interpretation by elaborating on what she does in her apartment: "I . . stay with my children talk with my children." With this utterance, she establishes herself as a family person through her work to strengthen ties with her children. In this way, she uses a micro-kinship strategy to align herself with the norms of the macro-level community.

Notable in Mrs. Rosales' and Mrs. Patterson's discussion is the linking of Mrs. Wallace's fearlessness with her ostensibly widely recognized identity as a female authority figure. In this way, Mrs. Patterson and Mrs. Rosales create a vision of fearlessness that is inherently female, a fearlessness that is fundamentally linked with, and put to use in the interests of, protecting community members. In contrast to the masculinist public discourse talk of crime and other dangers that we've seen in other chapters, the Danforth residents do not glorify elements of city life that can be dangerous. Rather, co-op members invoke the social interaction model of community problem-solving to diminish criminal or dangerous activities around their home, in the interests of creating a safe space for low-income community members. They portray community concern about crime and danger as legitimate positions, and in the process delink such concern from gentrifier interests. Fearlessness in this view is not the bravado to walk around at two o'clock in the morning as a sign of toughness, but rather a show of responsibility towards and care for the safety and well-being of one's neighbors.

From both the stories the Danforth members tell, and the activities the stories describe, we can see that co-op members build moral authority and power in two ways. The authority of Mrs. Wallace and Luisa within the Danforth relies on the reinforcement of the boundary between public and private, inside and outside. Conversely, the transference of their moral authority from the domestic sphere to the political sphere, and the transformation of this moral authority into political power, relies on a blurring of the boundary between public and private.

The Co-op vs. the Condo

Private space and co-op values

In the co-op stories, one of the most common ways of constructing the building as private space is through implicit contrasts of the co-op members with condo owners who moved in after the building was renovated. These contrasts take two forms: differentiation of the spheres which the members of the respective groups inhabit or from which they come, and differentiation of the two groups based on adherence to or deviance from the co-op value system.

Insiders and outsiders
In their descriptions of the building renovation and subsequent conversion of the units to coops and condos, both Mrs. Patterson and Sam dichotomize the old tenants and the new tenants in terms of a public/private distinction:

> Mrs. P: [There were] thirty cooperative units. And in order to <u>sell the other um units to the public</u> the building had to become converted to condominium because it would sell faster.

SAM: And <u>the families</u> flipped a coin [for a particular apartment]
        or, I don't know what we did, but anyway. Um, yeah so it
        worked out then- when we went to, the permanent situ-
        ation when we were s- began <u>selling this to the public</u>.

The labeling of potential condo owners as "the public" serves to align
these new residents with the world outside the Danforth, implicitly
distancing them from the Danforth community, the insiders. Both the
examples above set up an implicit contrast between condo owners
and co-op members. Because of this contrast, the labeling of the condo
owners as "the public" implicitly constructs the co-op community as
"the private." The construction of the co-op community as embodying the private is reinforced by Sam's labeling of the co-op members
as "the families," since, as we have seen, family life is aligned with
domestic life and hence a private sphere.

The distancing of the condo owners from the co-op community
is also achieved through use of the label *outsiders*, as in Mrs. Patterson's
comment below, where she criticizes the unfriendly behavior of the
new residents:

> But with <u>the people from outside who came in</u>, I don't know what
> they were thinking they- they're not friendly. You know.

In using the spatial metaphor *outsiders* to characterize the condo
owners, Mrs. Patterson, through implicit contrast, constructs the
building as *inside* space, and the original residents as *insiders*. The new
people are positioned as outsiders both geographically, through their
association with other places (i.e., the places they lived before moving into the Danforth), and morally, through their inappropriate social
behavior which does not conform with the co-op community's
values and norms of interaction.

In Mrs. Patterson's discourse, she frequently uses the label *outsiders*
in talk which criticizes condo owners' values. Condo owners' perceived lack of interest in participating in a community, their ignor-
ance of the history of the co-op and social structure of the co-op
community, and their frequently impersonal interactions with other
Danforth residents are frequent themes in co-op members' criticisms
of condo owners. We can see such criticism reinforced by use of the
distancing term *outsiders* in another remark made by Mrs. Patterson:

I was on the um, condominium board. Well, I don't want too say much, but uh, there were members from <u>outside</u>- you know- who bought the units here- the- condo units. And they were on the board, but um, there was some type of conflict where, right now, those people are not on the board. Yeah. Don't want to say too much!

Although she does not go into detail about the particular conflict, Mrs. Patterson constructs a negative moral positioning for condo owners through her invocation of a conflict and her implication that the conflict in question resulted in these owners' removal from the condo board.

Co-op vs. condo values

The negative positioning of condo owners and other non-co-op residents of the Danforth is frequently accomplished through narratives about residents who fail to show respect for the co-op members' claim to the building and their long tenure there. One common form is narratives about people questioning co-op members' residence status when they enter the building. Mrs. Patterson tells a series of three such narratives, one of which relates an experience that her daughter Grace had:

A fellow accosted my daughter and her friend one day outside in the, the little park at the side of the building and said, "Um, do you live here?" She said "Yes, my mother lives on the third floor." "I don't know, I've never seen you before."

This narrative both positions Grace positively as a person who adheres to the co-op value system at the same time as it positions the "fellow" negatively through his purported disregard for that system. These positions are first constructed through the contrast of the indefinite "*a* fellow" and the definite "*my* daughter." Discourse analyst Teun van Dijk[44] notes that vague identification terms are a typical narrative strategy to refer to members of out-groups,[45] and argues that this strategy serves as a means of distancing.

The distancing function of the indefinite and inexplicit "a fellow" is enhanced by the assignment of this character to what is called an *agentive* role in a violent action – as the agent or doer in "accosting" Mrs. Patterson's daughter. Negative positioning of the "fellow" is further enhanced through the contrast with the kinship term "my daughter." The contrast between indefinite and definite and between inexplicit and explicit also highlights the division between this fellow and Mrs. Patterson's daughter.

The inexplicitness of "a fellow" contrasts with "my daughter" in additional ways. First, the possessive *my* links Grace to Mrs. Patterson. In the talk before this narrative, Mrs. Patterson has already established a positive position for herself as a co-op member who exemplifies co-op values. Aligning Grace with her through the possessive, then, consequently creates a positive position for Grace. In addition to the possessive, the kinship term *daughter* incorporates Grace into the co-op family, thus constructing her as a member of the in-group.

Similarly, Grace is constructed as establishing her tie to the building through the utterance, "My mother lives on the third floor"; this strategy shows her as adhering to co-op norms by invoking family connection (a micro-kinship strategy). Sociolinguist Deborah Schiffrin observes that a mother constructing speech for her daughter that aligns the daughter with the mother's beliefs "portray[s] the daughter well within the family norms and practices," which consequently "constructs a position of mother/daughter solidarity and closeness."[46]

Similarly, with the utterance "my mother lives on the third floor," Mrs. Patterson positions Grace as a good daughter, respectful of the ties to her mother. And Grace's behavior as a good daughter in turn implies that Mrs. Patterson is a good mother, since it is she who raised Grace with these values. Mrs Patterson's portrayal of her daughter (which implies a portrayal of Mrs. Patterson herself) reinforces their roles as family people at the micro level, and this in turn reinforces their status as good members of the co-op family at the macro level. This all contributes to the positive positioning of Grace and Mrs. Patterson within the co-op's moral geography. Likewise, through implicit contrast, these utterances also contribute to the negative positioning of the kin-less "fellow" who accosts Grace in the story.

We can see the interaction of positive and negative positioning in Mrs. Patterson's next narrative of co-op member/condo owner interaction, co-narrated with Mrs. Rosales:

MRS. P: The impression I- I got with the people came after, they look down on you. As though they treat you with contempt! I don't understand, but my goodness. Let me tell you something. Mrs. Conway one day, I don't know what had happened to her keys, or if somebody . . her keys were stolen or something. She couldn't get into her apartment. So she sat down in front of the apartment. One lady who lives, I think the next apartment, she came in, and saw her, just-

MRS. R:	Just passed
MRS. P:	went on past, said, Whooo- you scared me! That was it! She did not say, Oh, excuse me, are you alright? Can I help, or can I do something for you? Not a word! But then, I was going out- coming upstairs, I usually walk up because I have this fear of being in the elevator, by myself. So I walked up. And I, as a habit, I looked through. the window, looked through. I saw, a leg protruding, you know the corner, on the floor! I opened the door! I said, Oh, that looks like Mrs. Conway's . . leg! I said, Mrs. Conway, what happened? Are you alright? So then she told me the story. And she told me, what happened to the neighbor.
MRS. R:	Yeah she, she was angry, yeah.
MRS. P:	Yeah. Until one day um, I mean the, and that person, is on the condo board. And, uh, for inspection,
MRS. R:	[laughs] Yeah!
MRS. P:	She was there to inspect the apartment, but Mrs. Conway told her, You, don't come in here.
MRS. R:	Yeah. And she told, You can come. Not her!
MRS. P:	And that was, that was bad.
MRS. R:	Yeah.
MRS. P:	I mean, they would see you, and they would not say, anything to you!

Mrs. Patterson starts this narrative with what narrative analysts call an *abstract*[47] (briefly, a summary introducing what the story will be about) that both positions the post-renovation residents negatively ("they look down on you," "they treat you with contempt"), and frames what is to come as discourse that will elaborate on this negative positioning. Mrs. Patterson next evaluates the abstract with the utterance "I don't understand," which portrays the new people's behavior as incomprehensible, hence adhering to a different value system than the (positively positioned) one she has already shown herself and her daughter to adhere to.

Mrs. Patterson next sets the scene in the narrative *orientation* or scene-setting, poising Mrs. Conway on the floor in front of her storyworld apartment, which she can't get into because she doesn't have her keys. The *complicating action* or plot then begins with "one lady who lives, I think the next apartment" entering the scene. Although the description of this figure is more explicit than the "fellow" from the previous narrative, she is still unnamed. In addition, Mrs. Patterson's explanation that she *thinks* the woman lives in the next apartment creates a weak anchoring for this woman within the building's community. This very generalized picture, in contrast with the definite "Mrs. Conway" further serves to position these two negatively and positively, respectively.

The force of the negative positioning of "one lady who lives the next apartment," and "a fellow," in contrast with the positive positioning of "my daughter" and "Mrs. Conway," is even more significant when we take into account that, as the main audience for these narratives, I knew the name of Mrs. Patterson's daughter, while I did not know who Mrs. Conway was. Thus, in the first case, Mrs. Patterson uses a micro-kinship strategy when she could just as easily have used her daughter's name. Likewise, in the second case, she chooses to use a definite and explicit referring term, despite the lack of preceding discourse to provide me with a referent for this name.[48] Thus, although this reference in actuality is less informative for me, the lack of a more general description of Mrs. Conway (i.e., the older woman who lives on the second floor) sets up Mrs. Conway's identity as something which should be given information, i.e., something which should be known, hence Mrs. Conway is an integral member in the co-op community.

When the neighbor enters the scene in the story, Mrs. Patterson sets her up as performing three actions – came in, went on past, said, "Whoo- you scared me." These actions are all evaluated as inadequate, with the utterance "That was it." Mrs. Patterson reinforces this inadequacy through contrast with the utterances that she *should* have uttered, in Mrs. Patterson's view: Can I help you, or can I do something for you? The neighbor's failure to ask the appropriate questions is further reinforced by Mrs. Patterson's evaluation that points out not only her failure to say the *right* thing, but her failure to say *anything* ("Not a word").

Next, with the contrastive marker "but" in "But then, I was going out- coming upstairs . . ." Mrs. Patterson structures a contrast between the neighbor's inappropriate behavior, and Mrs. Patterson's own appropriate behavior. Mrs. Patterson's evaluation of her own looking through the window of the hallway door to the hall as a *habit* again positively positions her as attentive to the building environment and on the lookout for anything out of the ordinary, much like the images of Luisa and Mrs. Wallace in the previous stories.

As she looks through the window Mrs. Patterson sees a leg. Her ability to identify this leg shows her as someone who knows the members of the building community so well that she can identify them based on a relatively anonymous part of anatomy. Likewise, the identifiability of Mrs. Conway's leg characterizes Mrs. Conway as someone whose interactions with other residents are so intensive or meaningful that she is able to be recognized by a relatively anonymous body part. This ready recognition also reinforces the contrast with the neighbor, who is barely recognized at all.

Mrs. Patterson's words to Mrs. Conway in the story also strongly contrast with the unnamed neighbor's utterance "You scared me." The neighbor is cast as simply remarking on a negative action caused by Mrs. Conway's presence in the hall, and her reported quote places her in the grammatical role of an *experiencer* (one who experiences something), rather than in any *agentive* role of taking any action to find out about Mrs. Conway's condition. Conversely, Mrs. Patterson indexes a relationship with Mrs. Conway by constructing herself in the storyworld as addressing Mrs. Conway by name; then she shows her concern for her neighbor's welfare with a quote asking what happened and if she was alright. The contrast of Mrs. Patterson's and the neighbor's reported speech reinforces their positions within the moral geography of the building.

The unnamed neighbor's negative positioning is further heightened by her being chastised by a respected co-op member when Mrs. Patterson narrates Mrs. Conway prohibiting the neighbor from going into Mrs. Conway's apartment.

Although Mrs. Rosales's contributions are fewer than Mrs. Patterson's in this co-narrated story, they serve equally important functions. First, in the utterance "just passed," Mrs. Rosales identifies ("passed") and evaluates ("just") the neighbor's breach of co-op norms. She then emphasizes the status of the behavior as unacceptable through her evaluation of Mrs. Conway's reaction to that behavior: "Yeah, she, she was angry, yeah." Mrs. Rosales's final evaluation comes in the form of elaboration of Mrs. Patterson's quote of Mrs. Conway's castigation, "You, don't come in here." Mrs. Rosales first enhances the force of the punishment through her agreement with Mrs. Patterson ("Yeah") and then through her elaboration, "And she told, You can come, not her!" This utterance works to position the neighbor negatively in two ways. First, through its elaborative function, it amplifies the negative force of Mrs. Patterson's utterance. Second, whereas the constructed addressee of Mrs. Patterson's utterance ("You, don't come in here") was the neighbor, Mrs. Rosales switches the addressee to the person who *is* allowed to enter the apartment ("You can come, not her"), and refers to the neighbor with the third person pronoun. The removal of the neighbor from the addressee role constructs her as someone to be ignored; thus the pronoun "her" serves as a distancing strategy.

After Mrs. Rosales's evaluation, Mrs. Patterson adds her own evaluation with a double narrative coda (the part of a narrative that drives the point home), first with the explicit evaluation "that was bad," and then with the final coda "I mean, they would see you, and they would not say anything to you!" This expression of outrage sets up the implicative that the appropriate behavior for neighbors when they see each other is to say something. Thus this coda implicitly chastises new residents for their inappropriate behavior. This negative positioning is again reinforced through the vague and distancing pronoun *they*, which contrasts with the more proximal generalized *you*.

Moral positioning and class identity

Implicit in the contrasts between co-op and condo people is a conflation of positive positioning and class alignment. Crucial to understanding the co-op stories is the recognition that it is condo *owners* who are shown to violate co-op norms, rather than the larger group of post-renovation residents, many of whom are *renters*. Their imputed disregard for the community ties that co-op members have built so meticulously goes hand-in-hand with what co-op members articulate as a wealthy attitude towards a home as a private refuge, rather than a place of community. (These class-correlated orientations to home are similar to what Brett Williams found in the neighborhood at-large in her ethnography of Mt. Pleasant in the 1980s.)

In co-op members' discourse, condo owners are positioned as representatives of the kinds of changes that are bringing about gentrification and threatening valued ways of life. Common in co-op members' talk are laments about neighbors who do not say good morning and do not talk in the elevator. These somewhat small behaviors serve as a gloss for a general orientation to apartment living that is at odds with co-op values. An excerpt from a conversation with Mrs. Patterson's son Kevin and his friend Maurice illustrates this. In this excerpt, we can also see that, in addition to class valences, gender and ethnicity are also important categories in delineating outsider behavior in the building. In fact, a major difference between stories about co-op members and condo owners is the role that ethnicity plays. While the co-op stories emphasize cross-ethnic ties and consequently downplay the role of ethnic differences, stories about condo owners not infrequently explicitly invoke ethnicity, particularly Whiteness. Class alliances seem to determine whether or not Whiteness is seen as a marker of separation; among co-op members, who align themselves with working-class struggles, ethnicity is backgrounded. Contrariwise, for condo owners who are talked about as displaying bourgeois interests, Whiteness does seem to work to separate condo owners from co-op owners.[49]

MAURICE:	There's a lot of new- once they renovated, a lot of new people come in. You know. And then it's like- a shock because- a lot of em treat you like- you know, s- you've been here for so long, you like, kind of like expect people to, open the door especially if it's somebody, who knows you live there, you know they just like-
KEVIN:	Oh the new people, the people who-
MAURICE:	just shut the door right in your in your face, I'll be like-
KEVIN:	Yeah. The old people who know you and stuff for- you know what I'm saying they know you and stuff but the new people that come up in here, man they rude!
GALEY:	Yeah?
KEVIN:	Yeah, th- Oh yeah! You know like sometimes I don't have my keys and stuff? <low pitch: Do you live here.> Yeah,

	for fifteen damn years! And you know they gonna check yourself!
MAURICE:	No, they just, /?????????/
KEVIN:	They don't hold that door because, I mean you gotta understand what, you know they don't know that, and they can't trust nobody given the fact that, you know that they don't /??????/ in the building and stuff you know what I'm saying, so you can't really- but still, man. =
MAURICE:	Yeah, that's true, too.
KEVIN:	= Sometimes they rude, though. And I would never do that to them! You know what I'm saying, I be living here, and, you're new. But I would still let you in, you know what I'm saying, because, I don't know, that's just how I am. You know.
MAURICE:	I mean I had people, just like, wait there, for like they, looking for their keys! Just to see if I'd get buzzed up. And then, you know, specially like, that one guy, he's like, like a nerdy guy?
KEVIN:	Is it a White dude?
GALEY:	Oh, Joe? I think his name's Joe, and he's a White, =
KEVIN:	White dude?
GALEY:	= White guy.
MAURICE:	White guy. You'd know him when you see him. He like deliberately- slams the door in your face and he will stay there- He'll literally- slam the door in your face and sit there. And look at you. And then when you get in the building. He will argue with you, and say, You God damn this, you /in now/. And he will talk under his breath, and if you say something to him like, What? What'd you say? He like- aaaaaagh!
KEVIN:	Yeah. Yeah yeah- You have some females in this building who are like that.
MAURICE:	But I had- people that- lived here- that- know that I live here-
GALEY:	Mm hmm
MAURICE:	That just slam the door in my face! Scah gzh:: You know? They've done- you know I came in so many times, they saw me bringing up,
KEVIN:	Yeah. Well they- I know you live here but uh, who are you again?

MAURICE:	Yeah, yeah. And they go- Do you live here? Like, ye:ah,. You saw me befo:re, just like, two days ago,.
KEVIN:	You know? I know your name is Maurice, you been living here for awhile but uh, what do you- want in this building?
MAURICE:	You know? So I just- I just, most of these times, I just- I don't even o- mess with the door! I just go straight to the buzzer. [laugh] Go straight to the buzzer and buzz up.
KEVIN:	Naw- I mean yeah, but then you have some people, not a lot of people, it's a few, who are Whites, and uh, they're real nice and friendly, you know what I mean, cause I guess they know I live here, they see me and- you're a pretty nice person and stuff like that, you know but- then you have some females, they don't even say hi or what- ever, nothing, and, you just keep on walking and I always try to say hi or whatever you know but- It's- I, I- I won't say it's a lot, it's a little bit.
GALEY:	Do you think it's like more White females than Black females that do that? That like don't say hi?
KEVIN:	Yeah. I mean even the Hispanic people will say hi. The Spanish people like real nice. They even you know, good morning or, on the elevator you'll talk- to uh -you know- whatever but- then you have you know you have some White people that are- you know they won't really- you know if you, if you push the issue and say you know like, Good afternoon or- I'm on the elevator I'm like, Okay bye, you know something like that you know what I mean I'll- go out of my way, and, I get a response, to that, so . . .

Kevin and Maurice's comments are typical of co-op discourse criti-
cizing new people, particularly condo owners, for an orientation of
individualism that disregards fellow building residents and disavows
the creation of social ties. Co-op members frame such behavior as
indicative of larger changes − and problems − in the neighborhood.
Mrs. Birch, for instance, another co-op member, remarks that "this
used to be a nice neighborhood; used to be, you knew everyone on
the street, and everyone greeted you." And her husband responds
that:

In this building– You know the same things are beginning to happen here that happened in Adams Morgan. You used to walk down the street at any time and you'd meet a person, you– you either spoke or you nodded you know I– um – let them know you saw them and you– You treated them as a member of the Adams Morgan family. And one day I nodded like that at a lady with – you – Uh-oh! Well the same thing is beginning to happen in this building. You could be on the elevator, somebody run and jump on the elevator with you and he won't open his mouth. But he'll open his mouth to me cause I'll stick my mouth in his ear there, Hello:! . . But as far as this community is concerned, I– I think this community is at– at a da:ngerous point. A very dangerous point in our existence here.

Here Mr. Birch signals community ties through the kinship metaphor in "the Adams Morgan family," which is under threat from new ways of being, symbolized by greeting practices (or lack thereof). Mr. Birch links not saying hello with demographic and social changes in Adams Morgan and the precarious status of the low-income co-op amidst the influx of more and more high-income residents, as well as a desire among some co-op members to reconfigure the co-op so that members would be able to convert their units into condominiums or sell their apartments at market rates.

Social Interaction vs. Individualism: the Struggle for Community

Danforth co-op members articulate the struggle to own their building as a struggle of poor people to empower themselves and their community. The contrast of the people who came in after the renovation, able to buy a condo without any of the inherent struggle – and critically without a struggle that both relied on and reinforced community ties – highlights the class conflicts inherent and implicit in apartment building interactions. The class conflicts in the microcosm of the Danforth serve as a representative of the class conflicts inherent in life in Mt. Pleasant at-large. Such conflicts point to larger disagreements over the public vs. private orientations discussed in chapter 3. Through the use of micro and macro family strategies and narratives about patrolling the building and creating order through informal social control, Danforth co-op members outline a set of values that promotes the social interaction model of community life. They emphasize the importance of social ties in forming a strong community, and a strong community in turn is shown to be critical for accomplishing political goals as well as creating, as Mrs. Birch says, "a nice neighborhood" – a place where people know who you are and will look out for you. These neighborhood residents are concerned about crime and danger – they do not valorize it – but their approach to dealing with it is to become involved, and to take responsibility for dealing with it by interacting and getting to know their neighbors. The fearlessness that they attribute to Mrs. Wallace and Luisa, the matriarchs of the building, is not about creating neighborhood legitimacy through the maintenance of a tough, masculinized demeanor. Rather, their fearlessness is a quality ideologically linked with a communal orientation that emphasizes the importance of looking out for the well-being of one's neighbors, and that is discursively linked with female roles such as mother.

A similar social interaction orientation can be seen in co-op members' suggestions for dealing with the spate of building robberies described in the beginning of this chapter: co-op members campaigned for building residents to interact with people in the building so that they would know who lived there and who didn't, know who frequently came to visit which neighbors, etc. This stood in stark contrast to the condo's campaign for increased security, which consisted in trying to get money to install a new, high-tech key-card system. The co-op members' approach implicitly constructs the individualistic, law-and-order attitudes of the condo owners as outsider behavior to be disdained and lamented.

The Danforth co-op members strategically manipulate discourse of public and private in their efforts to create a community. In descriptions of organizing and of interactions with public institutions, members blur the boundaries of public and private space to define concerns about housing and family as *community issues* that concern the larger community and are integral to the public good.

Public and private are ideological constructs that can be joined or separated for different purposes. While the blurring of public and private can lead to successful community organizing, the separation of the spheres can be equally strategic. In the co-op members' delineation of co-op values, for example, they invoke a more complex usage of public and private. While their focus on social control and community ties emphasizes an orientation towards public interaction, at the same time they inscribe their building as private space – separate from "the outside" and "the public" – in order to establish ownership claims over it. Ironically, in this case, members of "the public" who subsequently move into the building can only join the ranks of "the private" by embracing a value system which is oriented towards "public" life, interaction, and community building. As Mr. Birch implies, these conflicting value systems are at the center of tensions within the larger neighborhood sphere about gentrification and the kind of place that Mt. Pleasant should be.

Notes

1   Condominiums, or condos for short, are buildings in which people directly own individual apartments. Conversely, in cooperatives, co-op members own shares in the cooperative as a whole. People generally form limited-equity co-ops as a means to preserve affordable housing; such co-ops are sold (and must be re-sold) below market rate, making them available to people with low incomes.

2   This came about with the Supreme Court's ruling in the case of *Bolling v. Sharpe*; see chapter 2.

3   See chapter 2 for a discussion of demographic shifts in the neighborhood.

4   Goode (1988:57)

5   Williams (1977)

6   Simons and Shaffer (1979)

7   My variable use of first-name and title-last-name pseudonyms in this chapter reflects the prevalent naming practices among co-op members, as well as the way that I myself address co-op members in conversation.

8   In DC it is very difficult for prospective buyers to secure mortgages for co-op housing.

9   Because members of the co-op association own shares in the cooperative but those in the condominium own their own apartments, I refer to the first group as "co-op members," and the second as "condo owners."

10 The majority of the original co-op members were poor in the late 1970s, at the time of the housing struggle. In the ensuing years, however, a number of them became middle class, and a few upper-middle class.

11 For many years, there were loopholes to this law, however; up until May 2005, landlords could sell up to 95 percent of a building with-

out having to invoke the right of first refusal (Pohlman 2003). The DC City Council closed the loophole by passing the Rental Housing Conversion and Sale Act of 2005.

12 Ackelsberg (1988)
13 McIlhenny (1997)
14 Gal (2002)
15 Clark (1993:134)
16 I use the term *stories* here to refer to a wider range of discourse than the term *narrative* would entail. In this analysis, the category of *co-op stories* includes all talk of life during the co-op struggle, including, e.g., narratives, pseudo-narratives (cf. Labov 1972), and answers to questions that I posed about the co-op in interviews.
17 E.g., Schiffrin (1996), Linde (1993), Tannen (1989)
18 Martin (2002:334)
19 Martin (2002), Taylor (1999)
20 Sharoni (1997)
21 Blee (2002)
22 Bao (1997)
23 Lakoff and Johnson (1980)
24 Smith (1986, 1992)
25 Quinn (1991:65)
26 Williams (1977)
27 Simons and Shaffer (1979)
28 Williams (1977)
29 While homes are often considered to be a domain of female authority, however, feminists like Maria Rosa Dalla Costa, Selma James, and Gillian Rose have pointed out that the home can also be a space of subjugation, exploitation, or violence against women by men.
30 Williams (1988:61)
31 Martin (2002)
32 Martin (2002:304)
33 Leavitt and Saegert (1990:132)
34 Clark (1993:140)
35 Again, I follow co-op convention in referring to Luisa by first name and Mrs. Wallace by title and last name.
36 "Meg" is Margaret Malone, a co-interviewer in the interview which this example comes from. An earlier analysis of this example appears in Modan and Malone (1993).
37 Tannen (1989)
38 As mentioned earlier, this is a particularly useful strategy for combating the "urban frontier" discourse which can discursively marginalize people at risk of being pushed out of gentrifying neighborhoods.

39 Although Sam was very involved in the legal aspects of the struggle, he did not represent the co-op in court; the co-op's main lawyer did not live in the building.

40 Sam, on the other hand, told me that he didn't think the metaphor should be taken so literally.

41 Gal (2002:80)

42 See Fraser (1993).

43 Eckert (1989:256)

44 van Dijk (1984:87)

45 van Dijk focuses on the use of pronouns such as "they" to introduce new figures in narratives, with no antecedents. The term I am analyzing here, "a fellow," is somewhat more explicit than an antecedent-less pronoun would be in the same slot. However, it is nevertheless vague enough, particularly in contrast with the explicit *and* definite "my daughter," to be classified as the same type of strategy as the pronouns which van Dijk analyzes.

46 Schiffrin (1996:180)

47 In this analysis I use the narrative categories outlined in Labov (1972). An *abstract* is a description at the beginning of a narrative of what the narrative will be about. An *orientation* sets the scene in which the narrative occurs. *Complicating action* consists of utterances in a temporal sequence that make up the plot. *Evaluation* strategies highlight certain aspects of the complicating action, and can be expressed through various linguistic forms, such as lengthened vowels, marked pitch, negation, or explicit utterances such as "I couldn't believe it!" The *conclusion* explains how the complicating action came to a close, and the *coda* reiterates the point of the story and reconnects the narrative to the larger conversational context.

48 Alternatively, this strategy also works to position me as an insider, by imputing to me knowledge about Mrs. Conway.

49 Whiteness was the only ethnicity that came up in condo stories.

CHAPTER 7

HOME TIES, WINDS OF CHANGE

May 2005

It's spring on the cusp of summer, and I'm back in Mt. Pleasant. I'm living in one of the last of the group houses of the old Mt. Pleasant, a grand Victorian with unruly lilies and a crumbling stoop. The furniture is old, cozy but worn, and on humid, breezy days you can still catch a trace of that ineffable group house scent, some mysterious mix of patchouli, curry, plant soil, and marijuana, testament to past generations of hippie cooperative living.

The house, too, is on the cusp. Although the floors tilt a little and the freezer drips, the lighting fixtures, all original, are in perfect condition, and the woodwork – floors, moldings, and chestnut paneling in the dining room – has been lovingly restored. We are periodically cautioned to make sure that casters are securely anchored under all the furniture legs.

Our landlord, ex-CISPES[1] activist turned organic farmer, is raising the rent next month to cover his property taxes which have doubled in the past four years. But Joe is a decent guy; he's charging us less than the real-estate-speculating landlord of the group house up the street. Joe is from the first wave of group house landlords, former residents who held on to their property because of their ties to Mt. Pleasant, and kept abreast of what was going on in the neighborhood and in their tenants' lives, even the former ones. "Seth's in Khazakhstan," he informs me one day. "Julia's daughter just turned two." Joe comes down to the house every month or so from his farm in Maryland to cut the grass, catch up with old friends, and fix anything that needs fixing in the house he raised his daughter in. When the harvest is good, he brings us sweet vine-ripened cantaloupes, or bushels of heirloom tomatoes. "This neighborhood's getting worse," says Joe. "Too many people with money coming in. And too many cars."

It's Saturday morning, and I walk up the street to check out the farmer's market. On the steps that double as a stage at the back of the park, Vietnamese grandmothers watch over their grandchildren climbing on the wrought-iron fence. They needn't worry, though, as Ernesto,[2] playing with his daughter Reina, is making sure that none of the clambering boys climbs too high or jumps too far. "You know what you're doing, right? Be careful." "I know what I'm doing, I'm seven!" scoffs one of them, although his sister deflates his pride by confiding to Ernesto that Thanh is only six. In back of the grandmothers a trio of White guys with fuzzy hair plays jazz under a shaded canopy.

The market has changed since last year. Most of the sellers now accept food stamps, and there's more advertising in Spanish. But it's only the Spanish flyers that mention WIC and FMNP Senior,[3] and only the English flyers that promote sorbet and quiche.

At the farmers' stands are berries, free-range veal and beef, a wide range of lettuces – a large bag of arugula goes for 5 bucks – and everything is organic. The customers are mostly White, and there are lots of strollers. It's not the same Whites from the old days, though; fashions have moved from hippie to hip, though in a Washington bureaucrat sort of way (punctuated by the musician types still modeling the pierced/tattooed tank top look). Carla, the woman[4] who used to take her kids on pilgrimages to Baltimore's Little Italy, says to me, "I know this is such a yuppie market, but the produce is really good." We both buy $4 loaves of fresh-baked olive bread.

When I get home, I find a folded yellow flyer lodged in the door. It boldly asks:

I open the flyer and read further.

Our house is on the cusp. It could make someone a lot of money. But the neighborhood is no longer on the cusp: the tide has turned, new neighbors willing to spend lots of money are replacing old neighbors who can't as the whole city moves east in search of housing that is, at best, less unaffordable.

Since the late 1990s – the turning point for gentrification here in Mt. Pleasant – much has changed, and people have dealt with it – have been able to deal with it – in different ways. Some, who were lucky enough to have bought before the boom or to get a reasonable rent locked in, have stayed. Others have moved east to Columbia Heights, Petworth, and Shaw, or out of the DC diamond to Maryland and Virginia. Some of those have moved back, finding suburban life not for them, but most in this group find it a struggle to maintain the same standard of living that they had even half a decade ago.

I close this part of the book by stepping back to give a space to the stories and updates of my neighbors in their own voices[5] – how they have dealt with gentrification, what they think about the shifts, and what they want you to know about urban life – and urban change – in Washington, DC.

David

I came to this country in like '96, I lived in Los Angeles for four months and then I came to Mt. Pleasant in November of 1996. We have relatives here. So it was easy for us to come, we had somebody to help us out and check things out for us. I lived in an apartment building on Mt. Pleasant St. for two years, then I moved a couple blocks up. Basically I've lived here for seven years.

I just recently moved- three months ago I moved to Rockville? I moved because I got a better job. And I don't have a car, so it was easier for me just to move over there. It was cheaper, in terms of transportation. And it's funny, cause you know when you live in a place like Mt. Pleasant for so long, you take a lot of things for granted. In Rockville, everything is like, everything's closing, everybody's going home, everything is like- dying. Sometimes I get freaked out, you know I don't see people like look around for somebody to- It's so quiet. Silence is scary. It's like, let's make some noise! And then some-body comes out, Shut up! That's nice. Thank you very much . . . The people are completely different. I mean, not, you know- I just moved there, I haven't been there that long but, but you know like- people don't talk as much as in DC. The interactions that you have with the people- it's different, somehow. Everybody has their own group, they don't mix that much. People are more uptight. But like I said, I've just been there a couple months, I'm still adapting myself to the place. That's just my observation so far. But I'm working, I'm chilling, I'm working there.

I miss the movement in Mt. Pleasant. In Mt. Pleasant I was used to coming out, like at twelve-thirty, one in the morning, go to the store and be able to- there's always something going on. So it's a city thing, there's more movement here, you know more things going on. And, also um, you know like in Maryland if you want to get to some place you need to get in a car. Or even the bus or the metro is kind of like, it's a longer trip, and you have to wait and, because every-thing's farther, you have to wait longer for the buses. Transportation in DC is faster.

I grew up in Mt. Pleasant- since I was 13 until now- so it has a sentimental value. You know, me and my friends, my cousin, we used to hang out- I was one of the kids who was always, always, always, hanging around on Mt. Pleasant [St.] and playing, you know foot-ball, playing in the street. For me, Mt. Pleasant was always like a safe haven, and basically I was- I was sort of confined to DC, not even DC I was confined to Adams Morgan, Mt. Pleasant, and Georgia Avenue, for all my teenage years. Of course I went to the mall, of course I went to the beach, you know but uh- generally I didn't get out of DC. And I never felt the need, you know like some people are like, Oh, I want to get out of this place, I want to get out of this place. I never felt that need to get out. It's funny that now I'm getting out because of my job situation and because of- I'm older now, I can do more stuff, you know I make my own money so I can decide I want to do this, I want to that. And I've been getting out, I've been, expanding my horizons on a small scale. And I like that, but it's funny that [even though I moved] I never felt the need to leave. I feel com-fortable here. I feel like, DC's a place I feel like I belong to, and that's why I was never, like, I want to get out of here.

In Mt. Pleasant, I came to know what diversity means. Cause in LA I was like in a small space in my mind and I didn't get out of that, so this is why DC became so essential- no not essential, but like important for me. In Mt. Pleasant, we're in the middle. You go **that** way, to Georgia Avenue, it's mostly like, African American people. And if you walk **this** way, it's mostly White. And this is the line that divides the whole city. It's a melting pot, because it's like- boom! Here everyone comes together, and they interact. By necessity. Maybe that's why we fight so much. I mean there's a lot of fights in DC you know, but it's part of the- it's part of the blending, it's part of people getting together. We don't always get along, but we're interacting.

Mt. Pleasant has so many people in one little place, I was learning from everyone. It taught me about other cultures, other people- that you gotta know a person, and what they're about, before you make a comment. And try to interact. Otherwise, you could get your ass kicked! In other places, you know, if you were in Mexico City, if you never got out of Mexico City, you might not respect people from San Salvador. You might not respect people from anywhere else, because you wouldn't have a clue what they're about. I mean, you can study geography, and you can learn about the whole world, but in Mt. Pleasant you really learn what people are about. Now I'm curious about people, you know? I might find out that I don't **like** them, and I **hate** them, but, you know, that's also part of humanity.

Another thing that's unique about Mt. Pleasant is that we have rich people, um, **really** rich people, we have poor people, and we have flat broke people. In the same place. You know, we have these ugly buildings, and then back there we have those houses, really nice colors and everything. Usually [in other places] they're more separated- You know, this is a **really** really rich neighborhood, and this is a **really** really poor neighborhood. But in Mt. Pleasant you get to see everything. People with the money, people with no money, and people with some money. It's something to pay attention to. Like how can rich people and poor people and broke people be in the same place and not have some kind of a, big, issue. I mean there are fights, of course, but they also blend, there's blending. Pretty much everybody in Mt. Pleasant is laid back. I guess because we live here we know each other, I mean you know if I see you in the street I would say, Hi hey, how you doing. Even the people that live back by Rock

Creek, you know, they're around, too. The people who live around here hang out here. Some people, like around Georgia Avenue or in Georgetown, they don't like to come over here because there's a lot of Latinos, there's a lot of Black people, this is part of the prejudice I'm talking about- There are some people who wouldn't even think about coming here. But the people who live around here, you know they hang out here. They go to the restaurants, they talk to people, they're laid back.

With the whole gentrification thing right now, though, things are gonna change. Supposedly it's gonna be like a second Georgetown. You know a really commercial place, we're gonna get a [live] theater, a movie theater, brand new schools, mini-mall, everything. You have the metro right there, who would not want to live in this. But then people can't afford to live here anymore it's like, nobody cared about this neighborhood before, now with all this stuff, we won't be able to afford it, we won't be able to enjoy it. And I'm gonna be the outsider! You know like, I used to live there! Well, not anymore. A lot of people say they gonna try to stay as long as possible. Even if it kills them. You know like to pay the rent and stuff like that. They want to- they definitely want to- stay here for awhile. But, you know. Like I said it's a matter of money, it's not even a matter of other people taking over. It's money taking over. And if you don't have the money then . . .

And whoever can't afford to live here anymore, What are they gonna do, they're gonna move to Maryland. They're moving to Maryland. A lot of people have moved to Maryland already. And what is gonna happen is like a domino effect, cause with all the people going **there**, and the people that **used** to be there, they feel like, hold up- hold up- It's gonna be the same thing. It's gonna cause commotion over there because it's gonna be a lot of people coming in, and then some people won't like it so they're gonna start- let's go someplace else. It's crazy.

Right now, everywhere you go there's construction. Which is good for me because I'm in that business! But eventually everything's gonna be finished, and eventually there isn't gonna be that much space. So, we are talking about a lot of expensive condominiums, all over DC, like, **a lot**! So, I guess a lot of professional people are gonna start moving in, we're gonna get a lot of upper income people here. It's gonna happen, and it's happening already. In like a two-year period of time, the rent went from 600 to 900. You gotta have two jobs. Just to not be broke. You know. And the buildings are not even that good. You know they're not worth nine hundred, a thousand dollars. If you want to get a two-bedroom apartment in DC, you're talking about twelve hundred, no, like thirteen hundred. For thirteen hundred in Maryland, you can get three bedrooms, and a backyard, and have your own parking space.

You know, I don't feel the change here yet, because for me it's not the place that makes the ambience, it's the people. And all my people are still here. A lot of people have moved out. A lot of people I know. But it was more like, you know people I **knew**, but not my close friends. But I know it's gonna feel different cause, like I said, a lot of wealthy people are gonna come in. And when they do, they're gonna change the whole set of rules. You know the whole atmosphere, they're gonna- you know already there's more police. Or maybe it's the same police but, they've become more aggressive when it comes to dealing with people. And, make no mistake, we don't- even **I** don't want drunk people on the street, because they're dangerous to people, and they are dangerous to themselves. But if you know the scene around here, you know that it's just a couple people, and it's the same people, that you need to watch out for. Most of them, they aren't gonna harm nobody. You know, they're the characters of Mt. Pleasant. A lot of those guys have been living here for 20, 30 years. And they have families, they have kids. They're part of Mt. Pleasant.

But I know it will change. And that's actually another reason why I moved out. I don't want to get to the point that I feel like, everybody's left and I'm still here. So I left before they left me! Mostly it was my job, and I was thinking, you know, it's good to see other places. But this is my place. Honestly, I could I could live my whole life in DC. It's that special. Of course I want to see other places, go back to LA, and I'd like to go to Spain, live in Spain for a few years. But if I want to settle down, I would settle here. I'd really like to some day, own a place in Mt. Pleasant. Or close to Mt. Pleasant. But it's gonna be hard. It's gonna be really hard.

What can I say about Mt. Pleasant? I was raised here, I love it here, and, I want to live here. Some day. After seeing other places, after I go around, this is the place I want to return home.

Gina

I was born in DC, I grew up pretty near the Maryland line, near Friendship Heights metro. And, it wasn't like "I'm gonna move to Mt. Pleasant," it was just, there was an opening in a group house, you know? I'd been living in an apartment in Dupont Circle, and the apartment got too expensive, I hung out [in this house in Mt. Pleasant] all the time anyway and they had an opening- somebody moved. So many people I knew lived in Mt. Pleasant- in group houses, so it was just kind of like, there's **bound** to be an opening at some point. So I moved into that house, I was there for like, two or three years, and then we all, in that house, moved to another house, where I lived for five years. So yeah, it wasn't really, Oh I want to move to Mt. Pleasant cause I want to move to that neighborhood? It was just like, that's where the group houses were. If you were more into the group house living thing, then usually there was just- something would come up in a Mt. Pleasant home.

I was still living in that house when I started going out with my now husband- we lived there together. After we decided to get married, we started to look for a place of our own. And I can remember thinking, you know we're **never** gonna find a house in this neighborhood, there's no way. And also in terms of where things were in Mt. Pleasant at that point, I mean I can just remember- going to these neighborhood meetings, the hostility and the hate and the, incredible sense of entitlement that just, permeated those- I was like- I gotta get out of here! There's so much tension and so much anger. And, um- this thing had happened right before we were leaving. We were in the process of looking for a house. And we had this great little corner market, and Paul went one morning and found Jean, the owner, who also lived next door, just totally in tears. Because she'd gotten this letter from one of the neighborhood groups saying that they were gonna protest her liquor license because she was disruptive to the neighborhood. They wanted to get her to stop selling singles [single cans of beer]. It was a form letter, you know, one of those things they have to do to protest a liquor license and get businesses to sign voluntary agreements- But Jean just took it incredibly personally. And it's just like, you know here's this complete lack of understanding. Like here's this person, whose whole life is this store. And this store that plays this incredible role in that part of Mt. Pleasant. That store was really a meeting place, where people interacted, and it was a model business. It was so ugly- it was like the classic example of how totally wrong, and adversarial those tactics are. Because here is this store, that was a total model business in the neighborhood it was totally connected with its neighbors. I mean people were **so** devoted to her, and, she was devoted to our neighbors. And if they had just gone about it by saying- if that's something that they wanted to pursue, if they had pursued it by going to the neighbors, trying to build relationships. You know, saying this is something that we're really trying- can we work with you, and Jean, you're an incredible business. You're a model business. Can you work with us? To help improve the other businesses. And just had an approach that wasn't this, us vs. them, adversarial, you are automatically a liability in this neighborhood. **We** as neighbors have to, confront and control you! It was just- it was **incredibly** ugly. And she, fought, and fought and fought. She had a lawyer, she had a- there was just a lot of people that, um, you know- helped her out, a lot of the neighbors, this really- **and** she had this petition, supporting her store, and supporting her, against those efforts. Twelve hundred people signed it.

It was weird because it was at this point where it was like, what I loved the most about the neighborhood, just like- all those people supporting Jean, and that little area of Mt. Pleasant I lived in and the way that a little business like that can become this sort of focal point where you meet people and you have conversations with them that you ordinarily wouldn't have. I mean that's the thing that I think it **is** important about those neighborhood businesses. But it was at this point where, we were thinking of moving. And we basically were just priced out of Mt. Pleasant. There was no way. So it was like, okay well let's, try to get closer. And it was literally like we would- park, at an open house. And it would usually be like a neighborhood more like you know in Columbia Heights.[6] And people would park for the open house, people would get out of their cars and **run** to the front door. And everybody would be eyeing each other and it was **so** ugly I was like, I can't deal with this anymore. And so we started looking in Takoma Park.[7] Because it seemed like maybe it would be a good thing to try to move out there. I had this idea, like we would just have a total sigh of relief out there. It was just so, nice, and the people, and street and that little main street in Takoma Park, you didn't see those like, looks of **disgust** on people's faces, and you know it was green, and- and I was just like, I'm gonna settle down in Takoma Park, I'm gonna garden, I'm gonna go to yoga all the time, I'm not gonna get involved in **any** neighborhood shit at all.

But it was a **really** incredibly hard choice. Because I had started working in the neighborhood a couple years earlier, and I really loved running into the people I worked with, right in my neighborhood, feeling that sense of connection. But we ended up doing it- we moved to like this idyllic little house. And in the beginning I remember feeling like- there was something nice about going home. And having it feel like a little refuge, you know like- okay I'm not there anymore. It was very calming. But, um, after about a year and a half, and after I had a baby, I was like- I can't live here anymore. I just- I mean I really liked it in a lot of ways, but I felt homesick. I was like, this is not- I **really** want to be living in the city. I **wanna** be engaged- in those struggles. And it was more than just that. I felt really isolated. Especially having a baby? And it's funny cause so many people are just like, when you have a baby, you want to live in the nice green, bucolic, Takoma Park. But I was just like, I want to be near my **friends**, I want to be able to walk to Mt. Pleasant, I mean I can't go to Mt. Pleasant St. and not see somebody I know. I wanted to have that social connection, and with people that I know from all these different categories of my life.

There's this sense on Mt. Pleasant St. that people that are on that street, they're not just there to consume stuff. They're there to socialize. To do their laundry. To go, you know Mt. Pleasant St.'s my favorite street in the whole city. Cause there's an energy on that street- and I just- I really wanted to live near it. And luckily we found a house right there.

So anyway, in September 2002 we moved. Back to a house a block away from the group house I'd lived in. It even had the same layout. Luckily it really was not that difficult to move back, because of what's happened in the real estate market, was to our benefit. We made enough money on our house in Takoma Park – we practically just traded houses.

It's funny because, so I live on the other side of 16th St., just a block away from Mt. Pleasant St.- and when I go to Mt. Pleasant St., I tend to see my neighbors more than I see a lot of those people from the, like, leafier parts of the neighborhood. But a lot of those people are like, like when I went to a meeting about that debate about having live music in restaurants on Mt. Pleasant St., some of the people against live music were like, you don't have any right to have any voice on this, because you don't live in Mt. Pleasant. So I feel like my voice is sort of diminished. In the eyes of some other people whose values about urban living are completely opposite of mine.

Some people have this whole idea, this driving agenda, that they have a right to be comfortable. And that, if they are made to feel uncomfortable- or if they just **feel** uncomfortable, they feel like it's somehow a violation against them. I mean like all those arguments about, not wanting to have even **unamplified** Mariachi bands. Why do they need to get rid of that? I mean it's totally because it makes them uncomfortable. But to me, what is so exciting about living, in a city, and why I wanted to move back from Takoma Park, is it's **because** there's something so much more invigorating about living in a place, where you're inundated with what's different from you- you might feel uncomfortable, you walk around and you feel uncomfortable, and then you move past that. And then you feel comfortable. When you cross a border and feel comfortable where you once felt uncomfortable. It's a humanizing process. To me living in Mt. Pleasant and living- and engaging- it's been something that's humanized me. And Mt. Pleasant St. has this kind of realness to it. And I think that realness is because people- like I said, cause people **use** it. To live their lives. Not just to consume stuff, but to- to live, and to be. And to connect with each other.

What's changed? Well, there's definitely, in the early to mid nineties, there was much more of a community of houses? And of group houses where artists and musicians were? I mean they're still there to some extent. Like the house I lived in is still a house that's pretty cheap rent, that people play music, and there's a similar house on Ingram St., it's sort of a long-term house like that, but there used to be **tons** of houses like that.

And there were so many incredible bands, and practice spaces and little, you know home recording studios in this neighborhood? There's such a secret history of that, that people don't know about. I mean like I saw Fugazi on 19th St.- they played a show cause they- cause a bunch of them lived there. And these really seminal bands like Bikini Kill played in this house on Williams St. that was called the Palace? And there were parties and shows- there were a lot of house shows. And really cool events. It was just- a very, very creative community and I still- that creative community still exists. But I think having those- having so many houses in the same neighborhood really facilitated an **extra** creative community. Because- you know, because of the space, because of the time people had with each other, because rents were low, people didn't have to work as much, there was just a lot more lingering time for people to be creative and do stuff. Also, there wasn't so much "ready made" entertainment- there weren't so many bars, you know people made their entertainment in their house. So it created a really vibrant, vital feeling.

But then, there's also things about it that I was like- there was also something missing, too. In that scene and in that community there's a kind of sense that you're in resistance. I mean it's a counter culture. And you're resisting social norms that are about conformity and materialism and, you know success and money. Really trying to build something that's more creative and vital and spontaneous. But it sometimes ended up feeling like- especially after I was starting to learn about some of the truly fucked up and oppressive things that were happening to people in our neighborhood- I mean this was around the time of [immigration reform and the city's big budget crisis]. That was when I really started thinking, let's use some of the resources- of putting on independent, do-it-yourself shows and introducing some of that vitality into neighborhood stuff, but infusing it with more of a politics. And that it's more than just a struggle about having to have a straight job versus being able to be more free and, dress however you want! But still taking that DC Punk thing, that intentionality about building a community.

But that's definitely changed, there are fewer of those houses, and that's had a big impact on people playing music. Like not being able to have practice spaces. A lot of people are like, well I have to move to Silver Spring[8] so I can have practice space. And then, other people would **never** move to Silver Spring but, they're in bands that have a band- the band has somebody that lives in Silver Spring. And there're a lot more people that live in apartments, that used to live in houses. So it's definitely affected the sense of community, in that scene.

On the one hand there's a lot of things are getting worse, gentrification has gotten worse, displacement has **really** pushed a lot, a **lot** of different kinds of people out. And I don't think it's just displacement, I mean people haven't all been forced to move out of the neighborhood, but a lot of people have been forced to have like 10 people living in an efficiency. I guess I **do** think it's probably cleaner and, safer, but that's because the crime rate went down in cities everywhere. I don't think about that too much. When I lived in Takoma Park I was always really freaked out by the woods behind our house. I mean I get sort of nervous in the country? About like you know just scary stuff in the woods.

Something to know about Mt. Pleasant and I think it's so, **cool** about it is geographical. It's the way that Mt. Pleasant St. isn't really a thoroughfare between two neighborhoods. It's kind of like a town center. It belongs to everyone and it belongs to no one. And, it's such a borderline too, cause it **is** sort of where there's a huge crevice, a gulf. You know, people living in, some of those apartments, six people in an apartment and then on the other side, people literally living in mansions. There's such a collision of all these different types of people and sometimes, and sometimes it's pretty ugly, but you know I think for the most part, people are interacting in their neighborhood to really build something. To not impose something, but to build something where- you don't even know what's gonna happen. There's so much that happens under the surface. There's ways of organizing and celebrating community that aren't just about imposing your set of preferences and values and fears on other people. And there's tons of examples of that in Mt. Pleasant. I think that a lot is at stake. When I think about the early nineties, what could have happened if people had been a little more organized, about like you know buying spaces to preserve affordable housing, or start businesses that could have been more supportive of kind of, an eclectic community. I think that everybody knew it [the real estate boom] was happening. And then it happened. And then, you know now people, now all that stuff is just out of reach. So yeah. I think those things should be actively resisted and challenged. And it **does** take stepping into some pretty toxic waters! But you can't do it with vengeance in your heart.

Yolanda

I lived in Capitol Hill, I was looking for another place, and Mt. Pleasant seemed like an interesting neighborhood. They had an apartment for rent, a basement somewhere, so we moved in. What I had heard about Mt. Pleasant was that it was a very family-oriented neighborhood, that it was very hard to find places to buy, that people when they moved in, they hardly ever moved out. So to me it seemed like it was a very stable neighborhood, and that people enjoyed living in it. And it was great! It was better than I had imagined it. You know, we moved in, we had a truck there, and, unloading stuff and people came by and invited us over for pizza. They were our neighbors and we stayed friends for- we're still friends, our kids still hang out. So that for me was the neighborhood. That was my introduction to it. The whole street that I lived on, there were a lot of kids, and they all played together and grew up together. Which was exactly what I had hoped for.

Also, Mt. Pleasant is beautiful. You know architecturally, Mt. Pleasant has this range of housing stock, that sort of goes through the history of DC. You know you have the big old farm houses, and then you have the rowhouses, and you have the apartment buildings, and so like the entire history of the city is encapsulated in this neighborhood. You can walk through the whole neighborhood and get a sense of what was there in 1850 and what was there in 1920 and 1970 and now. The housing is also in much better condition now. You know, I used to live on Huron St., years ago, the bottom of Huron was basically mostly boarded up houses. And dilapidated front yards. And the people who owned those boarded up houses, it was **really** hard to get them to- at least make sure that- when the roof collapsed, that the whole house wasn't collapsing, too. And now you walk past there it's been fixed up. The housing is taken care of. So, I think that is really nice to see. It also, of course means that the people change. And that's what I hear, too. But I don't live here anymore so it's- I left right before the **big** real estate boom. You know, not coming from the US, I remember thinking that I didn't understand the gentrification piece of it. Now I do better — being affected by it! I still think that it's always better to have a neighborhood in which the houses are not neglected. And are fixed up. It would be nice if they would make them available to people that don't have a lot of money!

The first project that I worked on in this neighborhood was a porch. A rear porch. And um, and actually the first few projects were small. They were porches, they were decks, porches and decks. You know and maybe an interior renovation. And then it started to become, **major** interior renovations. Last year I did a project for these people that bought their house the next corner over. You know they bought that house for over a million dollars! And they put in another, at least another a million into the house. And those are the kind of projects that people are doing now, where they're renovating larger portions of the house, because they can get an equity loan. I think a lot of people, it's easy for them to renovate a house now because it's worth a lot more. I mean there's people that I do work for now that, you know, they bought their house for 50,000 dollars, and they do a 200,000 dollar renovation!

I moved for personal reasons- it had nothing to do with the neighborhood. I wanted to change my living situation, and what went with that was that I could not afford to stay in the neighborhood. I looked. But I couldn't- I mean there was **nothing** for me. You know I had two kids and I worked in the house, there was nothing for me, under 2,000 dollars a month to rent. And uh, I just- you know I couldn't afford that so . . .

When I looked for another place, where I looked was motivated by what I could afford. And then it was motivated by that I wanted to stay as close as I could to Mt. Pleasant, for my kids. I had a friend who was renting the house I live in now for very inexpensive and, I jumped on it. I didn't think I could find **anything** within the Beltway[9] for less than that. Because I started looking outside of the Beltway, too.

Where I live now, it's very different than Mt. Pleasant. I don't think I've ever been as involved in a neighborhood as I was in Mt. Pleasant. And, I think that was partly because of the neighborhood. That you **could** get involved in it- it was in your face. You know, like there was, **this** person was doing **this**, and- everybody you met was in some sort of, you know. Group. Or organization. You know, Save the trees, Save the sidewalks, Save the- you know, it was- something!

When I moved to Mt. Pleasant, I had two young k- or one young kid and an older one, it was a really great place for kids. It was a great place for adults as well, with kids, and you could get involved in the neighborhood, and make it a better place, you had- you know you could walk to the bakery, there's places to walk to, there's places to buy things, you know I could hop on the bus and be at this job that I had for awhile, or work at home, and it was close enough to everything, public transportation was there, um, and if you wanted to get excited about something and change something, you could do that.

So it seemed- it seemed to feed me, it seemed to feed my kids, in that there were enough other kids around, there were playgrounds, and blackberries and, you know, junk food stores. And my kids've met interesting people. They were part of the neighborhood. When I was first living here, I mean this was still an area that, we had some kids living down the street that were walking to the neighborhood store with their 10 cents to buy chewing gum, and were attacked by somebody with a knife. So it was a neighborhood where you were thinking twice before letting your kid walk down the street alone. Of course I let them walk down the street alone! I just thought about it! I would, you know, go together. Or, you know, you warn them. You know. You can't really protect them from those things anyway. Carry a big knife and- or run! Or you know. Run. Give him your money. Give him your dime. Give him your chewing gum. But over-all it was a great place for them to grow up. There's still parents who-you have those parents that live in Bethesda and all these, really White places and they- in the beginning they had a hard time letting their kids come here. Thinking that it was dangerous. My kids just thought it was stupid! Stupid parents! I think it just solidified their idea that parents are stupid. And ignorant. You know and who knows what else.

I miss walking down the street and saying hello every 5 minutes to people that I know, or that I run into or, .I mean I used to walk- because I also worked a lot on Mt. Pleasant St., I could walk into any store and people would know me. It's a whole different place to live, when everybody knows you. Which also has its drawbacks- like that everybody knows you! There's no way to hide. Sometimes you didn't want to run into everybody, cause I had a bad day, and I just didn't want to talk to everybody and, you know, that wouldn't matter to **them**.

The change in Mt. Pleasant- well, I think, the thing for me is that change is inevitable. In any kind of city. You know, things change.

I mean- history kind of proves that. But I think that in Mt. Pleasant, change has occurred- I think people have been conscious of it. And they've been involved in it. And they've been for it or against it or, or in the middle of it. And to me, being engaged in your environment, no matter from what angle- the fact that you **can** be engaged in your neighborhood, and be involved in it and, in all aspects, I think is so important. You know the neighborhood was such an important part of who I became. I learned so much from being involved. I also learned how to become less involved! But, it told me that you can have an effect. That through your actions, through your knowledge, through your input, you can affect your environment. You know? And I think most people, or most neighborhoods perhaps, or specifically the neighborhood that I live in now, people are not involved- they're not involved in anything.

I think, specifically when change occurs in a neighborhood, it's important that people have a **say** in it. I mean, on my old street, for awhile there were people chaining themselves to **trees** so that they wouldn't be cut down. And no matter how many groups are against each other, and working against each other and hating each other and disliking each other, you know there's still dialogue, there's still, people have an opportunity to have an impact on where they live. I don't know why Mt. Pleasant became that way. But it seems to me that it attracts people that are interested in those kind of things. In fighting for something that they believe in. Or fighting against something they **don't** believe in, that's maybe more like it! Or fighting against **some**body they don't like. You know, that's probably **more** like it!

I think that if I'd lived in, sort of Bethesda or, you know, Rockville or something, I would have never have learned to become involved and what that means. It taught me to be able to articulate things, and it taught me to stand up for the things that I believe in. It also taught me sort of the limits of my- of how involved I want to be!

I think there are more interesting people per square inch in Mt. Pleasant than there are [anywhere] in the country! If you have an opinion, a strong opinion, move to Mt. Pleasant. Or if you want to change the world? I think that's what it is, maybe. Like, all politics is local. Here, you can actually touch that. That politics **is** local, and that you **can** affect your neighborhood by living here. And by affecting your neighborhood, you sort of affect the city. Although

DC's a hard city to affect. But you know, you **can** have a voice, you **can** have an impact on the environment you live in. Which in the end is the most important thing.

Notes

1 Committee In Solidarity with the People of El Salvador
2 whom you may recall from chapter 1
3 Women, Infants and Children food aid, Farmers Market Nutritional Program for Seniors
4 mentioned in the addendum
5 These stories come from follow-up interviews I conducted, which I explicitly told people I would be using to end this book, and in which I asked them what they would want the audience of this book to know about Mt. Pleasant. Because their responses were therefore more directly shaped to talk to the reader, I have chosen not to give background information on them myself, but rather to include any background information that they themselves gave within their stories.
6 the neighborhood just east of Mt. Pleasant
7 a neighborhood popularly considered to be left-leaning and somewhat hippie-ish, where many people leaving Mt. Pleasant have chosen to move to, just over the northeastern border in Maryland
8 the neighborhood in Maryland right next to Takoma Park
9 the highway that circles the city and the inner suburbs

PART II

THE MAKING OF *TURF WARS*

CHAPTER 8

THEORIZING DISCOURSE

Why Should We Care about Discourse?
A Slight Detour through Presidential Politics

I started studying discourse analysis when Bill Clinton was in the thick of his presidential primary campaign. During that time, I alternated between reading about multilingualism and turn-taking systems in sociolinguistics textbooks, and listening to presidential debates and congressional hearings on the local news. My entry into discourse analysis was concurrent with my baptism into the world of Washington politics.

When you start a graduate program in sociolinguistics, you can expect to spend a lot of time explaining to people – including most of your friends and family – just what it is that you've chosen to devote your energies to. I struggled to describe the relationship between language, culture and society, and the notion of the *discursive construction of reality*, in a way that people other than my classmates could understand. Ultimately, it was what was going on in the other part of my Washington experience that enabled me to do this – namely, the national healthcare debates that ensued during Clinton's presidential campaign and at the beginning of his presidency when Hillary Clinton took the helm of the administration's proposal to revamp the American healthcare system.

During the 1991 presidential primaries, healthcare was one of the country's most hotly discussed issues. In numerous surveys, "large majorities of the public rated health care reform among the most urgent problems facing the nation and voiced support for a plan that would provide medical insurance for all Americans."[1] At that time, 26 million people in the US went without insurance for some part of the year.[2] Compared with twelve of the major industrialized countries worldwide,[3] of which the United States had the highest gross national product, the US ranked highest on doctors' incomes and death rates of infants, 1–4-year-olds, and 15–24-year-olds, and lowest in average percentage of paid maternity leave.[4] Throughout the country, millions[5] were receiving their primary medical care in the emergency rooms[6] of overcrowded public hospitals that were facing severe budget cuts or the threat of closing.[7] Given public concern about a looming healthcare crisis, it was not surprising that healthcare reform was one of the lynchpins of Clinton's campaign, and one of his early initiatives when he took office in January of 1993. It seemed to me at the time that this would be a piece of legislation that would pass to wide popular acclaim. Even the American Medical Association, the Health Insurance Association of America, and the US Chamber of Commerce declared their support for employer-mandated healthcare, a key component of Clinton's proposal.[8]

Hilary Clinton headed up the president's task force to put a reform plan together, and in late September 1993 the administration introduced to Congress and the public what came to be known as "the Clinton plan." Within a month, it became clear that Republican politicians, strategists, and media personalities were developing a counter-campaign to build public opposition to healthcare reform. In early December, Republican advisor William Kristol (whom the conservative magazine *The New Republic* nicknamed "Dan Quayle's brain" when Kristol became vice-president Quayle's chief of staff[9]) sent out a memo to Republican members of Congress, advising that they vote against *any* health plan that the Clinton administration proposed, "sight unseen",[10] and that they promote the notion that "there is no health care crisis",[11] that the US "currently enjoys the finest, most comprehensive and most generous system of medical care in world history."[12] Kristol's rationale was that if healthcare reform passed, it would spur middle-class voters to vote for Democrat candidates, thereby strengthening the Democrat party.[13]

For my present purposes, what is important about the healthcare debate of the early 1990s is that the Republican campaign against the Clinton plan had everything to do with language. From the Senate floor to the talk show circuits to the direct mail flyers that people found on their doorsteps, the anti-reform campaign strategically used language to frame the Clinton plan as an assault on American values and Americans' interests. While on one front Republican Senator Phil Gramm of Texas was declaring that the United States had "the greatest medical system in the history of the world",[14] on another House Minority Whip Newt Gingrich (R) was decrying the healthcare plan as "culturally alien to America."[15] Gingrich and his Republican colleagues used phrases such as "central planning," "state monopoly,"[16] and "collectivized medicine"[17] to imply that the healthcare plan would transform the US into a socialist country. More explicitly, Gingrich complained that healthcare reform would bring "socialism, now or later,"[18] that "Bill Clinton is doing almost precisely the same thing we are telling Boris Yeltsin to stop doing."[19] And on the talk radio front, G. Gordon Liddy, architect-of-the-Watergate-scandal-turned-talk-show-host, exclaimed that

[Bill and Hillary Clinton] have buffaloed and deceived the American people into going along with [their healthcare plan]. They want to socialise the whole American economy, and they are starting by socialising 14 per cent of it."[20]

These utterances helped to *discursively construct* what many in this country came to consider the reality of the healthcare situation. (That Gramm's pronouncement of the US medical system as the best "in the history of the world" flew in the face of most measurements of the quality of a healthcare system had virtually no effect on the way that the public began to think about healthcare.)

Soon the American Medical Association and the US Chamber of Commerce reversed their positions supporting a mandate for employers to provide health insurance for their workers. The Health Insurance Industry Association not only reversed its position on this issue, but it created the organization that led the public relations campaign against the Clinton plan: The Coalition for Health Insurance Choices (CHIC).[21] This group funded and gave technical support to more than 20 separate groups working to defeat the Clinton plan. Blair G. Childs, the leader of CHIC, advised the smaller coalitions CHIC was working with to use words that you've identified in your research . . . There are certain words that . . . have a general positive reaction. That's where focus group and survey work can be very beneficial. "Fairness", "balance", "choice", "coalition", and "alliance" are all words that resonate very positively.[22]

Republican politicians employed similar tactics, painting the Clinton healthcare plan as something suspicious and inherently bad, by linking it discursively with controversies that had nothing to do with healthcare. For example, in March of 1994, Representative Lamar Smith (R-Texas) directed members of the House, along with their press secretaries and assistants, to focus on "Whitewater and Healthcare."[23] In other words, he directed them to connect healthcare with a suspicious private land deal that had occurred in the Ozarks in the late 1970s. If such a connection could be made in people's minds, then the negative connotation of Whitewater could rub off onto Clinton's healthcare reform plan.

And such a connection indeed *was* made: All over the country, people flooded the editorial pages of small and large newspapers with letters expressing sentiments like the following, from the *Chicago Sun-Times*:

> Let me see if I have this straight: We want our **health care** system to be run by the same people who gave us the Postal Service, Medicare and Medicaid, the Vietnam War, Watergate, the S&L scandal, the House banking scandal, etc.
>
> Next thing you know, the Clinton administration is going to tell us that organized crime is going to run the banking system, and the Colombian drug lords are going to operate our pharmaceutical industry.
>
> Conrad Gurtatowski, Calumet City

The memo that Lamar Smith sent out included soundbites for people to use in speeches and media commentaries. A few weeks later, conservative radio talk show host and provocateur Rush Limbaugh did Smith and Childs one better by declaring on his show that "Whitewater is about healthcare." One might think that listeners would find dubious a connection between individual people's investment in land and a government's policies for its constituents' health, but

Limbaugh's characteristic linguistic flair proved incredibly effective, particularly because his treatises were coordinated with Childs' and CHIC's pressure campaigns: Limbaugh's speeches to his audience were punctuated by anti-Clinton-plan advertisements that provided a toll-free phone number. People who called this number were given more ammunition against the plan, and then directly connected to their representatives' offices.[24]

That the Republicans and their allies were successful in shaping public opinion through language can be seen perhaps most clearly in the *Wall Street Journal*'s poll asking respondents to evaluate five healthcare plans. When respondents were given a description of the contents of Clinton's plan, 76 percent said it had "great appeal." However, when they were explicitly told that it was "The Clinton Plan," approval dropped 30 to 40 percentage points.[25] The success of the Republicans in convincing people that Clinton's plan was a frightening example of Big Government invading individual freedom perhaps explains the letter that Congresswoman Pat Schroeder (D-Colorado) received from a constituent, telling her to "keep the government's hands off my Medicare."[26]

On September 26 of 1994, George Mitchell (D-Maine), Senate Majority leader, announced the death of the administration's health-care initiative. That this was largely a result of Republican efforts can be seen by Senator Bob Packwood's (R-Oregon) remark to his colleagues that "We've killed health care reform. Now we've got to make sure our fingerprints are not on it,"[27] and Senator Phil Gramm's more wholehearted embrace of his role: "I am certainly proud of my part of killing the Clinton plan in all of its incarnations."[28]

Since Bill Clinton began to talk about healthcare in 1991, the number of uninsured people in the US has risen by one million or more every year. In 2003, the latest year for which data are published, it rose by 1.4 million, to a total of 45 million people without health insurance. On other measures of healthcare, compared to the thirty other OECD[29] countries, the United States ranks highest in per capita pharmaceutical spending, private insurance costs, obesity; among the highest for teen pregnancy[30]; above the OECD median in infant mortality and low birth weight, below the OECD median for life expectancy, immunization, and acute care hospital beds and doctors per capita, and lowest of all OECD countries on public health spending.[31] Yet in the popular consciousness, Congress did a good thing by shooting down what many still consider to be Clinton's ill-conceived and dangerous ideas for reform. The linguistic tactics of players like Blair Childs, Lamar Smith, William Kristol, and Rush Limbaugh were successful. As a beginning student of discourse analysis in the early 1990s, I learned from the healthcare debates as clearly as from anything I was reading in my studies, that discourse matters.

Defining *Discourse*

Big D *and* little d

It's worth pausing here to talk about what exactly discourse *is* – how various theorists conceptualize the term, and how I'm using it in this study. *Discourse* is a term that scholars from different disciplines use to mean different things. Social theorists commonly use the term to mean *a way of talking or writing about a particular topic that is connected with various ideologies.* James Gee notes that linguists tend to refer to this definition of discourse as *big D Discourse.*[32] As Gee explains,

> Discourses are ways of being in the world, or forms of life which integrate words, acts, values, beliefs, attitudes, social identities . . . A *Discourse* is a socially accepted association among ways of using language, of thinking, feeling, believing, valuing, and of acting that can be used to identify oneself as a member of a socially meaningful group or "social network", or to signal (that one is playing) a socially meaningful role.[33]

What characterizes the *big D* approach is an interest in the ways that people represent the social world through discourse, and the ways that those representations rely on or construct certain ideologies. Scholars who take a *big D* approach tend to focus on the *general content* of that talk, writing, or signing, and typically pay little attention to linguistic structure. Some scholars who take a *big D* approach to discourse analysis are interested in the ways of using language in a very general sense, such that the approach is often abstract rather than empirically grounded (based on observation or experience) in analysis of actually occurring texts.[34]

In recent years, scholars in many fields outside of linguistics have taken to analyzing representations of people or events that occur in discourse. This has become such a prevalent approach that it's commonly referred to as the "discursive turn" in social sciences and humanities. Where social science studies generally are interested in the interrelationship between social categories – age, race, geographical boundaries, etc. – and phenomena in the world – crime, mental health, television viewing, etc. – social scientists taking a discourse approach do not take social categories or real-world phenomena as natural or given. Rather, they are interested in studying how such categories and phenomena came to be constructed – through language – and how those categories promote certain power relations and biases. A scholar taking a discourse approach to healthcare in the US, for example, might want to know how discourses about American healthcare maintain or threaten the interests of some groups over others. A study of age discrimination might involve how attitudes about aging are encapsulated in the retirement policy documents of corporations, or how ideas about aging are promoted in cosmetics and pharmaceuticals advertising. Theorists interested in racial inequality might ask what criteria scientists and governments have historically used to delineate racial groups, and how those criteria have been promoted in political speeches or the writing of laws. A criminologist might study the discourses that influence people's ideas about what counts as crime, what shapes people's views about whether or not smoking pot, smoking crack, or snorting cocaine should be crimes, and what the various punishments for these should be.

Social scientists who take a discourse approach to the study of social behavior tend to focus on the content of discourse, while generally paying little attention to the organization and structure of linguistic form.

What distinguishes a linguistic approach to discourse is its focus on the structure and organization of discourse – characteristic of the *little d* approach. Although linguists may be interested in the connections between language and ideology that *big D* approaches focus on, we use the term *discourse* in a narrower and somewhat more technical sense. At its most basic, *discourse* from a linguistic perspective is language above the utterance[35] level. Language is a system of smaller units that speakers combine to make larger units – sounds (*phonemes*) are combined to make meaning units (*morphemes*, for example *unit* and *s* in the word *units*) which are combined to make words. Words are combined to make utterances, which finally combine to make discourse.

Discourse is not just a collection of random utterances, however. To qualify as discourse, utterances that are grouped together must have some relation to each other. In other words, any given utterance in a chunk of discourse exists within what we can call a wider linguistic context. Thus, as sociolinguist Deborah Schiffrin[36] notes, a given utterance derives its meaning from its position in a sequence of other utterances, as well as from its grammatical structure. At the same time, that utterance also shapes the meaning context for following and previous utterances.

In analyzing utterances in their linguistic context, analysts trained in this tradition pay close attention to linguistic form as well as linguistic content. For example, if a parent tells a child jumping on a bed to stop and the child responds, a linguist would be interested to know if the way the parent phrases the comment influences the way the child responds: Does the parent structure the utterance as a directive ("Stop jumping on the bed"), a request ("Please stop jumping on the bed"), a hint ("It's not really a good idea to jump on the bed"), or an explanation ("Jumping on the bed is gonna ruin the springs")? Further, what are the social consequences? Does the child consider one phrasing more authoritative than another? Would a child whose parents gave directives understand an uncle's hint as an actual command? Would a child whose parents gave hints consider an aunt's command forms to be rude or mean?

Sociolinguistically oriented analysts also attend to the social context that an utterance exists in. Sometimes utterances hang together because of the relationship between words or linguistic structures – for example, the relationship between *book* and *it* in the utterances, "Where's the *book*? *It's* on the table." (M.A.K. Halliday and Ruqaiya Hasan[37] refer to this relationship as *cohesion*). However, in all but the most banal cases of language use, situational or world knowledge is critical for understanding what Halliday and Hasan call the *coherence* among utterances. Any chunk of discourse both gains its meaning from, and shapes the meaning of, the larger social context within which it's situated.[38]

This social contextedness means that linguistic interactants must bring with them – and thus engage – social knowledge, attitudes, and values when they interpret and produce discourse. At the same time, certain discourse structures promote certain perspectives, while backgrounding others. For example, as in the analysis of the grant proposal for public toilets, nominalization (the turning of a verb into a noun) and passive voice obscure who the performers of actions are: Compare the utterances, "A shooting occurred last night" (a nominalization of the verb *shoot*) to "a high school student was shot" (passive voice) to "a police officer shot a high school student" (active voice).

It is at the nexus of ideology and linguistic structure that *big D* and *little d* discourse can come together: Since any utterance is necessarily socially contexted, every actual series of utterances involves and invokes a particular world view and value system. *Big D* Discourses are also related to *little d* discourses in that a social group's *general* ways of speaking, and the world views encoded in and promoted by those ways of speaking, are built up through an accrual of actual *little d* discourses over time.[39] It is through hearing and participating in actual linguistic interactions that speakers acquire the *big D* Discourses of the groups they belong to. And it's through their subsequent use of those abstract-level Discourses in *actual* discourse that the ideologies embedded in Discourses get perpetuated or contested.

Like *big D* analysts, in the present study I'm concerned with ideology. At the same time, however, I am interested in how ideologies are encoded and promoted in specific, actual instances of *situated interaction* – that is, interactions that are situated within specific social contexts. I maintain a *big D* interest in the way that particular instances of discourse about urban life are indicative of larger, more general ways of talking about urbanness at the wider societal level. At the same time, I follow a *little d* methodology by analyzing how linguistic content, form, and context shape the meanings of particular utterances.[40]

Functionalist Approaches to Discourse: Performance, Performativity, and Practice

Thinking about the Clinton healthcare debates made me interested in the functions of discourse – I didn't want to think about discourse as simply an object that existed out there, an object that somehow was formed through an abstract system of language rules that existed in people's heads. Rather, I wanted to study how it was that people *did things* with language. I became more and more interested in what's come be called a *practice-based approach* to analyzing discourse. The discursive practice perspective has grown out of a branch of the philosophy of language called *speech act theory*. In philosophers J.L. Austin's and John Searle's influential work in the 1960s and 1970s, including Austin's book *How To Do Things With Words*, these scholars critiqued language philosophers' preoccupation at the time with the way that language conveyed truth or falsity. Austin argued that not all utterances could be interpreted as true or false, and that instead of thinking about utterances in those terms, it was more interesting to think about utterances in terms of what they accomplished. Austin theorized that utterances were *performative* – that by their uttering, they performed an effect on the world – they brought a state of affairs into being, rather than simply reflecting a state of affairs. One of the classic examples is the utterance, "I now pronounce you married," that (under certain circumstances) accomplishes the marriage of two people. Searle went on to theorize how utterances were successful or unsuccessful, based on whether or not certain conditions were met. For example, who can be vested with the authority to utter these words in a binding way? How many people can be married to each other? Does the sex or gender of those to be married matter?

Searle's interest in the micro-level mechanics of how individual utterances succeeded or failed to accomplish things within particular social contexts is indicative of a *little d* approach to discourse. The philosopher Judith Butler, also interested in the performative aspect of utterances, took a *big D* approach to this question, and drew on speech act theory to develop the more widely ranging *theory of performativity*. Butler's theory of performativity was more centrally concerned with how people doing things with discourse and other symbolic systems brought ideologies and ways of understanding the world into being, reinforced them, or changed them.

Butler's *big D* approach considered not just what people said, but extended Austin and Searle's original scope of inquiry to other forms of practice such as clothing choice or participation in certain kinds of activities. Butler was particularly interested in the ways that people construct, reinforce, or change gender roles through repeating or changing actions (including utterances) over time. Take, for example, a group of people in the US who frequently curse. If this group also, say, tends to sit on a bus seat with legs widespread, wear neckties,[41] and use the lower part of their voice's pitch range – all practices that in the US tend to be associated with men – then the combination of those symbolic practices might lead to an interpretation of those group members as masculine – whether they are women or men. If the group curses a lot but in most other ways performs actions that over time have come to be associated with femininity – so that they are perceived by and large as feminine – then this group's cursing might be seen as non-normative gender behavior. If enough people who performed "feminine" practices began to curse, however, then over time cursing might cease to be an activity associated with gender. (And one could argue that this is what has happened in the US over the past 30 or so years in some social groups.) Butler emphasized that people are constrained to perform the activities and actions that are associated with their sex, however, in that there are all kinds of negative consequences for acting like a woman if people think you should act like a man, or acting like a man if people think you should act like a woman.

Butler's work became extremely influential for theorists of language and gender, who took her philosophical approach to the issue and applied it to microanalyses of people speaking in gendered ways. One of the leading scholars in this area is the sociolinguist Deborah Cameron, who has helped to shift the field from an approach where, as she explains, "people talk the way they do because of who they (already) are" to one where "people are who they are because of (among other things) the way they talk."[42]

In the late 1990s, at the time that I was doing my fieldwork, linguistic anthropologists and sociolinguists were taking an interest in connections between interpersonal or group relations and social identity. For me, this was exciting because it created a space for thinking about people's agency – about our own roles in creating our social worlds, our choices, the ways that larger institutions constrain our choices, and how we respond to those constraints. Sociolinguists like Penelope Eckert and Sally McConnell-Ginet were developing a practice-based approach to sociolinguistic analysis, an approach that drew connections between discourse's performative nature and people's social identity. This approach gave me a way to think about how our portrayals of ourselves as certain kinds of people, as well as others' portrayals of us, constrain the choices that we have.

The practice-based approach has its roots in sociologist Pierre Bourdieu's *Outline of a Theory of Practice*. Bourdieu argued that it is not the case that communities follow a set of fixed rules for the various rituals of day-to-day life, but rather that rules emerge out of certain practices that form a person's *habitus*. A habitus, briefly stated, is the whole of a person's commonsense environment, the practices that seem like the natural or right or sometimes even the only way to do things – from holding a fork to riding a bus to running a political campaign. Habitus also includes a person's *dispositions*, or tendencies to think and act in certain ways. Bourdieu used *habitus* as a way to explain how choice and agency are constrained: Although we may think that the practices we choose – what music we listen to, who we choose as romantic partners, how we dress, what we read – is purely a question of free choice, Bourdieu found that free choice did not explain the similarities of people's choices within particular demographic groups. Bourdieu argued that it is our habitus that constrains our choices – our social practices – such that these demographic patterns emerge. Bourdieu's focus on the ways that social structure and organization grow out of social practices (actions which people perform in social interaction), and the way that this notion was developed within sociolinguistics, was very important in my thinking about how to characterize Mt. Pleasant in terms of community.

Discourse and Community

Traditionally, sociolinguists and linguistic anthropologists have used the framework of a *speech community* to analyze the groups they have studied. The role that theorists assign to speech or language in defining a group as a speech community varies. For sociolinguist William Labov, the notion of *speech community* is closely tied to linguistic criteria. In Labov's view, members belong to the same community if they share norms for producing and evaluating linguistic features. Labov conducted a landmark study of speech in New York City, in which he was concerned primarily with micro-level features such as what it means to pronounce an *r* sound after a vowel in a word like *author*, or to leave the *r* out.[43] According to such criteria Mt. Pleasant really couldn't be analyzed as a speech community: Mt. Pleasantites as a group have such divergent linguistic backgrounds, and many have moved not just to the neighborhood, but to the city, region, and country, in teen years or adulthood, long after their linguistic systems were more or less set (although of course speakers accommodate to others, and occasionally speakers do exhibit changes in their underlying linguistic system at a late age).

Linguistic anthropologist John Gumperz had a slightly broader approach to the linguistic criteria needed to define a community as a speech community. Drawing on research from India to Europe and the United States, Gumperz emphasized that, although people had to share some basic ways of comprehending the social meaning of language (for example, what values or meanings a group gives to being a monolingual Spanish speaker or a monolingual Guaraní speaker), members of speech communities need not actually speak the same language. For Gumperz, speech communities are primarily defined by the interaction of their members, where that interaction is more intensive than interaction with other groups. (In other words, strength of interaction serves as a boundary between speech communities.[44]) Although with some finessing I felt like I could make this definition work for Mt. Pleasant, it still didn't really seem to fit. Mt. Pleasant was such a heterogeneous and multilingual neighborhood, and a neighborhood where lots of people did not interact intensively, that it didn't really make sense to me to use these criteria as the main ones to define the neighborhood as a linguistic community.

Still, my intuition was that there *was* a community here, and that there was some type of language use that corresponded to being part of that community. I knew there was something that people were doing with the way they talked about the neighborhood that drew them together as members of a community, even when they didn't agree. It was here that a practice-based approach became useful.

The connection between practice and community was explicitly articulated by the education theorists Jean Lave and Etienne Wenger in their work on situated learning.[45] In seeking to understand how people gain knowledge, Lave and Wenger examined a number of different occupational and social groups including butchers, midwives, and recovering alcoholics, and found that it was through watching and participating in practices that were situated within social interactions that people learned new skills or knowledge. Lave and Wenger also found that what people learned depended on where they were in the hierarchy of the group.

Penelope Eckert and Sally McConnell-Ginet took Lave and Wenger's idea of *community of practice* and used it to investigate the relationship between linguistic behavior and the formation of social groups in a suburban Detroit high school. What was especially appealing to me about their approach was that for them, the notion of *place* was an integral part of community formation, and that they also connected practice to social identity. I was drawn to their work because they argued that "sociolinguists need some conception of community that articulates place with practice."[46] This made me think that their approach would be particularly useful for working out how it was that Mt. Pleasant counted as a community. And they had a definition of *community of practice* that really seemed to fit well with the way that I perceived community interaction in Mt. Pleasant, and that had a role for language, but was flexible about what that role was:

> [a] community of practice is an aggregate of people who come together around mutual engagement in some common endeavor. Ways of doing things, ways of talking, beliefs, values, power relations – in short, practices – emerge in the course of their joint activity around that endeavor. A community of practice is different as a social construct from the traditional notion of community, primarily because it is defined simultaneously by its membership and by the practice in which that membership engages.[47]

Viewing people in Mt. Pleasant as members of a community of practice worked, because it highlighted people's participation in what I came to call *discourses of place* as a type of what Eckert and McConnell-Ginet referred to as "social engagement." Although the particulars of how people talked about the neighborhood differed, people in Mt. Pleasant were united by their common endeavors to define their neighborhood as an urban place and themselves as urban people. In other words, a critical mass of people who lived or hung out in the neighborhood were very much engaged in the practice of defining what kind of place the neighborhood was, and who was a "real" or "fake" person. And I was surprised at the pervasiveness

of this engagement across all different spectrums in the neighborhood – age, ethnicity, politics, reasons for living in the neighborhood, etc. Viewing Mt. Pleasant as a community of practice enabled
me to draw connections between the ways that people talked about
the neighborhood and the ongoing struggles I witnessed (and sometimes took part in) over claims to space and rights to community
membership. (For more on the distinction I'm making between "community" and "neighborhood," see the discussion of those terms in
the addendum.)

The practice-based approach also resonated with my training in
interactional sociolinguistics, a perspective that views discourse as meaning deriving not only from the social and linguistic context, but also
from the *use* that speakers put discourse to in interactions with other
people.[48] For example, when a teenager showing off to friends in
his car yelled out the window to me one day, "Hey Baby, want a
ride?", it had a very different meaning than when my 65-year-old
female neighbor yelled the very same thing to me the next week as
she slowed her car down to signal that she was actually offering me
a ride. As I got more immersed in my fieldwork, I started to see
more and more clearly how discourse meaning was connected to
speakers' goals, as well as to a speaker's social identity. This led me
to want to investigate how and why people within a community create social identities for themselves and others in interactions.

Community-based research

I had developed an interest in language and community early in my
graduate studies in DC at Georgetown University, when I took a
field methods course with the sociolinguist Peter Patrick. I have to
admit that back then, "field methods" sounded incredibly boring –
that is, until I found out what it actually was. I had come to grad
school because I was interested in how language worked as a system
and what the social consequences were of the ways that people used
language, but I hadn't really considered in any kind of systematic
way how the methods that a researcher used might impact the kind
of linguistic data that a researcher had access to. In college I had
done research projects that involved analyzing newspaper articles, or
asking fellow students outside the library what kind of metaphors

they used to describe mental illness (i.e., "not playing with a full deck," "taking a ride on the Disoriented Express"), but I had never done a project that involved trying to get complete strangers to sit down with me, let me tape them for long stretches of time, and introduce me to their friends so that I could do the same thing with them.

In the field methods class, Peter set out to teach us the basic tools of the trade by having us conduct a semester-long community-based research project.[49] The "field" for this project was two DC neighborhoods – Mt. Pleasant and the adjacent Adams Morgan, where I had just moved upon coming to DC. The class was split into groups of three and four, and each group chose two blocks to focus on. One of the blocks that my group chose was the block I lived on. In the classroom we covered practical skills, such as learning how to find the range that our tape-recorders and microphones would pick up, and we debated other scholars' ideas about theoretical dilemmas, like whether or not the talk that happens in a sociolinguistic interview (a loosely structured, informal interview) is the same as the talk in a spontaneous conversation[50] or the extent to which ethnographers should begin research with specific hypotheses in mind, versus just going in and starting to talk, and letting the research questions emerge as you learn new things about life in the community under study.[51] We put our evolving ideas about fieldwork to the test by going out "in the field,"[52] writing about what happened, and coming back into the classroom to share our results. We conducted interviews and discussed the different approaches we had each used in writing up an interview report. (Do you talk about the surroundings where the interview took place? Describe the backgrounds of the interviewer and interviewee? Include the questions you asked along with your interlocutor's responses?) And we learned that mistakes are part of the game. One friend of mine was captivated by an afternoon gardener who regaled her with richly detailed narratives of his childhood in the same house that he was now living in, but an hour and a half into the interview my friend noticed that the battery box on the tie-clip microphone attached to the man's shirt-collar was open and the battery was sitting on his shirt. In my enthusiasm to fill out all the information on the information forms we were supposed to turn in with every interview, I found out the hard way that older women may find it quite insulting and inappropriate for someone much younger to ask their age.

When I first went out into the field, I was intently focused on asking questions "in the right way," which to me meant in a way that would get people talking so that I as the interviewer could fade into the background and just follow their lead, hoping that they would develop their own topics which I could just pursue with follow-up questions. (This was the classic sociolinguistic interview technique that William Labov had developed, and it was designed to get a maximum amount of unmonitored speech from participants, as well as to yield discourse that was not influenced by what participants thought interviewers wanted to hear.) But slowly I began to realize that the kinds of things people told you, and the general reactions they had to you, had a lot to do with what kind of person they thought you were. I first grasped this idea in the abstract while reading linguistic anthropologist Charles Briggs' book *Learning How to Ask*,[53] in which Briggs describes how people in his research site did not respond to interviews with the kind of information that he was hoping to get, and that it was not until he started learning woodcarving from a respected woodcarver, and the woodcarver during these carving sessions talked about many of the topics that Briggs had been curious about, that he realized how much the social context − in this case, what linguists call the *speech event* − influences everything from topics that are likely to be discussed to norms for who can talk when and who can say what.

In discussing Briggs' work in class, Peter encouraged us to consider the social identities we brought with us (or that were imputed to us), as well as the associations we formed in the communities we were working in, as part of the social context which would influence how people interacted with us, linguistically and otherwise. I still remember two stories he told us to illustrate these points: When he had taken a field methods class himself as a student, two of his classmates started to become friendly with a group of young men who spent time on a certain street corner in the neighborhood the students were working in. While other students in the class were starting to build a rapport with multiple people in the neighborhood, these first two students found that no one else in the neighborhood wanted to talk to them. After some investigation, they finally discovered that the men they had first made a connection with turned out to be heroin junkies whom no one in the neighborhood wanted to have anything to do with, so by extension people in the neighborhood wanted to have nothing to do with these students. Peter also told us that when he began his fieldwork in urban Jamaica, he found that people in the neighborhood he was working in thought he was a Mormon missionary because he was a White guy who rode a bicycle, since the only White people who rode bicycles in that area were Mormon missionaries.

These stories provided me with an insight into the importance of the way I presented myself, but this didn't really become real to me until I experienced it myself. And while the examples we'd been discussing in class had to do with how people presented themselves, my fieldwork group's interactions with community members also taught us that you can't always control how people will read you, regardless of how you present yourself.

The relationship between an informant and a researcher is an inherent component of any kind of research, even experimental research – if I walk into a psychology lab to take part in a study where every part of an experiment is controlled, that in itself is a certain kind of social context, and the way I behave in that experimental context, with that particular researcher, is not necessarily the same as the way I would behave in a similar real-life situation interacting with a different person in my everyday life. A fundamental tenet of ethnographic research is that there exists no neutral position for a researcher – if you are engaged in social interaction, you are part of that interaction, and who you are is going to affect the kind of data you have access to. The key to good ethnographic research is accepting this, because if you learn to be reflective about what exactly your position is and how people are reading you, you can gain a lot of insight into norms of interaction and values in the community you're studying. Different researchers have different kinds of access to different communities, and every researcher will have access to some aspects of a community that other researchers do not have access to. My field-methods group comprised three people – Limin Zheng, a Chinese man in his early 30s, Lourdes Pietrosemoli, a Venezuelan woman in her 40s, and me. As a group, we were able to gather lots of different types of information because of the ways that people responded differently to us. From Limin's interactions we found out about tensions among local merchants and fears of the changing business landscape, when a store owner responding to a phone call from Limin thought that he was a Korean businessman who wanted to buy him out. Lourdes exploited her status as someone who had not grown up in the United States and was not planning to stay, to probe into community members' attitudes about local race relations. Because many community members assumed that she did not know very much about the history of race relations in DC, and because people seemed to read her as someone who did not have a stake in local race relations in the same way as she would have if she'd been planning to stay in the US, many informants gave her mini-lectures on relations between Blacks, Whites, and Latinos, in much more detail and with much less concern for voicing stereotypes of these groups than they showed when talking to either me or Limin, who people read as long-term residents of the Washington area. My own contribution was information about race-inflected tensions between owners and renters and between longtime and newer residents, gleaned from numerous stories told to me about irresponsible White group house kids who never shoveled the snow in front of their houses.

Reading sociolinguistic and anthropological studies about communities at the same time as I was finding my way through the difficulties and pleasures of fieldwork opened a new universe for me, as it showed me the complexities of even the simplest interactions – how even a small act like how two people acknowledged each other as they passed on the street could shed light on gender relations, fears about neighborhood change, economic inequalities, or conflicts over what counts as proper behavior in public space.

Reading theory and watching it play out in real life on the streets of my own neighborhood gave me a feeling akin to what I had felt walking the Stations of the Cross in Jerusalem. (Even as a Jew, there was something undeniably stirring about tracing the footsteps of such a historically and spiritually significant figure as Jesus.) Seeing theory play out for real in Mt. Pleasant gave me the feeling that there was a deep and layered meaning under the surface of every seemingly mundane act that I saw on the street, a meaning that could be unpacked in unexpected ways by detailed observation and careful analysis. This really hit home when I read Brett Williams' *Upscaling Downtown*, an ethnography of Mt. Pleasant in the 1980s.

Among the aspects of neighborhood life that Williams investigated were friendships among children of different ethnic and/or economic backgrounds. She detailed the ways that young children forged friendships out of the cultural preoccupations that they shared – one of which turned out to be characters from television shows. While playing She-ra and He-man was shaping kids to be good consumers, at the same time the creativity of the play reshaped television-toyland into a distinctive community activity. As Williams noted, "children's commodities are unlike many that adults learn and consume because they are deeply communal and participatory. They link children across all the boundaries that divide adults."[54] But Williams also chronicled how those boundaries came to weigh down on kids: Cross-ethnoracial and cross-class friendships grew weaker as children grew older, and as more economically well-off parents placed their children in structured after-school activities and in private schools or in public schools "across the park."[55] Detailing how children grew to be aware of ethnoracial categories and how their friendships started to take on different valences as their class and ethnoracial backgrounds influenced their academic and social trajectories, Williams poignantly illustrated the difficulty of negotiating between individual and group identities. As I read Williams' analysis, I came to see kids jumping from porches to sidewalks not simply as play, but more clearly as stories about the commercialization of culture. Laughing and yelling in alleys above wheel-less cars on cinderblocks and among tomato plants heavy with fruit were no longer simply neighborly interactions to me; I came to see them as narratives about ethnicity, class, and inequality in American society.

I had a similar revelation later on, when I read Olivia Cadaval's book, *Creating a Latino Identity in the Nation's Capital*. In this book, Cadaval traced the history of the DC Latino festival, from its beginnings in Mt. Pleasant and Adams Morgan, through to its move downtown to Pennsylvania Avenue. By analyzing the connection of the festival in its multiple incarnations to the shifting demographics of the Latino community and the disputes about how best to represent the community and gain representation for Latino interests in the city at-large, Cadaval elucidated how cultural celebration is embedded with politics, and that politics, moral values, and economics are entwined with each other and with the symbolic systems (the elements of a parade, the words of a poem) that people use to articulate them.

Later I read urban anthropologists' work on patterns of participation and exclusion in urban neighborhoods undergoing rapid change due to shifting demographics and new urban development policies – Roger Sanjek's work on cross-racial alliances and local politics in a neighborhood undergoing demographic shift[56] and Steven Gregory's work on African American civic institutions and struggles over neighborhood space,[57] both in Queens, New York, and Jeff Maskovsky's research on community responses to public and private urban planning initiatives in a gentrifying neighborhood in Philadelphia.[58] Taking a more discourse-oriented approach, urban sociologist Christopher Mele[59] illustrated how the language of the media, real estate industry, and neighborhood residents supported or fought patterns of investment and disinvestment in New York City's Lower East Side over the course of the 20th century. Making connections between my work and these studies, I began to see how the goings-on in Mt. Pleasant fit into a larger American story about how people dealt with neighborhood change in the urban US, and that telling Mt. Pleasant's story could provide insight into creating and preserving community ties and communal life.

Living in Adams Morgan and Mt. Pleasant while I was studying about language and community identity pushed me to pay attention to the mundane, ordinary activities that my neighbors and I performed on a daily basis, and to think about them as complex and full of multiple meanings. Scholars like Williams and Cadaval showed in a very concrete way what anthropologists mean when they talk about "theorizing the everyday." It's by building theories about the meanings of everyday interactions that we can get at the relationship between the *big D* and the *little d* – that we can come to understand how individual acts cohere over time to form, reinforce, or change larger social structures like ethnic and class relations. Once I got to the stage of doing my own in-depth research, what was really exciting about being in Mt. Pleasant was discovering that community identity was such a strong concern of so many people in the neighborhood, which meant that everybody around me was theorizing the neighborhood. What this book is meant to be is my reflections about my community's various theories of what it means to be an authentic urbanite, who gets to define that in what kind of settings, and what's at stake in whose definitions win out.

Ideology

What it means to be an authentic urbanite is a question of both identity and ideology. Identity started to be an important framework for analyzing discourse in the late 1990s. A common critique that people levy against discourse research on identity is that the inquiry is sometimes limited to questions about the *mechanics* of identity construction – what discourse strategies people use in creating identities – and does not investigate the real-world *consequences* of identity construction.

Research on the mechanics is important because we can't understand conflicts about identity if we don't understand the nitty-gritty of how people construct identity in the first place. But I wanted to explore the material effects of identity constructions – how did they impact events in the real world? How did they relate to relations of inequality? These questions were compatible with the goals of critical discourse analysis (CDA). I was attracted to CDA because this branch of analysis has an explicit political goal of addressing real-world problems of power distribution and inequality, and the ways in which people perpetuate inequality through discourse – particularly public discourse which reaches a wide audience. To get at these questions, critical discourse analysts focus on the ideological components of texts as well as the circulations of texts through space and time. This turned out to be a good framework for me for articulating how different views of urbanness and of Mt. Pleasant circulated through the neighborhood, and how they interacted with each other.

I was particularly influenced by the work of Teun van Dijk and Ruth Wodak. Wodak's discourse-historical approach[60] seeks to elucidate not just how discourses shape and are shaped by the sociopolitical contexts of the societies in which they are used, but the approach also focuses on tracing the historical development of such discourses. In addition, it emphasizes the importance of ethnographic fieldwork, to get a sense of how texts get produced and what they mean to the people who produce and interpret them.[61]

Teun van Dijk's theory of social cognition[62] strongly informed the way that I thought about the connections between discourse and ideology. As van Dijk explains, ideologies are *socially shared* belief systems that people use to evaluate the world around them. He characterizes these systems as based on cognitive models that are stored in memory and updated, maintained, and/or revised through social interaction. Key to van Dijk's work is the evaluative function of ideologies. In addition to ordering knowledge and beliefs, ideologies, through their evaluative function, help people to interpret and make decisions about the ways in which they and others act upon and interact with and within various kinds of social environments.

The work of scholars specifically studying ideologies of language was particularly useful because it promoted the view that, although ideologies are learned, reinforced, or contested through social interaction, this does not mean that ideologies are universally shared within a group. Charles Briggs noted, for example, that

> cases in which one ideology appears to dominate, provide[ ] fascinating vantage points from which to examine how ideologies of language, to paraphrase Clifford Geertz (1966), become both constructions of and for social inequality, provided that scholars become critically aware of [. . .] the ways that dominance over competing ideologies and practices is naturalized.[63]

For the purposes of analyzing Mt. Pleasant, this perspective helped me to focus on the ways that dominant and non-dominant ideologies interacted with each other – how people espousing what I came to call various *ideologies of place* (more on that term later) were in conversation – and contestation – with each other, and how people used each others' views to articulate their own ideologies about what kind of place Mt. Pleasant was and who belonged or did not belong there.

A recognition of the contested nature of ideologies enabled me to better understand relationships between ideology and power. As linguistic anthropologist Susan Gal has noted,

> the power of [ideological] signifying practices resides not only in their ability to constitute social groups and subjects (positionality), but also in their ability to valorize one position, one group, and its practices or knowledge over that of others; to formulate – but also to elide, preclude, or disable – possible forms of action.[64]

This perspective highlighted the relationship between practices – the activities on the street that I had been thinking about – and ideology: Ideologies classify, interpret, and lay the groundwork for specific actions (including discursive actions). In analyzing local practices, I started to think about how community members' ideologies – their evaluative belief systems about what should or should not occur in neighborhood space – shaped how they chose to act, and how they interpreted others' actions.

Notes

1   Bok (1998)

2   Bennefield (1995). Statistics are for people uninsured for at least one month. From 1991 to 1993, the median period without insurance was 7.1 months.

3   Canada, Denmark, Finland, France, Germany, Japan, the Netherlands, Norway, Sweden, Switzerland, and the United Kingdom

4   Wolff et al. (1992)

5   for example, in 1998, 2 million children alone

6   Halfon et al. (1996), Lieberman et al. (2004)

7   cf. Walls et al. (2002)

8   Starr (1995)

9   This quip is characteristic of a prevalent public and media discourse at the time that depicted Quayle as not particularly intelligent.

10   Source Watch (2005)

11   Starr (1995), Public Broadcasting System (PBS) (1996)

12   Novak (1993)

13   PBS (1996)

14   *Postgraduate Medicine* (1994)

15   McGrory (1993)

16   Ibid.

17   Dewar (1993)

18   Broder (1993)

19   McGrory (1993)

20   Usborne (1993)

21   Source Watch (2005)

22   Source Watch (2005)

23   In the Whitewater scandal, Bill and Hilary Clinton were accused and then cleared of illegal activities relating to their land investments in the Whitewater Development Corporation in Arkansas.

24   Source Watch (2005)

25   Starr (1995)

26   Bok (1998). Medicare is government-funded health insurance for seniors.

27   Clymer (1994:36). In fairness to Packwood, Clymer reports that when Packwood was asked if he had made these comments and what they meant, he replied, "I don't know," and added, "I don't remember what I say from one day to the next."

28   Clymer (1994:36)

29   Organization for Economic Co-operation and Development, which includes Australia, Austria, Belgium, Canada, Czech Republic,

Denmark, Finland, France, Germany, Greece, Hungary, Iceland, Ireland, Italy, Japan, Korea, Luxembourg, Mexico, Netherlands, New Zealand, Norway, Poland, Portugal, Slovak Republic, Spain, Sweden, Switzerland, Turkey, United Kingdom, United States.

30 National Center for Health Statistics (2001)

31 Teen pregnancy statistic from UNICEF Innocenti Research Center, cited in Nationmaster.com US healthcare statistics. All other statistics OECD (2005).

32 The terms *big D Discourse* and *little d discourse* are used to refer both to types of discourse themselves, and to analytical approaches to analyzing discourse.

33 Gee (1990:142–143)

34 By texts, I mean specific instances of discourse that have in some way been bounded and set up as objects of commentary or analysis, for example through telling a story about a remark someone made, or transcribing a chunk of discourse. For a fuller discussion of text and discourse, see Bauman and Briggs 1990.

35 Functional linguists, those who study actually-occurring language and the relationship between language structure and function, use the term *utterance* to highlight the primacy of spoken or signed language over writing, and in recognition of the fact that much that is said or signed does not follow the abstract grammatical conventions of an idealized, well-formed sentence. Researchers also use the term *utterance* to highlight that an analysis is based on actually-occurring language, rather than on a made-up sentence that *could* be uttered, but wasn't. Use of the term thus distinguishes the empirical data-collection approach from research that either posits the existence of an abstract, ideal speaker in a homogeneous speech community, and/or which tends to build theory based on introspection or grammaticality judgments, rather than on an analysis of actual language use. For a fuller discussion of the distinction between utterance and sentence, see Fasold (1990).

36 Schiffrin (1994)

37 Halliday and Hasan (1976)

38 There are different schools of thought on what qualifies as context. Some scholars, such as conversation analysts, only consider the immediate context of the specific situation in which a linguistic interaction occurs and the social information that participants themselves explicitly reference. Others, such as linguistic anthropologists and critical discourse analysts, consider the larger social forces and ideologies in circulation in the community or society within which the interaction is located.

39 See Giddens (1984) on the theory of structuration.

40 Because the line between *big D* and *little d* discourses is not clear, and because as explained above each type entails the other, in the present study I refer to both types as *discourse* (with a small-case *d*).

41 It is difficult to come up with examples of "masculine" behavior that are not also inflected by other social factors such as class or formality, as the examples of cursing and wearing neckties make clear. Although the example of widespread legs on a bus seat may seem odd, I include it because, at least in DC, it is one of the few behaviors I have observed that on the whole seems to cross lines of age, race/ethnicity, class, and sexuality. Similarly, studies have shown that using the lower portion of one's pitch range is characteristic of men across social groups.

42 Cameron (1997:49)

43 Labov (1972)

44 Gumperz (1971)

45 Lave and Wenger (1991)

46 Eckert and McConnell-Ginet (1992:95)

47 Eckert and McConnell-Ginet (1992:95)

48 Antaki, Condor, and Levine (1996), Schiffrin (1994), Gumperz (1982)

49 The design was loosely based on William Labov's field methods course in the Linguistics Department at the University of Pennsylvania. For more on this approach, see Labov (1984).

50 cf. Wolfson (1976)

51 cf. Spindler and Spindler (1987)

52 In anthropology this phrase is apt to connote the exoticness of "foreign," inscrutable places, a throwback to the colonial history of anthropology when the discipline, as it developed in the West, was concerned with coming to understand the ways of non-Western peoples who were also usually colonial subjects. Although there is a long history of US ethnography, until the late seventies and early eighties it was somewhat on the margins of the discipline. This changed in the late seventies and eighties, when anthropology started to problematize its connection to colonialism and a focus on "exotic Others." In the US, this self-reflection resulted in the field as a whole according greater recognition to North American Anthropology and of the idea that conducting fieldwork in your own back yard (or in my case, front stoop) is just as important and illuminating as traveling to another continent to study an unfamiliar culture.

53 Briggs (1986)

54 Williams (1988:119)

55 See chapter 2 for a discussion of this expression.

56 Sanjek (1998)

57   Gregory (1999)

58   Maskovsky (2006, 2001)

59   Mele (2000)

60   cf. Reisigl and Wodak (2001)

61   CDA, which typically analyzes such texts as newspaper articles or media broadcasts, has been criticized (along with other analyses of media language) for doing little in-depth analysis of the way that a text gets produced (for example, what the editorial process is leading to the generation of a news story) or how readers or listeners interpret a text. The discourse-historical approach avoids such pitfalls. See also Spitulnik (2001).

62   cf. van Dijk (1998, 1995)

63   Briggs (1998:230–231). See also Schieffelin and Doucet (1998), Gal (1993).

64   Gal (1993:321)

CHAPTER 9

GEOGRAPHY AND SOCIAL LOCATIONS

Positioning

An important idea in interactional sociolinguistics is that people use particular discourse strategies to align or oppose themselves to each other, or to articulate their relation to the information they are conveying. For example, do they articulate themselves as having a stake in what they're saying, or do they distance themselves from it, conveying the idea that they're "just the messenger"? A commonly used framework to analyze this kind of stance-taking is Erving Goffman's notion of *footing*. As Goffman explains it, footing is "the alignment we take up to ourselves and the others present as expressed in the way we manage the production or reception of an utterance."[1]

Footing was a useful tool that I used to focus on the stances that people took towards each other the in face-to-face interactions I was studying. For example, in contentious town hall meetings about alcohol sales policies or trash cleanup, sometimes one member of a civic organization would take an aggressive stance that characterized all merchants as irresponsible, while another member of the same group would take a more conciliatory approach, averring that their group shared many of the same interests as many of the merchants and that they could work together. Using the concept of footing, I was able to examine how these divergent stances could work in tandem in a meeting to create an image of a civic group as pushing for radical change, but at the same time having the best interests of the community at heart. (Of course, discourse strategies don't work in a vacuum. These strategies could only work to create an image of a group having a neighborhood's best interests at heart (rather than their own personal interests) as long as that was reflected in the projects that a group pursued. If they pursued projects that many in the community considered to be only in the interests of White, monied property owners, or against the interests of immigrant merchants, then those projects would trump any discourse strategies in creating an image of a civic group.)

While footing was a useful concept for analyzing face-to-face interaction, however, as I started analyzing the data I was collecting I found more and more that I was interested not in the stances that speakers themselves took up, but in the stances they constructed for other people they were talking about who were not present, as well as the ways that they aligned people to places. Rom Harré, Bronwyn Davies, and Luk van Langenhove's concept of *positioning* was well suited for investigating this kind of stance-taking.

These researchers' model of *positioning* views stances as positions that are dynamic and emergent in discourse, a perspective which fits well with a practice-based approach. Positioning develops the analysis of stance-taking in two other ways. First, it adds an explicitly moral framework. When we construct stances for ourselves and others, we articulate a moral aspect of that stance; we could say that creating stances is a way of positioning people along moral axes of, for example, goodness, or justness. Second, the concept of positioning allowed me to examine stances that speakers set up for other people or things that may or may not be present in the interaction at hand. It follows from this point that positioning is relational; the positioning of one person implicitly positions other people.[2] Furthermore, since positioning can be applied to entities other than humans, using the concept enabled me to talk about alignments and oppositions to *places*.

Harré and his colleagues' discussions of positioning relied to a great extent on spatial metaphors, but they were not interested in actual spatial relations. To use positioning fruitfully in a context where I wanted to analyze how people positioned themselves in relation to concrete spaces and places, I needed a way to ground a theory of positioning, as it were. It was here that Jane Hill's concept of moral geography became extremely useful. As I discussed in chapter 3, a moral geography is an interweaving of a moral framework with a geographical territory. In her essay "The Voices of Don Gabriel," Hill used the concept to analyze the connections between political economy, morality, community boundaries, and space in a story that Don Gabriel, an elder in a Mexicano[3] (Nahuatl) peasant community near the city of Puebla, Mexico, told to Hill about his son's murder. In telling the story, Don Gabriel mapped positive values of community-mindedness, reciprocity, and kinship ties onto his home and village, while he linked negative values of greed, competitiveness, and individualism, as well as disorder and danger, with outlying areas and more urban places. Don Gabriel emphasized the distinctions between these parts of the moral landscape by mixing Spanish into his talk about outsiders and outlying areas, while his descriptions of home and village were all in Mexicano. These delineations added a moral layer to the political economic geography of the area, which distinguished the peasant village's collectivism from the capitalist system of the Spanish-speaking areas.

Before reading *Voices of Don Gabriel*, I had been thinking about Mt. Pleasant in a fairly insular way, only considering how talk of Mt. Pleasant related to goings-on in the neighborhood itself. Hill's framing of *moral geography* at first did not exactly seem to fit my case, because I was not contrasting different areas. But after reading this essay, I started to notice more and more that Mt. Pleasant discourse was full of references to other places, most noticeably "the suburbs," as well as other areas of the city. And just as Don Gabriel had done, people in Mt. Pleasant used negative characterizations of these other places to bolster the positive qualities of the place they associated themselves with. With Hill's concept of moral geography, I was able to *spatialize* the notion of social positioning – to think about how social positioning worked in relation to real geographical space – and to start theorizing about how social positioning was accomplished through the discursive strategy of contrast. It also seemed that the concept of moral geography could be productively applied to the kind of social and moral positioning that I was finding in discourse that was limited to the subject of Mt. Pleasant, where people interwove moral frameworks into their discussions of the neighborhood, applying those frameworks wholesale without differentiating between different spaces within the neighborhood.

Thinking about how Hill's work could geographically inform Harré and colleagues' conceptions of social positioning sparked a train of thought that led me to concentrate more systematically on sociolinguistic and linguistic anthropological investigations of how people take up stances in relation to particular places. There is very little work within these fields that has set out to investigate place identity as a central concern, and indeed, as Rudolf Gaudio notes,[4] spatial aspects of linguistic interaction have been virtually absent as components of sociolinguistic theories of language in use.[5] However, because many studies are situated within particular geographical communities, people's orientations to places invariably become part of many analyses at some level, even if implicitly. This is especially true in the branch of sociolinguistics called *variation analysis*.

Variation analysts study how variants of the same linguistic feature pattern in relation to other linguistic features and to social features. For example, the final sound in the word *writing* has two variants in American English – the final sound in *sin*, and the final sound in *sing*.[6] Which variant you get might depend on the part of speech of the word you're looking at (with the word *building*, you're more likely to hear the *sin* sound in "I'm building (verb) a house," than you are in "that's a big building" (noun)), or it might depend on what sound follows the *-ing* ("I'm building glass houses" vs. "I'm building steel houses.")[7] But the patterning of variants is more often than not likely to be influenced by all kinds of social factors. With verbs ending in -ing, for example, you're more likely to get (the sound represented by) "ng" than "n" in female speech, upper class speech, and formal situations.[8]

Variation analysis has a historical link with dialectology and dialect geography research, since regional variation is one kind of variation. Perhaps also because of this connection, variation analysts are often concerned, at least implicitly, with places. Most of these studies have focused on the connection between pronunciation and social features that are important in particular communities. Some researchers have studied how pronunciation patterns along social networks, or the friendship, work, or family circles that exist in a community. For example, Lesley Milroy[9] found that, in communities in the Belfast area in Northern Ireland, people who had dense networks that were concentrated in geographical spaces – having relatives in the same neighborhood, participating in neighborhood-based activities – had pronunciations that were considered more vernacular (that differed from what was considered the regional standard). And because networks often tended to be gender-based (either because men in some neighborhoods worked together while women worked at home, or because friendships were built around same-gender relationships), pronunciations ended up patterning according to gender, too.

In her research on Jocks and Burnouts in a suburban Detroit high school in the early 1980s,[10] Penelope Eckert found a similar correlation between social groups, gender, relationships to places, and pronunciation. For the purposes of my own research, what interested me about Eckert's work was the importance of geography for the pronunciations she was studying. Detroit is an area undergoing a change in vowel pronunciation called the *Northern Cities Chain Shift*.[11] (The sounds associated with the shift are sometimes what people think of as a Chicago accent.) As is common of many sound changes, the Northern Cities Chain Shift jumped first to urban centers, and then spread from those areas to the suburbs. Eckert found that the *burnout* students, a group of working-class students who opposed themselves to school activities and thought of themselves as more related to Detroit, pronounced the newer parts of the sound shift at higher rates than the jocks, a group of middle-class students who were more invested in school activities such as (but not limited to) sports. These newer changes were more commonly heard in Detroit, so using the newer vowel pronunciations was a way to show one's connection to Detroit – a way for these suburban kids to create an urban identity. What was even more interesting was that the burnout girls used the new vowels at even higher rates than the burnout boys. Boys were also able to align themselves with urbanness through activities, like driving to Detroit and spending time there, but girls were more constrained by their parents – they were not allowed to go to Detroit alone. To explain the distinction between boys' and girls' pronunciations, Eckert reasoned that, since the girls were more limited in participating in activities that could give them an urban status, they used "urban" vowel pronunciations as the symbolic capital that gave them an air of Detroitness.

Although she didn't frame it this way, I found Eckert's work to be important in thinking about how people articulate relationships between cities and outlying areas, and their own relationships to both. These questions are also relevant for variation research in places where economic incentives have impelled people to leave their hometowns for higher-paid work in more metropolitan areas. For example, in a study of vowel pronunciation in Martha's Vineyard, an island off the coast of Massachusetts, William Labov[12] found that speakers with positive attitudes about the island pronounced words like *house* and *kind* with a vowel sound somewhere between the broadcast news pronunciation of these sounds and the vowel in the stereotype of the New York pronunciation of "bird." This pronunciation was common among older people on the island, and a strong marker of the local accent. But it was also indicative of a particular orientation to the island – among young people, this pronunciation was highest among those who had left the island and then decided to return. And the pronunciation was highest among fishermen, who were dedicated to a traditional way of life and opposed themselves to summer tourists.[13] Similarly, in a study of dialect variation in Thyborøn, Denmark, Lisa Lane[14] found that it was women who worked outside of the village who had the most traditional, Thyborøn-identified accents. Lane's analysis of this phenomenon was that it was *because* of their ties outside of the village that these women needed to create a Thyborøn identity linguistically.

Conversely, in her work in Valladolid, Mexico, Julie Solomon[15] found that Spanish speakers in rural Yucatan in Mexico who had what she called a *cosmopolitan orientation* pronounced the sound represented by 'll' in words like *silla* (chair) more similarly to the way it was pronounced in nearby urban areas.[16] For people in the village where Solomon worked, the pronunciations of the city also invoked the economic opportunities of the city, while people associated the more local, older pronunciation with poverty, rurality, and lack of education. What these studies showed, if implicitly, is that place-identity is part and parcel of linguistic variation.

The connection between people's pronunciations and their affiliations with certain places is often under speakers' level of consciousness. However, particular pronunciations sometimes become emblematic of local identity in the popular mind, and this view can even propel a particular pronunciation to become the most common variant in a community. Barbara Johnstone, Neeta Bhasin, and Denise Wittkofski[17] argue that this is exactly what happened with the 'ah' sound in words like "downtown/dahntahn" in Pittsburgh. The "ah" pronunciation is an older variant that dialectologists might predict would be likely to fade away and be replaced by the more widespread "ow" pronunciation. Johnstone and her colleagues argue that the "ah" sound has stayed around *because* it is such a strong symbol of being a Pittsburgh person, and that's something that many Pittsburghers are invested in.

The variationist work that deals with place identity is important because it highlights that people's connections to places are communicated in even the smallest details of their day-to-day interactions. Particularly because most of these studies (with the exception of Johnstone, Bhasin, and Wittkofski) did not set out to investigate place identity per se, this body of research makes clear that place identity is one of the major criteria by which people categorize the world and articulate their place in it; as these studies found, place plays as much of a role in people's relations to their social worlds as categories like gender and class. Seeing the role that place identity played in the findings of these studies made me feel that I was onto something. But I couldn't apply these studies in any direct sense, because to do variationist research that looks at such micro-level linguistic features, you have to be working with people who are part of the same speech community in the narrow sense. In a community like Mt. Pleasant where people don't share the same dialect (let alone the same language), people will not share the same set of options of pronouncing certain sounds. I wanted to study how place identity emerged at a larger linguistic level, so I next turned to research on discourse (in the sense of language above the sentence-level) to see how discourse analysts had grappled with place identity.

It turned out that place identity was salient at every level of linguistic analysis. At the most macro level of *language variety*, for example, linguistic anthropologist Norma Mendoza-Denton has found that choice of language gets filtered through alliances to various places.[18] Mendoza-Denton studied two groups of Latina gang girls in Northern California, the Norteñas and the Sureñas. Although girls in these groups had similar family backgrounds, linguistic repertoires, and immigration histories, and they lived in the same neighborhoods, at the macro level the groups had quite different linguistic practices: Norteñas spoke predominantly English and code-switched into Spanish, while Sureñas spoke predominantly Spanish and code-switched into English.[19] As the groups' names might suggest (*norte* translates as *north* and *sur* as *south*), these linguistic practices were tied up in the ways that the two groups aligned to particular places: Norteñas considered themselves to be from the North and constructed a US Chicana identity for themselves, while Sureñas identified with the South and Mexico. For these girls, the politics of language had everything to do with the politics of place.

At the discourse level, deixis[20] seemed like an obvious place to look for place identity, since place identity is related to locations and to how places are located in relation to other places, and those relationships are encoded in deictics; we create closeness or distance by referring to something *here* or *there*, as *this* or *that*.

The work of linguistic anthropologists on deixis provided examples of the ways that deictics encode social relations among people and between people and spaces, and how these social relations consequently construct places. For instance, Alessandro Duranti[21] analyzed how Samoan parents in suburban Los Angeles use the deictic directive "sit down" with their children, which is meant to be interpreted specifically as "sit on the floor." This command recalls behavior appropriate within houses in Samoa, and in doing so it constructs a Samoan place within a suburban American built environment.

The sociolinguist Deborah Tannen's work also sheds light on how the ways that people talk about places shape the identities that they convey to others in conversations. In her study on conversational style and miscommunication,[22] she found that, when Jewish New Yorkers living in California talked about geography in Manhattan and events that took place in New York, they used a high level of cooperative overlapping speech[23] and other features that were characteristic of New York Jewish conversational style. Tannen herself did not frame her investigation as being about identity and place alignments, but her analysis makes clear that sharing stories about New York and using New York Jewish conversational style to tell those stories enabled these participants to create and bond around a shared New York identity.

People also create identities in relation to multiple places. Linguistic anthropologist Rudolf Gaudio's study of Nigerian Hausa 'yan daudu (men who act "like women")[24] is a case in point. In the Hausa language, verbs can take suffixes that indicate motion towards a particular location (or *deictic center*).[25] Motion away, however, is not indicated by any suffix; in linguistic terms, motion away is *unmarked*. The 'yan daudu who Gaudio spent time with frequently traveled from one place to another, to find work or avoid persecution. In the stories they told about these journeys, Gaudio found that speakers alternated between using verbs with "motion-towards" suffixes and verbs without, thereby creating stories that had a strong sense of movement. With this verbal system, 'yan daudu created cosmopolitan identities based on travel to and alignments with *multiple* places at the same time. Although English does not have the same grammatical resources that Hausa has, this work helped me hone in on the way that Boaz, the Israeli merchant in chapter 3, was creating similar multiple alignments in a story told in English to create a transnational identity.

I found that these studies helped me in thinking through how to investigate the ways that people constructed their identities through alignments to place, but they didn't provide a model for systematically investigating place identity itself. In the mid-1990s, most of the discourse studies out there tended to look at the identity of a place as already existing, and as a backdrop against which people created their own identities. When I started my research there was very little work within sociolinguistics and linguistic anthropology that focused on the identities of places as a central concern, and since that time there hasn't been much more. Among the earliest work to investigate place identity as a central theme was Keith Basso's research on Western Apache place names and stories about particular places.[26] By assigning place names that invoked past events and keeping those events alive through storytelling, the speakers Basso studied imbued the landscape with cultural meaning; places served as markers of community history, and as symbols of community values that were embedded in local evaluations of events that were associated with those places. Because places were laden with values, the invocation of place *names* could recall those values, and be used to socialize community members into appropriate behavior. Like Hill's work, what was key for me in Basso's research was that it highlighted the link between places, morality, and social action.

Other work on place names illustrated the way that people use discourses of place to promote particular points of view in community disputes over rights to space, something that became more important in my research as I started comparing the views expressed in the sociolinguistic interviews I was conducting. For example, linguistic anthropologist Karen Blu[27] found that Blacks, Whites, and Lumbee Indians in Robeson County, North Carolina used different town names and names for geographical features. She also described how, in storytelling, Whites tended to focus on physical, visually observable aspects of space, whereas Blacks and Indians focused more on social space (for instance, areas where a high proportion of group members lived). These North Carolinians used these various discourse orientations to space to reinforce or contest views of their own and other ethnic groups' connections to the landscape.

Even though studies like Basso's and Blu's focused more explicitly on the identity of places themselves, they tended to frame the discourses of place that they were analyzing as *reflecting* a given group's or speaker's notion of place, rather than actively *constructing* it. I was more interested in focusing on the active construction, and there was not a lot out there within discourse analysis. Some exceptions, however, were William Leap's and Barbara Johnstone's work.

Leap's research on intersections of place and ethnoracial identity[28] was useful in thinking about how different people constructed community boundaries. Leap asked White and Black gay men to draw and discuss maps of Gay DC, and he found that the two groups drew maps which highlighted different parts of the city, and talked about Gay DC in quite different ways.

Barbara Johnstone[29] was also interested in the active construction of place identity. Focusing on intertextuality (the way that textual elements travel across multiple texts), Johnstone revealed how residents of Fort Wayne, Indiana, picked up parts of newspaper stories about a local flood in their conversations and other writings. Her work was important to me for thinking about how discourses in a community circulate and build up to create a public community story and a shared identity – in the case of these Fort Wayne residents, a particularly "heartland" identity.

You may have noticed that I've been using the term *place* in a somewhat loose, undefined way. This is because, by and large, sociolinguistic and linguistic anthropological literature does not take pains to operationalize or define what *place* means. Although the literature in my field had helped to articulate the relationships between person and place identity, even the work that explicitly focused on place generally did not analyze or theorize just how place construction happened.

It was somewhat randomly that I would stumble upon research which would lead me to conceptualize *place* as an analytical concept, and to think more systematically about the process of place identity construction.

From Matt Groening to Cultural Geography (Procrastination Pays Off)

Before Matt Groening created the TV show *The Simpsons*, he was busy with two rabbit-like characters jumping into and out of all kinds of hellish situations. When I was in graduate school, the one that really spoke to me was his book, *School is Hell*. My favorite installment was, of course, "Lesson 19: Grad school (Some People Never Learn)" (Figure 9.1).

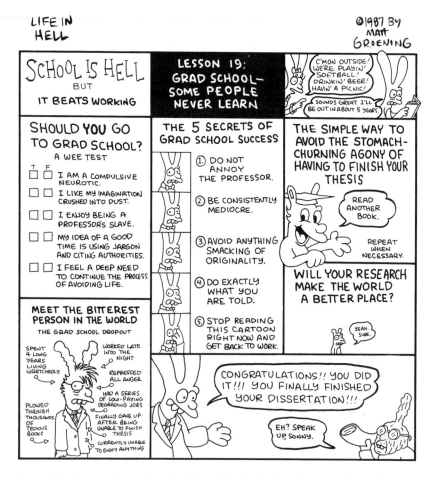

Figure 9.1   Reprinted from *School is Hell* published by Pantheon Books, a division of Random House, Inc. New York © 1987 Matt Groening Productions, Inc. All Rights Reserved. The Simpsons © and ™ Twentieth Century Fox Film Corporation. All Rights Reserved.

It was the middle of spring, I had a conference presentation to write, and I had already laid in bed long enough for my snooze alarm to go off three times. Finally I dragged myself into the dining room to turn on my computer, and proceeded to write a sentence, make some tea, rewrite the sentence, get some potato chips, delete the sentence – twice – and rewrite it in its original form. Before getting some more potato chips.

At 11:30 a.m. I wasn't quite ready to call it a day, however, so I decided to follow Matt Groening's advice and READ ANOTHER BOOK. Which meant a slow, meandering walk down to Adams Morgan, where I could browse at my leisure in Idle Times Books, and still feel like I was working.

It was here that I came across a copy of cultural geographers James Duncan and David Ley's edited volume *place/culture/representation*. Shaking me out of my procrastinatory haze, this book gave me a whole new insight into the interactions I'd been analyzing in Mt. Pleasant. It awakened me to the world of cultural geography, and inspired me to see all kinds of connections between that field and the discourse analysis work that I was engaged in.

The writers in Duncan and Ley's book took a *hermeneutic approach* to studying geography – an approach that "recognizes that [scholarly] interpretation is a dialogue between one's data – other places and other people – and the researcher who is embedded within a particular intellectual and institutional context."[30] These authors were not interested in simply describing or mapping a geographical terrain, but rather sought to interrogate such descriptive and mapping practices. The contributors to Duncan and Ley's volume understood *place* as coming into being through (among other factors) people's perceptions, and those perceptions as shaped by the production and reproduction of symbolic systems such as maps, photographs, discourse. In this view, places were entities that were struggled over; they were contested terrains that were shaped by and reflected unequal power relations and the (multiple and sometimes contradictory) interests of some people or groups over others. This approach fit very well with the tenets of ethnographic discourse analysis, as well as the goals of critical discourse analysis. What it added was a systematic investigation of the history, interests, and symbolic processes that contributed both to the ways that environments got built or changed, and the mentalities that shaped those choices.[31]

The theorizings of urban anthropologists on connections between culture and the built environment also held great interest for me. Margaret Rodman argued that a separation between the cultural and the physical precludes a complete analysis of place. Using as an example her work in housing cooperatives in Toronto, she showed that one could only understand the geography of the cooperative if one analyzed the actual physical space, the ways people used the spaces for purposes both intended and unintended, and the meanings that they attributed to the spaces.[32] Similarly, Setha Low pointed out the problems of a theoretical framework that regards physical spaces as being distinct from the way that people experience them. The form that a given space takes tells stories of the people who have shaped and interacted with it, just as a space's form contributes to the future experiences that people will have there:

> Explaining built form in its relation to culture provides us with clues to meaning encoded in historically generated spatial forms. The built environment not only reflects sociocultural concerns but also shapes behavior and social action; thus, embedded in these design forms is a living history of cultural meanings and intentions.[33]

Although geographers and urban anthropologists rarely analyze discourse at the *little d* level, these scholars' focus on the connections between form, use, and meaning[34] resonated with me as a discourse analyst.

Finding the Scaffolding

Conducting research is somewhat like a scavenger hunt – you have a conversation with someone or you pick up a book in a library or bookstore, and your interest gets sparked in a certain topic. You learn of a researcher working on that topic, and you read their work. In their book or article or essay, they have a "literature review" section, where they talk about other people who have shaped their ideas. So you turn to the work of those people, and then in turn you find out about the theorists who have shaped these scholars' thinking. As I started reading more and more cultural geographers and urban anthropologists, what kept coming up again and again were the theories of Henri Lefebvre from his book, *The Social Production of Space*.[35] Lefebvre's work has been enormously influential in the interdisciplinary field that's come to be called *Space and Place Theory*. Theorists of space and place explore, from multiple perspectives, how space and culture/society mutually constitute each other. Another way to articulate this interest is as an interest in the *social construction of place*.

Lefebvre's theory of social space considers what he calls *social spaces* (roughly the same thing as what I've been referring to as *places*) to be amalgamations of the social, the mental, and the material (i.e., physical). He considers these components to be inseparable, making up an indivisible social whole. However, for the purposes of understanding how social space works, he devised an approach that does in fact separate them out for heuristic purposes.[36] This approach consists of three elements: *spatial practice*, *representations of space*, and *spaces of representation*.[37]

Spatial practice

Lefebvre defines spatial practice as

> a projection onto a (spatial) field of all aspects, elements and moments of social practice.[38]

Spatial practices are the everyday practices that people perform in any given area; these will be considered by some as appropriate for that place, and by others as inappropriate. In other words, actions are evaluated based (in part) on where they occur, and places are evaluated in part through the actions which are carried out there.[39] Over time, the concert of spatial practices that people perform and evaluate in a particular place constructs sets of assumptions about what constitutes normative behavior for that place. As Lefebvre explains it,

> Spatial practice ensures continuity and some degree of cohesion. In terms of social space, and of each member of a given society's relationship to that space, this cohesion implies a guaranteed level of *competence* and a specific level of *performance*.[40]

In using the notions of *competence* and *performance* (loosely borrowed from the linguist Noam Chomsky, as Lefebvre points out), Lefebvre points to the importance of both action and interpretation in people's constructions of places. We can consider *performance-based spatial practices* to be activities, events, and interactions that either occur within a geographical area (such as playing soccer in a park or drinking beer at a bus stop) or outside of it (such as deciding at a city council meeting to rezone a neighborhood street for commercial uses). *Competence-based spatial practices* involve being able to "read" a place – for example to know if a place is safe or unsafe, or what kinds of activities are appropriate there.

Although in some senses it's useful to make a distinction between action and interpretation for the purpose of analysis, it is important to keep in mind that – as the linguistic anthropologist Dell Hymes[41] points out in his discussion of linguistic performance and competence, and as Lefebvre implies with his emphasis on the unity of space – performance and competence are integrated with one another, since a person's performance of a given action – boarding a bus through the front door, asking for a bus transfer when getting on rather than when getting off – is a demonstration of that person's linguistic and socio-geographic competence. By demonstrating through your actions that you have competence in knowing how to "read" a particular place, you are also (re)constructing ideas about normative, appropriate behavior.

The cultural geographer Tim Cresswell illustrates this point nicely in his example of behavior in a church:

> Our actions in places are evidence of our preferred reading. Kneeling in church is an interpretation of what the church means; it also reinforces the meaning of the church.[42]

Even spatial practices that contest dominant ideas about how to use a space – such as drinking beer on a street corner – may reconstruct normativity in a given place by highlighting the spatial norms that are being transgressed. If such practices continue over time, they may change the dominant orders. (This is a model of spatial order that has much in common with Butler's notion of performativity, discussed earlier.)

Of course, spatial practices do not in and of themselves constitute places. The practices themselves are mediated by cultural interpretations and judgments,[43] as well as the symbolic means – discourse, maps, policy documents, paintings – that we use to represent those interpretations and judgments. When we add interpretation and representation to the mix, we arrive at the second and third elements in Lefebvre's triad: *representations of space* and *spaces of representation*.

Representations of space and spaces of representation

Representations of space are a society's dominant systems of knowledge about spaces and dominant ways of conceiving of and evaluating spaces. For Lefebvre, representations of space are those representations conceived and put forth by the people that a society endows with professional power over space – urban planners, architects, policy makers, engineers, surveyors, etc. These "professionals" have the power to translate their representations into actual built form by, for instance, designing a city land parcel.[44] An important concern of Lefebvre's was how representations of space promoted capitalist interests.[45] He considered the interests that representations of space represented as opposed to conceptions rooted in *lived space* – which he called *spaces of representation*.

Where representations of space were conceived somewhere in an office by people who did not have intimate, lived knowledge of geographical areas, spaces of representation in contrast were the conceptions of space that were born out of people's day-to-day experiences in and with those areas. For Lefebvre, people experienced spaces of representation through the symbolic systems and images that they used or saw in interpersonal interactions; spaces of representation were connected to real life in a more direct way than the dominant representations of space, and for Lefebvre they could be used to oppose the representations of space that served the interests of the powerful in society at the expense of the people whom the representations of space necessarily marginalized. But spaces of representation themselves are also shaped by representations of space, and both are shaped by – and in turn shape – spatial practices. The three points of Lefebvre's conceptual triangle are always active, influencing and influenced by each other, and combining to produce social spaces (or what I have been calling *places*). This process of back-and-forth influence implies a tension among the elements that together make up social space, and that tension means that social space is not static; at some times spaces of representation might be more prominent in a community's vision of its common space, at other times spatial practices might be more prominent. It's important to keep in mind, however, that the usefulness of thinking of these elements separately is in that it can help to build an analytical understanding for theorizing how space works. As Lefebvre emphasizes, in practice, in daily life, these elements are mutually constitutive and cannot be so easily separated.

The tension that binds the three elements of the triad together seemed to describe well the ebbs and flows in the ongoing process of place-making in Mt. Pleasant. As a discourse analyst my attention, not surprisingly, was drawn to the role that discourse played in the triad. It was by reading Lefebvre[46] that I came to think about my neighbors' use of discourse as not just a form of *social* practice, but more specifically as a form of *spatial* practice.

It's important to keep in mind that discourse *itself* is not a practice; rather, *use* of discourse is a practice, and discourse is a symbolic system. Symbolic systems are systems in which the parts of the system stand for, or represent, something else – an object,[47] an idea, etc. As a symbolic system, then, discourse is a form of representation. It is, in fact, one of the key forms of representation in Lefebvre's representations of space. Although Lefebvre does not focus on discourse per se in his explanation of spaces of representation, he does include as a key element "complex symbols and images of [a space's] 'inhabitants' and 'users'."[48] Discourse must surely fall under this rubric, as it is a system made up of complex symbols and used by inhabitants of spaces. This means that discourse is located in two of the three components of Lefebvre's model. From a discourse analytic perspective, a different way to think about these components might be to consider both spaces of representation and representations of space as subsets of a larger category of *representation*, with the subsets being distinguished by who uses the representations – those with power over a space vs. those who live in or use a space (in other words, dominant discourses vs. counter-discourses). Let me explain why I think this particular configuration might be beneficial for an ethnographic discourse analysis of place-making.

The urban sociologist Manuel Castells has noted that Lefebvre theorized from a purely philosophical perspective, rather than one growing out of empirical investigation. Castells explained that the reality of place-making down on the ground was much more complex than the world predicted by theories like Lefebvre's, and argued for theory-building that was grounded in and in conversation with empirical research of actual people and places.[49]

Along the same lines, from an ethnographic perspective, the distinction that Lefebvre's triad implies between the discourse of planners (generally empowered) and the discourse of city inhabitants (often in marginalized positions) is not likely to be so cut and dried. Take for example the case of a neighbor of mine in Mt. Pleasant. Anna was an urban planner who worked at a local community development corporation, or CDC. She was also an immigrant who had lived in Mt. Pleasant (with the exception of her time in college and graduate school) since she had moved to the US at age 15. In her work, the way that she represented the neighborhood was informed by the tools and discourses of urban planning, as well by her experiences as an immigrant teenager and adult in the neighborhood. In one of the projects that Anna worked on, she conducted participatory planning workshops with local teenagers in which they drew and then discussed maps of the neighborhood. The CDC could then use the teenagers' visions to shape future neighborhood projects.[50]

Shortly after one of these workshops, a group of the teenagers involved gave a presentation on their summer activities to a community development funder that had contributed a large sum of money to the youth center the teenagers attended.[51] They decided to organize their presentation around mapmaking: They used their maps to explain the circumstances of local youth and the reasons behind youth center program initiatives. Then they themselves conducted a mapping workshop: They directed the funders to draw maps of the neighborhood where the funding office was, as a way to get the funders to reflect on their own lived, daily experiences in that neighborhood.

In these examples, Anna's contributions to her employer's community development initiatives are firmly grounded in both the science of urban planning and her personal history in the neighborhood;[52] the teenagers' maps use the technology of planning and geographical sciences and the vernacular artforms of the street (graffiti, Old English lettering); and the community development funders drew on their personal, day-to-day interactions in participating in the funding follow-up meeting structured by the youth. Are what are created in these interactions representations of space, or spaces of representation?

Once you start to analyze real-life examples of place-making, it becomes harder to tease these apart. I would also argue that it's also not necessarily a worthwhile endeavor per se, although in some cases it might be beneficial. For example, if one was interested in how children learned to represent space, it might be useful to investigate the relative influences of formal education in reading maps (representations of space) vs. informal socialization listening to their relatives give directions (spaces of representation).

What I *do* think worth teasing apart, however, are psychological experiences and other interpretations of space (ideologies, attitudes, etc.) that exist in the mind, as opposed to both representations (including discourse) and physical characteristics of an area. Lefebvre seems to combine and conflate these under the category of *spaces of representation*. As he explains, a space of representation is

> space as directly *lived* through its associated images and symbols, and hence the space of "inhabitants" and "users", but also of some artists and perhaps of those, such as a few writers and philosophers, who *describe* and aspire to do no more than describe. This is the dominated – and hence passively experienced – space which the imagination seeks to change and appropriate. It overlays physical space, making symbolic use of its objects.[53]

In this description, a space of representation includes the qualitatively different phenomena of experiences and imagination, physical objects, and the symbols and images (including symbolic uses of the physical objects).

From the earlier discussion of discourse it should be clear that discourse is closely linked to ideologies, and that ideologies are formed through lived experiences. However, discourse and ideology are not inseparable, as is illustrated by the fact that a given stretch of discourse can have multiple meanings based on the knowledge and value systems that an individual brings to an interpretation of that discourse. Take, for example, the term *representations of space*. For someone well versed in Lefebvrian analysis, this term is closely connected with the dominant forces in a society, as well as with capital. To some people, a scholar's use of this term might signal a Marxist analysis. People not familiar with Lefebvre, on the other hand, would have no reason to think that the term conveyed anything about social or power relations.

From a discourse perspective, it is useful to distinguish symbolic systems from ideologies or perceptions of lived experiences. Separating out analytical categories for symbolic systems, mental apparatus (ideologies, interpretations, imagination), and physical characteristics of space can help to focus on how these interact with each other. If these elements of place-making are collapsed into one category, we run the risk of not paying attention to each of them individually. To go back to a previous example, making these separate categories can help us understand how it comes to be that the utterance "Hey Baby, want a ride" can take on different meanings and shape or reinforce the status of an area as a place of neighborly concern or of gendered intimidation depending on, for example, the accent that it's uttered in (part of the form of the symbolic system), the location from which it's uttered (physical space), or the ideas that a listener has about what constitutes aggressive behavior in public space (the mental realm).

In his Lefebvrian analysis of street protests sparked by a police officer's shooting of an African American teenager in Lexington, Kentucky,[54] the urban geographer Eugene McCann emphasizes that Lefebvre's theory of the production of social space is deeply concerned with the details of everyday life. McCann cautions that, in order for an analyst to really engage lived experience as an integral part of an investigation of place-making, the model "must be transported from one context to another with care and sensitivity,"[55] contextualized within the social and political relations of the area under study.[56] Somewhat along the same lines, I want to argue that a researcher's methodology and focus of analysis will necessarily also shape how she or he uses Lefebvre's approach to examine a particular place. Overall the elements of the model provide a very fruitful framework for analyzing how discourse (and its use) interacts with other representational systems and spatial practices, as well as with interpretations and attitudes towards spaces. However, for an analysis that focuses on discourse, I find it more useful to chunk the pieces of the model somewhat differently.

We all organize the world in different ways; we break it up into different categories, and decide what goes into which category based on the backgrounds and the experiences that we bring to any interpretation of the world. This is as true for scholars as it is for inhabitants of a neighborhood. For someone like Lefebvre, who had such a strong interest in the interaction of space as conceived from above (by officials and professionals) with space as lived on the ground (by inhabitants and users), it made sense to draw the line between the categories *representations of space* and *spaces of representation* based on the relationship of spatial actors to a given space (distant or intimate) and the power which society vested in them over the space. For me, because my training conditioned me to hone in on the interaction of *discourse* with other social phenomena, it made sense to have a unified category of discourse, which was separate from categories of other social phenomena.

So rather than separate the two types of discourse based on their users, it made more sense to me to have a unified category in which discourse and other symbolic systems could be grouped – a category that we could call *representations*. And rather than combine symbolic systems with the mental components that contribute to the production of social space, it worked better for me to make that a separate category, which in this study I've referred to as *ideologies of place*. I recognize that Lefebvre's notions of imagination and (interpretations of) lived experience are not exactly the same as ideologies. However, because they are all *ideas* about space that contribute to the production of social space, I've found it logical to group them together. I chose to label this group *ideologies* because my neighbors' ideologies about places played such a key role in shaping both the ways that they used space and the ways that they talked or wrote about spaces.

It was clear that the way my neighbors represented the neighborhood were deeply connected with their ideologies about places. I was keenly aware in my fieldwork that my neighbors were using the ideologies underlying local discourses about urban living to classify, interpret, and lay the groundwork for actions that they and others witnessed and performed in various spaces within the neighborhood. For example, ideologies about home as refuge or as place of community-building informed how my neighbors responded to kids playing in apartment building halls, or whether they criticized others for not engaging in conversation while doing laundry in the laundry room. Through such examples, I came to see that spaces become certain kinds of places through the combination of people's spatial practices (including discursive practices, like yelling at kids in the hall or chatting with them in the laundry room) and the ideological systems that they use to evaluate the practices that they and others perform.

To sum up, then: as social actors, we choose our spatial practices and interpret our own and others' spatial practices based on ideologies of place,[57] i.e., evaluative belief systems about what should or should not occur in a particular locale. Through these actions, the ideologies that support or oppose them, the symbolic systems used to represent those ideologies, and the actual physical contours and contents of spaces (another example of the combination of use, meaning, and form) we construct what Lefebvre called *social space*. In this study I chose to use the term *place* rather than space, however, for two reasons.[58] First, because it is the more common use,[59] and second, to distinguish my work from linguistic work that focuses more narrowly on how language encodes spatial relations per se (e.g., When giving directions from one place to another, do people use cardinal directions (north, south) or relative directions (left, right)? How do languages signify the distance between a speaker and an object? Does a language just have *this thing* (for an object close-by) and *that thing* (for something farther away) like English, or *kore* (*this thing close*), *sore* (*that thing far from me and close to you*), and *are* (*that thing far from both of us*) like Japanese[60]?).

Space, Place, and Discourse

Many theorists interested in what can be called the *social construction of place* have focused on discourse as an object of analysis. Of particular relevance to my work is discourse research in gentrification studies. For example, cultural geographers Caroline Mills[61] and David Ley[62] have examined texts like real estate advertisements and interviews with residents in Vancouver and other urban Canadian locations. The work of both of these theorists showed how market-oriented real estate and commerce constructed images of urbane and sophisticated neighborhoods, images which new or prospective residents could use to construct identities for themselves as sophisticated cosmopolitans.

Ley brought a political economic angle to such analysis; by tracing the patterns of occupational tenure in gentrified or gentrifying neighborhoods – the order that people with different professions moved into gentrifying neighborhoods (artists, social workers, teachers, lawyers, etc.) – Ley argued that gentrification in many urban neighborhoods in the US and Canada has its roots in the aesthetics of the college-educated counter-culture young people (such as artists or students) who moved into rundown but vibrant city neighborhoods instead of the suburbs that they disdained as homogeneous, sanitized, and soul-killing. Ley argued that each occupational wave made a neighborhood seem more appealing to the next wave, and that current residents' aesthetics could be commodified and co-opted to sell a "lifestyle" to prospective residents. This described exactly the history of Mt. Pleasant since the early 1970s, and propelled me to think about the economic consequences of the discursive images that people constructed of Mt. Pleasant as a bohemian, activist, or hip neighborhood.

Sociologist Christopher Mele made a similar argument in his historical analysis of the images that residents, the real estate industry, and media outlets presented of New York's Lower East Side from 1880 to 2000. He found that, while residents often promoted an image of the neighborhood as tough or artsy or alternative, real estate executives commodified that image in order to sell up-market residential and retail space.

Geographer Neil Smith has also made connections between investment and disinvestment patterns and discourse in the Lower East Side.[63] Smith generally takes a materialist approach to gentrification, focusing on gentrification as rooted in urban economic and political restructuring. However, in two essays which are a somewhat uncharacteristic departure from his overall approach, Smith analyzed studies of texts like real estate advertisements, apartment building and retail shop names, and media discussions of gentrification. His analysis showed that metaphors of wilderness, the frontier, and the wild west fostered an image of gentrifiers bravely setting down camp in barren and unknown territory, thereby giving gentrifiers a "cutting edge" identity as cultural trailblazers.[64] At the same time, it rendered invisible the people who were already living in gentrifying neighborhoods and whose housing tenure was severely threatened by the growing real estate increases brought about in no small part by the cachet that came with the ostensible excitement of that untamed frontier.[65]

Placing People on the Margins – Geographic Themes in Exclusionary Talk

Another area of research in which discourse has been a central data source is that of processes of social and geographic marginalization. This was a major trend that I found in my own data, and scholars across different disciplines noted the phenomenon in a multitude of different settings. Reading studies from different fields, conducted in different places and with different research focuses and goals, I found that talking about geography turns out to be a very common way to set up a moral and deictic center and then distance other people from that center. A case in point is the story that Don Gabriel told to Jane Hill, where, as Hill showed, he mapped positive values onto areas that he aligned with himself – for example his home and village – and linked negative values associated with outsiders with outlying areas and urban places.

The prevalence of this phenomenon can even be seen in the spatial metaphors that analysts themselves use to describe it – a moral center, the periphery, marginalization, distancing.[66] And space itself can be used as a metaphor, as linguistic anthropologists Elizabeth Keating and Alessandro Duranti have shown. In their work in the Polynesian islands of Pohnpei and Samoa, respectively, these analysts found that, in public and ritual events, people with high-status social positions (again, note the spatial metaphor *high*) physically occupy spatially higher positions (sitting on a platform, for example) in the spaces in which events occur. So through practices like sitting on a platform while others sit on the floor, people imbue spaces with meaning.

The work on geographic marginalization highlights two tactics that speakers take. In the first type of marginalization, speakers compare places to each other without talking explicitly about the people who inhabit those places. Instead, attitudes about inhabitants are often subtly conveyed through an *implicit* connection between the place and the people who live there. One study where this phenomenon can be seen[67] is geographer John Dixon and colleagues' analysis of newspaper articles and letters to the editor about a squatter camp in the Cape area of South Africa.[68] The writers of these texts presented the squatter camp as an "alien place," a disordered and dirty built environment which did not fit in with the writers' constructions of the surrounding area as a site of "natural beauty." Although the writers did not explicitly mention the race of people living in the squatter camp, they used discourses that had strong associations with apartheid-era ways of talking about Blacks; through this strategy, they implicitly racialized the squatter-camp debate – but, like the writers in the Mt. Pleasant public toilets grant, in an off-record way.

While many researchers have analyzed marginalizing discourses of place within a particular locale, others have examined this type of discourse across national boundaries. The discourse analyst Shi-xu, for example, examined contemporary Dutch writing on traveling in China,[69] and found that the authors in question used descriptions of 19th-century Europe to describe Chinese cities. Shi-xu argued that this approach constructed China as a sort of backwards and primitive Europe.

The second tactic that speakers use to geographically marginalize others is to explicitly invoke and critique people in their talk about places. Many researchers have noted the use of geographical themes, particularly in media writing, to label people who perform frowned-upon acts as people who come from somewhere else. For instance, the geographer Tim Cresswell noted that, in stories by New York City newspaper writers,

> graffiti and its creators were associated with other places in order to present them as aberrant and deviant. Graffiti was associated with the third world in order to emphasize its apparent disorder.[70]

Cresswell also found this guilt-by-association-with-other-places in British media accounts critical of a group of nuclear weapons protesters who had organized as the *Greenham Common Women's Peace Camp*. Media writers and pundits related the women's actions to ties to the Soviet Union, thus calling into question their allegiance to Britain. Similarly, the geographer Susan Ruddick found that media accounts of a shooting in an upscale Toronto coffee-shop focused on the Jamaican identity of the shooter. Ruddick noted that this characterization of the event and its participants led to the event becoming a lightning rod that brought to public discussion Toronto residents' tensions and disagreements about immigration policy, race relations, and the contested image of Canada as a multicultural nation.[71]

In the present study I have strived to bring together the *big D* discursive-construction-of-place concerns of urban anthropologists and cultural geographers, with the *little d* sociolinguistic and linguistic anthropological interest in connections between language structure, meaning, and use, and to combine these approaches with an ethnographic attention to the ways that specific interactions, occurring within particular spaces and times, influence and are influenced by the larger sociopolitical world. The linguistic, anthropological, and geographical research on place identity shows not only the critical role that language has in shaping place identities, but also the extent to which your words can have an impact when you have the power to broadcast them and the authority to make people pay attention to you.

Places are not neutral, and their meanings are not fixed. Rather, place identities are created through social – and linguistic – interaction. Place meanings are contested, and they serve the interests and agendas of those who create them. If we want to create communities that serve the interests of justice and equality, then we need to consider what's at stake in the ways we talk about places, and find discourses that can sustain the kind of society that we want to live in. It's my hope that this study of Mt. Pleasant has brought that point home.

Notes

1 Goffman (1981)
2 Said (1978) made this point in his theorizing of *orientalism* and the *Other*. In an analysis of colonial attitudes towards the Middle East and Asia, Said illustrated how Western lawmakers, writers, artists, scientists, and others constructed images of colonial subjects as exotic, emotional, dangerous, etc. By means of contrast, these images allowed people in the Imperial centers to construct Westerners as civilized, rational, self-controlled, etc. and worked to create a rationale for Western colonial endeavors.
3 Hill (1995)
4 Gaudio (2003)
5 Notable exceptions are ethnography of communication and work on deixis and linguistic encoding of spatial relations.
6 Although using the "sin" variant is sometimes referred to as "dropping your g's," it's worth pointing out that for the majority of English speakers there is no actual "g" sound in words like "sing." The sound

is similar to a "g" in that the tongue touches the back of the roof of the mouth, but it's a nasal sound like an "n," because when you make it air goes through your nose and not your mouth.

7 The final sound in *sing* (rather than the one in *sin*) is more likely to occur in "building glass," because the "g" in glass is similar to the sound of "ng" than it is to the sound of "n." It's the other way around in "building steel," because the "s" sound is more similar to the "n" sound than to the "ng" sound.

8 See Fischer (1958), Trudgill (1974), Kiesling (1998).

9 Milroy (1987)

10 Eckert (2000, 1989)

11 At the time of this writing, the American *Public Broadcasting System's* webpage with supplementary materials for the documentary *Do You Speak American* has an activity where visitors to the site can hear the sounds of the Northern Cities Chain Shift. Of the five examples in the activity, the first four represent the Chain Shift. http://www.pbs.org/speak/ahead/change/vowelpower/vowel.html

12 Labov (1972)

13 A follow-up study by Renée Blake and Meredith Josey in 2003 found that the vowel in *kind* was moving away from the traditional pronunciation. They attributed this to rising economic status among Islanders, and more positive attitudes towards tourists and the mainland, which young people saw as a place of economic opportunity.

14 Lane (1998)

15 Solomon (2000)

16 A sound somewhere between "y" and the sound represented by "s" in *measure*. Community members with a more local orientation pronounced this sound more like a "y."

17 Johnstone, Bhasin, and Wittkofski (2002)

18 Mendoza-Denton (1999)

19 At the more micro level, however, Mendoza-Denton found that the variation in the girls' speech cut across groups; when it came to English vowel pronunciation, the core gang girls in each group sounded like each other, and different from the more peripheral, *wannabe* girls in their same group.

20 Deixis is discussed in the analysis of the grant proposal in chapter 4.

21 Duranti (1997)

22 Tannen (1984)

23 Specifically, she refers to the strategy these speakers use as *cooperative overlap*. Tannen considers both interruption and cooperative overlap to be subsets of the neutral category of *overlap*. She distinguishes between

interruption and cooperative overlap to make the point that when the speakers in her study overlapped each other, they evaluated it positively as a show of involvement and interest. Tannen emphasizes that this is not the same as the notion of *interruption*, which she defines as a bid to take the floor, and which in popular conceptions is often considered to be a negative, non-cooperative discourse feature.

24 Gaudio (1997)
25 In Hausa, virtually any verb can take the "towards" suffix, not just "motion" verbs like "walk" or "run."
26 Basso (1996)
27 Blu (1996)
28 Leap (1996)
29 Johnstone (1990)
30 Duncan and Ley (1993:3)
31 See also Lees (2004), Beauregard (1993).
32 Rodman (1993:126)
33 Low (1993:75)
34 The geographer Edward Soja also promotes the idea of lived, experienced place, with a focus on practice, in his influential concept of "thirdspace." See Soja (1996).
35 Although Lefebvre wrote this book (in French) in 1974 and a few scholars writing in English engaged his ideas (most notably Manuel Castells and David Harvey), the book's greatest impact in the Anglophone world occurred after it was translated into English in 1991.
36 I'm thankful to Eugene McCann and Annemarie Bodaar for emphasizing that, despite his triad, Lefebvre strongly believed that that space cannot be divided up into smaller segments, or separated from society.
37 Although Lefebvre's translator Donald Nicholson-Smith translates Lefebvre's original term *espaces de la représentation* as *representational spaces*, I adopt Rob Shields's translation *spaces of representation* because it is less confusing when comparing with *representations of space*. (See Shields 1998.)
38 Lefebvre (1991:31)
39 Cresswell (1996) also makes this point.
40 Lefebvre (1991:33)
41 Hymes (1974)
42 Cresswell (1996:16)
43 It's worth pointing out that our sensual experiences in space – what we hear, smell, or feel – also influence how we perceive that space as a particular kind of place.
44 cf. Shields (1991)

45 One of Lefebvre's main goals was to emphasize that relations of production had a strong spatial component, at a time when Marxist theorists were not paying a lot of attention to space.

46 along with the cultural geographers Tim Cresswell and David Sibley, and urban sociologist Rob Shields

47 From the perspective of the linguist Ferdinand de Saussure, a symbol more specifically conveys the mental representation stored in our minds of an object, rather than the object itself.

48 Lefebvre (1991:39)

49 Castells (1978, 1997). Other critiques that Castells makes of Lefebvre's work, as well as Lefebvre's responses, can be found in Castells (1977) and Lefebvre (1987). For further discussion of these scholars, see also Merrifield (2002).

50 See Schaller and Modan (2005).

51 The youth center had been a partner in the participatory planning project, and the workshops had taken place there.

52 The conceptions of some civic group members provide another example of the interrelatedness of these categories. Some of these community members' lived experiences of place were closely connected with dominant discourses. For instance, their notions of the borders of the neighborhood corresponded with the official borders decreed by the city. However, no one saw the space as ahistorical or homogeneous, features of *abstract space* that Lefebvre notes are common for representations of space. Also, generally even for the members of what would otherwise be thought of as the bourgeois class, the struggles over space were not primarily about property values. Finally, even those in more powerful and connected positions constructed their notions of place just as much through their lived experience on the streets of Mt. Pleasant as those in marginalized positions. The situation has changed somewhat since 2000, however, with new residents who do voice explicit concerns about property values and economic investments. These concerns are characteristic of the concerns of capital that Lefebvre notes are part and parcel of abstract space, and in that sense some of the more recent constructions of place in Mt. Pleasant may fit more closely with the concept of *representations of space*.

53 Lefebvre (1991:39). Lefebvre also remarks here that spaces of representation "tend towards more or less coherent systems of non-verbal symbols and signs." However, since so many representations of space contain both verbal and non-verbal elements – take for example the grafitti'd wall on the front cover of this book – it seems fruitful to consider fully how these work in tandem, rather than focusing on images and non-verbal symbols.

54 McCann (1999)
55 McCann (1999:164)
56 Specifically, McCann argues that any complete analysis of place-making in US cities must address the role of race and race relations, even though this is an aspect of urban organization that Lefebvre ignored.
57 along with other ideologies, such as ideologies of gender
58 It's important to note that both the definition of the term *place* and philosophies about what the study of place should include are contested. For a comprehensive discussion of theory of place, see Cresswell (2004).
59 For a fuller discussion of how theorists have used the term *space* and what problems the term presents, see Shields (1991:30–31).
60 This is a simplified explanation of Japanese demonstratives. For a more comprehensive discussion, see Hamaguchi (2001).
61 Mills (1993)
62 Ley (1996, 2003)
63 Smith (1986, 1992)
64 This terminology is mine, not Smith's.
65 Although Smith and Ley both examine the role of discourse in gentrification processes, they differ in terms of what they believe drives gentrification. While Smith focuses on real estate speculation and investment that combines with real estate discourse to create new real estate markets, Ley is interested in the cultural as well as economic processes that drive gentrification, including gentrifiers' desires for a certain kind of lifestyle or identity, which gentrifying neighborhoods tap into. See Bourassa (1993), Lees (1994), Ley (1987, 1996), Smith (1979, 1987, 1996).
66 See Mitchell (2000) for a discussion of geography metaphors.
67 This is not an exhaustive list, but rather some key examples to convey a sense of the kinds of research that people have conducted on this topic.
68 Dixon, Reicher, and Foster (1997)
69 Shi-xu (2005)
70 Cresswell (1996:154)
71 Ruddick (1996)

ADDENDUM: DEFINING TERMS

In discussions about community formation, race and ethnicity, and geography and landscape, researchers often use key terms in multiple ways. This addendum explains how I am defining the terms I've used in the ethnography, and why I've chosen some terms over others.

Community and Neighborhood

A central issue in researching a heterogeneous group of people who live in the same area is how to define a spatialized community. In this study, I use the term *spatialized community* to mean a group of people organized around common interests (loosely defined), who participate in social networks or in interactions with social institutions that are located within a particular geographical area. This definition makes it possible to distinguish between a place, on the one hand, and the people who are connected it, on the other.

Whereas the notion of *community* focuses on people linked through social networks, the term *neighborhood* refers more directly to the geographical space with which a community is aligned. These terms provide a helpful way to distinguish between *residence* and *participation* in a place. Because community is defined through social networks, it is possible to be a member of a geographical community without actually living in the geographical terrain. Likewise, it is possible to live in a neighborhood without being part of the community. In this study, I focus on community members, many of whom do indeed live in Mt. Pleasant, although a number of them do not. Among those in this research who do not, most (but not all) have either lived in the neighborhood at some point, or have run or worked in neighborhood businesses.

In his work on nationalism and national identity, the political scientist Benjamin Anderson develops the concept of *imagined communities* as spatialized communities in which members

> will never know most of their fellow-members, meet them, or even hear of them, yet in the minds of each lives the image of their communion . . . All communities larger than primordial villages of face-to-face contact (and perhaps even these) are imagined.[1]

As Anderson documents, the promotion of shared language varieties (like sacred languages used in religious activities) and the mass circulation of linguistic texts (like newspapers) have historically played an integral role in the process of community formation, whether on the local or national level. In the case of newspapers, for example, people began to feel a sense of communitas based on practice (through the shared action of reading the same newspapers), code (through a spreading competence in emerging standard languages that were being pushed by institutions promoting nationalist projects), and content (through recognition of common stories and themes being written and talked about).

Similarly, Mt. Pleasant comes to be an imagined community through the connection that residents feel with each other. This connection emerges first out of the idea of a shared geographical territory (whether through residence in neighborhood housing, or through using the space, e.g., by managing a business or socializing on Mt. Pleasant St.); and second, through participating in institutions (broadly defined) which in various ways are seen to be linked to Mt. Pleasant – such as subscribing to the neighborhood email list, participating in social networks of people who spend time together, shopping at Mt. Pleasant stores, or patronizing community-based organizations serving neighborhood constituents.

Through interaction with neighborhood institutions, Mt. Pleasant community members participate in circulating discourses about neighborhood life and local goings-on, thus creating a *community of practice*. (For more on this concept, see chapter 8.) Following the work of education theorists Jean Lave and Etienne Wenger[2] and sociolinguists Penelope Eckert and Sally McConnell-Ginet,[3] I use this term to highlight the active nature of community creation:

> [a] community of practice is an aggregate of people who come together around mutual engagement in some common endeavor. Ways of doing things, ways of talking, beliefs, values, power relations – in short, practices – emerge in the course of their joint activity around that endeavor. A community of practice is different as a social construct from the traditional notion of community, primarily because it is defined simultaneously by its membership and by the practice in which that membership engages.[4]

The notion of *community of practice* is a crucial tool to unite discursive and social geographic views of place identity. Viewing Mt. Pleasantites as members of a community of practice highlights their participation in discourses of place as a type of social engagement. Although the particularities of their practices may differ, Mt. Pleasantites are united by their common endeavors to define their neighborhood as an urban place and themselves as urban people. Furthermore, across lines of ethnicity, class, gender, age, and political ideology, community members share similar discourse strategies and themes in their characterizations of the community, even when they use those themes to construct identities for Mt. Pleasant that diverge widely from one another.

Many of the perceptions associated with particular communities are linked to characteristics of the geographical places that those communities inhabit. Because we are talking here of spatialized communities, the spatial characteristics of the areas that communities are associated with play an important role in community definitions. In Mt. Pleasant, especially prominent in this regard are actual interactions in the neighborhood's public spaces and discussions of such interactions. As geographer Susan Ruddick notes in her analysis of race, class and gender in public space, "interactions in and *through* public space are crucial to the formation and maintenance of social identities."[5] Communities exist in dialectical relationships with places. By that I mean that there is a two-way relationship: our notions of people's social identities are often influenced by what we think about the places we associate them with, just as our understandings of certain places are likewise shaped by what we think about the people who populate them.

Terms for Ethnic Groups

In common parlance as well as academic scholarship, people use the terms *race* and *ethnicity* to mean multiple things, and sometimes use the terms interchangeably. Following the work of linguistic anthropologist Bonnie Urciuoli[6] and cultural theorist Jon Stratton,[7] I take *race* to be a term applying to groups that a nation-state considers to be so different from the dominant culture that the dominant culture deems it impossible for them to be part of the 'mainstream'. Ethnic distinctions, on the other hand, suggest, in the words of Stratton, "a group's divergence from the dominant culture . . . but also their underlying similarity."[8] However, not all theorists make this distinction. Stratton also states that a common conceptualization of race is of race as a superordinate category that encompasses multiple ethnicities. In Mt. Pleasant, however, people use *race* and *ethnicity* interchangeably. In addition, groups that might be thought of as subgroups of superordinate racial categories (such as Vietnamese vis-à-vis Asian) are discussed within the same taxonomic framework, and at the same taxonomic level, as groups that in other research are sometimes considered superordinate categories (Black and White) or which cross superordinate categories (Latina/o). Because of the fluidity of the terms, and because locally the borders between groups can be fluid, I avoid the term 'race' and use instead 'ethnoracial' or 'ethnic'.

In addition, I've chosen to use terms that are commonly used in the neighborhood to refer to the four major ethnic groups in the neighborhood: *African American*, *White*, *Latino*, and *Vietnamese*. Although these terms do not adequately capture the full range of ethnoracial demographics in Mt. Pleasant, they do represent the major ways in which Mt. Pleasantites delineate the neighborhood's ethnic makeup.

Although in Mt. Pleasant the term *Black* is quite common, I use *African American* to distinguish descendants of those brought to the US as slaves, on the one hand, from African, Afro-Caribbean, or Afro-Latino voluntary immigrants and their descendants, on the other. African Americans are members of the majority ethnic group in DC, while

African, Caribbean, and Latin American immigrants participate in distinct communities. At the same time as I make this distinction, however, it's important to recognize that African, Caribbean, and Latin American immigrants, and particularly their children, also participate in African American communities, and do not always draw a distinct boundary between immigrants and non-immigrants of African descent.

Although the term *European American* is more analogous to *African American*, this phrase is virtually never used in local parlance, therefore I use the more pervasive *White* – but, following common neighborhood usage, I employ it to refer particularly to European Americans (descendants of people who immigrated from Europe to the US), and not, for example, to white-skinned Latinos. Again, this is somewhat of a simplification of ethnoracial dynamics in Mt. Pleasant, as some Mt. Pleasantites – particularly Latinos raised in Latin America – consider white-skinned Latinos to be both Latino *and* White.[9] In Mt. Pleasant, there is generally no community-wide discourse about more specific White ethnicities, most likely because of the historical dearth of European immigrant communities in Washington (as described in more detail in chapter 2). Thus, although individual Whites may have strong ethnic allegiances, there are not the kinds of large-scale local ethnic communities that exist in other Northeast and Mid-Atlantic cities. One Italian-American community member originally from New York periodically takes her children to Philadelphia or Baltimore, the closest cities with Italian-American communities, so that they gain more familiarity with Italian-American culture.

In Mt. Pleasant, the term Latino refers primarily to people of Latin American descent, regardless of phenotype. Sometimes the determinants of membership in this community are linguistic, rather than only geographic, as people from Spain may be considered part of the Latino community in some contexts. In this vein, the term *Hispanic* is also common in the neighborhood, as is the term *Spanish*. Although because of its "o" ending *Latino* is a masculine term, for ease of reading I use it instead of the more inclusive but jarring-to-the-eye *Latina/o* or *Latin@*. Since much of the public discourse discussed here refers to Latino men in particular (see chapter 4, especially), it would be awkward to use the feminine *Latina* as a generic term. However, I use the feminine when talking about Latina women specifically.

While the terms *African American*, *White*, and *Latino* can reference American-identified individuals, this might seem to be less the case with the term *Vietnamese*. I use this term rather than a more US-identified reference such as *Vietnamese American* because that term is generally not used in Mt. Pleasant, by either in-group or out-group members. The majority of Vietnamese in Mt. Pleasant arrived in the US in the late 1980s and early 1990s. As the tenure of the Vietnamese community lengthens and members raised in the US grow in number, terms like *Vietnamese American* may become more widely used.[10]

Public Discourse

This ethnography examines the discourse strategies and themes that community members use in their talk and writing to position themselves and other community members as certain kinds of people (and as more or less authentic *Mt. Pleasant people*) and the neighborhood as a certain kind of place. I examine a fair amount of private discourse in this study in order to provide some background on the community and to show how ways of conceptualizing the neighborhood circulate through various speech events. But I focus on public discourse, because that is the discourse that is most shared by community members. Public discourse is closely linked to public space; they are both elements in the public sphere. It is in public space and in public discourse that disparate people can come across each other and interact, where members of communities can debate and negotiate values, behaviors, and impending changes. In this way, the public sphere is a critical aspect of participatory democracy, so a focus on public discourse and public space allows us a window into the process of negotiation of communities. As scholars like political scientists Nancy Fraser[11] and David Lowery,[12] linguistic anthropologist Rudolf Gaudio,[13] and urban planner Tridib Banerjee[14] have noted, however, public spaces are not wholly open to "the public"; identities such as race, class, and gender often serve to exclude people from access to public space and consequent access to public discourse. In Mt. Pleasant as in the city at-large, this has become increasingly the case since the late 1990s, when public–private development initiatives such as Business Improvement Districts have limited access to public space and put control of public space into the hands of private security forces. Nevertheless, public spaces often serve as the medium through which community members do identity work (as Susan Ruddick notes), and discourse about public space plays an especially important role in processes of marginalization. So if we're interested in understanding the connection between identity and political participation in community formation, a focus on discourses of public space is crucial.

The definition of public discourse that I am using for the purposes of this study is discourse that can reach an audience which is, in principle, open to anyone. This means that the speaker or writer cannot be sure who the audience includes, as in a public meeting or a conversation on the street that anyone might overhear. Likewise, public discourse tends to occur in spaces (material – like streets, or virtual – like newspapers or electronic listservs) that in principle anyone has access to. Again, though, in reality access to public space is often limited to certain types of people; some people might not feel comfortable in a town hall meeting in a library basement that follows Roberts' Rules of Order, while others might feel uncomfortable walking through a park where men in ragged clothes are sitting on the benches. (And, of course, the different types of comfortableness and uncomfortableness different people feel goes directly to what kind of access to power they have; the consequences of not feeling comfortable in a park are obviously much different from the consequences of not feeling comfortable in a town hall meeting.)

Such constraint of public space means that speakers or writers often have a more limited implicit audience in mind, based on who they think will have access to the space. For example, anyone in Mt. Pleasant is free to join the Mt. Pleasant listserv. However, one must have particular material resources (computer access and leisure time) and linguistic resources (English literacy) in order to read the list, and a certain sense of empowerment in order to post to the list. Thus, writers to the list impute, among other characteristics, a certain class background to the list membership. This can be seen in the disparate ways that ads requesting different kinds of services tend to be written. While patterns of job queries are not hard and fast, the tendency is for jobs requiring more education (such as music or language teachers) to include list readers as potential employees, while queries for skilled trades or relatively unskilled services, such as plumbers or housecleaners, tend to ask other list members for recommendations of people they have used in the past. For example:

> I am looking for someone who can do basic yard/alley clean-up, to be paid by the hour. Right now I would like to hire them to simply rake all the leaves/pull weeds, cut wood trees in the 3200 block alley between Summers and Frazier.[15] Also perhaps to rake the 3200 block of Summers. If anyone knows of a reliable person please respond. Thank you.

Ads seeking the services of more white-collar workers tend to include such people as potential email addressees:

> I'm looking for someone who could help me brush up on my Russian. I've studied the language for four years and spent some time living in Kiev. I'm flexible with time and cost. Please contact Sarah at 202-986-9866 or email.

Another aspect of the distinction between public and private is economic: Canonically, private spaces are privately owned and overseen, while public spaces are owned and overseen by the state. However, in the 1990s this relationship became more complicated in DC, as public–private partnerships developed between the city and private organizations or businesses, leading to phenomena such as private security forces who patrol theoretically public streets. In addition, in Mt. Pleasant, public events are often held in privately owned venues, such as restaurants or churches. So the boundary between public and semi-public becomes blurred. Some of the data I analyze, such as a play for which the audience had to pay admission, could perhaps be better described as semi-public discourse. But community members don't tend to make a distinction between public and semi-public discourse. (For instance, the status of talk at an open meeting held in the basement of the public library, and a meeting held in a church rec[16] room for which the meeting group pays a small fee, is seen to be the same.) Therefore, in this study I do not distinguish between these two kinds of talk. Rather, I make a distinction between public talk to a (semi) anonymous audience, vs. private talk to a specific, known audience.[17]

Place and Space

Following a strong trend in cultural geography, I use the term *place*, rather than *space*, to refer to geographic areas that are socially experienced and interpreted. While I use *space* to refer more specifically to the physical features of a geographic area, a *place* is a space that has cultural meaning (although what that meaning is may be strongly contested). As many scholars of place have noted, spatial features or parameters of a given area of course play an important role in the ways that area will be conceptualized and experienced. However, not *all* interpretations of spaces rely on spatial relations. I use the term *place*, then, because it allows for a framework where physical spatial relations may be more or less relevant in people's interpretations of what a given area is like. A more in-depth discussion on the concept of *place* can be found in chapter 9.

Notes

1   Anderson (1991:6)
2   Lave and Wenger (1991)
3   Eckert and McConnell-Ginet (1995, 1992; see also Eckert 2000)
4   Eckert and McConnell Ginet (1992:95)
5   Ruddick (1996:135; emphasis in original)
6   Urciuoli (1996)
7   Stratton (2000)
8   Stratton (2000:227)
9   I use a capitalized *White* to refer to the ethnic group, and a lower-case *white* to refer to skin color.
10   This study has a strong focus on public discourse, and events that were part of the public story of the neighborhood. Because during the time period of this study Vietnamese community members were by–and-large not participants in the neighborhood's public discourse, they do not appear prominently in these pages. A more extensive discussion about Vietnamese conceptions of the neighborhood can be found in Schaller and Modan (2005).
11   Fraser (1993)
12   Lowery (1988)
13   Gaudio (2003)
14   Banerjee (2000)

15 The names of small side streets in this study are pseudonyms.

16 room for recreational activities, meetings, parties, etc.

17 It could of course be argued that all the data discussed here is public talk, as informants knew their talk might be read at a later point in a book like this. However, my sense is that it is the immediate context/audience that is relevant to speakers.

BIBLIOGRAPHY

Ackelsberg, Martha A. 1988. Communities, resistance, and women's activism: Some implications for a democratic polity. In Bookman, Ann, and Sandra Morgan (eds.). *Women and the politics of empowerment*. Philadelphia: Temple University Press. 297–313.

Anderson, Benedict. 1991. *Imagined communities: Reflections on the origin and spread of nationalism*. London: Verso.

Anderson, Kay. 1988. Cultural hegemony and the race-definition process in Chinatown, Vancouver: 1880–1980. *Environment and Planning D: Society and Space* 6:127–149.

Antaki, Charles, and Ivan Leudar. 1996a. Backing footing. *Theory and Psychology* 6(1):41–46.

Antaki, Charles, and Ivan Leudar. 1996b. Discourse participation, reported speech and research practices in social psychology. *Theory and Psychology* 6(1):5–29.

Antaki, Charles, Susan Condor, and Mark Levine. 1996. Social identities in talk: Speakers' own orientations. *British Journal of Social Psychology* 35:473–492.

Asher, Robert L. 1967. Mt. Pleasant: Troubled, polyglot in-town neighborhood. *Washington Post*. December 19.

Baker, Donald P. 1978. Race issue enters fight to ratify D.C. voting. *Washington Post,* October 1.

Bakhtin, Mikhail Mikhailovich. 1981. *The dialogic imagination: Four essays*. Holquist, Michael (ed.). Emerson, Caryl, and Michael Holquist (trans.). Austin, TX: University of Texas Press.

Banerjee, Tridib. 2001. The future of public space: Beyond invented streets and reinvented places. *APA Journal* 67(1):9–24.

Bao, Xiaolan. 1997. Chinese mothers in New York City's sweatshops. In Jetter, Alexis, Annelise Orleck, and Dianna Taylor (eds.). *The politics of motherhood: Activist voices from left to right.* Hanover, NH: University Press of New England. 127–140.

Barrett, Rusty. 1999. Indexing polyphonous identity in the speech of African American drag queens. In Bucholtz, Mary, A.C. Liang, and Laurel Sutton (eds.). *Reinventing identities: The gendered self in discourse.* New York: Oxford University Press. 313–331.

Bass, Holly. 1997. Washington D.C. In Bock, Duncan (ed.). *Spin underground U.S.A.: The best of rock culture coast to coast.* New York: Random House. 385–405.

Basso, Keith H. 1996. *Wisdom sits in places: Landscape and language among the Western Apache.* Albuquerque: University of New Mexico Press.

Bateson, Gregory. 1972. *Steps to an ecology of mind.* New York: Ballantine.

Bauman, Richard. 2004. *A world of others' words: Cross-cultural perspectives on intertextuality.* Malden, MA: Blackwell.

Bauman, Richard, and Charles L. Briggs. 1990. Poetics and performance as critical perspectives on language and social life. *Annual Review of Anthropology* 19:59–88.

Bauman, Zygmunt. 1989. *Modernity and the Holocaust.* Ithaca, NY: Cornell University Press.

Beauregard, Robert A. 1989. Trajectories of neighborhood change: The case of gentrification. *Environment and Planning* A22:855–874.

Beauregard, Robert A. 1993. *Voices of decline: The postwar fate of US cities.* Oxford, UK: Blackwell.

Bennefield, Robert. 1995. *Interruptions in health insurance worsening, Census Bureau says.* Washington, DC: Public Information Office, U.S. Bureau of the Census.

Blake, Renée, and Meredith Posey. 2003. The /ay/ diphthong in a Martha's Vineyard community: What can we say 40 years after Labov? *Language in Society* 32(4):451–485.

Blee, Kathleen M. 2002. *Inside organized racism: Women in the hate movement.* Berkeley, CA: University of California Press.

Blommaert, Jan, and Jef Verschueren. 1991. The pragmatics of minority politics in Belgium. *Language in Society* 20:503–531.

Blu, Karen. 1996. "Where do you stay at?": Home place and community among the Lumbee. In Feld, Steven, and Keith H. Basso (eds.). *Senses of place.* Santa Fe: School of American Research Press. 137–165.

Bok, Derek. 1998. The great health care debate of 1993–94. *Public Talk: Online Journal of Discourse Leadership.* Philadelphia: University of Pennsylvania. http://www.upenn.edu/pnc/ptbok.html.

Bourassa, Steven C. 1993. The rent gap debunked. *Urban Studies* 30(10):1731–44.

Bourdieu, Pierre. 1977. *Outline of a theory of practice.* Cambridge, UK: Cambridge University Press.

Bowling, Kenneth R. 1991. *The creation of Washington, D.C.: The idea and location of the American capital*. Fairfax, VA: George Mason University Press.

Briggs, Charles L. 1986. *Learning how to ask: A sociolinguistic appraisal of the role of the interview in social science*. Cambridge: Cambridge University Press.

Briggs, Charles L. 1998. "You're a liar – You're just like a woman!": Constructing dominant ideologies of language in Warao men's gossip. In Schieffelin, Bambi B., Kathryn A. Woolard, and Paul V. Kroskrity (eds.). *Language ideologies: Practice and theory*. Oxford, UK: Oxford University Press. 229–255.

Brockett, Diane. 1978. How D.C. amendment passed in N.J. *Washington Post*. September 12.

Broder, David. 1993. Gingrich takes "No Compromise" stand on health care plan. *Washington Post*. October 15.

Butler, Judith. 1990. *Gender trouble: Feminism and the subversion of identity*. New York: Routledge.

Cadaval, Olivia. 1996. The Latino community: Creating an identity in the nation's capital. In Cary, Francine Curro (ed.). *Urban odyssey: A multicultural history of Washington, D.C.* Washington: Smithsonian Institution Press. 231–249.

Cadaval, Olivia. 1998. *Creating a Latino identity in the nation's capital: The Latino festival*. New York: Garland Publishing.

Cameron, Deborah, M.B.H. Rampton, Penelope Harvey, and Elizabeth Frazer (eds.). 1992. *Researching language: Issues of power and method*. London: Routledge.

Cameron, Deborah. 1997. Performing gender identity: Young men's talk and the construction of heterosexual masculinity. In Johnson, Sally, and Ulrike Hanna Meinhof (eds.). *Language and masculinity*. Oxford, UK: Blackwell. 47–64.

Carranza, Isolda E. 1996. *Argumentation and ideological outlook in storytelling*. Unpublished PhD. dissertation. Washington, DC: Georgetown University.

Castells, Manuel. 1977. *The urban question: A Marxist approach*. London: Edward Arnold.

Castells, Manuel. 1978. *City, class and power*. London: MacMillan.

Castells, Manuel. 1997. Citizen movements, information and analysis: An interview with Manuel Castells. *City* 7:146–147.

Clare, Elizabeth Slattery. 1988. Mount Pleasant: A neighborhood that lived up to its name. *Washington Post*. February 25.

Clark, Heléne. 1993. Sites of resistance: Place, "race" and gender as sources of empowerment. In Jackson, Peter, and Jan Penrose (eds.). *Constructions of race, place and nation*. Minneapolis: University of Minnesota Press. 121–142.

Clymer, Adam. 1994. Any additional delay for health bill means death for proposal this year. *New York Times*. September 18.

Connell, R.W. 1995. *Masculinities*. Berkeley: University of California Press.

Cresswell, Tim. 1996. *In place/out of place: Geography, ideology and transgression*. Minneapolis: University of Minnesota Press.

Cresswell, Tim. 2004. *Place: A short introduction*. Malden, MA: Blackwell.

Dalla Costa, James, and Gillian Rose. 1975. *The power of women and the subversion of community*. Bristol, UK: Falling Wall Press.

Davies, Bronwyn, and Rom Harré. 1990. Positionings: The discursive production of selves. *Journal for the Theory of Social Behavior* 20(1):43–63.

Davis, Angela. 1983. *Women, race and class*. New York: Vintage.

De Fina, Anna. 1999. *Immigrant identities: A discourse analysis of narratives told by Mexicans in the U.S.* Unpublished PhD. dissertation. Washington, DC: Georgetown University.

Dewar, Helen. 1993. Gramm sketches another GOP alternative. *Washington Post*. September 22.

Dixon, John A., Steve Reicher, and Don H. Foster. 1997. Ideology, geography, racial exclusion: The squatter camp as "blot on the landscape". *Text* 17(3):317–348.

Douglas, Mary. 1966. *Purification and danger*. London: Routledge and Keegan Paul.

Duggan, Paul, and Lonnae O'Neal Parker. 1995. On D.C. hot line, talking trash, traffic and other problems. *Washington Post*.

Duncan, James, and David Ley (eds.). 1993. *Place/culture/representation*. New York: Routledge.

Duranti, Alessandro. 1994. *From grammar to politics: Linguistic anthropology in a Western Samoa village*. Berkeley: University of California Press.

Duranti, Alessandro. 1997. Indexical speech across Samoan communities. *American Anthropologist* 99(2):342–354.

Eckert, Penelope. 1989. The whole woman: Sex and gender differences in variation. *Language Variation and Change* 1(3):245–267.

Eckert, Penelope, and Sally McConnell-Ginet. 1992. Communities of practice: Where language, gender and power all live. In Hall, Kira, et al. (eds.). *Locating power: Proceedings of the Second Berkeley Women and Language Conference*. Berkeley: Berkeley Women and Language Group. 89–99.

Eckert, Penelope, and Sally McConnell-Ginet. 1995. Constructing meaning, constructing selves: Snapshots of language, gender and class from Belten High. In Hall, Kira, and Mary Bucholtz (eds.). *Gender articulated: Language and the socially constructed self*. New York: Routledge. 469–507.

Eckert, Penelope. 2000. *Linguistic variation as social practice*. Malden, MA: Blackwell.

Emery, Fred A. 1932. Mt. Pleasant and Meridian Hill Park. In Morris, Maud Burr (ed.). *Records of the Columbia Historical Society*, Vol. 33–34. Washington: Columbia Historical Society. 187–221.

Evening Star. 1919. National representation for D.C. held to be near: Senator Champerlain and representatives Olney and Johnson assure Association of Oldest Inhabitants. December 9.

Fairclough, Norman. 1995. *Critical discourse analysis: The critical study of language.* London: Longman.

Farhi, Paul. 1990. Living on the edge in Mt. Pleasant: D.C. neighborhood's delicate racial balance is threatened. *Washington Post.* October 7.

Fasold, Ralph. 1990. *The sociolinguistics of language.* Cambridge, MA: Blackwell.

Fischer, John L. 1958. Social influences on the choice of a linguistic variant. *Word* 14:47–56.

Fraser, Nancy. 1993. Rethinking the public sphere: A contribution to the critique of actually existing democracy. In Robbins, Bruce (ed.). *The phantom public sphere.* Minneapolis: University of Minnesota Press. 1–32.

Gal, Susan. 1993. Diversity and contestation in linguistic ideologies: German speakers in Hungary. *Language in Society* 22(3):337–359.

Gal, Susan. 2002. A semiotics of the public/private distinction. *Differences: A Journal of Feminist Cultural Studies* 13(1):77–95.

Gale, Dennis E. 1976a. *The back-to-the-city movement . . . or is it?* Occasional Paper. Washington, DC: Department of Urban and Regional Planning, George Washington University.

Gale, Dennis E. 1976b. *Mt. Pleasant: Suburban village to urban neighborhood 1865–1970.* Manuscript. Historical Society of the District of Columbia.

Gale, Dennis. 1987. *Washington, DC: Inner city revitalization and minority suburbanization.* Philadelphia: Temple University Press.

Gardner, Carol Brooks. 1995. *Passing by: Gender and public harassment.* Berkeley: University of California Press.

Gaudio, Rudolf P. 1997. *Gender in motion through Hausa Muslim discourse and space.* Paper presented at the Panel on Language and Space: Cultural Spaces and Spatialized Identities, 96th Annual Meeting of the American Anthropological Association, Washington, DC, November.

Gaudio, Rudolf P. 2003. Coffeetalk: Starbucks and the commercialization of casual conversation. *Language in Society* 32(4):659–692.

Gee, James Paul. 1990. *Social linguistics and literacies: Ideology in discourses.* London: Falmer.

Gibson, Joshua. 1997. *State of the neighborhood: Observations and opinions from a summer's work with business owners.* Manuscript. Washington, DC: Latino Economic Development Corporation.

Giddens, Anthony. 1984. *The constitution of society: Introduction to the theory of structuration.* Berkeley, CA: University of California Press.

Gilliam, Dorothy. 1976. Mt. Pleasant: Washington's mix-and-match "suburb". *Washington Post.* September 18.

Glassner, Barry. 1999. *The culture of fear: Why Americans are afraid of the wrong things*. New York: Basic Books.

Goffman, Erving. 1981. *Forms of talk*. Philadelphia: University of Pennsylvania Press.

Goode, James M. 1988. *Best addresses: A century of Washington's distinguished apartment houses*. Washington, DC: Smithsonian Institution Press.

Goodey, Jo. 1997. Boys don't cry. *British Journal of Criminology* 37(3):401–418.

Gregory, Steven. 1999. *Black Corona: Race and the politics of place in an urban community*. Princeton, NJ: Princeton University Press.

Grice, H.P. 1975. Logic and conversation. In Cole, P., and J. Morgan (eds.). *Speech acts (Syntax and semantics, volume 3)*. New York: Academic Press. 41–58.

Gumperz, John. 1971. *Language in social groups*. Stanford, CA: Stanford University Press.

Gumperz, John. 1982. *Discourse strategies*. Cambridge, UK: Cambridge University Press.

Gurtatowski, Conrad. 1993. Washington can't cure health woes. *Chicago Sun-Times*. October 12.

Halfon, Neal, Paul W. Newacheck, David L. Wood, and Robert F. St. Peter. 1996. Routine emergency department use for sick care by children in the United States. *Pediatrics* 98(1):28–34.

Hall, Kira. 1995. Lip service on the fantasy lines. In Hall, Kira, and Mary Bucholtz (eds.). *Gender articulated: Language and the socially constructed self*. New York: Routledge. 183–216.

Halliday, M.A.K., and Ruqaiya Hasan. 1976. *Cohesion in English*. London: Longman.

Hamaguchi, Toshiko. 2001. *Co-construction of meaning in intergenerational family conversations: A case of the Japanese demonstrative pronoun "are"*. Unpublished dissertation. Washington, DC: Georgetown University.

Hamilton, Heidi E. 1996. Intratextuality, intertextuality, and the construction of identity as patient in Alzheimer's disease. *Text* 16(1):61–90.

Harmon, H.C., B.P. Davis, J.B. Bloss, S.G. Arnold, W.C. Lipscomb, Jr., and A.L. Sturtevant. 1876. *Annals of Mount Pleasant*. Washington, DC: O.H. Reed.

Harré, Rom, and Luk van Langenhove. 1991. Varieties of positioning. *Journal for the Theory of Social Behavior* 21(4):393–407.

Hill, Jane. 1995. The voices of Don Gabriel: Responsibility and self in a modern Mexicano narrative. In Tedlock, Dennis, and Bruce Mannheim (eds.). *The dialogic emergence of culture*. Urbana, IL: University of Illinois Press. 108–147.

Hill, Jane. 1998. Language, race, and white public space. *American Anthropologist* 100(3):680–689.

Hinton, Alexander Laban. 2005. *Why did they kill? Cambodia in the shadow of genocide.* Berkeley, CA: University of California Press.

Horton, Lois. E. 1996. The days of jubilee: Black migration during the civil war and reconstruction. In Cary, Francine Curro (ed.). *Urban odyssey: A multicultural history of Washington, D.C.* Washington: Smithsonian Institution Press. 65–78.

Hymes, Dell H. 1974. *Foundations in sociolinguistics: An ethnographic approach.* Philadelphia: University of Pennsylvania Press.

Jackson, Peter. 1998. Domesticating the street: The contested spaces of the high street and the mall. In Fyfe, Nicholas R. (ed.). *Images of the street: Planning, identity and control in public space.* London: Routledge. 176–191.

Jacobson, Matthew Frye. 1998. *Whiteness of a different color: European immigrants and the alchemy of race.* Cambridge, MA: Harvard University Press.

Johnstone, Barbara, Neeta Bhasin, and Denise Wittkofski. 2002. "Dahntahn" Pittsburgh: Monophthongal /aw/ and representations of localness in Southwestern Pennsylvania. *American Speech* 77(2):148–166.

Johnstone, Barbara. 1990. *Stories, community, and place.* Bloomington, IN: Indiana University Press.

Keating, Elizabeth. 1998. *Power sharing: Language, rank, gender and social space in Pohnpei*, Micronesia. New York: Oxford University Press.

Kennedy, George. 1950. Mt. Pleasant, founded by New Englanders, has interesting, well-kept history. *Evening Star.* November 20.

Kiernan, Michael. 1977. Why all those folks are moving. *Washington Star.* October 30.

Kiesling, Scott. 1998. Men's identities and sociolinguistic variation: The case of fraternity men. *Journal of Sociolinguistics* 2(1):69–9.

Koskela, Hille. 1997. 'Bold walk and breakings': Women's spatial confidence versus fear of violence. *Gender, Place and Culture* 4(3):301–319.

Kristeva, Julia. 1982. *Powers of horror.* New York: Columbia University Press.

Labov, 1972. *Sociolinguistic patterns.* Philadelphia: University of Pennsylvania Press.

Labov, William. 1982. *Objectivity and commitment in linguistic science. Language in Society* 11:165–201.

Labov, William. 1984. Field methods of the project on linguistic change and variation. In Baugh, John, and Joel Sherzer (eds.). *Language in use: Readings in Sociolinguistics.* Englewood Cliffs, NJ: Prentice-Hall. 28–53.

Lakoff, George, and Mark Johnson. 1980. *Metaphors we live by.* Chicago: University of Chicago Press.

Lakoff, Robin. 1975. *Language and woman's place.* New York: Harper and Row.

Lane, Lisa. 1998. Reflections of macro-social change: Linguistic, ideological and material orientations of women to their community. In Wertheim, Suzanne, Ashlee Bailey and Monica Corston-Oliver (eds.).

Engendering communication: Proceedings of the Fifth Berkeley Women and Language Conference. Berkeley: Berkeley Women and Language Group. 285–296.

Lave, Jean, and Etienne Wenger. 1991. *Situated learning: Legitimate peripheral participation*. Cambridge, UK: Cambridge University Press.

Leap, William. 1996. Fruit loops and naughty places: How the language of gay city reflects the politics of urban gay experience. In Warner, Natasha, Jocelyn Ahlers, Leela Bilmes, Monica Oliver, Suzanne Wertheim, and Melinda Chen (eds.). *Gender and belief systems: Proceedings of the Fourth Berkeley Women and Language Conference*. Berkeley: Berkeley Women and Language Group. 411–423.

Leavitt, Jacqueline, and Susan Saegert. 1990. *From abandonment to hope: Community-households in Harlem*. New York: Columbia University Press.

Lees, Loretta. 1994. Rethinking gentrification: Beyond the positions of economics and culture. *Progress in Human Geography* 18:137–150.

Lees, Loretta. 1998. Urban renaissance and the street: Spaces of control and contestation. In Fyfe, Nicholas R. (ed.). *Images of the street: Planning, identity and control in public space*. London: Routledge. 236–253.

Lees, Loretta. 2003. The ambivalence of diversity and the politics of urban renaissance: The case of youth in downtown Portland, Maine. *International Journal of Urban and Regional Research* 27(3):613–634.

Lees, Loreta. 2004. Urban geography: Discourse analysis and urban research. *Progress in Human Geography* 28(1):101–107.

Lefebvre, Henri. 1987. An interview with Henri Lefebvre. *Environment and Planning D: Society and Space* 5:27–38.

Lefebvre, Henri. 1991. *The production of space*. Donald Nicholson-Smith, trans. Cambridge, MA: Blackwell.

Levinson, Steven. 1983. *Pragmatics*. London: Cambridge University Press.

Ley, David. 1987. The rent gap revisited. *Annals of the Association of American Geographers* 77:465–468.

Ley, David. 1996. *The new middle class and the remaking of the central city*. Oxford, UK: Oxford University Press.

Ley, David. 2003. Artists, aestheticisation and the field of gentrification. *Urban Studies* 40(12):2527–2544.

Lieberman, Charles, Eric Hays, and Matthew Newman. 2004. *Using hospital emergency rooms for routine care*. California Institute for County Government Brief. Sacramento: California Institute for County Government.

Linde, Charlotte. 1993. *Life stories: The creation of coherence*. Oxford, UK: Oxford University Press.

Low, Linda, and Howard Gillette, Jr. 1988. Mt. Pleasant: Community in an urban setting. In Smith, Kathryn Schneider (ed.). *Washington at home: An illustrated history of neighborhoods in the nation's capital*. Northridge, CA: Windsor Publications.

Low, Setha. 2001. The edge and the center: Gated communities and the discourse of fear. *American Anthropologist* 103(1):45–58.

Low, Setha. 1993. Cultural meaning of the plaza: The history of the Spanish-American gridplan-plaza urban design. In Rotenberg, Robert, and Gary McDonogh (eds.) *The cultural meaning of urban space*. Westport, CT: Bergin and Garvey. 75–93.

Low, Setha M. 2003. *Beyond the gates: Life, security, and the pursuit of happiness in fortress America*. New York: Routledge.

Low, Setha M, and Denise Lawrence-Zúñiga. 2003. *The anthropology of space and place: Locating culture*. Malden, MA: Blackwell.

Lowery, David. 1998. Consumer sovereignty and quasi-market failure. *Journal of Public Administration Research and Theory* 8(2):137–172.

Mackenzie, Suzanne, and Damaris Rose. 1983. Industrial change, the domestic economy and home life. In Anderson, J., S. Duncan, and R. Hudson (eds.). *Redundant spaces in cities and regions? Studies in industrial decline and social change*. London: Academic Press. 155–200.

Manning, Robert D. 1995. Washington, D.C.: The social transformation of the international capital city. In Pedraza, Silvia, and Ruben G. Rumbaut (eds.). *Origins and destinies: Immigration, race, and ethnicity in America*. Belmont, CA: Wadsworth. 321–336.

Martin, Deborah G. 2002. Constructing the "neighborhood sphere": Gender and community organizing. *Gender, Place and Culture* 9(4):333–350.

Maskovsky, Jeff. 2006. Governing the "new hometowns": Race, power and community in the new inner city. *Identities: Global Studies in Culture and Power* 13(1):73–100.

Maskovsky, Jeff. 2001. The other war at home: The geopolitics of US poverty. *Urban Anthropology* 30:215–238.

McCann, Eugene J. 1999. Race, protest and public space: Contextualizing Lefebvre in the U.S. city. *Antipode* 31(2):163–184.

McGrory, Mary. 1993. Gingrich's buzzword pudding. *Washington Post*. October 15.

McElhinny, Bonnie S. 1995. Challenging hegemonic masculinities: Female and male police officers handling domestic violence. In Hall, Kira, and Mary Bucholtz (eds.). *Gender articulated: Language and the socially constructed self*. New York: Routledge. 217–244.

McIlhenny, Bonnie. 1997. Ideologies of public and private language in sociolinguistics. In Wodak, Ruth (ed.). *Gender and discourse*. London: Sage. 106–139.

Mehta, Anna, and Liz Bondi. 1999. Embodied discourse: On gender and fear of violence. *Gender, Place and Culture* 6(1):67–84.

Mele, Christopher. 2000. *Selling the Lower East Side: Culture, real estate and resistance in New York City*. Minneapolis: University of Minnesota Press.

Mendoza-Denton, Norma. 1999. Fighting words: Latina girls, gangs, and language attitudes. In Galindo and Gonzalez-Vasquez (eds.). *Speaking Chicana: Voice, power and identity*. Tucson, AZ: University of Arizona Press.

Merrifield, Andy. 2002. *Metromarxism*. New York: Routledge.

Merry, Sally Engle. 1981. *Urban danger: Life in a neighborhood of strangers*. Philadelphia: Temple University Press.

Middleton, DeWight R. 1986. The production and management of fear in urban contexts. In David Scruton (ed.). *Sociophobics: The anthropology of fear*. 122–141.

Mills, Caroline. 1993. Myths and meanings of gentrification. In Duncan, James, and David Ley (eds.) *place/culture/representation*. New York: Routledge. 149–170.

Milroy, Leslie. 1987. *Language and social networks, 2nd edition*. Oxford, UK: Blackwell.

Mitchell, Don. 2000. *Cultural geography: A critical introduction*.

Modan, Gabriella, and Margaret E. Malone. 1993. *The Danforth: Co-construction of community through talk of struggle*. Paper presented at City Voices Pre-session, Georgetown University Roundtable on Linguistics, Washington, DC.

Moeller, Gertrude L. 1989. Fear of criminal victimization: The effect of neighborhood racial composition. *Sociological Inquiry* 59(2):209–221.

Monk, Janice. 1992. Gender in the landscape: Expressions of power and meaning. In Anderson, Day, and Fay Gale (eds.). *Inventing places: Studies in cultural geography*. Melbourne: Longman. 123–138.

Monroe, Tony. 1993. Rebirth in Mt. Pleasant: New businesses help cover up scars of '91 riots. *Washington Times*. September 3.

Montgomery, David, and D'Vera Cohn. 1995. Waiting for a shutdown; Reality of likely furloughs sinks in for U.S., D.C. workers. *Washington Post*.

National Center for Health Statistics. 2001. *Births to Teenagers in the United States, 1940–2000*. National Vital Statistics Reports. 9/25/01.

National Public Radio. 1999. *The 1990 Census*. Washington, DC: Metro Connection, WAMU radio. February 20.

Novak, Robert. 1993. GOP paper denies health care crisis. *The Buffalo News*. December 15.

Ochs, Elinor. 1992. Indexing gender. In Duranti, Alessandro, and Charles Goodwin (eds.). *Rethinking context*. Cambridge, UK: Cambridge University Press. 335–358.

Ohlemacher, Stephen. 2005. Big cities ride daily population yo-yo. *The Atlanta Journal-Constitution*. October 21.

Organization for Co-Operation and Economic Development (OECD). 2005. OECD Health Data 2005: How does the United States compare? http://www.oecd.org/dataoecd/15/23/34970246.pdf.

Pohlman, Robert. 2003. Cooperatives: Affordable housing tool. *DC North*. August 2003.

Postgraduate Medicine. 1994. Editorial: Quotes worth remembering about the health security act. *Postgraduate Medicine* 95(1):14.

Public Broadcasting System. 1996. Newshour Online: A detailed timeline of the healthcare debate portrayed in *The System*. *Newshour Online*. http://www.pbs.org/newshour/forum/may96/background/health_debate_p age2.html.

Quinn, Naomi. 1991. The cultural basis of metaphor. In Fernandez, James (ed.). *Beyond Metaphor: The theory of tropes in anthropology*. Stanford, CA: Stanford University Press. 56–93.

Reel, Monte. 2003. Charmed . . . they're sure; in D.C., he began to compliment, and they began to grin. *Washington Post*. June 1.

Reisigl, M., and Ruth Wodak. 2001. *Discourse and discrimination*. London: Routledge.

Richardson, Lynda. 1990. Mt. Pleasant residents kindle community spirit. *Washington Post*. February 10.

Rodman, Margaret. 1993. Beyond built form and culture in the anthropological study of residential community spaces. In Rotenberg, Robert, and Gary McDonogh (eds.). *The cultural meaning of urban space*. Westport, CT: Bergin and Garvey. 123–138.

Rowan, Carl. 1978. Justice and D.C. representation. *Washington Star*. August 30.

Ruddick, Susan. 1996. Constructing difference in public spaces: Race, class and gender as interlocking systems. *Urban Geography* 17:132–151.

Sacco, Vincent F. and William Glackman. 1987. Vulnerability, locus of control, and worry about crime. *Canadian Journal of Community Mental Health* 6(1):99–111.

Said, Edward W. 1978. *Orientalism*. New York: Pantheon.

Sanjek, Roger. 1998. *The future of us all: Race and neighborhood politics in New York City*. Ithaca: Cornell University Press.

Schaller, Susanna, and Gabriella Modan. 2005. Contesting public space and citizenship: Implications for neighborhood Business Improvement Districts. *Journal of Planning Education and Research* 24:394–407.

Schell, Lawrence M. 1980. Cities and human health. In Gmelch, George, and Walter P. Zenner (eds.). *Urban life: Readings in urban anthropology*. Prospect Heights, IL: Waveland Press. 18–35.

Schieffelin, Bambi B., and Rachel Charlier Doucet. 1998. The "real" Haitian Creole: Ideology, metalinguistics, and orthographic choice. In Schieffelin, Bambi B., Kathryn A. Woolard, and Paul Kroskrity (eds.). *Language ideologies: Practice and theory*. Oxford, UK: Oxford University Press. 285–316.

Schiffrin, Deborah. 1981. Tense variation in narrative. *Language* 57(1):45–62.

Schiffrin, Deborah. 1994. *Approaches to discourse.* Malden, MA: Blackwell.

Schiffrin, Deborah. 1996. Narrative as self-portrait: Sociolinguistic constructions of identity. *Language in Society* 25(2):167–203.

Schwartz, Barry. 1976. Images of suburbia: Some revisionist commentary and conclusions. In Schwartz, Barry (ed.). *The changing face of the suburbs.* Chicago: University of Chicago Press. 325–340.

Schwartzman, Jason. 2005. Crime tears at seams of vibrant community. *Washington Post.* September 25.

Selassie, Bereket H. 1996. Washington's new African immigrants. In Cary, Francine Curro (ed.). *Urban odyssey: A multicultural history of Washington, D.C.* Washington: Smithsonian Institution Press. 264–275.

Shandler, Philip. 1969. The silent minority. *Washington Star.* January 5.

Sharoni, Simona. Motherhood and the politics of women's resistance: Israeli women organizing for peace. In Jetter, Alexis, Annelise Orleck, and Dianna Taylor (eds.). *The politics of motherhood: Activist voices from left to right.* Hanover, NH: University Press of New England. 144–160.

Shields, Rob. 1991. *Places on the margin: Alternative geographies of modernity.* London: Routledge.

Shields, Rob. 1998. *Lefebvre, love and struggle.* London: Routledge.

Shi-xu. 2005. *A cultural approach to discourse.* Basingstoke, UK: Palgrave.

Shuman, Amy. 1992. "Get outa my face": Entitlement and authoritative discourse. In Hill, Jane H., and Judith T. Irvine (eds.). *Responsibility and evidence in oral discourse.* Cambridge, UK: Cambridge University Press. 135–160.

Sibley, David. 1988. Purification of space. *Environment and Planning D: Society and Space* 6:409–421.

Sibley, David. 1995. *Geographies of exclusion: Society and difference in the West.* New York: Routledge.

Silverstein, Michael. 1976. Shifters, linguistic categories, and cultural descriptions. In Basso, K., and H.A. Selby (eds.). *Meaning in anthropology.* Albuquerque: University of New Mexico Press. 11–56.

Simons, Lewis M., and Ron Shaffer. 1979. Antioch lost money on contract with Pride firm. *Washington Post.* November 14.

Singer, Audrey, Samantha Friedman, Ivan Cheung, and Marie Price. 2001. *The world in a zip code: Greater Washington, D.C. as a new region of immigration.* Washington, DC: The Brookings Institution Center on Urban and Metropolitan Policy.

Singer, Audrey, et al. 2003. *At home in the nation's capital: Immigrant trends in metropolitan Washington.* Brookings Greater Washington Research Program. Washington: The Brookings Institution Center on Urban and Metropolitan Policy. June.

Skogan, Wesley G. 1986. Fear of crime and neighborhood change. In Reiss, Albert J. Jr., and Michael Tonry (eds.). *Communities and crime*. Chicago: *University of Chicago Press*.

Skogan, Wesley, and Michael Maxfield. 1981. *Coping with crime: Individual and neighborhood reactions*. Beverly Hills: Sage.

Smith, D.J., and J. Gray. 1985. *Police and people in London*. London: Gower.

Smith, Kathryn Schneider. 1988a. Georgetown: Port town to urban neighborhood. In Smith, Kathryn Schneider (ed.). 1988. *Washington at home: An illustrated history of neighborhoods in the nation's capital*. Northridge, CA: Windsor Publications. 19–29.

Smith, Kathryn Schneider (ed.). 1988b. Introduction. *Washington at home: An illustrated history of neighborhoods in the nation's capital*. Northridge, CA: Windsor Publications. 9–14.

Smith, Neil. 1979. Toward a theory of gentrification: A back to the city movement by capital not people. *Journal of the American Planning Association* 45:538–548.

Smith, Neil. 1986. Gentrification, the frontier, and the restructuring of urban space. In Smith, Neil, and Peter Williams (eds.). *Gentrification of the city*. Winchester, MA: Allen and Unwin. 15–34.

Smith, Neil. 1987. Gentrification and the rent gap. *Annals of the Association of American Geographers* 77:462–465.

Smith, Neil. 1992. New city, new frontier: The Lower East Side as wild, wild west. In Sorkin, Michael (ed.). *Variations on a theme park: The new American city and the end of public space*. New York: Hill and Wang. 61–93.

Smith, Neil. 1996. *The new urban frontier: Gentrification and the revanchist city*. London: Routledge.

Smith, Susan. 1987. Fear of crime: Beyond a geography of deviance. *Progress in Human Geography* 11(1):1–23.

Soja, Edward. 1996. *Thirdspace: Expanding the geographical imaginations*. Oxford: Blackwell.

Solomon, Julie. 2000. *Phonological and syntactic variation in the Spanish of Valladolid, Yucatan*. Unpublished dissertation. Palo Alto, CA: Stanford University.

SourceWatch/Center for Media and Democracy. 2005. Coalition for Health Insurance Choices. http://www.sourcewatch.org/wiki.phtml?title=Coalition_for_Health_Insurance_Choices.

Spindler, George, and Louise Spindler. 1987. *Interpretive ethnography of education: At home and abroad*. Hillsdale, NJ: Erlbaum.

Spitulnik, Debra. 2001. The social circulation of media discourse and the mediation of communities. In Duranti, Alessandro (ed.). *Linguistic anthropology: A reader*. Malden, MA: Blackwell.

Stallybrass, Peter, and Allon White. 1986. The city: The sewer, the gaze and the contaminating touch. In *The politics and poetics of transgression.* Ithaca: Cornell University Press. 125–148.

Starr, Paul. 1995. What happened to health care reform? *The American Prospect* 2:20–31.

Stoler, Ann. 1990. Making empire respectable: The politics of race and sexual morality in 20th-century colonial cultures. In Bremen, Jan, Piet de Rooy, Ann Stoler, and Wim F. Wertheim (eds.). *Imperial monkey business: Racial supremacy in social Darwinist theory and colonial practice.* Amsterdam: Vrije Universiteit Press.

Stratton, Jon. 2000. *Coming out Jewish: Constructing ambivalent identities.* New York: Routledge.

Tannen, Deborah. 1984. *Conversational style: Analyzing talk among friends.* Norwood, NJ: Ablex.

Tannen, Deborah. 1989. *Talking voices: Repetition, dialogue, and imagery in conversational discourse.* Cambridge, UK: Cambridge University Press.

Tannen, Deborah. 2004. Marked women. In Valentine, Tamara M. (ed.). *Language and prejudice.* New York: Longman. 129–134.

Taylor, Ralph B., Stephen D. Gottfredson, and Sidney Brower. 1984. Block crime and fear: Defensible space, local social ties, and territorial functioning. *Journal of Research in Crime and Delinquency* 21(4):303–331.

Taylor, Verta. 1999. Gender and social movements: Gender processes in women's self-help movements. *Gender and Society* 13:8–33.

Trudgill, Peter. 1974. *The social differentiation of English in Norwich.* Cambridge, UK: Cambridge University Press.

Tuan, Yi-Fu. 1979. *Landscapes of fear.* New York: Pantheon.

Urciuoli, Bonnie. 1996. *Exposing prejudice: Puerto Rican experiences of language, race, and class.* Boulder, CO: Westview Press.

U.S. Census Report. 1990. Washington, DC: U.S. Census Bureau.

Usborne, David. 1993. Sound-biters hound Clinton; Radio and TV talk-show hosts have become the new opinion formers in the US. *The Independent.* October 3.

Valentine, Gil. 1989. The geography of women's fear. *Area* 21(4):385–390.

van Dijk, Teun A. 1984. *Prejudice in discourse.* Amsterdam: Benjamins.

van Dijk, Teun A. 1987. *Communicating racism: Ethnic prejudice in thought and talk.* Newbury Park, CA: Sage.

van Dijk, Teun A. 1993. *Elite discourse and racism.* Newbury Park, CA: Sage.

van Dijk, Teun A. 1995. Discourse semantics and ideology. *Discourse and Society* 6(2):243–289.

van Dijk, Teun A. 1998. *Ideology: A multidisciplinary approach.* Thousand Oaks, CA: Sage.

Walklate, Sandra. 2000. Trust and the problem of community in the inner city. In Hope, Tim, and Richard Sparks (eds.). *Crime, risk, and insecurity*. London: Routledge. 50–64.

Walkowitz, Judith. 1992. *City of dreadful delight: Narratives of sexual danger in late-Victorian London*. Chicago: University of Chicago Press.

Walljasper, Jay, and Daniel Kraker. 1997. Hip hot spots. *Utne Reader* November–December:57.

Walls, Craig A., Karin V. Rhodes, and Jae J. Kennedy. 2002. The Emergency Department as usual source of medical care: Estimates from the 1998 National Health Interview Survey. *Academic Medicine* 9(11):1140–1145.

Washington Post. 1961. Mt. Pleasant citizens plan a "Georgetown". August 22.

Washington Post. 1978. Voting for the District – on the merits. September 2. (Reprinted without byline attribution or original date from the *Greensboro Daily News*.)

Washington Star. 1978a. Splendid: 67 to 32. August 23.

Washington Star. 1978b. A crucial vote for DC. July 24.

West, Cornell. 1993. *Race matters*. Boston: Beacon Press.

Williams, Brett. 1988. *Upscaling downtown: Stalled gentrification in Washington, D.C.* Ithaca: Cornell University Press.

Williams, Juan. 1977. Antioch Law School seeks to shed landlord role; Antioch Law in a battle with its own tenants. *Washington Post*. August 26.

Wilson, Elizabeth. 1992. *The sphinx in the city: Urban life, the control of disorder, and women*. Berkeley: University of California Press.

Wolff, Michael, Peter Rutten, Albert Bayers III, and the World Bank Research Team. 1992. *Where we stand: Can America make it in the global race for wealth, health, and happiness?* New York: Bantam.

Wolfram, Walt. 1993. Ethical considerations in language awareness programs. *Issues in Applied Linguistics* 4:225–255.

Wolfson, Nessa. 1976. Speech events and natural speech: Some implications for sociolinguistic methodology. *Language in Society* 5:189–209.

Youth Action Research Group (YARG). 2003. *Youth voices heard*. Washington, DC: YARG.

INDEX

existential constructions 156
exotification 173

Fasold, Ralph 293 n. 35
fear 100–110, 116
  and ethnicity 110–111,
    115–117, 120–122
  and gender 88–89, 98,
    110–111, 117, 122, 127,
    131–133, 207, 228–231, 243
  and social ties 104–105
  and suburbs 110–111, 115,
    125, 129–133
fearlessness *see* fear
fieldwork 284–289, 294 n. 52;
  see also ethnography
filth 100, 138, 141–145; *see also*
  disorder, noise
fluid signifiers 156, 164
footing 296–297; *see also*
  alignment
fractal recursivity 101–103
framing 151, 176–179, 187–188,
  190, 192–196, 235, 271
Fraser, Nancy 226 n. 42, 331
functional approach to linguistics
  283, 293 n. 35

Gal, Susan 101, 102, 208,
  225–226, 291
Gardner, Carol 118–119
Gaudio, Rudolf 299, 303–304,
  331
gender
  and ethnicity, divided loyalties
    123–124
  and fear *see* fear and gender
  and public space *see* public
    space and gender
  and suburbs *see* suburbs and
    gender
gendered practice 278–289

gentrification 31 n. 2 (def.),
  317–318
Goffman, Erving 296
Goodey, Jo 127
Gray, J. 126
Gregory, Steven 288–289
Grice, J.P. 149
Gumperz, John 281

habitus 280
Hall, Kira 131
Halliday, M.A.K. 276
Hamaguchi, Toshiko 325 n. 60
Hamilton, Heidi 10
Harré, Rom 297, 298
Hasan, Ruqaiya 276
heterogeneity 98–100, 116, 130
Hill, Jane 90, 177, 297–298, 304,
  319
Hinton, Alexander 141
historic present tense *see* tense
homogeneity *see* heterogeneity
  valuing of 155, 169 n. 45
Hymes, Dell 310

identity research 289–290
ideology 290–291
indefinite *see* definite/indefinite
indexicality def. 106–107,
  145, 158, 159, 164; *see also*
  indexing
  direct 107
  indirect 108
indexing 182, 186, 190, 217,
  219, 225–226, 237, 319–320;
  see also indexicality
indirect discourse 177, 192–193,
  194; *see also* voicing, reported
  speech
inexplicit reference *see* reference,
  inexplicit
interactional sociolinguistics 283